T0238544

Lecture Notes of the Institute for Computer Sciences, Social Informatics and Telecommunications Engineering   95

Joy Ying Zhang   Jarek Wilkiewicz
Ani Nahapetian (Eds.)

Mobile Computing, Applications, and Services

Third International Conference, MobiCASE 2011
Los Angeles, CA, USA, October 24-27, 2011
Revised Selected Papers

 Springer

Volume Editors

Joy Ying Zhang
Carnegie Mellon University, Silicon Valley
Moffett Field, CA 94035, USA
E-mail: joy.zhang@sv.cmu.edu

Jarek Wilkiewicz
Youtube / Google
Mountain View, CA 94043, USA
E-mail: jarekw@google.com

Ani Nahapetian
University of California, UCLA
Los Angeles, CA 90095-1596, USA
E-mail: ani@cs.ucla.edu

ISSN 1867-8211   e-ISSN 1867-822X
ISBN 978-3-642-32319-5   e-ISBN 978-3-642-32320-1
DOI 10.1007/978-3-642-32320-1
Springer Heidelberg Dordrecht London New York

Library of Congress Control Number: 2012943584

CR Subject Classification (1998): C.2, H.4, I.2, D.2, H.3, H.5

Typesetting: Camera-ready by author, data conversion by Scientific Publishing Services, Chennai, India

Printed on acid-free paper

Springer is part of Springer Science+Business Media (www.springer.com)

Preface

MobiCASE 2011, the Third International Conference on Mobile Computing, Applications, and Services, was held in Los Angeles, CA, October 24–27, 2011. The conference was sponsored by ICST and technically co-sponsored by the IEEE Computer Society and the Create-Net in association with the European Alliance for Innovation (EAI). MobiCASE was also sponsored by AT&T, IBM Research, Samsung, Slalom Consulting, and Carnegie Mellon University Silicon Valley.

The aim of MobiCASE conferences is to provide a platform for researchers from academia and industry to advance mobile applications and services research, an exciting area that has attracted significant attention from the community in recent years. The first MobiCASE conference, MobiCASE 2009, was held in San Diego, October 26–29, 2009; the second, MobiCASE 2010, was held in Santa Clara, October 25–28, 2010.

This year, the conference received 50 submissions and the Program Committee selected 18 papers after a thorough review process that are included in this volume. Extended versions of selected papers are invited for publication in the ACM/Springer *Mobile Networks and Applications* (MONET) journal.

In addition to the regular papers included in this volume, the conference also featured two keynote speeches: "Building Billows—The Present and Future of Gaming in the Mobile Cloud" by Dan Galpin from the Android team, Google, USA, and "Participatory mHealth: Opportunities and Challenges" by Deborah Estrin of the UCLA Computer Science Department.

The Technical Program Committee decided to give the Best Paper Award to Oren Antebi, Markus Neubrand, and Arno Puder of San Francisco State University for their paper "Cross-Compiling Android Applications to Windows Phone 7."

I would like to thank the Organizing Committee members, Session Chairs, the Technical Program Committee members, and all the authors and reviewers who contributed immensely toward the success of this event.

Also, on behalf of the Organizing Committee and the Steering Committee of MobiCASE, I would like to thank the ICST for sponsoring this event, in particular the staff members who worked very hard to make MobiCASE 2011 happen. We very much look forward to another successful conference in 2012 and in the forthcoming years.

November 2011   Joy Ying Zhang

Organization

Steering Committee Chairs

Imrich Chlamtac	President, Create-Net Research Consortium, Italy
Thomas Phan	Samsung R&D U.S. Labs, USA
Petros Zerfos	IBM T.J. Watson Research Center, USA
Martin Griss	Carnegie Mellon University, USA

General Chairs

Ani Nahapetian	Cal State Northridge and UCLA, USA
Jarek Wilkiewicz	YouTube/Google, USA

Technical Program Chair

Joy Zhang	Carnegie Mellon University, USA

Technical Program Committee

Sasan Adibi	Research In Motion, Canada
Murali Annavaram	University of Southern California, USA
Jörgen Björkner	Telepo, Sweden
Chris Boulton	NS Technologies, UK
Philip Brisk	UC Riverside, USA
Jian Chen	Chinese Academy of Sciences, China
Ling-Jyh Chen	Academia Sinica, Taiwan
Jing Chong	China Mobile Research Institute, China
Pablo Najera Fernandez	University of Malaga, Spain
Jason Hong	Carnegie Mellon University, USA
Roozbeh Jafari	UT Dallas, USA
Won Jeon	Samsung Research, USA
Minkyong Kim	IBM T.J. Watson Research, USA
Andrew Lippman	MIT, USA
Gustavo Marfia	University of Bologna, Italy
Tammara Massey	Johns Hopkins University, USA
April Mitchell	HP Labs, USA
Giovanni Motta	Google, USA
Junaith A. Shahabdeen	Intel, USA
Jie Tang	Tsinghua University, China

Vincent S. Tseng   National Cheng Kung University, Taiwan
Alireza Vahdatpour   University of Washington, USA
Alexander Varshavsky   AT&T Labs, USA
Pablo Vidales   Deutsche Telecom R&D, Mexico
Lebing Xie   MobisCloud, China
Guang Yang   Nokia Research, USA
Yu Zheng   Microsoft Research Asia, China

Workshop Chairs

Soheil Ghiasi   UC Davis, USA
David Brunelli   University of Trento, Italy

Publicity Chair

Jennifer Wong   SUNY Stony Brook, USA

Demo and Exhibit Chairs

Giovanni Pau   UCLA, USA
Claudio Palazzi   University of Padua, Italy

Industry Track Chair

Kristoffer Gronowski   Ericsson Research Silicon Valley, USA

Local Chair

Foad Dabiri   UCLA, USA

Sponsorships Chair

Daniel Maycock   Slalom Consulting, USA

Workshop on Software Engineering for Mobile Application Development Program Committee

Tony Wasserman   Carnegie Mellon Silicon Valley, Chair, USA
Ray Bareiss   Carnegie Mellon Silicon Valley, USA
Adam Blum   Rhomobile
Ralf Carbon   Fraunhofer IESE, Germany

Table of Contents

Track V: Mobile Web and Services

Track VI: Tools for Mobile Environments

Track VII: Mobile Application Development Issues

Poster session

SensCare: Semi-automatic Activity Summarization System for Elderly Care

Pang Wu, Huan-Kai Peng, Jiang Zhu, and Ying Zhang

Carnegie Mellon University, Moffett Field, CA 94035, USA
{pang.wu,huankai.peng,jiang.zhu,joy.zhang}@sv.cmu.edu

Abstract. The fast growing mobile sensor technology makes sensor-based lifelogging system attractive to the remote elderly care. However, existing lifelogging systems are weak at generating meaningful activity summaries from heterogeneous sensor data which significantly limits the usability of lifelogging systems in practice. In this paper, we introduce SensCare, a semi-automatic lifelog summarization system for elderly care. From various sensor information collected from mobile phones carried by elderlies, SensCare fuses the heterogeneous sensor information and automatically segments/recognizes user's daily activities in a hierarchical way. With a few human annotations, SensCare generates summaries of data collected from activties performed by the elderly. SensCare addresses three challenges in sensor-based elderly care systems: the rarity of activity labels, the uncertainty of activity granularities, and the difficulty of multi-dimensional sensor fusion. We conduct a set of experiments with users carrying a smart phone for multiple days and evaluate the effectiveness of the automatic summary. With proper sensor configuration, the phone can continue to monitor user's activities for more than 24 hours without charging. SensCare also demonstrates that unsupervised hierarchical activity segmentation and semi-automatic summarization can be achieved with reasonably good accuracy (average F1 score 0.65) and the system is very useful for users to recall what has happened in their daily lives.

Keywords: Sensor-based Elderly Care, Structured Activity Recognition, Activity Summarization, Lifelog.

1 Introduction

In year 2020, 71 million Americans will be officially considered as elderly (65 years or older) according to the projection of US Census Bureau. This accounts for 20% of the nation's total population [17], a staggering increase from 10% in 2010. Numbers from [17] also shows that about 80% of aging adults have one chronic condition, and 50% have at least two. With such chronic conditions, most elderlies require some levels of care to assist their daily living. Statistics also shows that there are fewer young and middle-aged adults living with their parents and provide care to them. The situation is even worse in rural area where low population density and large catchment areas combine with lack of service access and reimbursement in creating barriers to community-based elder care [4].

J.Y. Zhang et al. (Eds.): MobiCASE 2011, LNICST 95, pp. 1–19, 2012.

Aging-in-place [1] has become increasingly popular in recent years as many elderly prefer to age in their own houses instead of relocating to nursing homes. Aging-in-place has the advantage that senior or elderly person can continue to live in their own surroundings without making a drastic change and maintain their valuable social networks. The success of aging-in-place depends on the telecare and other assistive technologies where elderly can access the care services remotely and promptly when needed. The fast development in mobile sensing technology and remote healthcare technologies has started to bridge the gap between the needs of age-in-place and current healthcare system where doctors and caregivers have to physically meet the patient for any checkups and diagnosis.

In this paper, we describe SensCare, a semi-automatic system that provides solutions to an important scenario in elderly care: automatic generation of meaningful activity summaries from mobile lifelogs. SensCare aims at reducing human annotation effort in activity summarization. With mobile sensors constantly logging the elderly users' daily activity, SensCare automatically recognizes the daily activity of the user and generates a meaningful hierarchical summary. An effective summary can help the elderly better understand his/her behavior so as to improve his/her well-being. It also helps doctors to diagnose causes of an elderly's medical conditions and allows remote family members to keep up with the life of the elderly. For instance, a senior suffered with insomnia carries a mobile phone with him constantly. He puts the phone under the pillow when he goes to bed. The accelerometer embedded in the phone records the motion in the night which reflects his sleeping quality. Such an automatic summary is valuable since the elderly himself cannot provide accurate quantitative answers. This summarized data, such as the average sleeping hours in the past week, wake up frequencies etc. can be accessed by the remote caregiver to evaluate the effectiveness of medicines the doctor has prescribed and by family members remotely to see how the elderly is doing.

The rest of paper is organized as follows: Section 2 presents a hypothetical before-and-after scenario to illustrate how the SensCare system would be used. We describe the system design in Section 5. This section also discusses potential limitations of the system. In Section 6, we present experimental result with data collected over 5 days and compare algorithms proposed in SensCare with other methods. In Section 7 and 8, we will go through the related works and summarize our works and guide to the future challenges of the system.

2   Scenario for Semi-automatic Activity Summarization

Many elderly hypertension patients are recommended to exercises regularly to control their high blood pressure in addition to a heart-friendly diet and taking drugs at regular basis. To qualitatively evaluate physical exercises performed by an elderly, doctors usually ask them questions during their office visits such as "Which exercises do you perform on a daily basis?" "How long does it last?" etc. In many cases, elderly patients cannot remember detailed information and can only provide rough answers like "I walk to office everyday and it takes about 20 to 30 minutes." or "Well, I went hiking with my family last weekend and had spent a whole afternoon there." Yet, "20 to 30 minutes" is too rough and it is unclear as to how many hours in the "whole afternoon" did the elderly patient actually hike . The unreliable data leads to unreliable assessment by doctors.

With SensCare (Figure 1), elderly users carry mobile devices constantly to collect data about their daily activities. The collected data is uploaded to the cloud and SensCare will automatically segment the data into a hierarchy of activities. Users can view this hierarchical segmentation in a calendar layout on their PC or tablet devices. They can annotate some activities such as "walk in the park" on the calendar. Users' annotations are also uploaded to the cloud (a backend system) for the system to propagate the annotation to all similar activities in the lifelog. After users annotate a few instances of their "useful" activities such as "walking", "hiking" and "driving", SensCare will recognize these activities and label them automatically in the future. SensCare segments the lifelog in an unsupervised manner, so users only need to annotate activities of interest to them.

SensCare gives caregivers more accurate information of users' daily activities and when combined with other sensor information such as the blood pressure measured by the in-home device, the doctor can come up with a better plan to improve the elderly's lifestyle in order to help his hypertension condition.

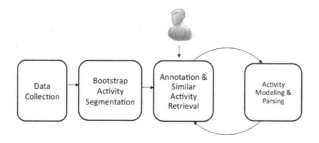

Fig. 1. The system workflow of SensCare

3 Activity Summarization through Unsupervised Hierarchical Activity Segmentation and Recognition

The purpose of activity summarization in SensCare is to automatically generate a list of activities that a user did by the end of a day when all sensors' data is uploaded. It is more useful if the summarization is hierarchical, i.e., users can zoom in a high-level activity, e.g., "played tennis from 9am to 10:30am", and see more fine-detailed activities such as "warm up, 9am to 9:05am", "tennis game: 9:10 to 9:30", "break: 9:30 to 9:40", "tennis game: 9:40 to 10:15".

Supervised activity recognition approaches can recognize a few activities specified in the labeled training data. However, labelled training data is very expensive to collect. It is also infeasible to predict what kind of activities users might be interested in the future. Supervised activity recognition is unlikely to answer questions like "What costs me most of the time this morning" or "How many hours did I spend on the road to grocery stores last month?", unless the system is trained with labeled data to address these questions.

Although it is impractical to enumerate all activities, we can detect the boundaries for different activities without any training data and then categorize similar activities, which will provide part of the semantic information. In SensCare, activity summarization is achieved through the combination unsupervised activity segmentation and activity recognition.

When all sensor data is uploaded, SensCare first quantizes each sensor readings to discrete labels called *behavior text*. This text-like symbolic representation allows the SensCare system to use some well-established algorithms from statistical natural language processing field such as Information Retrieval (IR) and Text Summarization to process the sensor data. We also apply heterogeneous sensor fusion (Section 4) to fuse multi-dimensional sensor data such as information from accelerometers and GPS into a single dimensional behavior text string for the convenience of handling multiple sensor input. The unsupervised hierarchical segmentation segments the input behavior text string into a hierarchy of shorter segments, each, hopefully corresponds to a meaningful activity at different granularities. With annotations provided by the user on some instances of the past activities, SensCare can recognize those activities similar to the labeled ones and assign meaningful labels to them, e.g., "play tennis".

In SensCare, we developed two methods for unsupervised activity segmentation: top-down segmentation by detecting activity change and the smoothed Hidden Markov Model (HMM).

3.1 Top-Down Activity Segmentation through Activity Change Detection

The underlining assumption of this segmentation algorithm is that when a user switches his/her activity at time t, there should be a significant change from behavior text string $[t - w, t - 1]$ to string $[t, t + w]$. For a window size w, define the "change of activity" at time t as:

$$H(t, w) = -logS([t - w, t - 1], [t, t + w - 1]), \quad (1)$$

where $S(P, Q)$ (Eq. 3) measures the similarity between behavior text string P and Q.

The higher the value of $H(t, w)$, the more likely is the user to have changed his/her activity at time t. Figure 2 shows an example of H values at each data point given different window sizes for a segment of behavior text.

Notice that: (1) peaks of activity change identified by larger windows are also peaks identified by smaller windows but not vice versa; and (2) activity changes

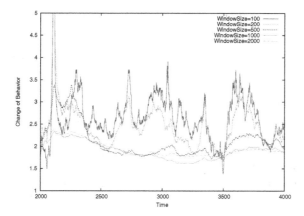

Fig. 2. Activity changes calculated by different sizes of sliding windows

over larger windows are smoother than smaller windows. Intuitively, larger window size captures changes of larger-scale activities whereas smaller window captures changes of smaller activities. Based on these finding, we first segment the lifelog data using large window sizes and then recursively segment the data using smaller windows. This results in a hierarchical segmentation of lifelogs which allows the user to efficiently browse through the lifelog and annotate activities of his/her interests.

3.2 Smoothed HMM Segmentation

Hidden Markov Model (HMM) has been widely used in text string segmentation and labeling. After specifying the topology of a Markov model, an HMM can be trained on unlabeled sequences of text through the Baum-Welch algorithm [3]. which estimates model parameters such as the probability of emitting a symbol from a certain state and the transition probability from one state to another. A trained HMM can then be used to "parse" a sequence of text and estimate the most likely "states" sequence (e.g., "S1 S1 S1 S2 S2 S1 S1 S3 ...") that generates the observed text. "state" is then used as the label for each observed symbols or in our case, the underlying activity for the observed sensor readings. When the state labels changes, we consider the underlying activity has changed and segment the data to reflect this change. For example, segmenting the data as [S1 S1 S2] [S2 S2] [S1 S1] [S3 ....

In our implementation, each state in the HMM emits single behavior text symbols. This leads to a problem where HMM segments the input data into too many activities. To smooth out these noise, we apply a sliding window of size $2w$ over the recognized state sequence. At time t, we use the dominant activity symbols within the window $[t - w, t + w]$ as the smoothed activity symbol for time t and segment the sequence to activities over the smoothed activity/state symbols.

3.3   Activity Recognition

The purpose of activity recognition is to assign semantic meanings to the segmented activities. In SensCare users can annotate some instances of activities after the automatic segmentation. For unlabeled activities, SensCare will search through the labeled activities and assign the label of the most "similar" labeled activity to the unlabeled ones. As all sensor data has been converted to a single dimension behavior text, similarity between two activities can be calculated by the distance of their corresponding behavior text strings.

Inspired by the BLEU metric [20] where averaged n-gram precision is used to measure the similarity between a machine translation hypothesis and human generated reference translations, we use *averaged n-gram precision* to estimate the similarity between two lifelog segments.

Assuming that P and Q are two activity language sentences of the same length l. P is the sequence of P_1, P_2, ..., P_L and Q is the sequence of Q_1, Q_2, ..., Q_L. Denote the *similarity* between P and Q as $S(P,Q)$. Define the n-gram precision between P and Q as $\mathrm{Prec}_n(P,Q) =$

$$\frac{\sum_{\tilde{p} \in \{\text{All } n\text{-gram types in } P\}} \min(freq(\tilde{p}, P), freq(\tilde{p}, Q))}{\sum_{\tilde{p} \in \{\text{All } n\text{-gram types in } P\}} freq(\tilde{p}, P)}, \tag{2}$$

and the similarity between P and Q is defined as:

$$S(P,Q) = \frac{1}{N} \sum_{n=1}^{N} \mathrm{Prec}_n(P,Q) \tag{3}$$

$\mathrm{Prec}_n(P,Q)$ calculates the percentage of n-grams in P that can also be found in Q and $S(P,Q)$ averages the precision over 1-gram, 2-gram and up to N-gram. In our experiments, we empirically set $N = 5$.

4   Heterogeneous Sensor Fusion

Different types of sensors capture different aspects of users' activity. Combining information from multiple sensors helps to disambiguate activities that are similar to each other on certain aspects. Activities such as *"Driving"* and *"Eating"* are very similar to each other if we only look at their accelerometer readings. If we include the location/speed information, these two activities can be well distinguished.

Different sensors have different data representation and semantic meanings. Most sensor fusion approaches first classify single sensor readings and then combine classification results from multiple sensors to derive high-level meanings. Other approaches [15] directly concatenate features from different sensors and train activity classifier using the combined feature vectors. Both approaches work for certain applications but lack flexibility. For Multiple Sensor Fusion techniques, the problem typically has a "tracking" nature: given a set of interested quality and input sensors, they fuse the sensors to better model the interested quality. Thus, these approaches are inherently application specific, depending on the mapping relationship between the input sensors and the interested quality.

Based on the behavior text representation, we propose to fuse heterogeneous sensor information in a more principled way where sensor readings are concatenated as a new unit to reduce the conditional entropy of the whole data set for a certain task. In this paper, we use GPS and accelerometer readings as example to illustrate our sensor fusion approach.

After quantizing the GPS coordinates to behavior text, we calculate the mutual information between each accelerometer label and GPS labels. If they are not correlated, i.e, with low mutual information value, we concatenate the two together into a new label, otherwise we drop the GPS label when the mutual information is high. The intuition is that when two types of sensor highly correlate to each other such as the "running" motion always occur in the gym, then there is no need to use both information to represent this activity, whereas "sitting" motion occur with many locations: living room, study room, cafe etc., we need to combine these two information to distinguish different ways of "sitting" which can be "sit on coach and watch TV in the living room" or "sit in front of the laptop and surf the web" or "sit in a cafe and chat with friends."

Mutual information is defined as:

$$I(A;G) = H(A) - H(A|G) \tag{4}$$

where $H(A)$ is the marginal entropy of label A in accelerometer text, $H(A|G)$ is the conditional entropy of label A and G. The conceptual process is illustrated in following figure:

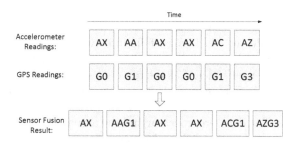

Fig. 3. Conceptual sensor fusion process

5   SensCare System

SensCare is based on a non-intrusive mobile lifelogger system designed using a blackboard architecture [22]. SensCare consists of two groups of components: the *blackboard* which acts as a centralized context data storage and message router, and *satellite applications* that provides or consumes context data, or perform system reconfiguration (Figure 4).

As shown in figure 4, the conceptual blackboard consists with three major components: event controller, raw data storage and activity data storage.

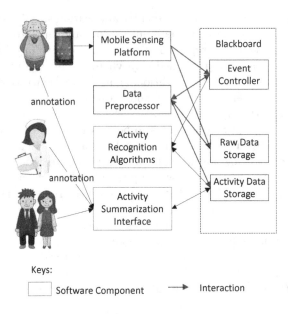

Fig. 4. System architecture

The *raw data storage* stores the unprocessed context data received from sensing platform. The *activity data storage* saves intermediate data generated by activity recognition applications or user's annotation results. The third component, *event controller*, acts as a message router and controller of the system. It receives events from one application then dispatches it to another if there is an application subscribing to that message.

Components outside the blackboard falls into two categories: context/event provider and consumer. A typical context provider is a mobile sensing platform, which is carried by the user and acts as the raw data source of the system. Some of the components are in both classes, for instance, the activity summarization interface will both consume the preprocessed data and provide user annotation to activity data storage. The data preprocessor and the activity recognition algorithm work together in an activity recognition loop and provide initial segmentation for users' annotation. Activity indexing and similar activity retrieval applications are helpers to reduce the human effort in activity summarization (annotation) process. After all, activity data will be displayed on the summarization interface to key parties in healthcare network, including the elderly, his family members and caregivers. The following sections will provide more details of these key components.

5.1   Smart Phones as Mobile Sensing Platform

There are two typical approaches of traditional sensor-based monitoring system: "Smart Home" [21] and wearable sensing platforms.

Smart Homes have sensors mounted on walls and ceilings or have them built in furnitures and appliances. With a rich set of sensors, this approach can collect a wide varieties of lifelog data for further analysis. However, deploying such a system is expensive.

Wearable sensing platforms [11] attach low-cost-light-weight sensors such as EEG and ECG to the human body to measure users' body information like brainwave and heart-rate. However, most of these devices are invasive and uncomfortable to wear [16].

For elderly healthcare, we believe three aspects of the mobile sensing platform are important to the success of sensor-based elderly care systems:

– Mobility. The sensing platform will be embedded in devices that users can naturally carry at daily basis. The device should be lightweight and provide a user friendly interface to configure. The power should last at least one day without charging with sensors activated.
– Sensing capability. The sensing platform should have sufficient types of sensors to capture different aspects of a patient's activity.Many mobile sensing platforms in the market has only one or two types of sensors (e.g., accelerometer only FitBit). As shown by our own work and by others(e.g., [14] and [12]) using multiple types of sensors usually leads to much higher activity recognition accuracy.
– User acceptance. The sensing device should not significantly disturb users' normal life. Comfortableness, appearance and privacy are important for users to accept the technology. For most elderly users, wearing an uncomfortable device over 8 hours per day will make them rejecting the technology. Similarly, wearing several wired sensors around the body or carrying a sensing platform with camera might lead to embarrassment in social events.

Based on these criteria, we choose smart phones as the mobile sensing platform for SensCare. Smart phones are affordable to most users. They do not need any special deployment or configuration to get their embedded sensors work. Smart phones have built-in network connections for data transmission and they usually have programming interfaces for developer to write new applications. Though it would be ideal to extend the sensing capability with other wearable sensors such as EEG or ECG and transmit the data to smart phones via bluetooth.

We developed the mobile sensing client on an Android phone. The mobile sensing client records the following information: 1) 3-axis accelerometer for motion, 2) Magnetometer for the azimuth value of phone's heading direction. 3) GPS coordinates for outdoor locations, 4) Microphone recordings for sound (we only use sound information for ground truth annotation in this paper), 5) Rotation matrix of the phone derived from the accelerometer reading and the g-value[1], 6) Ambient light , 7) Temperature sensor for environment temperature, and 8) WiFi signal strength for indoor location. All these sensory data are recorded with their sampling time-stamps. The data is saved in CSV format and is transmitted to the raw context data storage on the server side using the HTTP protocol via wireless connections.

---

[1] We used Motorola Droids which do not have gyroscope sensors. The orientation of the phone is estimated by the Android SDK based on the accelerometer readings and the gravity g-value.

5.2   Interactive Activity Summarization Interface

After the data is processed on the server side, SensCare displays all segmented/recognized activities on the web using a personal calendar system. The user can browse through the calendar, select and annotate automatically identified activities, or create/identify a new activity when the automatic activity segmentation fails to do so. Users can also view the hierarchical structure of their daily activities (Figure 5), which will provide them more choices on granularity for activity annotation as well. A color code is assigned to each activity so the user can easily distinguish between different activities. To better visualize activities by their semantic meanings, we use the same color for similar activities on the calendar. Once the user annotates one activity on the calendar, the description of the activity, e.g., "playing tennis", will be propagated such that all similar activities will all be labeled as "play tennis."

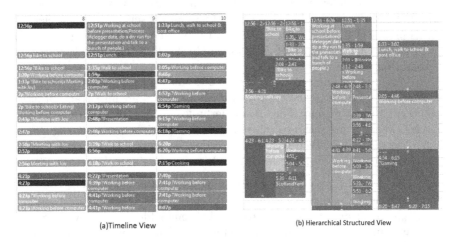

(a)Timeline View   (b) Hierarchical Structured View

Fig. 5. Personal calendar based timeline under different views

6   Experiments and Evaluation

6.1   Experiments Setup

The sensing client runs on a *Motorola Droid*. Table 1 shows sensors used and their sampling rates. Although video and audio data should help, we decided not to use them in SensCare for three reasons. First of all, the media stream will create a large data storage and transmission overhead, which greatly reduces the battery life. Another reason is privacy concern, especially for recording video. In addition, we realized that capturing video on Android requires the application stays on foreground, which will prevent the user using other functionalities of the phone.

We collected 36 hours of real life data in 5 continue weekdays from two graduate students to verify and analyze the system[2]. The data collection process lasts

---

[2] We are planning to collect data from elderly participants to study more realistic data for elderly care.

Table 1. Sensors on the mobile client and their sampling rate

Sensor	Sampling Rate
Accelerometer, magnetometer	
Ambient light, temperature	20Hz (every 50 ms)
Microphone	8KHz
Camera	
GPS, WiFi	every 2 minutes

about 7 hours each day. To simulate the lifestyle of an elderly, users are asked not to perform strenuous physical activities. Table 2 is a summary of activities done by the user.

User carried two phones during the data collection stage (Figure 6). One was tied to the user's right arm and another phone was used in the normal way: most of the time the phone was in user's pocket and from time to time the user took it out to make phone calls or check emails.

By the end of each day, the user will use the web interface to annotate his activities during the day in three settings:

Fig. 6. Two phone positions in experiments

– Based on the unsupervised segmentation results, label each identified activity. User will based on his memory and the coloring of the activity to assign the "meaning" of the identified activity.
– Without looking at the unsupervised segmentation, the user listens to the recorded audio and creates from scratch his daily activity summary on the calendar. This segmentation/annotation is used as the ground truth in our experiments.

The goal of the experiments is to evaluate 1) whether the automatic activity segmentation matches the ground truth, and 2) whether the similar activity coloring scheme and the automatic activity recognition through similar activity label propagation helps the user to recall what has happened before.

Table 2. Activity instance count and their average time

Activity	Instance Count	Avg. Time per Instance (minutes)
Walk	7	50.29
Working on Computer	15	66.07
Cooking	4	19.75
Eating	9	20.78
Washing Dishes	2	4.5
Cycling	2	21.5
Video Gaming	2	47.5
Presentation	2	29
Having Class	2	79
Meeting	2	69.5
Talking to Somebody	5	15
Driving	3	8.67
Printing Paperwork	1	44

6.2   Evaluation Metric

We evaluate the accuracy of the activity segmentation and recognition by calculating the F-Score of user's annotation with the ground truth.

Each identified activity in system's annotation A is a triple of $< s, t, l >$ where s is the starting time of the activity, e is the ending time and l is the label of the activity such as "walking". Similarly, we can represent each activity in the ground truth G also as a triple of $< s, t, l >$.

For each activity A in the system's annotation, if there exists a ground truth activity G such that $A_l = G_l$, i.e., the two activities have the same label, and $A_s = G_s \pm \Delta$ $A_e = G_e \pm \Delta$ where two activities have roughly the same starting time and ending time within the allowed margin Δ, then we consider a matches the ground truth activity g and is a true positive (Figure 7). With the precision and recall value calculated for each activity type, we can estimate the harmonic mean and report the F1 score. High F1 scores indicate the system's segmentation/label matches the ground truth.

6.3   Impact of Phone Position in Activity Recognition

We first compare whether the position of the phone has any impact on the activity recognition. Figure 8 shows that system performs better when the mobile phone is attached to users right arm. But for some specific events, like cycling and walking, right arm setting performs worse than pocket setting. It makes sense because arms are relatively stable while riding the bike yet legs are moving more frequent and regularly. In the case of walking, the motion pattern of arms is not as unique as the motion pattern of legs. For events that are closely related to hand movements, like cooking, the right arm setting performances better.

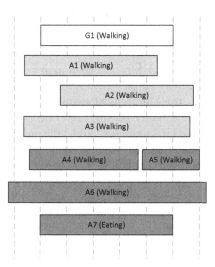

Fig. 7. Ground truth labeled as G_1 with three true annotations(A_1-A_3) and four false annotations(A_4-A_7)

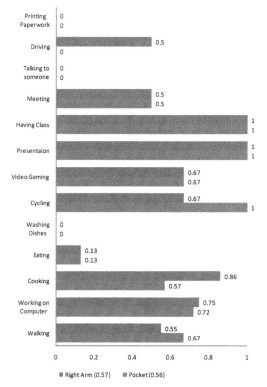

Fig. 8. F1 score of user annotations on pocket and right arm datasets, produced by only using accelerometer data. For pocket dataset, the overall F-Score is 0.57, while the score of right arm dataset is 0.56.

6.4   Hierarchical Activity Recognition vs. Smoothed HMM

We also compare the performance between the hierarchical activity segmentation with the smoothed single-layer HMM. From the best performance of HMM, we set the number of states in HMM to 10 and set the smoothing window size to 800 (around 6 minutes) empirically. Averaged over all activity types, HMM performs worse than the hierarchical segmentation approach (Figure 9). In particular, HMM performs badly on high-level activities such like *"Having Class"*, *"Meeting"*, *"Working on Computer"* and *"Presentation"*. These activities are usually composed by multiple low-level activities and have multiple motion patterns. HMM doesn't have the capability to merge these similar pattern to a higher level activity.

We found that HMM's inability to provide detailed activity structure information also hinders the user to annotate lower level activities. For example, from HMM's segmentation the user can only annotate *"Working Before Computer"* but cannot label sub-activities like *"Writing Paper"* *"Data Preprocessing"* and *"Activity Annotation"* (Figure 10).

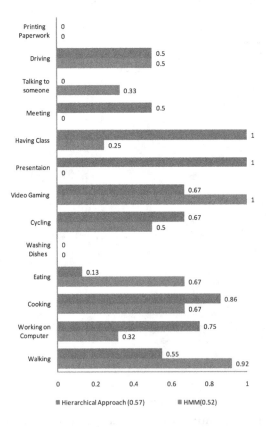

Fig. 9. The F-Score of user annotation on Hierarchical activity segmentation result vs. HMM, on right arm dataset, motion only

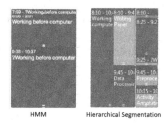

HMM   Hierarchical Segmentation

Fig. 10. Single level activity segmentation might lost information regards of lower level events

6.5 Power Consumption

To achieve ubiquitous sensing, selected sensors on the smart phone need to work continuously. With all sensors active, the sensing application can drain the battery very quickly. We estimate how long the mobile sensing platform can continuously monitor the user.

We exam the battery life under three sensing configuration sets. The first one keeps all sensors on; the second one keeps all sensors on except the camera. In the third setting, both camera and microphone are turned off.

Experiments show that the phone can only work for 3 hours without charging if all sensors were turned on. With the camera turned off, it can work for 8-10 hours, which is long enough for daily activity monitoring. The smart phone can work for more than 24 hours if microphone is turned off.

6.6 Sensor Fusion

As shown in Figure 9, unsupervised activity segmentation using accelerometer sensor only fails to identify activities such as *"Washing dishes"*, *"Driving"* and *"Talking to somebody"*. By analyzing the original lifelogs, we noticed that these activities don't differ significantly motion-wise from their preceding and following activities. For instance, *"Driving"* is usually followed by *"Having dinner"* whose motion signatures are similar to *"Driving"* . Using motion-only information, the system can not separate these activities from each other and these activities are recognized as one super-activity such as "driving, then having dinner". This is common for events that last less than 15 minutes.

We experiment with sensor fusion of combining motion sensors with location information. Instead of simply concatenate the two sensor into one, we use the mutual information criterion to fuse two sensors only when needed (Section 4). Figure 11 compares results of using motion only information and "motion plus location" fusion for activity segmentation. In general, sensor fusion significantly improves the recall for location related activities such as "driving" and "eating". In motion only segmentation, these two activities are usually concatenated into one. After introducing the GPS location information, the system is now able to distinguish them. Similarly, with motion-only information, "meeting" and "talking" are usually recognized as *"woking on computer"*. Combined with location information, they can now be identified correctly.

However, we do notice sensor fusion causes lower activity segmentation when location information should not be used to identify an activity. In particular, for activities that occur at different locations such as "working on computer" and "cycling" , there is no need to distinguish "working on computer at room 101" vs. "working on computer at room 102", or "cycling on Castro street" vs "cycling on Liberty Ave.". But for the overall performance, the sensor fusion result is superior than motion only activity segmentation (Figure 11).

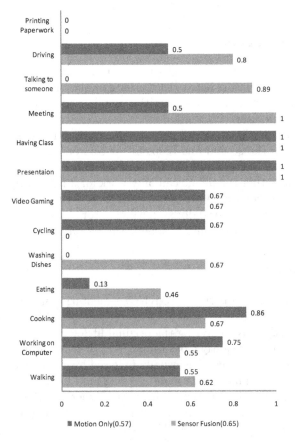

Fig. 11. A comparison of motion only and sensor fusion activity annotation results, on right arm dataset

7   Related Work

There are many works try to recognize user activity from accelerometer data [5,13]. The most successful and exhaustive work in this area is made by

Bao et al. [2]. In their experiments, subjects wore 5 biaxial accelerometers on different body positions as they performed a variety of activities like walking, sitting, standing still, watching TV, running, bicycling, eating, reading etc. Data collected by the accelerometers was used to train a set of classifiers, which included decision trees (C4.5), decision tables and nearest-neighbor algorithm found in the Weka Machine Learning Toolkit [23]. Decision tree classifiers showed the best performance, recognizing activities with an overall accuracy of 84%. However, most of the investigated algorithms are supervised and would be hard to be applied to applications like *SensCare*, since collecting enough trainning data is difficult under such a real world application senario, and it's impractical to train models for all possible activities in human's life.

The sequential and temporal characteristic of activity makes dynamic models such as the Hidden Markov Model (HMM) widely used in activity recognition. To overcome some of the shortages of HMM, like performance degrades when the range of activities become more complex or long-term temporal dependency exists between activities that makes Markov assumption difficult to deal with [6], variations of HMM were developed such as Layered HMM [19], Switching Hidden Semi-Markov Model (HSMM) [6] and Hierarchical Hidden Markov Model (HHMM) [7] for sensor-based activity detection. Although building HMM family models don't need labeled training data, however, it requires to predefine the number of state as an parameter for model training. In activity recognition's perspective, for HMM based systems, the number of activities needs to be a prior knowledge, which might only be true under certain application senarios. On the other hand, the EM algorithm employed by HMM for parameter estimation is a performance bottleneck for model trainning. Our experience with Hierachical HMM has indicated that it is still hard to scale up to efficiently handle the data size as what SensCare needs to process.

There are several works try to model activities using language-based techniques. Such techniques include suffix-tree [10], probabilistic context-free grammar [9,18], and a decision-tree-based [8] method. While all these techniques are hierarchical, they are either supervised or require a lot of human intervention.

8   Conclusion

In this paper, we introduce SensCare, an activity summarization system using smart phones to provide summarization for elder healthcare systems. We evaluate the feasibility of using smart phones as sensing platform regarding of user acceptance, privacy, power consumption and the impact of phone position on activity detection.

An unsupervised hierarchical activity segmentation algorithm was used in the system to overcome challenges like detecting activity with rare labeled data and unknown activity granularities. We compare the performance of selected algorithm with a single-layer Hidden Markov Model. Result show that the structural activity segmentation significantly improves the annotation quality.

A heterogeneous sensor fusion technique is used to improve the activity segmentation. Experiments over five days of real life dataset indicate that activity segmentation based on sensor fusion is much better than using motion infomration only.

For future work, we will investigate a more principled method for sensor fusion to determine which sensor types should be fused to best describe an activity. We will use all sensor information collected in our future experiments and work with our partners in elderly care to test the system with elderly users.

Acknowledgement. This research was supported in part by CyLab at Carnegie Mellon under grants DAAD19-02-1-0389 and W911NF-09-1-0273 from the Army Research Office and the awards from Google Research and Cisco Research.

References

1. Aging in place. Journal of Housing for the Elderly,
   http://www.seniorresource.com/ageinpl.htm
2. Bao, L., Intille, S.S.: Activity recognition from user-annotated acceleration data, pp. 1–17. Springer (2004)
3. Baum, L.E., Petrie, T., Soules, G., Weiss, N.: A maximization technique occurring in the statistical analysis of probabilistic functions of markov chains. The Annals of Mathematical Statistics 41(1), 164–171 (1970)
4. Buckwalter, K.C., Davis, L.L.: Elder caregiving in rural communities (2001)
5. Bussmann, J.B.J., Martens, W.L.J., Tulen, J.H.M., Schasfoort, F.C., van den Berg-Emons, H.J.G., Stam, H.J.: Measuring daily behavior using ambulatory accelerometry: The Activity Monitor. In: Behavior Research Methods, Instruments, & Computers, pp. 349–356 (August 2001)
6. Duong, T.V., Bui, H.H., Phung, D.Q., Venkatesh, S.: Activity recognition and abnormality detection with the switching hidden semi-markov model. In: Proceedings of the 2005 IEEE Computer Society Conference on Computer Vision and Pattern Recognition (CVPR 2005), vol. 01, pp. 838–845. IEEE Computer Society, Washington, DC (2005)
7. Fine, S., Singer, Y., Tishby, N.: The hierarchical hidden markov model: Analysis and applications. Machine Learning 32(1), 41–62 (1998)
8. Ghasemzadeh, H., Barnes, J., Guenterberg, E., Jafari, R.: A phonological expression for physical movement monitoring in body sensor networks. In: 5th IEEE International Conference on Mobile Ad Hoc and Sensor Systems, pp. 58–68 (September 2008)
9. Guerra-Filho, G., Fermuller, C., Aloimonos, Y.: Discovering a language for human activity. In: Proceedings of the AAAI 2005 Fall Symposium on Anticipatory Cognitive Embodied Systems, Washington, DC (2005)
10. Hamid, R., Maddi, S., Bobick, A., Essa, I.: Structure from statistics-unsupervised activity analysis using suffix trees. In: International Conference on Computer Vision (2007)
11. Harvard Sensor Networks Lab: Codeblue project: Wireless sensor networks for medical care, http://fiji.eecs.harvard.edu/CodeBlue
12. Huynh, T., Fritz, M., Schiele, B.: Discovery of activity patterns using topic models. In: Proceedings of the 10th International Conference on Ubiquitous Computing, UbiComp 2008, p. 10 (2008)

13. Lee, S.W., Mase, K.: Activity and location recognition using wearable sensors. IEEE Pervasive Computing 1(3), 24–32 (2002)
14. Logan, B., Healey, J., Philipose, M., Tapia, E.M., Intille, S.S.: A Long-Term Evaluation of Sensing Modalities for Activity Recognition. In: Krumm, J., Abowd, G.D., Seneviratne, A., Strang, T. (eds.) UbiComp 2007. LNCS, vol. 4717, pp. 483–500. Springer, Heidelberg (2007)
15. Maurer, U., Smailagic, A., Siewiorek, D., Deisher, M.: Activity Recognition and Monitoring Using Multiple Sensors on Different Body Positions. In: International Workshop on Wearable and Implantable Body Sensor Networks (BSN 2006), pp. 113–116 (2006)
16. Mundt, C., Montgomery, K., Udoh, U., Barker, V., Thonier, G., Tellier, A., Ricks, R., Darling, R., Cagle, Y., Cabrol, N., Ruoss, S., Swain, J., Hines, J., Kovacs, G.: A multiparameter wearable physiologic monitoring system for space and terrestrial applications. IEEE Transactions on Information Technology in Biomedicine 9(3), 382–391 (2005)
17. National Center for Chronic Disease Prevention and Health Promotion: Improving and Extending Quality of Life Among Older Americans: At A Glance 2010 (2010), http://www.cdc.gov/chronicdisease/resources/publications/AAG/aging.htm
18. Ogale, A., Karapurkar, A., Aloimonos, Y.: View-invariant modeling and recognition of human actions using grammars. In: Workshop on Dynamical Vision at ICCV, pp. 115–126 (2005)
19. Oliver, N., Horvitz, E., Garg, A.: Layered representations for human activity recognition. In: Proceedings of the 4th IEEE International Conference on Multimodal Interfaces, ICMI 2002, pp. 3–8. IEEE Computer Society, Washington, DC (2002)
20. Papineni, K., Roukos, S., Ward, T., Zhu, W.: Bleu: a method for automatic evaluation of machine translation. Technical Report RC22176(W0109-022), IBM Research Division, Thomas J. Watson Research Center (2001)
21. Virone, G., Wood, A., Selavo, L., Cao, Q., Fang, L., Doan, T., He, Z., Stoleru, R., Lin, S., Stankovic, J.A.: A an advanced wireless sensor network for health monitoring (2006)
22. Winograd, T.: Architectures for context. Human-Computer Interaction 16, 401–419 (2001)
23. Witten, I., Frank, E.: Data mining: Practical machine learning tools and techniques with java implementations. The Morgan Kaufmann Series in Data Management Systems (October 1999)

Rankr: A Mobile System for Crowdsourcing Opinions

Yarun Luon, Christina Aperjis, and Bernardo A. Huberman

HP Labs,
Palo Alto, CA 94304, USA
{yarun.luon,christina.aperjis,bernardo.huberman}@hp.com

Abstract. Evaluating large sets of items, such as business ideas, is a difficult task. While no one person has time to evaluate all the items, many people can contribute by each evaluating a few. Moreover, given the mobility of people, it is useful to allow them to evaluate items from their mobile devices. We present the design and implementation of a mobile service, *Rankr*, which provides a lightweight and efficient way to crowdsource the relative ranking of ideas, photos, or priorities through a series of pairwise comparisons. We discover that users prefer viewing two items simultaneously versus viewing one image at a time with better fidelity. Additionally, we developed an algorithm that determines the next most useful pair of candidates a user can evaluate to maximize the information gained while minimizing the number of votes required. Voters do not need to compare and manually rank all of the candidates.

Keywords: ranking, mobility, crowdsourcing, incentives, user interfaces.

1 Introduction

Increasingly, businesses and organizations want to encourage innovation by soliciting new ideas from employees and customers. But that is the easy part—figuring out which ideas are the best is a time-consuming process, often handled by a single person or a panel of reviewers. While some campaigns invite large populations to help vote for the best ideas, it is less likely that many people will have time to thoughtfully consider a large number of ideas. Similarly, developers building a product or service face a deluge of feature requests. More and more are adopting so-called agile methodologies, which requires them to regularly prioritize open issues. And individual people also face dilemmas of selection, as for example a photographer trying to choose which out of dozens of shots to enlarge.

Given the gargantuan number of choices that firms and consumers face when dealing with information, it is necessary to develop efficient mechanisms for filtering and ranking the set of possibilities. And since consumers and members of organizations are often mobile, it is important to be able to gather their opinions/votes in a mobile setting. In other words, people should not be required to vote from their desktops.

We propose a mobile service, Rankr, which provides a lightweight and efficient way to crowdsource the relative ranking of ideas, photos, or priorities. Rankr is a service we created and deployed for deriving a rank ordering of multiple objects, suggestions or

J.Y. Zhang et al. (Eds.): MobiCASE 2011, LNICST 95, pp. 20–31, 2012.

websites that uses pairwise comparisons among them. Unlike typical rank voting methods, voters do not need to compare and manually rank all of the candidates. Moreover, pairwise comparisons are well-suited for devices with smaller screens.

Given the votes that others have already cast, Rankr automatically determines the next most useful pair of candidates a user can evaluate to maximize the information gained while minimizing the number of votes required. This ensures that the mechanism scales beyond traditional voting schemes while enabling the crowdsourced ranking of many items–many more than any one user could be expected to evaluate.

We implemented our solution as a mobile service that systematically displays a pair of items side by side. A user (which could be an enterprise) interested in having people select the best among a collection of items, begins by organizing the items into a poll. The poll may be comprised of text descriptions (e.g., business ideas, slogans, feature requests) or media (e.g., photos). Each poll is easily accessible through a range of devices, such as a desktop browser and any mobile device.

The wide accessibility of Rankr together with the fact that each user is not required to perform a large number of comparisons make our solution very effective for crowdsourcing the ranking of items. Users who have idle time can easily get into the system, perform as many comparisons as they wish, and have their work recorded by the system. Rankr scales well not only to users who spend a lot of time using the mobile service, but also to users who only spend a small amount of time (e.g., while waiting in line at the grocery store or while waiting for the train). These design decisions lend themselves to the philosophy that a user can contribute his or her opinion with very little effort and time.

2   Related Work

A variety of prior solutions exist to crowdsource opinions. Most of these approaches evaluate each item on its own without comparing it to other items. For instance, Starbucks allows consumers to suggest ideas and vote "up" or "down" on ideas of others at "My Starbucks Idea".[1] Dell offers a similar service called IdeaStorm on its webpage, where people can promote or demote ideas.[2] However, when the goal of the evaluation is to get a ranking of the items, it is important to see how different items compare to each other. The simplest way to achieve this is through pairwise comparisons.

The method of paired comparisons [2] presents items in pairs for comparative judgment to one or more judges. The outcomes of the pairwise comparisons are then used to assign a score to each item. The estimated scores can in turn be used to rank the items. The Elo method addresses the problem of estimating the scores using data from pairwise comparisons under specific assumptions about the underlying distribution [3].

The Elo method has been used in a variety of settings, most notably for ranking chess players, and has recently been applied for ranking in twitter-like forums [8]. It has also been used for eliciting preferences from pairwise comparisons of pictures in a matching game [5]. Pairwise comparisons are also used by FotoVotr[3] for its weekly photo contests

---

[1] http://mystarbucksidea.force.com/

[2] http://www.ideastorm.com/

[3] http://www.fotovotr.com/

and by the dating site OkCupid[4] to obtain a ranking for potential profile pictures of a user; however, we do not know what algorithms are used by these websites.

In this paper, we use the Elo method to rank items of various types (such as business ideas, priorities or agile feature requests) in a mobile setting. We use ordinal pairwise comparisons, but note that the problem of obtaining aggregate rankings from cardinal pairwise comparisons has also been studied [6].

The problem of obtaining an aggregate ranking that represents the preferences of a group of people accurately and fairly is a central question in social choice theory. The difficulties in accomplishing this task are illustrated in Arrow's impossibility theorem [1], which states that when voters have three or more distinct alternatives, no voting system can convert the ranked preferences of individuals into a community-wide ranking that meets a certain set of criteria. On the other hand, it is possible to get a satisfactory aggregate ranking under certain assumptions on individual preference [7]. However, here we do not consider these concerns of social choice theory. Moreover, we do not require knowledge of the complete preferences of each user. Instead, each user may only perform a few pairwise comparisons which are used to obtain an aggregate ranking with the Elo method.

Our approach is also related to conjoint analysis, a statistical technique used in market research to determine how people value different features that make up an individual product or service [4]. Rankr, however, focuses on ranking items and does not consider how individual features of an item affect people's preferences.

3   Design

Rankr is a mobile service that displays a pair of items side by side. A user interested in having people select the best among a collection of items begins by creating a set of them which Rankr can then access. The collection may be comprised of text descriptions (e.g., business ideas, slogans, feature requests) or media (e.g., photos). We refer to such a collection as *a poll*. In the case of photos, they can be uploaded to the desktop version of Rankr. Polls that are text based can be created via the desktop or mobile version.

The creator of the poll then sends a link to a list of people, asking them for help in evaluating the items. When a recipient clicks on the Rankr link, s/he is presented with a pair of items and is asked to select the item that is better with respect to some criterion. For instance, in the case of photos, the question could be: "Which photo would look better in a desk frame?" Some other examples are shown in Figure 1. After the user chooses one of the items, the page performs an AJAX reload with another pair so that s/he can continue voting on pairs if s/he wants to. In order to avoid biases, because the order in which items are presented/loaded can vary due to the asynchronous nature of the Internet, in the Rankr prototype, we insured that both images were loaded and then presented simultaneously to the user.

Given that we are interested in aggregating opinions from a large and heterogeneous crowd, we allow users to enter and leave the system at any time, having completed an

---

[4] http://www.okcupid.com/

(a) A poll that ranks pictures.

(b) A poll that measures brand awareness.

(c) A poll that helps a company prioritize how it could improve employee satisfaction.

Fig. 1. Examples of polls

arbitrary number of votes. In order to obtain a ranking of the items, we associate a score with each item. Once a user compares two items, the scores of those items are updated.

Users are able to see the relative rankings of the items they vote on at any time during the voting process (Figure 2). The rankings show the current rank of the item as well as its points. Points are a simplified representation of the difference between the items with the highest and lowest scores.

In Section 3.1, we discuss the user interface. In Section 3.2, we describe the algorithm that updates the items' scores in order to produce a ranking. In Section 3.3, we present the results of an internal pilot study. In Section 3.4, we discuss incentives for participation.

3.1   Interface

We produced a design that is intuitive for the user when s/he has to choose between two items. As a starting point, we chose to focus on the best way to display two images. To help solve this problem, usability tools, in particular a cognitive walkthrough, paper

Fig. 2. The ranking of a list of items from a poll

prototypes, and a task analysis were employed. The cognitive walkthrough explored different ways to display two images side by side and yielded four possible interaction models. These models were translated into paper prototypes using Balsamiq[5], printed, and then cut. A usability study was conducted and the favored paper prototype was implemented. Next, a task analysis was done on the hi-fi prototype to insure the system was operating as intended and to seek further guidance on the next iteration of interface design. We will discuss in further detail the usability studies using paper prototypes and the task analysis.

Paper Prototype. The four prototypes had a different interaction model for how the images would be displayed (Figure 3). One of the prototypes simply displayed both images side by side (Figure 3(a)). The remaining prototypes predominately displayed one of the images while giving cues to the second image (Figures 3(b), 3(c), 3(d)).

Six participants, recruited through availability sampling, between the ages of 20 and 50 with varying experience with touchscreen smartphones interacted with the lo-fi prototototypes. The study revealed that participants unanimously *preferred viewing both images at the same time rather than viewing the images separately at higher fidelity.*

---

[5] http://www.balsamiq.com

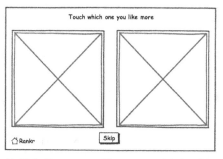

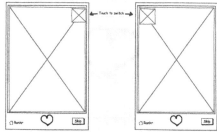

(a) **Pair Prototype:** Pictures are side by side.

(b) **Thumbnail Prototype:** One of the images takes up the majority of the screen. A thumbnail version of the other image is displayed in the corner.

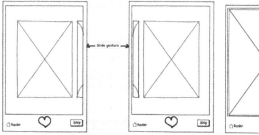

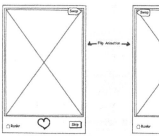

(c) **Gallery Prototype:** One of the images takes up the majority of the screen. The second image is partially visible to either side of the image in focus. This interface suggests the user is viewing the images in a gallery.

(d) **Button Prototype:** One of the images takes up the majority of the screen. Also displayed on the screen is a labeled button (e.g., "swap"). Clicking the button switches the image to the other item.

Fig. 3. Paper Prototypes

It is interesting to note that all participants acknowledged the multi-touch reverse pinch gesture as a method to zoom in on the image to increase its fidelity.

A secondary goal of the paper prototypes was to determine an intuitive interaction model for the user to select the image they prefer. Possible methods included an icon by each picture the user would select to indicate the preferred item or a direct touch to select the image. Possible choices for the icon included a heart, a thumbs-up, or a smiley face (Figure 4). Out of the three, users preferred the heart icon. However most participants felt that the most intuitive interaction was to directly touch the image they preferred.

Task Analysis. The results of the task analysis were used to inform the next stage of design as well as provide a sanity check on the current system. Four participants, recruited through availability sampling, with familiarity of touchscreen smartphones between the ages of 20 and 40 were asked to do simple tasks using a first generation Nexus phone running Android 2.3. The four tasks were:

Fig. 4. Users were asked which icon best represented the action of preferring one image over another. Although users liked the heart icon the best, most users wanted to directly touch the image to indicate preference.

1. Choose a poll
2. Make pairwise comparisons
3. Skip a pair
4. View the rankings of the poll

Even though there were no cognitive mismatches between the system design and the user's conceptual model of how the system should operate, participants felt the interface was too information scarce and wanted to be more informed about their decisions.

The word "points" was confusing to users. They did not understand how points were being calculated nor how the points should be interpreted. To address this issue, we could look into a more intuitive way to display the scores and potentially explain to users how points are calculated.

3.2   The Algorithm

We now describe how the results of comparisons are used to (1) rank the items and (2) select the next pair to be compared.

Comparisons are translated into a rank ordering through the Elo method [3], which is used for calculating the relative skill levels of players in two-player games such as chess. A score is associated with every item, which increases whenever the item "wins" in a pairwise comparison and decreases whenever the item "loses" in a pairwise comparison. The magnitude of the increase (resp., decrease) depends on the difference between the score of the item and the score of the item that it defeated (resp., was defeated by). Winning against a high score item results in a larger increase than winning against a low score item. With the goal of achieving more accuracy at the top, the algorithm is more likely to select items with higher scores for the next comparison.

Let s_i be the score of item i. Suppose that item i is compared with item j. Let y be the indicator of whether item i is selected in the pairwise comparison between i and j (that is, $y = 1$ if item i is selected and $y = 0$ if item j is selected). After the comparison, the score of item i is updated according to:

$$s_i \leftarrow s_i + K \left(y - \frac{1}{1 + e^{s_j - s_i}} \right), \tag{1}$$

where K is a scaling parameter, often referred to as the "K-factor."

Fig. 5. Users can see the personal history of comparisons of a particular item from the results screen. This feature was heavily requested by participants in the task analysis.

The idea behind the Elo method is to model the probability of the possible outcomes of a pairwise comparison between item i and item j as a function of the scores of the two items. For instance, if the score of item i is greater than the score of item j, then item i should have a larger probability of being selected in a pairwise comparison between the two items. The update rule given by (1) is derived under the assumption that an item with score s_i is selected against an item with score s_j with probability

$$\frac{e^{s_i}}{e^{s_i} + e^{s_j}} = \frac{1}{1 + e^{s_j - s_i}}.$$

While Elo is a method to calculate relative scores of items, it is not a ranking algorithm per se, in that it does not specify which two items should be in the next ballot. The easiest method would be to pick randomly these two items each time a user is willing to perform a comparison; however, this does not give preference to the top items. Since we are interested in identifying accurately the top items, rather than obtaining a reliable complete ranking, for the next comparison we preferentially select items which have high scores at the time the ballot is requested. This selection algorithm does not alter the Elo method, but rather considers the scores returned from the Elo method in determining the next ballot.

3.3   Pilot Test

The objective of the internal pilot was to gather perception of the best ping pong players out of 12 colleagues in addition to discovering any problems in the Rankr service. The poll was setup as a 12-item poll with each item being a ping pong player. A total of 278 comparisons were made from 8 participants who completed on average 35 comparisons or 53% of the total available ballots[6]. We discovered through the pilot that people were uncertain when to stop voting due to lack of a progress bar, and participants were confused when the lowest ranked item had 0 points when they knowingly voted for the item. The feedback from the pilot will help inform the next iteration of design.

3.4   Incentives for Participation

In certain cases, it may be useful to introduce an incentive mechanism that will induce people to volunteer their pairwise comparisons of whatever set of items or ideas they are presented with, and ideally convey a truthful opinion of what they think is best.

One such mechanism gives a reward to whoever ranks highest the item that all other participants also consider the most desirable. So all participants are not only choosing what they think is most desirable but also what they think others will find attractive and desirable. A variant of this mechanism would have the participants paying a small amount of money to enter into this "game" and receive the total amount collected as a prize. The introduction of a monetary reward could encourage the participants to think carefully about their choices. Alternately, the evaluation of these items can be done quickly and independently so that these comparisons could be farmed out to workers on a service like Amazon's Mechanical Turk.[7] Users could also be incentivized to do comparisons in exchange for having others evaluate their own items, in a tit-for-tat scheme. These could naturally be combined: users could rank friends' content just to be helpful, or rank strangers' content to earn credits for getting their own content evaluated, or pay to have other users evaluate their content.

---

[6] A 12-item poll will have $\binom{12}{2}$ or 66 combinations.

[7] https://www.mturk.com/mturk/welcome

4   Implementation

Rankr is implemented as a mobile web service using the jQueryMobile[8] framework, an extension of the jQuery framework. The jQueryMobile framework is designed to create a unified user interface across popular mobile browsers. The decision to develop Rankr as a mobile web service versus a mobile application was intentional. We wanted Rankr to reach as many mobile users as possible while minimizing the development time for each mobile platform. Additionally, because Rankr only requires minimal user input for pairwise comparisons to be made (i.e., screen taps from the user), the benefits of developing Rankr as a mobile application, such as access to the mobile devices' hardware instruments (e.g., accelerometer) are not needed.

The server handles authentication and, for general purposes, serves a single page containing "mini mobile pages" to the mobile device with accompanying CSS and JavaScript files. Aside from the first page load, further communication between the mobile device and the server is done with AJAX requests using JSON.

Rankr has been verified to look and work the same on Android 2.0+, BlackBerry 6.0+, iOS 3.0+, and WebOs 1.4.1+ which confirms jQueryMobile's success in creating a unified user interface independent of mobile device.

The Rankr server runs on a combination of Ubuntu, Apache, Python, and Django. These specific software packages were chosen out of convenience and familiarity.

5   Future Work

Having completed the initial stages of development, we now intend to open Rankr to a larger user base to stress test the system. This would also involve running additional usability studies with a larger sample size.

In terms of specific improvements to the interface, we plan to integrate a more intelligent method to display images to maximize the real estate of the small screen (Figure 6, 7). Moreover, we are considering to incorporate sound and video in order to have multimedia polls where users could potentially compare a text item versus an audio item.

In the Rankr prototype, we insured that both images were loaded before presenting the images to the user in order to eliminate biases that could arise if one image is loaded before the other. Research into measuring other potential user biases because of how items are presented is needed. For instance, a user may be more or less likely to select an image because of its size, or users may behave differently when images are top-aligned (as in the current implementation) versus middle-aligned.

Focusing on the mechanism of pairwise comparisons, we could potentially use Rankr as a tool for profiling. As an example, consider a firm that wants to cluster consumers with respect to their preferences. The firm can ask consumers to do a few pairwise comparisons between specific products or more general categories. Using the results, the firm can cluster consumers into different types, and suggest different products to consumers of different types.

---

[8] http://jquerymobile.com

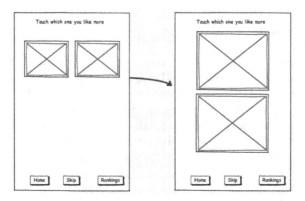

Fig. 6. In portrait mode, items will be stacked vertically

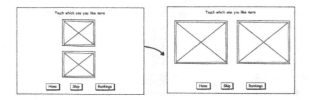

Fig. 7. In landscape mode, items will be stacked horizontally

6   Conclusions

In this paper, we have presented Rankr, a mobile service that ranks items through pair-wise comparisons. Our service has a number of advantages. First, it is accessible from any smartphone. Second, it has an intuitive interface. Third, it scales well irrespectively of how many comparisons each individual user performs, as long as all users in aggregate complete a sufficiently large number of comparisons. These properties make Rankr very effective for crowdsourcing the ranking of collections of items.

Acknowledgements. We would like to thank the following people for their contributions: Mike Brzozowski and Alex Vorbau whose early development work helped make Rankr a reality; Hang Ung for his efforts in the algorithm and implementation; and Thomas Sandholm for his thoughtful insights.

References

1. Arrow, K.J.: Social Choice and Individual Value. Wiley (1963)
2. David, H.A.: The Method of Paired Comparisons. Oxford University Press, New York (1988)
3. Elo, A.E.: The rating of chess players: Past and present. Arco Publishing, New York (1978)
4. Green, P.E., Srinivasan, V.: Conjoint analysis in marketing: New developments with implications for research and practice. The Journal of Marketing 54(4), 3–19 (1990)

5. Hacker, S., Ahn, L.V.: Matchin: Eliciting user preferences with an online game. In: Proc. of the SIGCHI Conf. on Human Factors in Computing Systems. ACM (2009)
6. Hochbaum, D.S.: The separation, and separation-deviation methodology for group decision making and aggregate ranking. In: Hasenbein, J.J. (ed.) TutORials in Operations Research, INFORMS, Hanover, MD, vol. 7, pp. 116–141 (2010)
7. Mas-Collel, A., Whinston, M.D., Green, J.R.: Microeconomic Theory. Oxford University Press (1995)
8. Sarma, A.D., Sarma, A.D., Gollapudi, S., Panigrahy, R.: Ranking mechanisms in twitter-like forums. In: Proc. Conf. on Web Search and Data Mining (2010)

Data Fusion for Movement Visualization in a Remote Health Monitoring System

Armen Babakanian[1] and Ani Nahapetian[2]

[1] University of California, Los Angeles
Los Angeles, CA, USA
[2] California State Northridge, Northridge
Northridge, CA, USA
`ani@csun.edu`

Abstract. In this paper, we present a data fusion visualization infrastructure for sensor signals from a remote health monitoring system. The infrastructure involves wireless interfacing with the embedded sensor system, known as the Smart Shoe. It fuses and filters the data measured and then uses it to visualize with a graphics display the extracted walking and movement patterns. The various features of the visualization infrastructure are presented, along with the implementation challenges and details.

Keywords: Medical Embedded Sensing Systems, Remote Health Monitoring, Wireless Health, Visualization.

1   Introduction

The proliferation of low-cost sensors and wireless connectivity is helping to introduce real-time and remote health monitoring for a wide array of patients. A variety of sensored devices exist that can unobtrusively be incorporated into patient life and then wirelessly transmit data to caregivers and healthcare professionals.

In this work we focus our data fusion and visualization infrastructure on the Smart Shoe embedded sensor system. The Smart Shoe is a lightweight sensing system aimed at extending fall risk analysis and human balance monitoring outside of a laboratory environment.

The current system monitors walking behavior to generate fall risk estimates, by using collected ambulation data values to extract correlations with features identified by geriatric motion experts as precursors to balance abnormality and fall risk [13] [14]. Additionally, the Smart Shoe has been used for neuropathy management [3] [4] and can be used for fine-grained weight fluctuation detection, which has been shown to be important for weight and cardiovascular system monitoring.

In our infrastructure, we wirelessly collect raw sensor signals from the Smart Shoe, either through a handheld device gateway or directly using the computer used for visualization. The data is them filtered and fused to enable graphical visualization of the walking and movement patterns of the Smart Shoe sensor system.

J.Y. Zhang et al. (Eds.): MobiCASE 2011, LNICST 95, pp. 32–40, 2012.

There are three distinct advantages to the use of a visualization approach for data analysis in this scenario. First, the visualization enables physicians and caregivers to assess walking patterns in a convenient and affordable manner. The graphics software includes features such as changing the angle of view, which would impossible to do in any other context. Potential views include, separating one shoe from the other, looking under the soles of the shoe while walking is taking place, and examining the movement of the foot from the side.

Second, the visualization software enables the researchers and caregivers to assess the quality of the data collected from the Smart Shoe system in an efficient manner. With visual inspection invalid data values can be easily spotted, and thus removed to prevent skewing of the data analysis results. The sheer volume of data collected using the Smart Shoe specifically, and all other embedded health sensing systems generally, is astounding. Ensuring the validity of the data values can be an intimidating task; however, it is critical in health applications, considering that medical decisions for medication, hospitalization, and limitation of mobility can results from the assessment of the Smart Shoe system data values. By enabling a fast and efficient visualization of the data results, human users can reliably identify any abnormalities in the sensor data collection.

Finally, the infrastructure presented in this work has been used for Smart Shoe system development. The visualization and data fusion software and algorithms have been used to further enhance the development of the sensor system, including modifications to the placement of the system sensors and testing of the Bluetooth wireless transmission.

In the remainder of this paper, we present in detail the system infrastructure and components, with a special focus on the data fusion and graphics infrastructure.

2   Related Work

The Smart Shoe developed at UCLA has been used for various other applications. These include application to balance and fall risk assessment [13] [14], as well as monitoring foot placement in patients suffering from neuropathy [3] [4]. Smart Shoe data has also been used for event detection algorithm development and experimentation [15].

There exist other research systems that have examined visualization of movement and gait patterns in patients. With the Smart Cane system [1] [9] [17], the motion of the cane was displayed on a tablet PC for the purpose of system development and demonstration.

There exist various visualization software systems that visualize gait pattern data, but not using a graphics interface as we have done. These include [12], which uses a graph structure to display course-grain changes in gait over time. Dejnabadi et al carryout full gait visualization using accelerometer and gyroscope data, but no data from pressure sensors [5].

Data fusion in other embedded sensor systems has been explored previously. Projects include the environmental monitoring systems [6] [7] [8] [10] [16] and the in-home patient monitoring systems [11].

3   System Infrastructure

3.1   Smart Shoe

The Smart Shoe, shown in Figure 1, is an orthotic shoe developed at UCLA [3] [4] [13] [14]. Through the use of 3-axis gyroscope, 3-axis accelerometer, and a few well-placed pressure sensors, shown in Figure 2, the Smart Shoe is able to monitor foot motion and pressure distribution to evaluate the state of a patient. It wirelessly connects via Bluetooth to smart phones or other computing devices for data processing, visualization, and network connectivity.

The Smart Shoe is a lightweight infrastructure aimed at extending fall risk analysis and human balance monitoring outside of a laboratory environment. It is also used for detecting balance trends over time and alerting patients of improper foot placement. Additionally, the Smart Shoe can be used for fine-grained weight fluctuation detection, for weight and cardiovascular system monitoring.

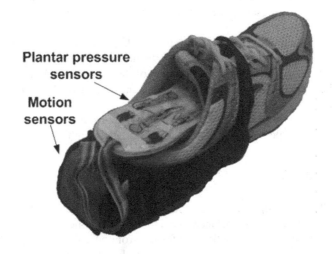

Fig. 1. Smart Shoe System [15]

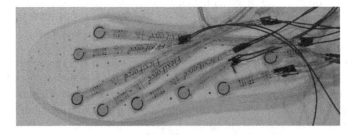

Fig. 2. Smart Shoe Insole Pressure Sensor Locations [14]

3.2   Overall System Functionality

A high-level overview of the overall functionality of the visualization infrastructure presented in this paper is given in Figure 3. As shown, sensor signals from the Smart Shoe are wirelessly transmitted to a computer, where visualization and data storage can be accomplished. The transmission of the data can be done in one of two ways. Using the Bluetooth transmitter on the smart shoe, sensor data can be transmitted directly to the computer.

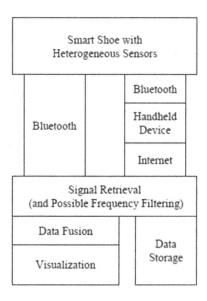

Fig. 3. Top-Level View of the System Interactions, from Sensor Data Collection to Wireless Transfer, to Visualization and Storage

Additionally, data from the smart shoe can be sent to a handheld device, including a smart phone. The data can then be transferred to a remote server or the computer with the visualization software. The advantage of this approach is that the computer with the visualization software does not need to be in the presence of the Smart Shoe. To the contrary, caregivers can visually monitor the motion of the patient remotely and conveniently.

Previous to our visualization infrastructure, data collected from the Smart Shoe was collected from the sensor system and then archived. The results were then used for various applications, including imbalance detection and activity monitoring. However, with this additional work, the data can be fused for data visualization using a user-friendly and interactive graphics interface.

3.3   Data Fusion

The sensors used in the Smart Shoe are heterogeneous, including accelerometers, gyroscopes, and pressure sensors. Additionally, the sensor signals are transmitted over a wireless connection either directly or indirectly to a computer. Transmission over the Bluetooth connection can be lossy. Additionally, the data collected from the various sensors are not necessarily time-synced with each other. All of these challenges with the sensor signals require post-processing of the data using a data fusion approach. Using statistical inference and model generation, x-y-z movement in space is created for eight data points. These values are then used for the visualization software.

3.4   Graphical Component

In this section, we present the interactive graphics visualization component of our infrastructure. Screenshots from the software developed is given in Figure 4. The Figures 4a and 4b demonstrate two different screenshots over time, as the patient moves the left foot to walk.

It is possible for the user of the software to change the angle of view, using mouse clicks and keyboard clicks. As shown in Figure 4, a view of foot motion from the bottom of the shoe can be shown, a perspective that would physically not be possible.

The dynamic pivot feature allows for the view changes. A grey bar at the end corner of the screen is used to represent the current location of the pivot. The location can be selected from a range of values, and with more than two values selected the center of mass of those selected points is calculated. In other words, the shoe is given three rotational values (x,y,z), and the values entered by the user are used to determine the point around which to pivot the shoe.

The user can modify is the number of feet that are to be viewed at a time. One or both feet can be viewed at a time.

It is possible to change the quality of the shoe graphics. With an online execution of the software, data filtering is used to limit the computation complexity of the data fusion, and hence enable online interaction between the visualization software and the Smart Shoe. In the case of offline visualization, the highest quality of visualization is to be used, for the most precise and complete examination of the data.

A summary of the interactive software features developed are given in Table 1. Additionally, we have uploaded two videos of the software execution to You Tube [18] [19]. The videos demonstrate a range of views that are possible, as well as the quality of the graphics software developed. They also highlight the ease with which invalid data values can be spotted.

The software takes into account collision detection with the ground. Specifically, it corrects for missing or flawed data, where the data appears to demonstrate that the shoe is moving past the ground. This collision detection algorithm can be used outside of the visualization software, in dynamic calibration of the sensors, specifically for the accelerometers. In the case of ground collision detection, recalibration of the sensors is signaled and carried-out without halting data collection. A related approach for in situ calibration of sensor systems has been examined before [2].

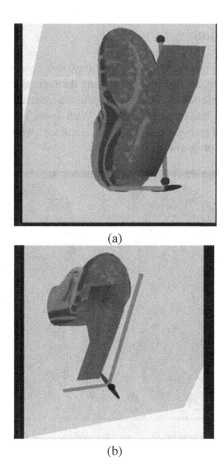

(a)

(b)

Fig. 4. Graphics Visualization Software Screen Shots: Demonstrating the Change in Shoe Movement as the Patient Walks

Table 1. Graphical Software Feature List

Feature Name	Feature Description
Dynamic Pivoting	Changing the view from which the shoe(s) can be viewed
Shoe Number	Displaying one or both feet to the screen at a time
Graphics Quality (i.e. online or offline execution)	Decreasing the quality of the animation by filtering the data values, for the sake of a more responsive online version of the software.
Data Source (i.e. remote or local)	Using data values collected using the machine's Bluetooth connection or picking up data values off of a remote server (which were collected from the Smart Shoe using a handheld device in the field).

4   Implementation

The implementation of the visualization involves two related parts, first fusing the heterogeneous sensor signals and then displaying them graphically.

The graphics are implemented with a polygon structure across the sole of the shoe, with a relatively small number of polygons. With some iterative exploration, three polygons were found to provide enough visual accuracy, while still enabling efficient online execution of the program.

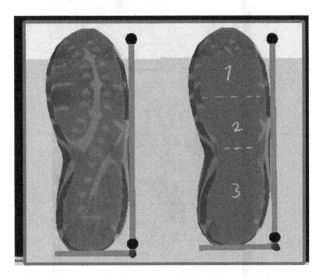

Fig. 5. Polygon Structure Overlaid the Shoe Graphics

Figure 5 demonstrates the locations of the polygons. As can be noted from the figure, the locations of the pressure sensors in the shoe insert, shown in Figure 2, are different from the end points of the polygons, displayed with red dots, in Figure 5. Additionally, the accelerometers and the gyroscopes are located at the back of the shoe, where there is no designated polygon.

As a result the graphics implementation required the manipulation and fusion of the data values obtained from the shoe sensors. Most notably the pressure sensor values and the movement sensor data was fused and then extrapolated to the eight movement points shown. The values of the movement points are then modified in the three-dimensional space, depending on the input sensor signals. The movement of the remainder of the shoe is dictated by the existing model for the shoe.

The red dots, which indicate the manipulation points, where chosen as they enabled full movement of the shoe. If desired, the third polygon can be extended to cover the bottom of the shoe completely. However, this is not the most natural point of motion for people.

5   Future Work

There exist several extensions to the work we are considering, in addition to the most general plan to apply our approach to other wireless health systems.

With the expansion of the Smart Shoe to fine-grain weight fluctuation detection, the data fusion approach can be leveraged for analyzing and visualizing patient weight changes and activity levels for the purpose of in-home congestive heart failure monitoring.

Finally, as a significant enhancement to the Smart Shoe, we plan to use our collision detection algorithm and software to enable dynamic Smart Shoe calibration to deal with accelerometer drift.

6   Conclusion

In this paper, we presented an efficient sensor data fusion and visualization approach, specifically for sensor signals collected from the Smart Shoe system. The system requirements that led to our fusion of non time-synced and heterogeneous sensor signals were presented. The various components of the infrastructure, including the data processing and graphical display were highlighted, including the implementation details of the graphics visualization.

References

1. Au, L.K., Wu, W.H., Batalin, M.A., Kaiser, W.J.: Active Guidance Towards Proper Cane Usage. In: 5th International Workshop on Wearable and Implantable Body Sensor Networks (BSN 2008), June 1-3 (2008)
2. Bychkovskiy, V., Megerian, S., Estrin, D., Potkonjak, M.: A Collaborative Approach to In-Place Sensor Calibration. In: Zhao, F., Guibas, L.J. (eds.) IPSN 2003. LNCS, vol. 2634, pp. 301–316. Springer, Heidelberg (2003)
3. Dabiri, F., Vahdatpour, A., Noshadi, H., Hagopian, H., Sarrafzadeh, M.: Electronic Orthotics Shoe: Preventing Ulceration in Diabetic Patients. In: 30th Annual International IEEE EMBS Conference, Vancouver, British Columbia, Canada, August 20-24 (2008)
4. Dabiri, F., Vahdatpour, A., Noshadi, H., Hagopian, H., Sarrafzadeh, M.: Ubiquitous Personal Assistive System for Neuropathy. In: The 2nd International Workshop on Systems and Networking Support for Healthcare and Assisted Living Environments (HealthNet), in Conjunction with ACM MobiSys, Breckenridge, Colorado (July 2008)
5. Dejnabadi, H., Jolles, B.M., Aminian, K.: A New Approach Measurement of Uniaxial Joint Angles Based on a Combination of Accelerometers and Gyroscopes. IEEE Trans. Biomed. Eng. 52(8), 1478–1484 (2005)
6. Ghiasi, S., Moon, H.J., Sarrafzadeh, M.: Collaborative and Reconfigurable Object Tracking. In: International Conference on Engineering of Reconfigurable Systems and Algorithms (ERSA), pp. 13–20 (June 2003)
7. Ghiasi, S., Moon, H.J., Sarrafzadeh, M.: Improving Performance and Quality thru Hardware Reconfiguration: Potentials and Adaptive Object Tracking Case Study. In: Workshop on Embedded Systems for Real-Time Multimedia (ESTIMedia), pp. 149–155 (October 2003)

8. Ghiasi, S., Moon, H.J., Nahapetian, A., Sarrafzadeh, M.: Collaborative and Reconfigurable Object Tracking. Kluwer Journal of Supercomputing 30(3), 213–238 (2004)

9. Lan, M., Nahapetian, A., Vahdatpour, A., Au, L., Kaiser, W., Sarrafzadeh, M.: SmartFall: An Automatic Fall Detection System Based on Subsequence Matching for the SmartCane. Bodynets (April 2009)

10. Mainwaring, A., Culler, D., Polastre, J., Szewczyk, R., Anderson, J.: Wireless Sensor Networks for Habitat Monitoring. In: ACM International Workshop on Wireless Sensor Networks and Applications (WSNA 2002), pp. 88–97 (2002)

11. Nahapetian, A., Chaudhry, S., Dabiri, F., Massey, T., Noshadi, H., Sarrafzadeh, M.: Wireless Body Sensor Enhanced Tracking for Extended In-Home Care. In: International Workshop on Wireless Sensor Networks for Health Care (WSNHC), Braunschweig, Germany (2007)

12. Noble, R., White, R.: Visualisation of Gait Analysis Data. In: 9th International Conference, Information Visualisation, London, July 6-8, pp. 247–252 (2005)

13. Noshadi, H., Ahmadian, S., Dabiri, R., Nahapetian, A., Stathopoulus, A., Batalin, M., Kaiser, W., Sarrafzadeh, M.: SMAER Shoe for Balance, Fall Risk Assessment and Applications in Wireless Health. In: Microsoft eScience Workshop (December 2008)

14. Noshadi, H., Ahmadian, S., Hagopian, H., Woodbridge, J., Amini, N., Dabiri, F., Sarrafzadeh, M., Terrafranca, N.: Hermes: Mobile Balance and Instability Assessment System. BioSignals (January 2010)

15. Vahdatpour, V., Sarrafzadeh, M.: Unsupervised Discovery of Abnormal Activity Occurrences in Multi-dimensional Time Series, with Applications in Wearable Systems. In: SIAM International Conference on Data Mining, SDM (2010)

16. Wang, H., Estrin, D., Girod, L.: Preprocessing in a Tiered Sensor Network for Habitat Monitoring. EURASIP JASP Special Issue of Sensor Networks 2003(4), 392–401 (2003)

17. Wu, W.H., Au, L.K., Jordan, B., Stathopoulos, T., Batalin, M., Kaiser, W., Vahdatpour, A., Sarrafzadeh, M., Fang, M., Chodosh, J.: SmartCane System: An Assistive Device for Geriatrics. In: Third International Conference on Body Area Networks (BodyNets 2008), March 13-17 (2008)

18. Short Visualization Software Demo,
    http://www.youtube.com/watch?v=PzVP-BPPvFo

19. Long Visualization Software Demo,
    http://www.youtube.com/watch?v=26XsurePm8g

Mobile MapReduce: Minimizing Response Time of Computing Intensive Mobile Applications

Mohammed Anowarul Hassan and Songqing Chen

Department of Computer Science,
George Mason University
{mhassanb,sqchen}@gmu.edu

Abstract. The increasing popularity of mobile devices calls for effective execution of mobile applications. A lot of research has been conducted on properly splitting and outsourcing computing intensive tasks to external resources (e.g., public clouds) by considering insufficient computing resources on mobile devices. However, little attention has been paid to the overall users' response time, where the network may dominate.

In this study, we set to investigate how to effectively minimize users' response time for mobile applications. We consider both the impact of the network and the computing itself. We first show that outsourcing to nearby residential computers may be more advantageous than public clouds for mobile applications due to network impact. Furthermore, to speed up computing, we leverage parallel processing techniques. Accordingly, we propose to build Mobile MapReduce (MMR) to effectively execute outsource computing intensive mobile applications. Based on the original MapReduce framework, a new scheduling model is built in MMR that can always leverage the best computing resources to conduct computation with appropriate parallel processing. To demonstrate the performance of MMR, we run several real-world applications, such as text searching, face detection, and image processing, on the prototype. The results show great potentials of MMR in minimizing the response time of the outsourced mobile applications.

1 Introduction

Mobile devices are getting more and more popular. According to International Data Corporation, the total number of smartphones sold in 2010 is 305 millions [5], which is a 76% increase from the previous year, and there are already over 4.6 billion mobile subscribers in the world and the number is still growing [6].

Different from traditional mobile devices (e.g., cellphones) that are mainly used for voice communication, mobile devices today are typically equipped with much more powerful processor and more sensors. Such increasing power of mobile devices has enabled fast development of mobile applications, such as picture editing, gaming, document processing, financial tracking [8]. Recently, Amazon released SDK for Android users [1] to develop mobile applications using Amazon cloud such as uploading images and videos to the Amazon cloud storage, and sharing game, movies, and other data among users.

J.Y. Zhang et al. (Eds.): MobiCASE 2011, LNICST 95, pp. 41–59, 2012.
© Institute for Computer Sciences, Social Informatics and Telecommunications Engineering 2012

However, constrained by the size and weight, mobile devices's processing power is still significantly lagging behind that of their desktop counterpart. Thus, many desktop applications, if running on mobile devices, can result in poor performance. For example, an OpenGL application on an Android phone can refresh slowly on the screen and drive the user away quickly. On the other hand, mobile devices are ultimately constrained by the limited battery supply and a computing-intensive application can quickly exhaust the limited battery power. Such a situation is worsened by the industrial trend to equip more sensors on mobile devices for a wider scope of non-traditional applications, such as environment monitoring [17], health monitoring [4,7], social applications [23,22], which are often more computing intensive.

From the resource perspective, a lots of research have considered to outsource computing intensive tasks to external resources [10,18,26]. For example, the virtual machine-based cloning approach [12] has been explored to clone the entire mobile environment to the cloud without worrying about modifying the application or dividing the job. Similarly, Zap takes a full process migration [25] approach with resource and process consistency. On the other hand, a number of job partitioning strategies have been proposed [28,14] to simplify the partitioning of the existing applications between the mobile device and the external computing resources.

While many existing schemes have focused on how to split the computing-intensive tasks and outsource to external resources, the impact of the network latency on outsourced applications has not been well investigated, which may be a dominant factor in the total response time to mobile users. For mobile applications, a minimal response time is not only critical to the users' experience, but also important for preserving the limited battery power supply on mobile devices. This is particularly true for delay sensitive and interactive mobile applications. When partial tasks of such applications are outsourced, it is critical to reduce the total response time to the user in order to maintain the QoS of the application. In this paper, we aim to minimize the response time of mobile applications from the users' perspective. Since outsourcing often involves both network transferring and computing, we first show that outsourcing to appropriate resources considering data affinity and network latency could be more advantageous than public clouds in reducing the overall response time. Furthermore, to speed up computing, we leverage parallel processing techniques. Accordingly, we design and implement Mobile MapReduce (MMR) based on the original MapReduce framework. In MMR, a new scheduling model is built that can always dynamically leverage the best computing resources, be nearby computers or public clouds, with the most appropriate parallelism considering the parallelization overhead [19] for any mobile application.

To demonstrate the performance of MMR, we have built a prototype and experimented MMR with several real-world applications, including text searching, face detection, and image processing. The results show that MMR not only outperforms on-device computing by 15 times and 20 times in terms of response time and the battery power consumption, respectively, but also outperforms public cloud like Amazon EC2 by 3 times and 4 times in terms of response time and the battery power consumption, respectively.

The remainder of the paper is organized as follows. We present our motivation of leveraging residential computers and MapReduce in Section 2. We present the design of MMR in section 3. Section 4 describes mobile MapReduce implementation. We present some preliminary evaluation results with several typical applications in Section 5. Some related work is discussed in Section 6, and we make concluding remarks in Section 7.

2   Background and Motivation

In this section, we present some background and our motivation with more details.

2.1   Nearby Computers vs. Public Clouds

To study the impact of latency on outsourcing to the public clouds and nearby residential computers, we have conducted some preliminary experiments with Amazon EC2 and our local computers. We use three approaches for an experiment to find a string in a text file: 1) Local Execution in Google Nexus One with Android 2.2 OS, 1 GHz CPU, and 512 MB RAM, 2) Outsourcing to Amazon EC2 with 5 GHz CPU, 1.7 GB RAM, and 300Kbps link speed and 3) Outsourcing to Residential Computers with 2 GHz CPU, 3.2 GB of RAM, and 10 Mbps LAN. Table 1 shows the user's response time when the same program is executed with different approaches along with the increase of the file size. As shown in the table, although EC2 has a much faster CPU, the response time is longer than if the job is outsourced to nearby residential computers because of the impact of network latency. Correspondingly, Table 2 shows energy consumed on the mobile device for executing the program with these approaches based on Power Tutor [9].

These results show that when outsourcing mobile computing tasks, the bandwidth consumption has to be taken into consideration and sometimes this may be a dominant factor. Under such situations, outsourcing to nearby residential computers may be more beneficial than to public clouds.

Table 1. Response Time (Sec)

File Size (KB)	Android	Amazon EC2	Residential Computers
10	0.0481	0.0146	0.0459
100	0.425	0.096	0.4245
200	0.424	0.971	1.300
400	0.465	1.600	1.300
750	0.480	3.400	3.300
1000	0.503	4.500	6.600

Table 2. Energy Consumption (J)

File Size (KB)	Android	Amazon EC2	Residential Computers
10	0.117	0.098	0.122
100	0.332	0.984	1.995
200	0.886	1.815	4.099
400	1.327	3.603	8.235
750	02.467	6.637	15.366
1000	3.092	8.823	20.583

On the other hand, if most of the data for the outsourced computing resides on the user's home computer, outsourcing to nearby residential computers may not outperform outsourcing to the user's home computer even if the home computer is far away. This is particularly true that today many mobile users synchronize their files with their home or office computers daily.

To demonstrate this, we experiment with compiling a Latex document with 10 files, each of 1.7 KB. In the experiment, the network speed to the farther home computer is 300 Kbps on average and to the nearby computer is 10 Mbps.

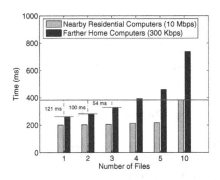

Fig. 1. Nearby Residential Computers vs. Farther Home Computer

Figure 1 shows the total execution time if 1, 2, 3, 4, 5, or 10 files needed to be transferred to nearby computers or home computers for compiling. The figure clearly shows that if the same number of files needed to be transferred, outsourcing to nearby residential computers is faster, but if the home computer only needs a small portion of the data to be transferred, then it performs better than the residential computers where the whole portion of the data needs to be sent.

The above preliminary results indicate that when outsourcing mobile applications, a scheduler should not only consider job types (such as CPU intensive or network intensive), but also the data affinity in order to minimize the impact of network.

2.2   MapReduce

As aforementioned, to speed up computing, we aim to leverage parallel processing. Since MapReduce is widely used today, we first briefly introduce the basics of MapReduce and then discuss why we adopt MapReduce.

MapReduce is a patented software framework introduced by Google to support distributed computing on large data sets on clusters of computers introduced from 2003 [16]. It is a programming model for processing and generating large data sets. Under MapReduce, the computation takes a set of input key/value pairs, and produces a set of output key/value pairs. The user specifies a Map function that takes an input pair to generate a set of intermediate key/value pairs. All intermediate values associated with the same intermediate key are grouped together and passed to the Reduce function. The Reduce function accepts an intermediate key and a set of values for that key. It merges together these values to form a possibly smaller set of values. In such an approach, applications are automatically parallelized and executed on a large cluster of commodity machines.

MapReduce has gained great popularity in practice. The openness of MapReduce and the simplicity of the interface allow users to develop many applications in MapReduce. Currently, there are more than 10,000 distinct programs using MapReduce[15]. MapReduce can partition the task into independent chunks and process them in parallel. In addition, the MapReduce framework deals with node failure so that re-execution of a task is minimized in case of failure. MapReduce has an open source implementation Hadoop, which we leverage in our work.

However, directly applying MapReduce for mobile computation outsourcing is not proper for a number of reasons. In the original MapReduce framework, Map and Reduce nodes are connected to each other, which is not always possible in our mobile computing environment. Furthermore, the HDFS in the original MapReduce contains the data prior to the job submission and computation, which is less likely to be practical in our mobile computing environment. That is, the data required for computing has to be transferred as well. On the other hand, the data size in our mobile computing is relatively small. It is only computing intensive relative to the slow CPU on mobile devices. Other than the above different design features, Hadoop is developed based on JVM, while Dalvik in our Android smartphone is a different platform that Hadoop is not compatible with or could be ported directly. Thus we will present later our framework that we modify from the original MapReduce in order to support our outsourcing.

3 Mobile MapReduce Design

We have shown in the previous section that nearby residential computers could outperform public clouds for some applications. Thus, from the users' perspective, it is necessary to consider all available computing resources for job outsourcing, including both residential computers and public clouds. That is, MMR should run on an architecture as shown in Figure 2.

As shown in this figure, in MMR, there is a resource overlay that a participating mobile user can leverage for computing in motion. The resource overlay consists of the normal user's residential (home) computers and public clouds. A user can register her home computer in the resource overlay (**Step 2**) through the rendezvous points (**Step 1**).

When a user leaves home, she can register her home computer on the resource overlay. When the user is on the road and wants to execute some computing intensive application, she starts the job with MMR running on her mobile device. The MMR client will contact the overlay (**Step 3**) by visiting a well-known bootstrapping site. Such contact could be done through the cellular connection if WiFi is not available. In the response to this request, the user is directed to the rendezvous point (**Step 4**). Based on the geographical location of the mobile user, a list of nearby residential computers and public cloud on the overlay are identified by the rendezvous point. The MMR scheduler running on the rendezvous point further selects some of these computers based on its scheduling policy.

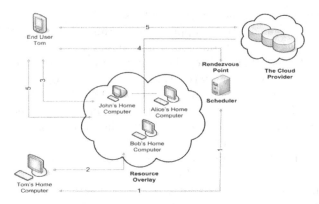

Fig. 2. Architecture of MMR

Once the list of residential and public cloud computers in the connectivity range is determined, the list of the machines is sent back by the rendezvous point to the mobile user (**Step 4**). From now on, all communications are done through WiFi connections. Based on the list, the mobile user connects to these computers and can start the execution. Note MMR scheduler may decide to execute part of the job on the mobile device. MMR then submits the job to an appropriate set of computers and gets back the result (**Step 5**). The MMR returns the final result to the user's application. Users' home computers operate in a P2P fashion with a credit system as proposed in [20].

With such an architecture, the most important component of MMR is the scheduler to find the most appropriate resources for outsourcing in order to minimize the response time.

In finding the most appropriate computer nodes to execute a particular task, the MMR scheduler considers the following:

1. Job Type: When requesting the computation outsourcing, the job type is determined. Based on both the CPU and the bandwidth demand and the data locations, nearby residential computers, public cloud or the user's home computers can be selected.
2. Node Status: Since MMR mainly targets delay-sensitive applications, the status of the selected computers may affect the response time. Furthermore, it is also important for the RP to maintain load balance across different residential computers on the resource overlay.
3. Network Bandwidth: In searching for the most appropriate residential computers for outsourced computation, the computer with the highest bandwidth is always selected first if other conditions are the same.
4. Parallelization Overhead: The execution time does not decrease linearly with the increase of parallelism. In addition to the Amdahl's law, work [19] has shown that further parallelization may degrade the overall performance of the system, which is true for MapReduce as well [2]. Thus this overhead is very important in MMR.

The RP considers these factors and employs a greedy optimization to select the best strategy.

To develop our algorithm, we start from the ideal case assuming each node has equal processing power, latency, and bandwidth. Let a be the node discovery and connection set up overhead, d the time to execute the computation on a single chunk of data in MMR, and bw the time to transfer one single chunk from the mobile device to the node which depends on the bandwidth from the mobile device to all the n nodes. Note that the size of a single chunk may vary from application to application. So, if the total number of chunks is C, then the total execution time is:

$$T = a \times n + \frac{C}{n} \times d + \frac{C}{n} \times bw, \tag{1}$$

In Equation 1, we assume these nodes have the same bandwidth with the mobile device. Here the time for discovering and connecting to neighboring nodes is linearly proportional to the number of nodes as the threading capability of mobile device limited by its CPU. Differentiating Equation 1 with respect to n, we get:

$$\frac{\mathrm{d}}{\mathrm{d}n}T = a - \frac{C \times (d + bw)}{n^2} \tag{2}$$

So we get the optimal degree of parallelism when:

$$n = \sqrt{\frac{C \times (d + bw)}{a}} \tag{3}$$

In practice, residential computers may not have the same CPU, latency, and bandwidth. So a, d, and bw are not the same for each node. Moreover, some nodes may have some chunks of the input data in prior. This is similar to Multiprocessor Scheduling [13], which is NP-Complete. We propose a greedy approach to find the optimal number of nodes based on the fact that, the T in equation 1 decreases first with the increase of parallelism, then starts to increase again [19].

Algorithm 1 shows the pseudo-code of the algorithm. In the MMR Scheduler, I represents the user's id, L is the location, which is required to find the nearby computers available for computation outsourcing. J represents the job. LC is the list of the available computers, which holds the following information for each node on the list: 1) i_c: computation power available on node i; 2) i_l: location of node i; 3) i_{bw}: the time to transfer one chunk of data from the mobile device to the node depending on the channel capacity from the mobile device to the node i; 4) i_{ds}: chunks of the data stored in prior for a job J in the node i; 5) C: total size of the input chunks of the input data; 6) cc: CPU cycle required for execution of each input chunks. Note that we assume profiling can be used to obtain these parameters for mobile applications.

Note that we include the mobile device and the home computer of the user as potential candidates to execute computation, as computation on them may be economical. As shown in the algorithm MMR Scheduler, in the first step, MMR finds the set of reachable computers nearby LC based on the location of the nodes and the mobile device (Line 1). We calculate a and d for each node,

---

Algorithm 1. MMR Scheduler(I,J,L,C,cc)

1: $LC \leftarrow$ The set of available computers nearby from I and L
2: **for** each node i in LC **do**
3:    add i to LC
4:    $i_a \leftarrow node\_connection\_overhead_i$
5:    $i_d \leftarrow cc/i_c$
6: **end for**
7: $n \leftarrow \|LC\|$
8: Calculate $a_t, d_t,$ and bw_t: the average of $i_a, i_d,$ and i_{bw} of all nodes i in LC
9: $op\_n \leftarrow \sqrt{\frac{C \times (b_t + bw_t)}{a_t}}$
10: **for** each i in LC **do**
11:    $Weight_i \leftarrow \frac{1}{i_a + i_d \times \frac{C}{op\_n} + i_{bw} \times \frac{C}{op\_n}}$
12: **end for**
13: Sort LC in decreasing order according to $Weight_i$
14: $a_{avg} \leftarrow i_a$ of first node of LC
15: $d_{avg} \leftarrow i_d$ of first node of LC
16: $bw_{avg} \leftarrow i_{bw}$ of first node of LC
17: $totaltime \leftarrow a_{avg} + C \times d_{avg} + C \times i_{bw}$
18: $count \leftarrow 1$
19: **for** $i = 2$ to n **do**
20:    $a_{avg} \leftarrow$ average of first i nodes' i_a
21:    $d_{avg} \leftarrow$ average of first i nodes' i_d
22:    $bw_{avg} \leftarrow$ average of first i nodes' i_{bw}
23:    $temptotaltime \leftarrow a_{avg} \times i + \frac{(C \times d_{avg})}{i} + \frac{C \times bw_{avg}}{i}$
24:    **if** $temptotaltime \leq totaltime$ **then**
25:       $totaltime \leftarrow temptotaltime$
26:       $count \leftarrow count + 1$
27:    **end if**
28: **end for**
29: **for** $i = 1$ to n **do**
30:    $C_i \leftarrow \frac{Weight_i}{\sum_{\forall i \in LC} Weight_i} \times C$
31: **end for**
32: Let $LCRD$ be the set of nodes having portion of the input data in prior
33: $m \leftarrow \|LCRD\|$
34: Sort LCRD according to i_{ds} in decreasing order
35: $j \leftarrow 1$
36: **for** $i = 1$ to m **do**
37:    **if** $j \leq count$ **then**
38:       $Time_i \leftarrow i_a + \frac{C_j - i_{ds}}{i_{bw}} + C_j \times i_d$
39:       $Time_j \leftarrow j_a + \frac{C_j - j_{ds}}{j_{bw}} + C_j \times j_d$
40:       **if** $Time_i < Time_j$ **then**
41:          First remove i from $LCRD$ and then Insert node i in between j and $j-1$ in LC
42:       **else**
43:          $j \leftarrow j + 1$
44:       **end if**
45:    **end if**
46: **end for**
47: **return** first $count$ nodes from LC

(Line 2-6) and the average of them (Line 8). Then we assign weight to different node based on the heuristics (Line 10-11). We first assume that we are in the ideal case where all nodes in LC have the same a, d, and bw: a_t, d_t and bw_t namely which are the average of those values for all nodes in LC. We also assume to use an optimal number of nodes if all of them have their average a, d, and bw. So, to process equal number of chunks $\frac{C}{op\_n}$, the time taken by each node is $i_a + i_d \times \frac{C}{op\_n} + i_{bw} \times \frac{C}{op\_n}$. where op_n is the optimal number of nodes according to Equation 3 (Line 9). The *Weight* of each node is the inverse of the time taken by each node to get and process the $\frac{C}{op\_n}$ number of chunks. Note that the more powerful and the shorter the latency a node has, the lower the time and the higher the *Weight*.

We sort the LC in decreasing order of weight (Line 13). Then we could find the minima of the curvature of the T in Equation 1 by adding one by one node for our computation (Line 19-28). Here we assume the a, d, and bw be the average of those values of the total nodes considered so far.

We also calculate the potential number of chunks to be executed by each node here based on the weight heuristic (Line 30). Then we find out the nodes having some chunks of the data in prior and sort them in decreasing order of i_{ds}(Line 34) in list $LCRD$ and give them priority if they have better performance considering affinity data (Line 36-46). The key point here is that, we first take the first node in $LCRD$ and take the first node of sorted LC and compare the total data transfer and execution time of the two nodes with the associated number of chunks of the node in LC and local data chunks. If the node from $LCRD$ takes less time than the node of LC, we move that node of $LCRD$ forward in the list LC before the current node and deal with the next node of $LCRD$ in the same way. Otherwise, we compare the node of $LCRD$ with the second node of LC in the same way until the list $LCRD$ is visited or we have taken the first *count* nodes from LC. In this way, we get the first *count* nodes having optimal parallelization and performance with respect to latency, computation power, and data location. The complexity of this algorithm is $\theta(n)$ for the first four loops, $\theta(n \log n)$ for the sorting, and $\theta(n + m)$ or $\theta(n)$ as $m < n$ for the nested loop (Line 36-46). The above algorithm deals with how to select the most appropriate computing resources for one job. If there are multiple jobs, MMR follows the original Hadoop fair scheduling policy for the queued jobs and then the MMR scheduler selects the best nodes for each job.

4 Mobile MapReduce Implementation

A major component of MMR is the modified MapReduce that considers user mobility and unreliability of residential computers. We modify the original MapReduce to incorporate these new functions as follows.

4.1 MMR vs. Hadoop

Our MMR implementation is based on the widely used open source Hadoop. From the perspective of the framework, MMR differs from the original Hadoop in the following aspects so that we need to modify the original Hadoop to accommodate these.

- *Dynamic Mobility Property of MMR:* In Hadoop, the master node has the worker list beforehand. It configures the network first before submitting any job. The worker nodes are responsible themselves to join the network. But in MMR we propose the framework for mobile users without persistent connections and the master node does not have any knowledge about the neighboring worker nodes.
- *Non-Distributive File System of MMR:* In Hadoop, HDFS [27] is used to store the input file. In MMR, the selected nearby residential computers do not have a copy of the input file until the file is transferred there. Thus, upon the response from the RP, the input data is first split and transferred to the selected worker node before the computation begins.
- *Handling Isolated Worker Nodes:* In MapReduce, the intermediate <Key,Value> pairs produced by the Map nodes are periodically written to local disk. The locations of these buffered key/value pairs on the local disk are passed to the master who forwards these locations to the Reduce workers. The Reducers use remote procedure calls to read the buffered data from the local disks of the map workers.

  In our resource overlay network, it is highly possible that the Map/Reduce nodes are not directly connected. So Reduce nodes cannot execute RPC to fetch the buffered data. In our framework, the Map node sends the list of <Key,Value> pairs to the master node who eventually forwards to the Reducers.
- *Node Failure:* MMR detects the failure of worker nodes with a timeout mechanism. Whenever the master node submits a job to execute to any worker node, it periodically contacts the worker node. The master node also gets the result back for small chunks of the job finished in that worker and saves it. Note that the worker node also gives a backup copy to the resource overlay. If it is the master node that loses the connection, then the resource overlay may give the result back to the master node based on the backup copy. If it is a crash of the worker node, then the mobile node finds another worker if any, or it executes the job locally (on the mobile device). After finding another machine (worker or local), it executes the remaining portion of the job. As the input data is partitioned into small independent chunks, the failure of any worker causes only re-execution of that portion of data.
- *Minimizing Intermediate <Key,Value> Transfer Overhead:* To minimize the transferring overhead, in MMR, the *MMR Combiner* is run over the <Key, Value> pairs produced by the Map nodes. For example: suppose we are searching for a rare string "MMR" in a large file. In the original MapReduce, the Map will emit < "MMR", "one" > every time it finds that string in the file. The Reducers would fetch the intermediate key/value pairs and merge them. In MMR, to reduce the data communication overhead, we propose that the *MMR Combiner* would integrate all the occurrence and finally send the result when it is finished for a particular split of input. If there are ten

"MMR" strings in the input split of the file, the node emits one < "MMR", "ten" > pair instead of sending ten < "MMR", "one" > pairs. This change causes significant improvement for data communication.

In addition, as the result of mobile application is comparatively small, so it is much faster to keep it in the cache rather than to write in local file system of the Workers. We also find that the system performs better when there is no replication factor like original MapReduce as the node failure is common in MMR. MMR uses a smaller block size, such as 512 KB, which is smaller than the original Hadoop (64 MB) due to the nature of the jobs on mobile devices. In practice, the block size can also be determined dynamically based on the input size, the reliability of nearby computers, the available network bandwidth, etc.

4.2 MMR Workflow

With the above modifications from the original Hadoop, in MMR, the mobile device works as the master node and the residential computers (including the home computer of the user in case) works as worker nodes. Each worker node may work as Map or Reduce. Figure 3 illustrates the similarities and the modification between MapReduce and MMR.

After exploring neighboring residential computers, the MMR Scheduler sends the list of the residential computers to the MMR running in mobile device. **(Step 1)**. MMR establishes connections between the master node running in mobile device and the worker nodes running in the residential computers. The nodes

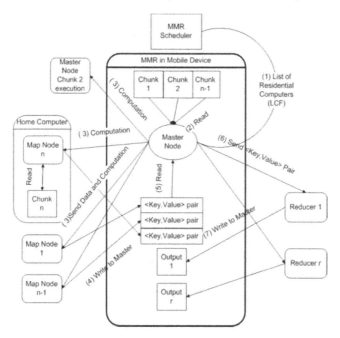

Fig. 3. MapReduce and MMR

may establish authentication and trust for this purpose. The name node and the job tracker of MapReduce starts on the master node. The name node divides the whole input data into **n** small chunks and read input chunks **(Step 2)**. It then sends the data and the computation to the appropriate data nodes **(Step 3)**. Note here that some data nodes may have some data in prior. These nodes are referred by the MMR scheduler so that only the computing program needs to be sent there, thus reducing the data transferring overhead. Some data chunks may be executed in the mobile device itself due to security reason. For all the other nodes, both computing program and data need to be sent over. The job tracker in the mobile device keeps track of the the processing progress of the job.

Currently we send the computation in serializable byte code from the master node to the data nodes. It also defines the output class key/value as well.

With the above interface, application developers can define the class of map, key/value and the input/output format. Thus the worker nodes do not have to know about the on-going computations and can offer unlimited types of services with its simple model without reconfiguring itself.

The data node receives the data portion in desired input data format and the task tracker starts the computation and sends back the output to the job tracker **(Step 4)**.

The job tracker saves the intermediate key/value results and marks the entry for that particular portion of the input data chunk as finished. The name node sends the next portion of the job to the data node and the task tracker starts computation for the next portion of the job.

This continues until the job is finished or any data node fails (e.g., a node is shut down or a node loses the connection from the name node). If any worker node fails, MMR tries to get the result for that data portion from the resource overlay or re-execute that portion of the job by exploring another worker node.

After finishing the Map part, the reducer may begin either on the mobile device or again in the nearby worker node acting as Reducer depending on the volume of computation. The master node reads the intermediate <Key,Value> pairs **(Step 5)** and sends them to the reduce nodes **(Step 6)**. After the computation is finished, reduce node sends the result back **(Step 7)**.

5   Preliminary Evaluation

5.1   Experiment Setup

In the experiments, we emulate a 3 user model and they have identical residential computers and mobile devices. We use Google Android Nexus One with 1 GHz CPU and 512 RAM as the mobile device for the local execution. We use 5 lab computers to emulate overlay residential computers that all have a dual-core CPU with 2GHz and 2 GB RAM for outsourcing and parallelization in residential computers. The EC2 instances rented are at Northern Virginia Data Center of Amazon. Each remote EC2 Ubuntu instance has a 5 GHz CPU with 1.7 GB of RAM. We use Power Tutor [9] to measure the power consumed by the applications running on the smartphone. The WiFi is 10 Mbps and the bandwidth from the Android Phone to EC2 instance is around 300 Kpbs on average. Note that we have also experimented with different network speeds. We omit their results for brevity.

We have conducted experiments with the following three applications.

- *Text Search* In this application, the user searches a string in a text file and the frequency of occurrence of that string is returned to the user. This simple string counting application takes an input file of 2.6 MB. We use string matching to find the total number of occurrence of that string in that text file.
- *Face Detection* In this application, we take a picture of a human face and try to match it with all the pictures in a folder previously taken. We use Cross-Correlation Function [3] to find the correlation between an image pair. Based upon that, we detect a particular person. We have each image in a different jpg file. The correlation between the files has been calculated by taking input from three different streams for 3 RGB values. The resultant size for the reference images is 575 KB in total and the newly taken image size is 145 KB. So the total size of the data file is 720 KB, and the computation program is 3 KB.
- *Image Sub Pattern Search* In this application, we take a picture and try to find the picture as a part of another large picture in a folder previously taken. We use Cross-Correlation Function [3] and 2D Logarithmic Search [21] to find the sub-image. We have each image in a different jpg file. The correlation between the files has been calculated by taking input from three different streams for 3 RGB values. The resultant size for the reference image is 1.7 MB, the newly taken image size is 260 KB, and the computation program is 4 KB.

We profile each application to deduce the average CPU cycle and data transfer requirement. We fed these profiling results and locations for the MMR Scheduler to find nearby residential computers to outsource computation. While profiling, we assumed that either there is no data is stored in prior in the residential computers or all the data are stored there. Upon this experimental set up we run each application in the following different environments.

- On-device*(OD)*: We run the application on the mobile device directly here.
- Computation+Data*(CD)*: Both the computation program and the data are outsourced to the residential computers here. The MMR in the mobile device gets connected to the resource overlay and the rendezvous point to explore the neighboring residential computers and outsource the computation with the data file.
- Computation+Data+Node Failure*(CD+F)*: This is to consider the node failure in the above environment to study the impact of node failure. When a node fails, MMR contact the resource overlay and the rendezvous point once again to find another neighboring residential computer and start the job from the failed point by outsourcing the data from the failed portion and the original computation program.

To emulate node failure case, we deliberately turn off one computer in the middle of an on-going computation when the computation is about 50% completed. Then MMR detects the failure based on timeout and it contacts resource overlay and rendezvous point to find another nearby residential computer.

– Computation*(C)*: We emulate the scenario when the selected residential computer is the user's home computer, which has the data of the task. The mobile device only needs to transmit the computation for the applications, which is small in size.
– Computation+Node Failure*(C+F)*: This is to consider the node failure in the above environment. Note that here for both the failed node and the new node, we outsource only the computation. We emulate the node failure case as we have done for CD+F.
– EC2 *(EC2)*: We outsource the computation to the remote amazon EC2 instances. We assume that EC2 is always available and 100% reliable.

In all these experiments, we mainly focus on the response time and the energy consumption on the mobile device. Since we use homogeneous machines for both residential computers and Amazon EC2 instances, our scheduler follows Equation 3. We further test with other parallelism levels in order to compare their performance.

5.2   Experimental Results

In this section, we describe the performance of the different approaches we have tested for the three applications. We repeat each experiment five times and present the average of the results.

Text Search. Figure 4 depicts the response time and the energy consumption of the text search application when it is executed on the Android and the computation is outsourced with and without parallel processing. In this experiment, the amount of data transferred is 2.6 MB when both computation and data are transferred, otherwise it is 1 KB if only the computing program is needed to

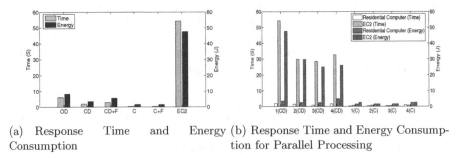

(a) Response   Time   and   Energy   (b) Response Time and Energy Consump-
Consumption   tion for Parallel Processing

Fig. 4. Text Search

be outsourced. In outsourcing the data file, it is divided into 512 KB chunks. So in the cases with node failure (CD+F and C+F), only one chunk is lost, which minimize the re-execution overhead.

In Figure 4, the left-y axis represents the response time while the right-y axis represents the corresponding energy consumption. Figure 4(a) clearly shows that outsourcing to EC2 results in the worst performance in terms of both the response time to the user and the amount of energy consumed, even worse than the on-device execution. Compared to the case when it is executed locally on the mobile device, outsourcing to the nearby residential computers results in 69% and 59% less response time and energy consumption, respectively, although outsourcing to nearby residential computers demand some bandwidth for file transferring. In the node failure cases where residential computers may not be reliable or the home user can depart a residential computer from MMR at any time, Figure 4(a) shows that the performance of outsourcing still outperforms the on-device computing in terms of both the response time and the total energy consumed on the mobile device, although there is a 47% and 61% increase compared to if there is no node failure.

When the computation is parallelized among multiple machines, Figure 4(b) shows the result. Again, the left-y axis represents the response time while the right one represents the energy consumption. The residential computers are identical with a 2 GHz CPU and 2 GB RAM. The rented EC2 instances have 5 GHz CPU and 1.7 GB RAM each. Without parallel processing, the response time may be well over the average connection time of a mobile user with a roadside WiFi ranges between 6-12 seconds [24]. This makes it impossible for a mobile user to get the result in time in the same communication session although EC2 has a faster CPU speed. This would be a critical problem for delay sensitive mobile applications when a user waits to get the result back. As shown in the figure, parallelization can clearly improve the performance when the number of computers is increased from 1 to 2 and 3. However, Figure 4(b) also shows that the response time and energy consumption first decrease with the increase of parallelization level, then it increases when the parallelization level increases (from 3 to 4 nodes). So here it is also important to calculate the the appropriate degree of parallelism to optimize the performance.

Again, in Figure 4(b), we also observe that the residential computers perform significantly better than EC2 when both the data and computation (CD) are outsourced. But when only the computation (C) is outsourced, they have similar performance.

Face Detection. Figure 5 shows the performance results when the face detection program is executed in different environments. In particular, figure 5(a) shows that executing on the Android takes the longest time of about 94.5 seconds. Not surprisingly, the corresponding energy consumption is the largest for the on-device execution.

Figure 5(a) also shows that both the response time and the energy consumption are reduced when the computation is outsourced. When the program is outsourced to the nearby residential computers, the performance improvement

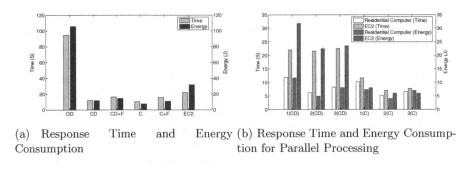

(a) Response Time and Energy Consumption

(b) Response Time and Energy Consumption for Parallel Processing

Fig. 5. Face Detection

is more pronounced than when the program is outsourced to EC2: on the residential computer, the response time is about 10.25 seconds and 11.90 seconds without or with the data transferred. Correspondingly, when the computation is outsourced to the nearby residential computer, the energy consumed is only about 23% and 36%, respectively, of the total energy consumption when we have on device execution without or with data transfer.

With the help of parallelization, the performance is better. Figure 5(b) shows the effect of parallelism on the response time and the energy consumption. However, as shown in the figure, although using 2 nodes to parallelize the computation does improve the user response time and the total energy consumption on the mobile device, the response time and energy consumption of the computation actually increase when the parallelization is further increased (from 2 nodes to 3 nodes). When the computing nodes have the data in prior, the performance is better than when the data need to be actually transferred before the computation. This indicates outsourcing computation to the nodes where data resides may be more beneficial than to the nodes with higher computation power without any data in prior. But again, an appropriate parallelization level is always desired as more resources may not improve the performance.

Image Sub Pattern Search. For *Image Sub Pattern Search*, Figure 6(a) shows that executing on the Android takes the longest time of about 163.9 seconds.

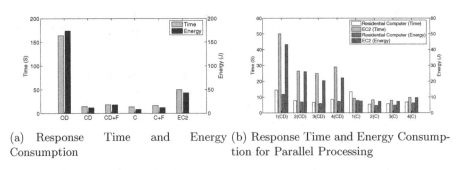

(a) Response Time and Energy Consumption

(b) Response Time and Energy Consumption for Parallel Processing

Fig. 6. Image Sub Pattern Search

In all the outsourcing scenarios, the response time is significantly reduced. Correspondingly, the energy consumption is the largest for the on-device execution. The reduction when the program is outsourced to the nearby residential computers is more pronounced than when the program is outsourced to EC2: on the residential computer, the response time is about 13.37 seconds and 14.52 seconds without or with the data transferred. Correspondingly, the energy consumed is only about 10% and 11% of the On-device (OD) computation, respectively, when the computation is outsourced to nearby residential computers. The node failure only causes 54% and 51% increase of the response time and the energy consumption compared to their counterpart without any node failure. These results are still much better than those when outsourcing to EC2.

Figure 6(b) shows the response time and the energy consumption when the computation is parallelized. When two and three nodes are used for computing, both the response time and the energy consumption on the mobile device decrease. However, when more nodes are used in the computing, performance degrades due to parallelization overhead. On the other hand without parallelization, the response time is more than 10 seconds, but with parallelization, the user gets the result back in 5 seconds, which is more feasible.

The experimental results show that while computation is outsourced to residential computers, the overall performance is better than when the computation is outsourced to EC2, though EC2 is much more powerful than nearby residential computers in terms of the CPU speed. The performance can be further improved when the computation is parallelized. The average gain for the response time and energy consumption is about 1.5 to 2 times compared to its single node computation on average. However, with parallel processing, appropriate parallelization is desired. This is because a certain level of parallelization can help reduce the response time and the total energy consumption on the mobile device, and further increasing parallelization level may actually degrade the performance. This is due to the fact that parallelization involves overhead, which may dominate under certain circumstances. Thus, in scheduling the execution of outsourced tasks, this must be taken into consideration as we have done in MMR scheduler.

6 Related Work

Plenty of research has been conducted to outsource computing tasks to external computing sources [10,18,26,11]. Typically, these schemes focus on how to properly split the job and deploy on the external computing sources. For example, studies [28,12] demonstrate the ability to partition the application and associate classes and thus outsourcing them. Rudenko et al. [26] suggest that if the total energy cost of sending the task else where and receiving the result back is lower than the cost of running it locally, then remote process execution can save battery power. Flinn et al. [18] also propose a similar idea, in which remote execution simultaneously leverages the mobility of mobile devices and the richer resources of large devices. Balan et al. [10,11] propose to augment the computation and storage capabilities of mobile devices by exploiting the nearby (surrogate) computers. Recently, MAUI [14] is proposed to partition the program dynamically and submit it on surrogate computers.

However, existing work has considered little about how to minimize the response time of the outsourced application, where the network latency may dominate. Considering network transferring and appropriate parallel processing, MMR partitions the data into small chunks to keep the re-execution tractable. Compared to MAUI [14] that requires modification of each application, MMR aims to work transparently with the existing over 10,000 programs developed based on MapReduce. In addition, compared with the partitioning overhead of existing approaches [28,14], the simple two methods Map and Reduce inherited from MapReduce offer an simple interface to be implemented in practice.

7   Conclusion

While mobile devices and mobile applications are getting more and more popular, effectively and properly executing these mobile applications is challenging. In this work, we focus on how to minimize the users' response time of these applications from the users's perspective. Considering both the network impact and the computing itself, we have designed and implemented Mobile MapReduce based on the original MapReduce framework for this purpose. Experimented on a prototype, Mobile MapReduce demonstrates that it can effectively minimize user's response time.

Acknowledgement. We appreciate constructive comments from anonymous referees. The work is partially supported by NSF under grants CNS-0746649 and CNS-1117300 and AFOSR under grant FA9550-09-1-0071.

References

1. AWS SDK for Android, http://aws.amazon.com/sdkforandroid/
2. BlastReduce: High Performance Short Read Mapping with MapReduce, http://www.cbcb.umd.edu/software/blastreduce/
3. Cross Correlation, http://en.wikipedia.org/wiki/Cross-correlation
4. Diamedic. Diabetes Glucose Monitoring Logbook, http://ziyang.eecs.umich.edu/projects/powertutor/index.html
5. International Data Corporation : Press Release, January 28- February 4 (2010), http://www.idc.com/
6. International Telecommunication Union : Press Release, June 10 (2009), www.itu.int
7. iPhone Heart Monitor Tracks Your Heartbeat Unless You Are Dead, gizmodo.com/5056167/
8. Mint, http://www.mint.com/
9. Power Tutor, http://ziyang.eecs.umich.edu/projects/powertutor/index.html
10. Balan, R., Flinn, J., Satyanarayanan, M., Sinnamohideen, S., Yang, H.-I.: The case of cyber foraging. In: Proceedings of the 10th ACM SIGOPS European Workshop, Saint-Emilion, France (July 2002)

11. Balan, R.K., Gergle, D., Satyanarayanan, M., Herbsleb, J.: Simplifying cyber foraging for mobile devices. In: Proceedings of The 5th International Conference on Mobile Systems, San Juan, Puerto Rico (June 2007)
12. Chun, B.G., Maniatis, P.: Augmented smartphone applications through clone cloud execution. In: Proceedings of the 12th Workshop on Hot Topics in Operating Systems (HotOS), Monte Verit, Switzerland (May 2009)
13. Crescenzi, P., Kann, V.: A compendium of NP optimization problems (1998)
14. Cuervo, E., Balasubramanian, A., ki Cho, D., Wolman, A., Saroiu, S., Chandra, R., Bahl, P.: MAUI: Making smartphones last longer with code offload. In: Proceedings of the 8th International Conference on Mobile Systems, Applications, and Services (MobiSys), San Francisco, CA, USA (June 2010)
15. Dean, J., Ghemaawat, S.: Mapreduce a flexible data processing tool. Communication of the ACM (January 2010)
16. Dean, J., Ghemawat, S.: Mapreduce: Simplified data processing on large clusters. In: Proceedings of the 6th Symposium on Operating System Design and Implementation (OSDI), San Francisco, CA (December 2004)
17. Eriksson, J., Girod, L., Hull, B., Newton, R., Madden, S., Balakrishnan, H.: The pothole patrol: Using a mobile sensor network for road surface monitoring. In: Proceedings of The 6th International Conference on Mobile Systems, Applications, and Services (MobiSys), Breckenridge, Colorado (June 2008)
18. Flinn, J., Narayanan, D., Satyanarayanan, M.: Self-tuned remote execution for pervasive computing. In: Proceedings of the 8th Workshop on Hot Topics in Operating Systems (HotOS), Schloss Elmau, Germany (May 2001)
19. Hart, J.M.: Data processing: Parallelism and performance. In: MSDN Magazine (January 2011)
20. Hassan, M.A., Chen, S.: An investigation of different computing sources for mobile application outsourcing on the road. In: Proceedings of the 4th International ICST Conference on MOBILe Wireless MiddleWARE, Operating Systems, and Applications (Mobilware) (June 2011)
21. Jain, J.R., Jain, A.K.: Displacement measurement and its application in interframe image coding. IEEE Transactions on Communications 29 (December 1981)
22. Kang, S., Lee, J., Jang, H., Lee, H., Lee, Y., Park, S., Park, T., Song, J.: Seemon: Scalable and energy-efficient context monitoring framework for sensor-rich mobile environments. In: Proceedings of The 6th International Conference on Mobile Systems, Applications, and Services (MobiSys), Breckenridge, Colorado (June 2008)
23. Liu, B., Terlecky, P., Bar-Noy, A., Govindan, R., Neely, M.J.: Optimizing information credibility in social swarming applications. In: Proceedings of IEEE InfoCom, 2011 Mini-Conference, Shanghai, China (April 2011)
24. Ott, J., Kutscher, D.: Drive-thru internet: IEEE 802.11b for Automobile Users. In: Proceedings of IEEE InfoCom, Hong Kong (March 2004)
25. Osman, S., Subhraveti, D., Su, G., Nieh, J.: The design and implementation of zap: A system for migrating computing environments. In: Proceedings of the 5th Symposium on Operating System Design and Implementation (OSDI), Boston, MA (December 2002)
26. Rudenko, A., Reiher, P., Popek, G.J., Kuenning, G.H.: Saving portable computer battery power through remote process execution. In: Proceedings of Mobile Computing and Communication Review, MC2R (1998)
27. White, T.: Hadoop: The definitive guide
28. Nahrstedt, K., Gu, X., Messer, A., Greenberg, I., Milojicic, D.: Adaptive offloading inference for delivering applications in pervasive computing environments. In: Proceedings of IEEE International Conference on Pervasive Computing and Communications (PerCom), Dallas-Fort Worth, Texas (March 2003)

Energy Efficient Information Monitoring Applications on Smartphones through Communication Offloading

Roelof Kemp, Nicholas Palmer, Thilo Kielmann, and Henri Bal

VU University Amsterdam,
De Boelelaan 1081A,
Amsterdam, The Netherlands
{rkemp,palmer,kielmann,bal}@cs.vu.nl

Abstract. People increasingly use a wide variety of applications on their smartphones, thereby putting an ever higher burden on their phone's battery. Unfortunately, battery capacity does not keep up with the energy demand of these applications. Various solutions have been proposed to get as much work as possible done with the scarcely available energy, among which offloading heavy weight computation to cloud resources.

In addition to offloading *computation* to cloud resources for computation intensive applications, we propose to also offload *communication* to cloud resources for communication intensive applications. In this paper we show that applications that monitor information on the Internet can offload the majority of their communication to cloud resources, thereby saving a significant amount of energy.

Along with discussing the principle of communication offloading, we detail the design and implementation of our communication offloading component that is part of the Cuckoo Offloading Framework. We evaluate this framework with an application monitoring a subsection of any given website based on image comparison and that communication offloading saves energy on the mobile device.

Keywords: communication, offloading, smartphone, energy efficiency.

1   Introduction

Today, smartphones have been widely accepted as primary personal communication devices. Key to this acceptance are improvements in phone hardware, such as better processors, integration of various sensors and higher quality touchscreens, together with improvements in mobile operating systems and networking technologies. These improvements have made the smartphone a compelling platform for a wide spectrum of applications, ranging from web browsers and games, to navigation and personal health applications, and much more. These applications increase the phone's energy consumption, while battery capacity remains limited and is not expected to grow significantly [14,16].

To address this energy problem, various solutions have been proposed on different abstraction levels, from low level energy efficient hardware components,

J.Y. Zhang et al. (Eds.): MobiCASE 2011, LNICST 95, pp. 60–79, 2012.

(e.g. modern low power smartphone processors) to increasing energy consumption awareness at the user level. Many solutions are orthogonal and can be used simultanuously. Ideally they will minimize the use of the scarcely available energy without reducing the user experience.

In this paper we will focus on energy efficiency solutions on the middleware level. One of the known solutions in this area is to offload intensive energy consuming computations from a smartphone to another computation resource, a technique known as *computation offloading* [12] or *cyber foraging* [3] and suitable for applications containing heavy weight computing, such as object recognition [10]. To ease the creation of these applications and to make intelligent run time decisions about whether or not to offload we created an offloading framework, called Cuckoo [8], which supports computation offloading. Although computation offloading can significantly reduce the energy footprint of compute intensive applications, those applications are not yet frequently used, and therefore the total energy saving is limited.

We therefore identified a class of applications that are, in contrast to the computation offloading applications, frequently used *and* involve significant communication, which is known to be very expensive in terms of energy consumption. This class of applications comprises *information monitoring* applications. These applications are typically continuously or periodically running, either as a home screen widget or as a background service, and monitor some source of information on the Internet. Examples are RSS readers, social network apps, sports score services, weather information widgets, traffic information widgets, and many more.

To find out whether certain information has been changed on the World Wide Web – inherently a *pull*-based architecture – these applications have to repeatedly pull a website to detect changes. Repeatedly pulling information – *polling* – from sources with an unpredictable update behavior has disadvantages. It will either cause unnecessary communication, in the case that information has not changed between two polls, or cause information on the device to be out of date, in case the information has changed, but no new poll has happened yet. Thus, setting the polling rate involves a tradeoff between energy efficiency on the one hand and accuracy on the other hand.

To avoid having this tradeoff, we introduce a new mechanism, *Communication Offloading*, that minimizes energy cost, while it maximizes the accuracy of monitoring applications. With this mechanism, communication intensive polling is offloaded to cloud resources, while communication between cloud and smartphone is done only when necessary with *push* communication.

To create a system that implements Communication Offloading several problems have to be addressed. In many cases, cloud initiated communication to a phone is difficult because of Network Address Translation and firewalls. Furthermore, the use of cloud resources involves additional cost and incurs scalability issues. Finally, having additional components in the cloud introduces end user problems such as vendor lock-in and privacy problems [9].

In this paper we will discuss the principle of Communication Offloading and how we added support for it into the Cuckoo offloading framework. We describe the design and implementation of our Cloud Based Push Framework, a fundamental component needed for Communication Offloading, and evaluate the framework using a real life example application that monitors images of arbitrary web pages.

The contributions of this paper are:

- We introduce a new mechanism for energy efficient information monitoring applications on smartphones, called Communication Offloading.
- We discuss the requirements for and an implementation of a Communication Offloading Framework, which enables developers to offload communication to the cloud.
- We present a Communication Offloading framework that enables easy implementation and execution of Communication Offloading applications and addresses the problem of maintaining connectivity between cloud and phone.
- We evaluate the Communication Offloading Framework with a real life application that does Image Based Website Monitoring and show that Communication Offloading is more energy efficient than the traditional approach.

This paper is organized as follows. Section 2 discusses the Communication Offloading principle. Section 3 details the background of our work. Next, in Section 4 we describe the requirements, design and implementation of our Communication Offloading Framework. In Section 5 we demonstrate the framework with a real life application and in Section 6 we evaluate the framework with measurements of example scenarios and provide insight in the energy saved by Communication Offloading. In Section 7 we discuss the related work and we give our conclusions in Section 8.

2   Communication Offloading

2.1   Target: Polling Applications

Communication intensive applications contribute significantly to the total energy consumed by applications. Depending on the type of network used for communication and the computation intensity of the associated pre and post processing by the CPU, communication is costs more in terms of mJ per second than heavy weight computation (see Figure 1). For example Google's Nexus One can scale its CPU clock frequency from 245 MHz to 1 GHz, where a higher clock frequency results in more energy consumption. Any combination of communication in combination with computation, however, is at least 11%, but up to 177%, more expensive than running the CPU at its highest frequency. Thus communication intensive applications are an even more interesting target for energy saving measures than computation intensive applications. Reducing the amount of communication and/or the complexity of the associated processing will lead to less energy consumption.

Within the class of communication intensive applications one can identify two subgroups, differing in whether the communication is predictable or not. On the

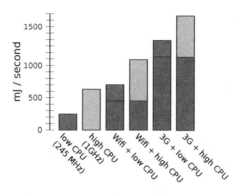

Fig. 1. Average cost of computation and communication on the Nexus One. Even the least energy consuming communication in combination with computation at the lowest clock speed is more costly than heavy-weight computation without communication. Values computed from an estimated fixed voltage of 3.8V and the manufacturer provided power profile which lists operations and the current they draw.

one hand there are the applications with unpredictable communication, such as web browsers, for which it is unknown beforehand when and which page will be requested to be retrieved, because this will be decided at run time by the user of the application.

On the other hand there are applications that do have a predictable behavior, typically monitoring a specific web resource with a fixed interval. These applications can be categorized as *information monitoring* applications (see Figure 2-i). Examples of such information monitoring applications are: weather notification, traffic monitoring, stock market monitoring, etc. and one can easily imagine many more applications. Many of these applications run permanently, for instance as a *home screen widget*.

In the remainder of this paper we will focus on permanently running information monitoring applications, since these applications consume a significant amount of energy and are therefore good candidates for energy saving techniques.

2.2   Pull versus Push

A naive energy reducing measure for information monitoring applications is to reduce the polling rate of the application. This will reduce the number of web requests and therefore the consumed energy. However, reducing the polling rate will also affect the accuracy. Information updates will be discovered later. Thus, using polling there exists a tradeoff between energy usage and accuracy of the information displayed.

Information monitoring applications pull information from web resources and then, when the data is locally available, inspect whether this data contains new information. If so, the application updates its state accordingly.

Note that, if the data on the web resource did not change during the polling interval, the energy spent on retrieving data from the resource does not affect the application's state and is thus effectively wasted. This energy waste is

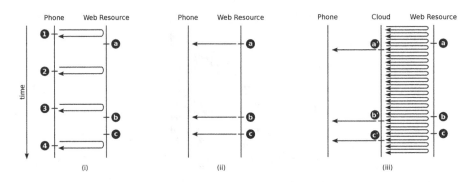

Fig. 2. Examples of Different Phone-Web Interactions. At the points (a), (b) and (c) the web resource updates its information. If the polling mechanism is used (i), updates are received on the phone after some delay – the time between (a) and (2), (c) and (4). Some updates are not received at all, e.g. (b). Using server based push notifications (ii), these situations will not happen. Cloud based push notifications (iii) use an intermediate cloud resource, that can poll the web resource at a much higher frequency and will therefore have a much shorter delay and is less likely to miss updates. Furthermore, the cloud based push mechanism moves energy expensive polling to the cloud.

unavoidable for phone based polling solutions, since in contrast to polling, information updates are irregular and unpredictable.

To prevent this energy waste, the phone ideally should communicate with the server only when data has changed. This can be done using a server based technique called *push notifications*. Then the server informs clients when specific data has changed (see Figure 2-ii). Push notifications are an excellent solution to have energy efficient applications on mobile phones that show web information.

Implementing push notifications, however, requires server code modifications and in many cases the application developer does not have the rights to alter code on the web server.

2.3   Our Proposal: Cloud Based Push

We propose a new alternative mechanism for information monitoring applications that exploits the energy efficiency of push notifications, but does not require any server code to be changed and thus can be used by third party developers.

We propose to add an intermediate cloud layer in between the client application on the phone and the code on the server. This intermediate layer consists of a small application that runs on a cloud resource. This cloud application communicates with the phone using the energy efficient push notification messages (see Figure 2-iii), while it uses polling at a high rate to retrieve updates from the web resource. Then, the energy is spent on the cloud, where energy is relatively cheap and abundant, while accurate information is available on the phone. There is no need to alter the code on the web server, instead a little extra code is put on a cloud resource. We call such an architecture *Cloud Based Push*, to underline the difference with existing server initiated push notification systems.

2.4   Requirements for Cloud Based Push

While individual developers could employ the principle of cloud based push themselves, the complexity of implementing such a system requires additional skills from developers and lengthens the development time in a market where rapid time-to-market is essential. Therefore, we believe that there is a need for a simple cloud based push framework. Furthermore, a single push framework allows multiple applications on a single phone to share the same push notification connection.

A cloud based push framework should consist of:

- a push system that deals with the communication between the phone and the cloud application.
- a component that maintains connectivity between cloud and phone
- a simple programming model where developers can plug in their monitoring code.

Furthermore, we favor code bundling for distributed applications, such that compatibility between the components is ensured and vendor lock-in is prohibited, thus we add a fourth requirement:

- a deployment system so that cloud code available on the phone and bundled with the client application can be deployed on cloud resources.

3   Background

We believe that the current generation of smartphones is ready to run real *smart applications* – applications that use personal, social and sensor information to make smart decisions to enrich and simplify the life of the user. While we already see some of these applications entering the markets today, there are still several problems for developers to create such applications, among which energy usage is a key problem. In order to ease the process of such applications we are building a toolkit called *Interdroid* (see Figure 3).

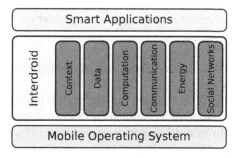

Fig. 3. Abstract overview of the Interdroid project. We strive towards a layer that enables application developers to use social and context information, intensive computing and communication, and data services while keeping energy usage to a minimum.

In this toolkit we offer developers easy ways to access social information and context information [19], to share, version and replicate information and to compute in an energy efficient way on this data. We use offloading to solve part of the energy problem in our toolkit.

3.1 Cuckoo

To encourage developers to use energy efficiency techniques, we strive towards a simple, complete and uniform platform at the middleware layer that we can offer to developers. This will maximize the probability that developers will really employ known energy saving techniques in their application, where time to market is short. In this section we outline our earlier work on offloading in the Cuckoo project [8], one of Interdroid's sub-projects.

Our initial effort in the Cuckoo Offloading Framework is a computation offloading component that can be used by developers to easily create energy efficient applications that contain compute intensive parts. The computation offloading component allows developers to generate both local and remote implementations of compute intensive code. The offloading component can then at run time decide to move heavy weight computation to remote resources, such as clouds.

In the Cuckoo offloading project we believe in a user centric approach, where the user experience should not degrade because of energy saving techniques. Therefore Cuckoo supports both local and remote implementations to have a fallback mechanism for the case when there is no network connectivity to the remote resource *and* to allow for remote implementations that take advantage of being different, for instance being implemented to use parallelism. Furthermore, Cuckoo bundles local and remote code on the phone and installs remote code when needed on the fly on remote resources, so that users are sure that their local code is compatible with the remote code.

4   Cuckoo Communication Offloading

We developed a communication offloading component as part of the Cuckoo Offloading Framework. The communication offloading component consists of:
- a Push Server that runs on cloud resources
- a Push Client library that handles the communication with this server
- a background application (service) that runs on the phone and manages the incoming push notifications.

In this section we will detail the different components, the design decisions and important implementation aspects.

We start with motivating our choice for Android as implementation platform, describe the traditional approach of writing an information monitoring app and explain what changes from a developers perspective.

4.1   Android: Implementation Platform

In order to make a real world implementation of the framework we have selected Android as our underlying implementation platform, because it is widely adopted, has support for existing Java libraries, such as the Ibis communication libraries [2] that we use for communication between the client and the server, and has been used for the earlier Computation Offloading component of the Cuckoo framework. Furthermore, Android supports multiple application types that could be used for web based information monitoring applications, namely:

- *home screen widgets*: lightweight applications that are permanently visible on one of the home screens.
- *background services*: applications with no UI that run in the background.
- *broadcast receivers*: lightweight applications that start when a particular broadcast message (*Intent*) is sent to the system.
- *activities*: regular applications that have a UI and execute a particular task, like listing email, capturing a photo, etc.

4.2   The Traditional Approach

When one writes a web based monitoring application for the Android platform, one would in general take the following approach. Depending on the type of application that wants to receive updates from the web resource, one creates such an application, be it a home screen widget, a broadcast receiver, or even an activity (although the latter is less likely, because of its short lived nature).

Then, to make sure polling happens in the background, one creates a service, which does the polling. This service will be started by either the widget, the receiver or an activity and then monitor the web resource. Once it finds an update it will send this update via an *Intent* message to the appropriate destination. The widget, broadcast receiver, or activity will receive this message and change its behavior according to the message (e.g. display the new information, alert the user, etc.). A schematic overview of this process is shown in Figure 4. Pseudocode for it is shown in Figure 5.

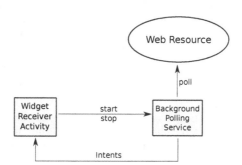

Fig. 4. Schematic overview of a traditional implementation of a monitoring app. An Android component (homescreen widget, broadcast receiver or activity) starts a service on the phone that repeatedly fetches information from a web resource. Once an update is found, an Intent message is sent back to the component.

```
/*********** Service Code ************/
MyService extends Service
// (2), change to MyService extends PushService

while (true) {
    info = poll("http://...");
    if (changed(info)) {
        sendIntent(...); // (3), change to push(...);
    }
    sleep(interval);
}

/*********** Widget Code ************/
onCreate() {
    startService(); // (1), change to startRemoteService();
}

onRemove() {
    stopService(); // (1), change to stopRemoteService();
}

onReceiveIntent() {
    updateUI();
}
```

Fig. 5. Pseudocode comparison between traditional and offloading code. The comment numbering corresponds with Figure 6.

4.3 The Offloading Approach

To make it as simple as possible for developers to use communication offloading, we retained the traditional approach as much as possible. Only a few parts in the source code have to be changed (see comments (1) to (3) in Figure 5). Furthermore the developer should add the Cuckoo libraries to the project.

Figure 6 shows the schematic overview of a web polling application that is based on communication offloading. It differs on four points from the traditional approach:

- (1) *Starting and Stopping*: Whereas in the traditional approach components would start and stop a local service, they now have to start and stop remote services.
- (2) *Remote Service*: Whereas the polling service was originally implemented to be executed locally, it now has to be implemented to be executed remotely. Although local code is compiled with the Android libraries and the remote code is compiled against the standard Java libraries, polling code typically does not involve Android specific code. Typically, the original local code and the new remote code are largely the same.

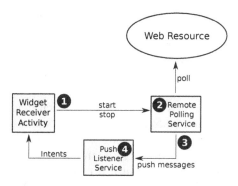

Fig. 6. Schematic overview of an implementation of a monitoring app using communication offloading. The same Android component as in Figure 4 starts and stops the polling, however, the polling now runs in the cloud. Once an update is detected in the cloud, the push listener service on the phone is notified.

- (3) *Informing the Source*: Traditionally, an Intent was sent to the source upon an update. With the offloading approach a message is sent over the network.
- (4) *Transforming the Push Message*: Once the push message is received by the Cuckoo provided listener service, the push message is translated into an Intent, which then as in the traditional approach is received by the corresponding Widget, Broadcast Receiver or Activity.

Our framework provides libraries with base classes that can be extended to implement remote polling services. The framework also provides a server application that can host the polling services, and both a push listener service application and a resource manager application that run on the phone.

4.4   The Push Server

The Push Server is the component of the framework that runs in the cloud and will poll the web resources. The Push Server has to be installed and started on a cloud resource either by a user or by the application provider, or a third party such as a network provider.

The requirements for the cloud resource to run a Push Server are minimal, since the Push Server is a regular Java application and can therefore run on any resource that has a Java Virtual Machine (JVM) installed. Furthermore, the resource needs to be permanently connected to the Internet.

Multiple resources can be bound to a phone, and multiple phones can be bound to a single resource. This allows users to use their own resources, such as home servers, together with resources provided by application providers.

Once a Push Server is up and running it can execute polling services. Such a service is the polling part of a phone application and will be implemented by the application developer and bundled with a web based monitoring application as a plugin for the Push Server. This code is thus available on the phone, while it needs to be executed on the Push Server. However, this code can be installed on the fly on the Push Server through Java's dynamic class loading mechanisms. Once installed and started, it will execute the polling code and each time an update of the particular web resource is detected, a push message is sent to the phone.

The Push Server maintains a bookkeeping of which devices are using which service and what their actual address is. If a service wants to send a push message to a phone, it will inform its hosting Push Server, which will take care of the delivery of the message. Messages might be not deliverable because the phone is temporarily unreachable, in such a case the Push Server informs the polling service, which can for instance use an exponential backoff algorithm for resending.

Scalability. Depending on who provides the resources that are used for communication offloading, the server might experience scalability issues. When the load on a Push Server becomes too high, one can use elastic computing such as offered by Amazons EC2 [1] and start a new Push Server instance in the cloud. To further improve scalability – in particular down-scaling – it is necessary to be able to transparantly migrate monitoring code from one Push Server to another, so that the number of instances and thus the cost can be kept at a minimum. At the moment Cuckoo does not support migration of monitoring code between Push Servers.

4.5   The Push Listener Service

Up to now we have seen that the phone application needs to be modified slightly to start a remote service running on a Push Server. Once an update is detected the service on the Push Server sends a push message back to the phone. In this section we will outline what happens when such a message arrives at the phone.

Our communication offloading framework provides a Push Listener Service, which runs in the background and waits for push messages to arrive. When such a message comes in, the Push Listener Service analyzes the message and transforms it into an Intent. Once this Intent is broadcast and subsequently received by the application, the application can handle the update. Typically, this will involve updating the UI or alarming the user through sound or vibration.

The Push Listener Service can temporarily be turned off by the user, because users may want to temporarily sacrifice the possibility to receive push messages to save energy.

4.6   Maintaining Connectivity

There is a distinct problem for cloud servers when it comes to sending push messages to mobile phones. First of all, phones inherently are mobile devices, they switch from network to network thereby often changing network address.

In order to send push messages a cloud server has to know the current address of a phone.

Even when this address is known, it is likely that cloud servers cannot reach a mobile phone, because it has limited inbound connectivity due to Network Address Translation (NAT), which is widely used for both Wi-Fi and 3G/4G access points. Access points that use NAT will hand out private IP addresses to connected devices. These addresses are only reachable in the local network and cannot be used by cloud resources outside this private local network to set up connections.

Although cloud resources cannot reach phones, phones can reach cloud resources. A solution to the aforementioned problems is to maintain an open bidirectional connection that is set up by the phone. To prevent such a connection from being closed due to protocol time-outs, keep-alive messages keep the connection active. In our framework we use the SmartSockets library [13] that provides a socket-like library that operates on top of an internal overlay network, which automatically keeps connections active.

Although we can keep connections active with keep-alive messages, eventually a phone switches to another network, and then the active connection is inevitably closed. Connection re-establishment therefore is an essential part of maintaining connectivity. In our implementation the Push Listener Service registers with the mobile OS to get notified of each network change and establishes a new bidirectional connection if the previous one is closed.

With the combination of keeping open connections using SmartSockets and reconnecting upon network changes, the cloud resource always has a means to send messages to the phone as long as the phone is connected to the Internet. The cost of maintaining an open connection through sending the keep-alive messages is very small for Wi-Fi compared to having an idle connection (see Table 1), for 3G it is significantly costlier, but still acceptable since it is a one-time cost and not a per app cost.

Table 1. battery cost of maintaining connectivity

	idle	open connection	overhead
Wi-Fi	2.18 %/hr	2.36 %/hr	0.18 %/hr
3G	3.03 %/hr	4.61 %/hr	1.58 %/hr

5   Image Based Website Monitoring

In order to demonstrate the Cuckoo Offloading Framework we made a compelling web based polling application. This application is called *Web Page Widget* and can be used to have a live view of a specific area of a website in a homescreen widget. Figure 7 shows screenshots of this widget.

The first screenshot shows one instance of the widget. This widget shows the output of monitoring a Dutch news website with live traffic information, weather information, the gas price and the stock exchange index value[1]. The

---

[1] http://www.nu.nl

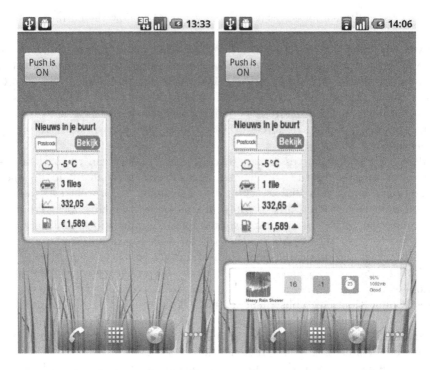

Fig. 7. Two screenshots of the Web Page Widget application. The first screenshot shows a single instance of the widget, the second shows the same widget half an hour later with updated values. Furthermore, a new instance of the same widget monitoring a different web resource is added. The screenshots also show the user control to turn delivery of push messages on or off.

second screenshot is taken about half an hour later and shows two instances of the widget. One of these is the same widget as in the first screenshot, but now with updated values. The other instance monitors weather information from the BBC weather webpage[2].

Each widget must be configured before it can be placed on a homescreen. The configuration consists of three steps and is visualized in Figure 8:

- *Select URL*: Select the URL of the webpage that is going to be monitored.
- *Select Area*: Select a rectangle around the area of interest on the webpage.
- *Select Scaling*: Select how the website area will be scaled in the widget area.

Once configured, the widget is placed on the homescreen and updates the part of the webpage in near real time whenever the contents of the website in that specific area change.

5.1   Implementation

While for some monitoring applications it is arguable to have server based push solution, that is the web site owner providing push support to mobile phones, it is

---

[2] http://news.bbc.co.uk/weather/forecast/101

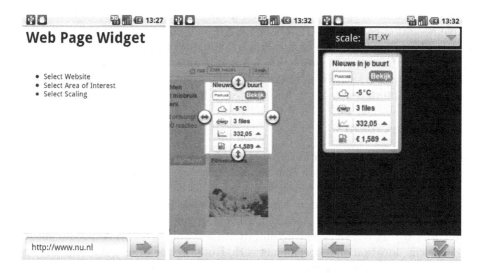

Fig. 8. Configuration of a Web Page Widget. First a URL of a to be monitored website is entered. Then this webpage gets rendered at the remote resource an image is sent back to the phone. The user now selects the area of interest. Finally, the user can specify how the image will be mapped onto the area on the screen.

clear that this application cannot be implemented with server based push. There is no single authority of all websites, so polling is the only way to implement such a monitoring application.

When we want to monitor websites we have to repeatedly execute HTTP requests. The data we get back is in HTML format and we can use text comparison to inspect whether it is the same as the previous value. Since we are interested in only a subpart of the webpage and there is no clear mapping to a rectangle on the screen and the HTML tags belonging to this rectangle, we render the webpage and then use pixel by pixel image comparison to detect changes. If a change is detected the widget is updated with a new image of the area of interest.

5.2   Traditional versus Offloading

When we implement this application in a traditional way, that is using polling and rendering on the phone itself, it will either drain the battery very rapidly or, when a low polling rate is used, have out of date information.

An offloading approach on the other hand will do polling, rendering and image comparison on the cloud resource and will only send the resulting image when it has changed. The size of the resulting image is significantly lower than the size of the HTML, images and scripts that are sent as a result of HTTP request, because it only covers the area of interest (AoI). Table 2 shows that for the two example widgets from the screenshots the images of the AoI are about 160 times (nu.nl) and 3000 times (bbc) smaller than the size of the full webpage. This alone will already save much of traffic to the phone. For instance, if the

AoI on the nu.nl webpage will change on average every 5 minutes, an offloading implementation can run for 12.5 hours and use an equal amount of data traffic as a single polling operation of a traditional implementation of this widget. Note that not only for this application, but for many monitoring applications users are interested in just a subsection of the overall information, however web resources do not offer interfaces to query for updates of subsections.

6   Measurements

Measuring energy consumption of mobile phones is a complicated task. First of all, there are many factors that influence the energy consumption. Some of these factors cannot easily be controlled, for instance the interference on the wireless network. Furthermore, measuring how much energy is consumed in a given period requires either special hardware or fine grained information from the hardware. Third, the resulting information is only valid for a specific phone on a specific location on a specific network. Running the exact same experiment from a different phone might give other results and going to another location (for instance closer to a cell tower) might also influence the experiment.

Although measuring energy consumption is a difficult task and measurements should be interpreted with care, we have executed several experiments to get insight in the energy cost of several operations related to communication offloading.

The phone we used for our experiments is a Nexus One, running on Android 2.2 with a 1.0 GHz CPU and a Li-Ion 1400 mAh battery. In our Wi-Fi experiments we used a 801.11n network, in the 3G experiments we used the Vodafone network in The Netherlands which uses HSDPA with a bandwidth up to 3.6 Mbps.

For each measurement we use the Android BatteryManager API to query the battery level, which runs from 100% (full) to 0% (empty). We execute our to be measured operation until the battery level has dropped by 5% and measure how long that takes.

In order to validate this methodology we have run a reference measurement to verify that the battery level as returned by the Android BatteryManager API indeed shows linear regression in time and is not merely a percentage of the maximum voltage of the battery, which is known to be non-linear. We found that the values reported by the BatteryManager indeed result in a linear correlation between energy use over time and the battery level.

6.1   Polling vs. Other Activities

Figure 9 shows the results of energy usage measurements of several common operations on smartphones. We found that video capture (720x480, H.264) is the most energy consuming operation, followed by browsing, which intensively uses the 3G radio, and navigation, which uses the GPS, the 3G connection and Bluetooth to stream the audio. Computationally intensive operations, such as playing a 3D racing game[3] also consume much energy, giving a total battery time of about 4 hours and 20 minutes for a user that just plays games.

---

[3] We used Raging Thunder Lite 2 from PolarBit.

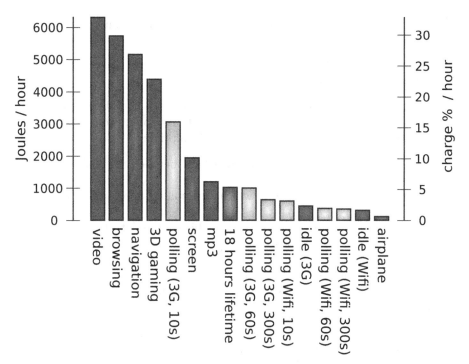

Fig. 9. Energy usage of various common smartphone operations. This graph shows the drop in the battery charge level and the Joules consumed for a particular operation in one hour.

Table 2. web page size vs. image size

source	web page size	AoI size	reduction
nu.nl	1.4 MB	9 kB	159x
bbc	0.9 MB	0.3 kB	3072x

When we look at the energy cost of polling, we see that using the 3G network in our case consumes much more energy than using the Wi-Fi network. Note that various network properties, such as distance to the access point, interference, etc. influence the energy cost. We also see that, like we expected, the energy cost of polling is reduced when the polling interval is reduced.

Although the energy cost of polling per hour is not that high compared to the other tasks, polling happens continuously, while other activities, such as video capture, browsing, navigation, mp3 playback happen only for a limited time. Furthermore, we measured polling for just a single application. If multiple applications are polling concurrently, the energy consumption will increase even more. If the compound number of polls from the various applications is one poll every 10 seconds and we use 3G, the phone will not last for longer than 6 hours and 15 minutes on a full battery. This is well below the lowest accepted operation time of about 18 hours, where a phone is charged every night. Though

Wi-Fi gives better results, one cannot expect that a smartphone user will only use Wi-Fi networks during an entire day.

6.2   Polling vs. Pushing

The amount of energy saved by switching from polling to cloud based push for a given application depends on the characteristics of that application. In particular the following variables influence the energy consumption:

- Average Update Rate (UR): The average time between two updates on the web page.
- Polling Rate (PR): The rate at which the polling application checks for updates.
- Data Reduction Factor: How many times bigger the data for a single poll request is compared to a push message.
- Processing Reduction Factor: How much more processing has to be done for a poll request compared to an incoming push message.
- Accepted Update Latency: The latency with which an update arrives on the phone.

We performed experiments to compare the cost of polling to cloud based push using our example Web Page Widget application monitoring the AoI on the nu.nl web page as shown in Figure 8.

For this application, the data reduction factor is 159 times (see Table 2). Processing using push notifications takes 0.072 seconds, which is updating an

Table 3. Polling vs. Pushing. This table shows how the important properties of monitoring cost with varying polling rates (PR) as a multiple of the update rate (UR) and for push. The values are based on a single widget running for 9h22m monitoring nu.nl. Wi-Fi (W) bandwidth is 623 kB/s, 3G bandwidth is 100 kB/s. Energy consumption is calculated based on the power profile. The lower the polling rate, the lower the energy cost, but also the more updates missed and the longer of a delay until updates are propagated to the phone. The push energy reduction factors include the one-time cost for the open connection (conn), the values between parenthesis are the reduction factors for each subsequent widget. For instance, a single widget with push uses 1.5 times less energy on 3G compared to polling with an PR of .57UR. A second push widget will reuse the existing open connection and therefore the additional cost the energy reduction is 241 times compared to an additional polling widget.

PR	2UR	1UR	0.57UR	0.1UR	push	conn
missed updates	69.3 %	52.9%	42.1%	18.6%	0.0%	-
update latency	138s	103s	60s	12s	0s	-
CPU time/hr	22s	44s	77s	443s	1s	-
Data size/hr	10.3 MB	20.6 MB	36.1 MB	206.5 MB	133 kB	-
batt. %/hr (W)	.11%	.23%	.40%	2.27%	.004%	0.18%
push energy reduction (W)	0.6x (28x)	1.3x (57x)	2.2x (100x)	12.3x (568x)	-	-
batt. %/hr (3G)	.69%	1.38%	2.41%	13.78%	0.01%	1.58%
push energy reduction (3G)	0.4x (69x)	0.9x (138x)	1.5x (241x)	8.7x (1378x)	-	-

image in a widget. The polling implementation has to do significantly more work, since it has to render the full web page and then extract the subimage, which takes in total approximately 3 seconds. The processing reduction factor therefore is 41 times.

We collected an update trace for the AoI on the nu.nl web page. The total trace time is 9 hours and 22 minutes, in which we detected a total of 140 updates, giving an average UR of 4 min 4 sec.

In the experiments we varied the PR of the polling version, which influences the accuracy and the energy consumption (see Table 3). If we apply a PR that is equal to the UR, we only see 66 out of the 140 updates (47%) and the average delay between the update and its appearance on the phone is 1:43 minutes, the energy consumed with polling is 0.9 (3G) to 1.3 (Wi-Fi) times more than with push.

Increasing the PR will decrease the average delay and the number of missed updates at the cost of spending more energy. If our accepted update latency is 1 minute, we have to set our polling rate to 0.57 times the UR. Using this polling rate, we will only see 58% of all updates and energy consumption goes further up to 1.5 (3G) to 2.2 (Wi-Fi) times more than push. When we also want to increase the number of updates we have to increase the polling rate even more. Polling 10 times during the average update interval results in only 18.6% of the updates missed and gives an acceptable age of only 12 seconds when an update arrives on the phone, but energy consumption is dramatic, especially when using 3G. In a single hour, about 14% of the battery will be spent on monitoring this web page, giving a maximum and unacceptable operation time of only 7 hours on a full battery. If we would have more widgets monitoring other web pages the energy consumption increases accordingly and operation time decreases even more.

Monitoring based on cloud based push however, has a much smaller energy footprint. Most of the energy consumed is spent on maintaining the connectivity. This cost however will not increase when multiple widgets are used on a single phone. The cost of running a single instance of a web page widget will only use 0.01% (3G) or even 0.004% (Wi-Fi) of the battery for a full hour. Even if one runs tens of web page widgets concurrently, the operation time of a full battery will only be limited by the small cost of a single open connection, while not missing any update and getting the updates instantly.

7   Related Work

Computation offloading is a well known technique in the field of distributed computing. Already in the era of dumb terminals, resource constrained devices used help from more powerful machines to execute certain tasks. With the introduction of resource constrained mobile devices, computation offloading has been used to allow compute intensive, memory intensive and energy intensive applications to run on mobile devices in such a way that the expensive part of the operation gets executed on remote resources. Before the introduction of cloud computing this technique was known as *cyber foraging* [17], where resource constrained mobile devices used nearby powerful machines – *surrogates* – to offload computation to. Later work, such as *CloneCloud* [5], uses cloud resources to support computation offloading. In [11] Kumar et al. discuss whether computation offloading can save energy for mobile devices. Some of the existing offloading systems rely on annotations by the developers, while others do automatic partitioning [7,6]. None of these systems support *communication* offloading and allow remote implementations to send push messages to the mobile device.

In this paper we introduce a communication offloading framework. Recently, we have seen a commercial company offering a push based app for Twitter updates, called TweetHook [18], where they run an intermediate layer application in the cloud to query the Twitter API. Google has also started a project called *PubSubHubbub* [15], which uses intermediate applications (hubs) to periodically query publishers of content. Once updates are found all subscribers are informed. PubSubHubbub requires subscribers to be at a fixed location and to be able to receive HTTP Post messages and is therefore not very suitable for communication offloading from mobile devices. PubSubHubbub hubs, however, are excellent sources of information where a communication offloading app can retrieve information from.

Whereas in this paper we use the Cuckoo Push framework, Google also offers a push service called Cloud To Device Messaging (C2DM) [4]. In our future work we will integrate Cuckoo and C2DM, and compare this to a pure Cuckoo implementation.

8   Conclusions

In this paper we proposed a new offloading technique to reduce the energy usage of information monitoring applications on smartphones. We offload expensive polling of web based resources to a cloud resource, that in turn sends push messages to the smartphone only when the information has changed. We have built an extension to the Cuckoo offloading framework to support this *communication offloading* and drastically simplify the process of developing such an application.

We evaluated the technique and the framework with an example application that does image based webpage monitoring and we showed that offloading polling to the cloud can have significant impact on the operation time of a single battery charge.

References

1. Amazon EC2, http://aws.amazon.com/ec2/
2. Bal, H.E., Maassen, J., van Nieuwpoort, R.V., Drost, N., Kemp, R., Palmer, N., Wrzesinska, G., Kielmann, T., Seinstra, F., Jacobs, C.: Real-World Distributed Computing with Ibis. IEEE Computer 43, 54–62 (2010)
3. Balan, R., Flinn, J., Satyanarayanan, M., Sinnamohideen, S., Yang, H.-I.: The case for cyber foraging. In: Proceedings of the 10th Workshop on ACM SIGOPS European Workshop, EW 10, pp. 87–92 (2002)
4. Android Cloud to Device Messaging, http://code.google.com/android/c2dm/

5. Chun, B.-G., Ihm, S., Maniatis, P., Naik, M., Patti, A.: Clonecloud: elastic execution between mobile device and cloud. In: Proceedings of the Sixth Conference on Computer Systems, EuroSys 2011, pp. 301–314 (2011)
6. Cuervo, E., Balasubramanian, A., Cho, D.-K., Wolman, A., Saroiu, S., Chandra, R., Bahl, P.: Maui: making smartphones last longer with code offload. In: Proc. of the 8th Int'l Conference on Mobile Systems, Applications, and Services, MobiSys 2010, pp. 49–62 (2010)
7. Giurgiu, I., Riva, O., Juric, D., Krivulev, I., Alonso, G.: Calling the Cloud: Enabling Mobile Phones as Interfaces to Cloud Applications. In: Bacon, J.M., Cooper, B.F. (eds.) Middleware 2009. LNCS, vol. 5896, pp. 83–102. Springer, Heidelberg (2009)
8. Kemp, R., Palmer, N., Kielmann, T., Bal, H.: Cuckoo: a Computation Offloading Framework for Smartphones. In: MobiCASE 2010: Proc. of The 2nd International Conference on Mobile Computing, Applications, and Services (2010)
9. Kemp, R., Palmer, N., Kielmann, T., Bal, H.: The Smartphone and the Cloud: Power to the User. In: MobiCloud 2010: Proceedings of the First International Workshop on Mobile Computing and Clouds (2010)
10. Kemp, R., Palmer, N., Kielmann, T., Seinstra, F., Drost, N., Maassen, J., Bal, H.: eyeDentify: Multimedia Cyber Foraging from a Smartphone. In: International Symposium on Multimedia, vol. 11, pp. 392–399 (2009)
11. Kumar, K., Lu, Y.H.: Cloud computing for mobile users: can offloading computation save energy? IEEE Computer 43(4), 51–56 (2010)
12. Li, Z., Wang, C., Xu, R.: Computation offloading to save energy on handheld devices: a partition scheme. In: Proceedings of the 2001 International Conference on Compilers, Architecture, and Synthesis for Embedded Systems, CASES 2001, pp. 238–246 (2001)
13. Maassen, J., Bal, H.: Smartsockets: solving the connectivity problems in grid computing. In: Proceedings of the 16th International Symposium on High Performance Distributed Computing, pp. 1–10. ACM (2007)
14. Palacín, M.: Recent advances in rechargeable battery materials: a chemists perspective. Chemical Society Reviews 38(9), 2565–2575 (2009)
15. PubSubHubbub, http://code.google.com/p/pubsubhubbub/
16. Robinson, S.: Cellphone Energy Gap: Desperately Seeking Solutions, Tech report, Strategy Analytics (2009)
17. Satyanarayanan, M.: Pervasive computing: vision and challenges. IEEE Personal Communications 8(4), 10–17 (2001)
18. TweetHook, https://tweethook.com/
19. van Wissen, B., Palmer, N., Kemp, R., Kielmann, T., Bal, H.: ContextDroid: an Expression-Based Context Framework for Android. In: International Workshop on Sensing for App Phones, PhoneSense (2010)

MapBiquitous – An Approach for Integrated Indoor/Outdoor Location-Based Services

Thomas Springer

Technische Universitt Dresden, Computer Networks Group,
01062 Dresden, Germany
thomas.springer@tu-dresden.de

Abstract. Nowadays, location-based services based on GPS and map data are commonly available. Since GPS does not work in buildings and map data provide geographic information only, such services are limited to outdoor scenarios. Large research effort has been carried out to explore indoor positioning and navigation systems but up to now mostly proprietary and isolated solutions have been proposed. In this paper, we introduce the MapBiquitous system as an approach towards an integrated system for indoor and outdoor location-based services. It is based on a decentralized infrastructure of building servers providing information about the building geometry, positioning infrastructure and navigation. Building servers are dynamically discovered and provided information is seamlessly integrated into outdoor systems by the MapBiquitous client. We discuss the general approach and architecture of MapBiquitous and present experiences of implementing the MapBiquitous concepts and location-based services on top of it.

Keywords: location-based services, indoor positioning, building model, OpenGIS, Android, MapBiquitous.

1 Introduction

Finding an indian restaurant nearby, navigating to a selected target address, tagging information to a particular location or presenting information about the building the user is in front of are location-based services (LBS) commonly available for outdoor settings. OpenStreetMap, GoogleMaps and other services provide the map data necessary to implement such services while GPS or WiFi positioning is used to determine the user's current location.

Similar use cases exist for indoor scenarios. Museum guides providing information about the objects in close proximity to the user, navigation within a building from room to room or finding a printer nearby are such use cases. They have been already implemented as research prototypes and some even as productive systems. The major difference between outdoor and indoor LBS is the lack of a well established and broadly used technical foundation for indoor services. While GPS and map services operate in a global scale, indoor positioning systems are based on proprietary infrastructures usually limited to single buildings

J.Y. Zhang et al. (Eds.): MobiCASE 2011, LNICST 95, pp. 80–99, 2012.
© Institute for Computer Sciences, Social Informatics and Telecommunications Engineering 2012

and information about building geometry is hardly available to the public. Thus, services like navigating from home directly to the right terminal in the airport, tagging information to a shop in a shopping mall, and more general setting up indoor location-based services in an interoperable and integrated manner are hard to implement.

In this paper we present the MapBiquitous system following an integrated approach for indoor and outdoor location-based services. The research explores concepts and standard technologies to allow the provision of LBS for indoor and indoor/outdoor scenarios in an interoperable way. Based on the main idea to provide the necessary data about building geometry and annotating it with information about positioning infrastructure, navigation and semantic location information outdoor and indoor positioning, navigation and information tagging should be seamlessly coupled.

The main contributions of the presented work are the decentralized system architecture, the approach for modeling and providing building data, including information for indoor positioning and routing based on open standards (namely WfS, GML and OpenLS Directory Service) and a concept for the creation of client applications with efficient access to decentralized building information and seamless integration into outdoor systems.

The paper is organized as follows: in section 2 related work is discussed. After discussing the requirements in section 3 we present the MapBiquitous approach and main architecture in section 4. In section 5 we report on the implementation of the MapBiquitous system and the experiences obtained by implementing LBS using MapBiquitous. We close the paper with a conclusion and outlook to future work.

2   Related Work

Location-based services are a topic of research with different aspects. Fundamental technologies are required to determine the position of objects, devices and persons and to set them into relation with reference systems, geographical data or building data. On top of such an infrastructure, concepts for data access and service architectures are investigated to create LBS.

Positioning Technologies: GPS is well established for determining locations in outdoor settings but does not work properly indoor [5]. Different approaches try to provide Indoor GPS based on additional infrastructure in buildings like repeaters or to improve GPS receivers to deal with the decreased signal strength in buildings. Approaches based on cellular networks work also in buildings but are not accurate enough for indoor services.

This is the reason of the many efforts to create indoor positioning systems. Many research projects try to exploit the WiFi infrastructure widely available in buildings and mobile devices. Different approaches mainly based on lateration or fingerprinting [7] exist. The major issue is that strength of WiFi signals in buildings is influenced by manifold factors, like material and constellation of walls, used device, and device direction. Therefore, calculating the distance for lateration based on signal strength does not yield accurate results. With finger-printing, actual signal strength values of all visible access points are recorded for reference points in the intended coverage area. After that setup phase client locations can be determined based on matching a current measured fingerprint with the stored fingerprints. This concept can produce more accurate results with the cost of a large effort for setup and maintenance of the fingerprint database. Anyway, issues like influence of device direction and different scales for signal strength in different devices still remain unsolved [3].

Alternative approaches based on an infrastructure use ultrasonic [17] or infrared signals [16,9] or use RFID technology to determine the position of a device. Dependent on the density and arrangement of beacons these systems can achieve high accuracy. Their major drawback is the high effort for installing an additional infrastructure. Hence, such systems are not widely deployed.

Inertial systems work without a pre-installed infrastructure. Based on a known starting location relative movements are tracked with a sensor fixed on the body or placed freely in the pocket and used to calculate the new location [18,14]. In [19] an approach is described to even avoid the knowledge of the initial location. A common issue of inertial systems is the integration drift, measurement errors add over time and constantly increase inaccuracy of the determined position.

In summary, non of the mentioned approaches is in a state to complement the globally available GPS for indoor positioning. Our approach does not introduce any new positioning method but integrates multiple positioning technologies. In addition, we provide the necessary information for positioning like access point locations, fingerprint records, or beacon information as part of the building model. Thus, as long as the user's device is able to interoperate with the positioning technology in a building it can dynamically obtain the necessary information and use that technology in the building.

Geographic Data Provisioning: A second major building block for LBS is spatial data to visualize locations and to attach semantic information to them. Geographic Information Systems (GIS) serve as data providers for geographic information for outdoor services. Under the term web mapping applications like OpenStreetMap or Google Maps provide access to geographic data like street maps and satellite imagery. Via APIs functionality like searching and routing is made available and can be integrated into custom applications.

In this context the Open Geospatial Consortium (OGC) specifies interfaces and protocols to support interoperable solutions for accessing spatial information and providing LBS. The Web Map Service (WMS) [4] is a OGC standard for offering geo-referenced map data as raster images. The Web Feature Service (WFS) [15] is a service to provide geographic features encoded in XML. Such features might be meta data provided in addition to map data for spatial analysis but also vector data represented in XML. Both services can be accessed via HTTP.

While WMS usually responses data encoded in GIF, PNG or JPEG, the default payload of WFS is Geographic Markup Language (GML) [10]. GML is also specified by OGC as an XML-based language for geographic features including representations of vector objects based on elements like point, line and polygon. Thus, GML is one option to model building geometry. CityGML, a particular schema definition for GML enables the modeling of 3D city models including buildings and their environment. In contrast to generic 3D vector formats like SVG or VRML, CityGML provides elements with the necessary semantics to represent and analyze city models including navigation functions. KML is used in Google Earth to model geographic features like geo-tags and routes, but it is a proprietary format.

In our approach we adopt WFS as a service for the provisioning of building information in GML format. Since both are OGC standards we ensure high inter-operability. In addition, WFS can be based on various data sources as backend. Available implementations usually support various data formats and databases. In this way, building data providers are not restricted to a particular format but can choose any format as long as it can be transformed into GML.

Service Engineering: Systems like MagicMap[1] or PlaceLab[2] integrate various positioning technologies for indoor and outdoor. Both systems use WiFi later-ation as main positioning method which require the availability of information about access point locations. Visualization of current location is based on floor plans which are provided as images. Thus, building geometry is not explicitly modeled in a standard format and the current semantic location is not known to the system. Locations are available based on a local reference system only.

In [13] a simple approach for indoor positioning and navigation based on dead reckoning and 2D barcodes is introduced. Users can download floor plans by reading a 2D barcode attached to publicly available maps in the building. With the download also the current position is provided. Due to the simplicity of the approach it could be adopted in any building. Anyway, building data is not explicitly modeled and positioning is limited to dead reckoning.

The REAL system [1] is a pedestrian navigation system which combines to sub-systems. The IRREAL (Infrared REAL) sub-system supports indoor posi-tioning and navigation while ARREAL (Augmented Reality REAL) offers the same functionality outdoors. The system combines infrared-based positioning and GPS. The system uses map data for outdoor and 3D data in a proprietary format for indoor locations. The system is based on dedicated hardware which is restricted to infrared and GPS. Thus, the approach is limited to buildings which are equipped with the infrared infrastructure. In addition, building models have to be provided in the special format.

In [3] a concept for campus wide positioning based on WiFi fingerprinting is explored. The user's position is visualized on a map or a floor plan. Both are based on proprietary data sources, the fingerprinting data is separately provided in a database. At all, the system is limited to the campus with all necessary geographic, floor and fingerprinting data available. Positioning is restricted to WiFi fingerprinting.

---

[1] http://www2.informatik.hu-berlin.de/rok/MagicMap/
[2] http://sourceforge.net/projects/placelab/

As a conclusion, to the best knowledge of the authors there is currently no single system providing a technological foundation for integrated indoor and outdoor LBS. Even if some of the technological building blocks are available and partial solutions like standard services and modeling language or integrated support for multiple positioning technologies have been investigated large research work has to be carried out. The introduced MapBiquitous system represents a first step towards that envisioned goal of seamlessly integrated indoor/outdoor location based-services.

3   Requirements

The goal of the MapBiquitous system is to provided indoor and outdoor location-based services in an interoperable and seamlessly integrated manner. In the following we analyze the requirements for such a system.

As discussed in the previous section, there is no single positioning technology which can be globally used. GPS is available outdoors and should be complemented with indoor technologies. Since there is no standard for indoor positioning available, *multiple positioning technologies* should be supported by the system (A1). To achieve a seamless integration, all positioning technologies should be accessible via a *uniform interface* (A2). In addition, during movement the user might enter different buildings and later on leave them to move on. Therefore, the system should support a *seamless handover between different positioning technologies* if the user enters a new area (A3).

By explicitly providing data about the building geometry, positioning infrastructure and navigation, geographic data available for outdoors should be complemented with appropriate indoor information. To achieve a wide adoption, the data modeling and provisioning has to be based on *open standards* (A4). For high interoperability, all data should share a *common reference system* to represent geometric coordinates (A5). To allow the representation of meaningful location information the provided building data should contain *geometric and semantic information* (A6). The creation of building models should be possible with *minimal effort* (A7). The *model should be generic* to allow the modeling of any necessary aspect not limiting its applicability to specific domains (A8).

Access to building models should be based on a *standard format and protocol* (A9). Even if creation and maintenance of building models requires effort, data should be provided with *high accuracy and timeliness* (A10).

The overall system should operate in the same manner like todays outdoor systems. To support a large number of users the system has to be *highly scalable* (A11). It has to be *highly available* with minimum down time (A12). Building data, supported positioning technologies and system architecture should be *highly extensible* to support the integration of new data and technologies (A13). Last but not least, the system should be *easily to be adopted and integrated into applications* (A14).

4   MapBiquitous Approach

The major objective for creating MapBiquitous was to provide a system for the seamless integration of building data and positioning information with existing outdoor technologies in a way that location-based services could be created on top of it. In the following we introduce the architecture and main components of MapBiquitous and discuss our design decisions.

The architecture of MapBiquitous is shown in figure 1. The system consists of a client and a server part. On server side we foresee a decentralized infrastructure of *building servers* which can be discovered based on a *directory service*. MapBiquitous clients basically consist of the three components *Loader*, *Renderer* and *Locator*. In addition, an internal representation of building data is stored in the *building data storage* on the client. The Loader is responsible for accessing the building servers. It loads and processes building data to fill the building data storage.

The Locator contains several modules to support different indoor positioning technologies. It accesses the information provided for positioning in the building. This can be for instance locations of the WiFi access points but also for infrared beacons or RFID tags in the building. The information is used to configure the associated positioning module which is than started to provide periodic location updates.

The location updates are received by the Renderer which is responsible for the visualization of location information. It adopts the concept of overlays to present map and building data in an integrated manner. The Renderer accesses the building data storage for rendering the building geometry and triggers the Loader in case of location updates for dynamic access to building data. It is notified by the Loader if new building data is available in the storage.

The building servers are responsible for providing building data for public access based on a standard format and protocol. They maintain information about the building geometry, positioning infrastructure and navigation for one or a set of buildings.

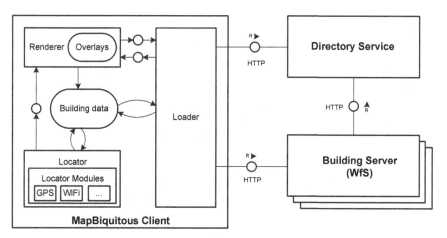

Fig. 1. Architecture of MapBiquitous

We decided to use a decentralized architecture to support high scalability (A11) and availability (A12) of the system and data. In contrast to a central server, with a decentralized architecture load is naturally balanced between the building servers and a single point of failure as well as a performance bottleneck are avoided. In case of failure of one building server only a single building or a small set of buildings is not available. All other data remains accessible.

Another reason for the partitioning of building data to decentralized servers is caused by the building data itself. Compared to map data, we assume a much higher change rate of building data. Even if the building geometry is stable, semantic information like usage of rooms and navigation information might change frequently. Furthermore, information about the positioning infrastructure will change over time, for instance if the WiFi infrastructure is updated. Moreover, building data is maintained by the owner or user of the building. Depending on the usage and type of the building we expect that the owner might want to decide if and what information about the building is provided to the public. We assume that owners want to keep control about the published data. A decentralized approach naturally supports these requirements since any building owner can decide by its own to provide a building server with the extend and level of detail he is willing to publish.

Issues of the decentralized approach might be the heterogeneity of technology, formats and quality of building data. Building data providers have to agree on common standards to offer their data in an interoperable way. It is up to the provider to keep the building data up to date and to provide accurate data. Even if these issues are challenging, we believe that they could be solved by establishing standard technologies. Because of the technological and administrative advantages we decided to follow a decentralized approach.

In the following sections we describe the introduced MapBiquitous components in detail.

4.1 Building Model

MapBiquitous should provide information about building geometry to complement the outdoor location information based on maps. Associated with that information data for indoor positioning and navigation should be provided. As previously discussed we propose a logic partitioning of building data at the granularity of buildings. Thus, each building is represented with its own self contained model. This model is layered as shown in figure 2. The concept foresees a layer for the building outline and one layer per floor. In the example we present the model of the computer science faculty building of TU Dresden which consists of the building outline, a basement and 4 floors. These layers cover the model of the building geometry per floor.

Rooms, floors and areas of stairs and elevators are represented as polygons. For representing the coordinates we use the World Geodetic System (WGS84). The WGS84 reference system has a global scale, thus allowing to use coordinates with a uniform reference system all around the globe (A5). WGS84 is also used by GPS and map services for representing locations. Thus, no mapping of coordinates

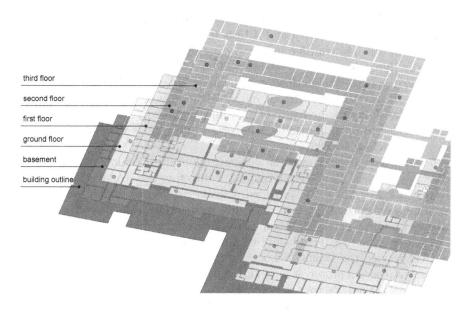

third floor

second floor

first floor

ground floor

basement

building outline

Fig. 2. Layered model of the computer science faculty building of TU Dresden

is required on client side. Especially, building geometry can be directly drawn on maps without complex pre-processing. In addition, semantic information like room number, type and usage of rooms is attached to the polygons (A6).

In addition to the floor plans additional layers are provided containing information for positioning and navigation. The idea is to add one layer per floor and positioning technology available in the building. Another layer is added per floor for navigation information. In this way, the building model can cover different positioning technologies in parallel and can be easily extended (A1).

For access building data is represented based on GML. It is a standard language specified by OGC for representing geographic features including vector objects based on elements like point, line and polygon (A8). For the client side, especially for mobile clients, GML is challenging because of the required XML processing. We decided to use GML for flexible and highly interoperable access to building models. In combination with WFS as service for access it is possible to support various internal representations of building data, which can be transformed into GML (A9).

4.2 Building Data Access

As described in the previous section building data is provided as vector data on distributed building servers. To access building data from a client, the building server providing the appropriate data has to be discovered. After that, building data has to be downloaded to be locally available at the client.

There are three methods for including building information into services and applications: embedded, initial URL and dynamic discovery. With the *embedded* method, building data is delivered and installed together with the service or application package. This is useful if LBS should be provided for a fixed set of buildings. In this way transfer and processing time is avoided.

A more dynamic way of accessing building data is to start with a *known building server URL*. As described, each building can contain links to neighboring buildings. Thus, starting with an initial URL close-by building data can be discovered avoiding the necessity of providing a directory service. This method can be applied to provide LBS for a larger set of buildings without the effort to provide a directory service.

The most flexible method is the *dynamic discovery* of building services using a directory service. As shown in figure 1 a directory service or a federation of directory services has to be provided. Clients can lookup building servers by providing their current location. The directory service responds with a list of URLs for building servers in proximity to the given location. Of course, building servers have to be registered before with their URL and location.

OGC specified the OpenGIS Location Service Specification (OpenLS) [8] to define interfaces and protocols for an interoperable service framework. One of the core services is the Directory Service which allows to register and lookup object or resources with location and further attributes. The OpenLS Directory Service uses WGS84 coordinates as well. Thus, coordinate transformations between different reference systems can be avoided (A5). We decided to use OpenLS Directory Service to support the dynamic discovery method in MapBiquitous because of these features and its availability as a standard (A4).

The WFS is the service of choice for accessing building data in MapBiquitous. WFS provides a simple protocol and interface for accessing geographical features based on HTTP. Its main operations are `getCapabilities()`, `describeFeatureType()`, and `getFeature()`.

Based on a given or gathered URL access to a WFS server starts with a `getCapabilities()` request to get information about the WFS server and a list of layeres offered for the associated building. For each layer name, title, projection and its extend are provided with the response. From the response . the available layers can be extracted. Information about the detailed layer type and content can be accessed using the `describeFeatureType()` operation. One request has to be send per layer. In this way, building geometry layers can be distinguished from positioning information and navigation layers without loading the whole content of the layers.

To access the complete layer data, a layer can be requested using the `getFeature()` operation. Thus, download of layer data can be accomplished step-wise, starting with the layer containing the building outline and the layer representing the current user location. In addition the layers providing information about positioning technologies supported by the client device can be loaded.

Hence, WFS allows the exploration and download of the provided features, i.e. building model layers, in a dynamic and selective way ensuring extensibility of and flexible access to the provided data based on a standard format and protocol (A9).

4.3   Client Architecture

As mentioned during the introduction of the architecture, the access, processing and visualization of building data is performed on the client side following the concept of a fat client. An alternative would be to process building information on the server side and to provide image data of maps with building data already projected on the map to thin clients. This would ease the implementation of clients, especially web clients. Ideally, an integration into existing map services could be achieved enabling the use of existing clients for map data.

Anyway, beside the visualization of building geometry information about positioning technologies is typically required at the client side to perform positioning. Therefore, existing clients would have to be extended or the functionality for positioning has to be separated from the visualization of the map and building data. Processing of building data at the server would also limit the flexibility of how building data could be used.

We decided to follow the approach of a fat client to support high flexibility for service creation with MapBiquitous. The main decision is to support layered vector data instead of pre-processed image data. If the provided building servers based on WFS are combined with map servers based on WMS the creation of web clients could be supported as well using the building data of MapBiquitous.

In the following sections we describe the client-side components in detail.

Building Data Storage. The core of the MapBiquitous client is the storage for building data on client-side. It is based on the location model depicted in figure 3. The location model is a hybrid model [2] which supports the representation of geometric as well as semantic location information. Especially, relations

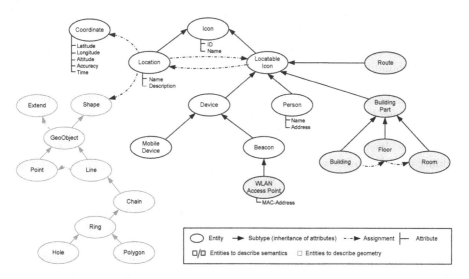

Fig. 3. Location model used as internal data representation in the client-side building data storage

between entities containing geometric and semantic information can be explicitly represented (A6).

The root element is `Item`. Every other entity directly or indirectly inherits from that element. Thus, each element has an id and name. The direct subtypes of Item are `Location` and `LocateableItem`. LocateableItem can be used to represent any object which can have a location like `Person`, `Device`, `BuildingPart`, or `Route`. A `BuildingPart` can for instance be a `Floor` or `Room`.

All named elements contain semantic information. The geometric information is represented by the elements derived from `Location`. The element `Coordinate` assigned to `Location` represents the geometric position of an `Item` with a latitude, longitude and altitude based on WGS84. Moreover, each `Coordinate` has a accuracy value and a time stamp.

The element `Shape` it the main element to represent the geometry of a `Location`. Based on the different subtypes arbitrary geometric structures can be represented using `Points`, `Lines`, `Chains`, etc. In this way building structure can be internally represented. The element `Extend`, assigned to each `GeoObject` represents the minimal and maximal values of coordinates of a `GeoObject`.

The presented location model integrates geometric and semantic infomation by assigning a `Location` to a `LocateableItem`. The location model is extensible and allows the representation of arbitrary geometric and semantic information.

Loader. The Loader component is responsible for discovering building servers and accessing building data. It is triggered by the Renderer to load data from building servers. Two cases are handled by different notifications. In case of a location change, the Renderer triggers the Loader to retrieve building data for a defined geo-window. This geo-window defines a geographic area by the minimum and maximum values for latitude and longitude. The loader starts with an lookup at the directory service to discover all building servers in the given area. Based on the lookup results the Loader than checks the building data storage for cached data. Data not available locally is requested from the building servers. For newly discovered buildings the loader requests the building outline and the description of available positioning information.

Further floor data and the layers for positioning technologies supported by the device are downloaded on follow-up requests by the Renderer. They are triggered when the device is in close proximity to a building or by user interactions.

After the download of building data XML processing is performed and new building data is stored in the building data storage. After that the Renderer is notified by the Loader about the availability of new building data.

Renderer. The Renderer is responsible for the integrated visualization of map and building data. The basic graphical layer presents map data. For the integration of building data the Renderer maintains a set of overlays. Based on WGS84 which are the common base for map and building data building geometry can be directly drawn on the map. The conversion of WGS84 coordinates to screen coordinates is usually provided by map-based views directly.

The Renderer accesses the building data storage to obtain the data about the building geometry. Based on the current view building data is represented in different levels of detail. For each level of detail a separate overlay is maintained. Based on the distance between the user position or focus point of the view buildings are represented in three different levels. For the lowest level of detail an icon is presented for each discovered building server (LOD1). For the next higher level of detail the building outline is drawn (LOD2). At the highest level of detail the complete floor plan is presented (LOD3).

In case of location changes and user interactions like changing the zoom level of the view or scrolling on the map the Renderer triggers the Loader to load building data. It gets notified by the Loader if new data is available in the building data storage.

Locator. The Locator is responsible for the positioning of the user device. It manages a set of locator modules which access to device hardware for positioning. They share a common interface for accessing location information (A1, A2). The Locator configures, starts and stops the Locator modules dependent on the proximity to buildings supporting the positioning technologies (A3). For instance, to save energy its useful to switch on WiFi and GPS only if needed. Indoors GPS can be usually deactivated while WiFi should be activated to get location updates.

The Locator accesses the building server storage to obtain the information required to configure the locator modules. For instance the WiFi access points and their locations are stored in the location model. In case of location changes the Locator sends notifications to the Renderer.

5 Evaluation

For evaluating our concepts we implemented MapBiquitous for desktop and mobile devices. To test the MapBiquitous system two applications were implemented, namely a WiFi analysis tool for the university campus and a location-based game. We report on the experiences made during the implementation of the MapBiquitous system and the applications.

5.1 MapBiquitous Implementation

MapBiquitous Server. MapBiquitous has been implemented using standard technologies on the server side. The directory service is based on the OpenLS Directory Service standard and provides an interface for registering and looking up resources with WGS84 coordinates and further attributes. The functionality has been implemented based on Apache Tomcat, MySQL and JSP. HTTP requests are processed by a JSP servlet, which parses the XML requests, extracts the geo-window, queries the database to get all available building servers in that area and generates the response messages.

For the provision of building servers the WFS implementation MapServer[3], particularly the package MapServer for Windows[4] is used. MapServer is an open source project running on different platforms including Microsoft Windows, Linux and Mac OS X. It supports a rich set of raster and vector data formats, geographic data sources and OGC standards (among them WMS, WFS, and GML). MapServer for Windows runs with Apache HTTP Server and PHP.

We currently provide building data for the campus of TU Dresden. Building geometry and semantic information about room numbers and usage of rooms is available from an internal database for building management maintained by TU Dresden. This data has to be modified to enable provision with WFS. For modification we use the open source tool Quantum GIS[5]. Information for positioning and navigation is currently added manually using Quantum GIS. We currently model the location of access points for WiFi positioning. According to the concept separate layers are introduced for access point locations for each floor. In addition we modeled fingerprint data and path information for navigation in separate layers. With Quantum GIS the internal representation of building data is transformed to ESRI shapefiles [6].

ESRI shapefiles consist of a main file (.shp) containing a sequence of records of geometric elements, a dBASE table (.dbf) containing the attributes of all geometric elements in the main file and an index file (.shx) which contains the information to assign the attributes to the geometric elements. Coordinates of geometric elements are represented based on WGS84.

The shapefiles can be directly used as data sources for MapServer. The configuration of MapService is performed based on a map file (.map). The map file contains all information about the data to be provided by WFS. It contains a link to the local shapefiles, a definition of the URL for accessing the building server, and information about the provides layers.

Currently all logic building servers are physically implemented on the same server. We provide building data for four buildings at the university campus, namely the computer science faculty, the mensa, the lecture hall and the "'Barkhausenbau"'', a complex building used by different faculties.

MapBiquitous Client. Two clients have been implemented for MapBiquitous: a desktop client and a client for mobile devices.

Desktop Client. The implementation of the desktop client (see figure 4) is based on Java Standard Edition. Visualization in the *Renderer* adopts the JXMapViewer component of the SwingX-WS-Framework by SwingLabs[6]. The component supports the visualization of maps from different providers, namely OpenStreetMaps, Google Maps and Yahoo Maps. On top of the map layer overlays can be created. The user interface allows interaction with the map and building data like zooming and dragging, searching for building servers, selection of layers for presentation (floor plans and WiFi access point locations).

---

[3] http://mapserver.org/
[4] http://www.maptools.org/ms4w/
[5] http://www.qgis.org/
[6] http://www.swinglabs.org

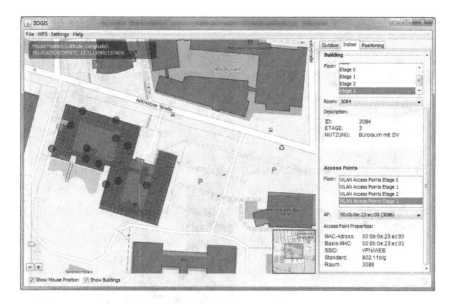

Fig. 4. Desktop client for MapBiquitous

The *Locator* supports GPS and WiFi positioning based on lateration. GPS Positioning has been tested with the Holux GPSlim236 device, an external GPS device which can be connected via USB or Bluetooth. The Bluetooth connection is mapped to a serial port. After defining a port for the connection to the GPS device, GPS location information can be accessed via a CommPort. WiFi positioning is based on PlaceLab. PlaceLab consists of the three components *Spotter* for accessing the WiFi adapter, *Mapper* for the provision of access point locations and *Tracker* for calculating the current position. The Mapper is connected with the building data storage of the client to allow access of the access point locations. With that information, the Tracker can be started to periodically calculate the current position of the device.

The *Loader* uses HTTP connections based on the java.net library for accessing WFS. DOM4J and XPathQueries is used for XML processing. All available data is loaded from building servers immediately after discovery. In this way after a short waiting time all building data is available.

Android Client. The mobile client was implemented using Android 2.2. The *Renderer* uses the `MapView` and `MapViewActivity` provided by Android to integrate Google Maps into applications. The MapView provides the possibility to create overlays which is used by the Renderer to integrate building data and map data. The user interface provides zooming and dragging for the MapView (see left part of figure 5).

During the implementation we noticed a limitation of the MapView regarding zooming. MapView only supports zooming up to level 19 (21 in satellite mode). Higher zoom levels can be set but zooming is not performed. This zoom level was not appropriate for presenting floor plan details. Thus, as a workaround

Fig. 5. Android client for MapBiquitous with MapView and overlays (left) and OpenGL view with floor details (right)

we implemented for the interaction with detailed floor plans a separate view based on OpenGL. The view allows the selection of building levels and rooms for visualization. Selected rooms are highlighted. If a room is selected, semantic information for the room is presented (see right part of figure 5).

The *Loader* of the mobile client has been optimized for the access of building data using wireless connections. Instead of loading the complete building geometry data at once, it is loaded stepwise and only if necessary for visualization. After discovering a new building server, the layer containing the building outline is loaded and processed. Only if the zoom level is high and the building is still visible floor plans are loaded. This is done dynamically based on the calculated current position. If the user is outdoors, the ground floor is presented. If the user is indoors, the current floor is determined as part of the user's location and only that floor is loaded. Anyway, to allow continuous positioning, all layers for positioning with the building are loaded at once. The implementation of XML processing is improved as well by using a SAX parser.

The *Locator* also supports WiFi positioning and GPS. For both technologies Android `Services` are implemented which can be shared between different apps. The services periodically calculate the current position of the device and propagate location updates via intents. These intents can be received by register-ing `BroadcastReceivers` for these intent types. GPS positioning is implemented using the `LocationManager` API provided by Android. WiFi positioning is im-plemented using PlaceLab in a version ported to Android. For porting PlaceLab to Android a new Spotter was implemented which accesses the `WiFiManager` API provided by Android.

The intents created by both services are received by the Renderer. The Ren-derer itself creates intents to trigger the Loader. Similarly, the Loader creates intents received by the Renderer if new layers are loaded, processed and inte-grated into the building data storage as described in section 4.3.

5.2   Applications Based on MapBiquitous

For testing the MapBiquitous system, we implemented two location-based ap-plications, namely a WiFi analyzer and a location-based game called LocPairs.

WiFi Analyzer. The purpose of the WiFi analyzer is to allow the testing of the WiFi infrastructure at the campus of TU Dresden. A network administrator should be able to perform measurements at reference points, access former mea-surements and analyze the infrastructure on the move to detect areas with low communication quality or unavailable access points. As shown in the left part of figure 6, the visualization of the app is based on MapBiquitous.

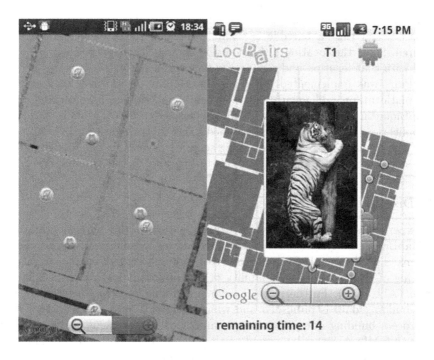

Fig. 6. MapBiquitous applications: WiFi-Analyzer (left) and LocPairs (right)

Because the WiFi infrastructure should be tested WiFi positioning has been switched off. We assume that the administrator can visually detect its location. Outdoor and indoor reference points can be defined directly by pointing on the floor plan or map. Similarly, former measurements are represented by icons directly on the map and floor plan. Details about measurements can be obtained by pointing to the assigned icon.

The WiFi-Analyzer is implemented by adopting the Android client of MapBiquitous. The Renderer has been extended with new functionality for visualizing the reference points and former measurements as well as for the interaction with the MapView to perform measurements at newly defined reference points. The Loader, Locator and the MapBiquitous server-side was adopted without any changes. For persistent storage of measurement data on a server, a separate web service was implemented.

LocPairs. LocPairs is a location-based game adopting the principle of the well-known pairs game. The playing field for LocPairs is an area inside a building. Pictures are represented by attaching 2D barcodes to doors of a floor. Scanning a barcode means uncovering a picture.

The game is played by two teams with two players each. Alternately, each team is in turn to find a pair of pictures. Players have to move to the right door within a limited time. If both players have reached the doors, they can scan the barcode and uncover the pictures. If they found a pair the can continue, otherwise it is the other teams turn.

The purpose of the game is to simplify the maintenance of a fingerprint database. Each time a barcode is scanned the fingerprint of that location is measured. Since the location of barcodes is known, the fingerprints can be assigned with that location and sent to the fingerprint database.

LocPairs was implemented based on the Mobilis plattform [12], a service-based platform for implementing mobile social applications. The Android client of MapBiquitous was integrated with the client-side services of Mobilis. To create the application, the Renderer was extended to create the map-based view for the game. The other views were added using separate activities. The MapBiquitous server-side was adopted as is and provided in parallel to the Mobilis server.

5.3   Discussion

The experiences and practical tests carried out with the implementation of the MapBiquitous system have demonstrated the feasibility of major design decisions. The decentralized architecture of building servers enables a natural balancing of the load, high availability of building data and robustness of the system (A11, A12). Furthermore, it allows building owners to decide if and which building data is published and which technologies are used to represent and process building data. The only technological requirement is the usage of WFS and GML. Anyway, by extending the Loader to support different modules for different formats and protocols even this requirement could be relaxed.

The decision to follow a fat client approach requires higher effort for creating clients. In addition processing of building data is performed mainly on the client side. Using WFS and GML as standard technologies requires XML processing which is challenging for mobile clients. In our first implementation of the Android client on a Nexus One Android device it took about 3 seconds to load and process the building outline and 40 seconds for the current floor plan. Loading and processing has been done in a sequential way. After the creation of parallel threads for loading and optimization of XML-processing using a SAX parser, times could be reduced to 1,5 seconds to load and process the building outline and about 8 seconds for the current floor plan. To further reduce waiting times for the user we implemented caching and prefetching of building data. In combination with the three introduced levels of details for presenting building data loading and processing is now transparent to the user. Advantages of the fat client approach are the higher flexibility for processing building data offered as vector data instead of raster images. In addition, positioning has to be performed on the client side anyway. With a fat client positioning and visualization can be implemented in a flexible way.

The consequent adoption of WGS84 simplifies the integration of building and map data because transformation of coordinates between different reference systems is avoided (A5).

The effort for creating and maintaining building models and information for positioning is high. For modern buildings digital building data might already exist. For public buildings data often exists for building management which is often already constantly updated as it is the case for our university campus. Anyway, updates usually have to be performed manually. Even worse, for WiFi infrastructures access point locations or fingerprinting data might not be available. Crowd-sourcing approaches as presented with OpenRoomMap [11] and the LocPairs application could help but need deeper exploration (A7, A10).

As a result of our experiments with WiFi positioning, accuracy of lateration based on known locations of access points is often to low for indoor applications. Caused be influences of device type, device orientation, access point constellation and moving persons in practice, WiFi based positioning is far away from accuracy in the range of meters. Approaches based on WiFi need further improvements and should be combined with alternative approaches like 2D barcodes, inertial positioning, Bluetooth or NFC.

The publication of building data causes security risks. For instance the knowledge about the usage type of rooms could motivate burglars. Furthermore, the availability of precise positioning technologies and indoor information influences privacy. Such information should not be published without the knowledge and agreement of the involved people. To avoid the publication of security sensitive building data, access control could be established for a subset of that data. By offering only a subset of data to the public such risks can be avoided.

6   Conclusion

In this paper a novel approach is presented to integrate technologies for indoor and outdoor location-based services in a seamless manner. We introduced a decentralized infrastructure of building servers providing explicitly modeled data about the building geometry, positioning and navigation. Building data is offered by open standards, namely WFS and GML to achieve high interoperability of the system. At client side building data is combined with map data for visualizing indoor and outdoor locations in an integrated manner. In addition, information for positioning is exploited at client side for indoor positioning with different technologies. The evaluation has shown that major design decisions are feasible and location-based services can be created adopting the MapBiquitous system. In summary, the presented work is a first step towards the envisioned goal.

Future work will address the named challenges to improve the MapBiquitous approach. Working towards an application for navigating within the campus of TU Dresden, data of all buildings has to be integrated into MapBiquitous WFS servers. Moreover, the issue of providing accurate indoor positioning has to be solved by following a WiFi fingerprinting approach. The work for navigation across buildings and outdoor is currently in an experimental state and has to be completed. With the availability of the campus navigation application we plan to carry out a field trial with a larger user group. Further research goals are the exploration of crowd-sourcing approaches as presented with the LocPairs application to decrease the effort for maintaining building, positioning and navigation data and the combination of indoor positioning approaches for device independent usage.

Acknowledgment. The authors would like to thank the many contributors of MapBiquitous. Jan Scholze developed the concepts and prototype of the initial system and desktop client during his student and master thesis. The students of the practical course on development of mobile and distributed systems implemented and evaluated the current Android prototype and the two introduced location-based services.

References

1. Baus, J., Krüger, A., Wahlster, W.: A resource-adaptive mobile navigation system. In: Proceedings of the 7th International Conference on Intelligent User Interfaces, IUI 2002, pp. 15–22. ACM, New York (2002)
2. Becker, C., Dürr, F.: On location models for ubiquitous computing. Personal Ubiquitous Comput. 9, 20–31 (2005)
3. Ching, W., Teh, R.J., Li, B., Rizos, C.: Uniwide wifi based positioning system. In: IEEE International Symposium on Technology and Society (ISTAS), pp. 180–189 (June 2010)
4. de la Beaujardiere, J.: penGIS web map server implementation specification, Open Geospatial Consortium Inc., Tech. Rep. OGC® 06-042, Version 1.3.0 (2006)

5. Dedes, G., Dempster, A.G.: Indoor gps positioning - challenges and opportunities. In: IEEE 62nd Vehicular Technology Conference, VTC 2005 Fall, vol. 1, pp. 412–415 (September 2005)
6. I. E. Environmental Systems Research Institute, Esri shapefile technical description, an esri white paper july 1998, Environmental Systems Research Institute, Inc. (ESRI), Tech. Rep. (1998)
7. Leppräkoski, H., Tikkinen, S., Perttula, A., Takala, J.: Comparison of indoor positioning algorithms using wlan fingerprints. In: Proceedings of European Navigation Conference Global Navigation Satellite Systems (ENC-GNSS 2009) (2009)
8. Mabrouk, M.: OpenGIS location services (openls): Core services, Open Geospatial Consortium Inc., Tech. Rep. OGC 07-074, version 1.2 (2008)
9. McCarthy, M.R., Muller, H.L.: RF free ultrasonic positioning. In: IEEE International Symposium on Wearable Computers, p. 79 (2003)
10. Portele, C.: OpenGIS geography markup language (gml) encoding standard, Open Geospatial Consortium Inc., Tech. Rep. OGC 07-036, Version 3.2.1 (2007)
11. Rice, A., Woodman, O.: Crowd-sourcing world models with openroommap. In: 8th IEEE International Conference on Pervasive Computing and Communications Workshops (PERCOM Workshops), March 29-April 2, pp. 764–767 (2010)
12. Schuster, D., Springer, T., Schill, A.: Service-based development of mobile real-time collaboration applications for social networks, Mannheim, Germany (2010)
13. Serra, A., Carboni, D., Marotto, V.: Indoor pedestrian navigation system using a modern smartphone. In: Proceedings of the 12th International Conference on Human Computer Interaction with Mobile Devices and Services, Ser. MobileHCI 2010, pp. 397–398. ACM, New York (2010)
14. Steinhoff, U., Schiele, B.: Dead reckoning from the pocket - an experimental study. In: 2010 IEEE International Conference on Pervasive Computing and Communications (PerCom), March 29-April 2, pp. 162–170 (2010)
15. Vretanos, P.P.A.: OpenGIS web feature service 2.0 interface standard, Open Geospatial Consortium Inc., Tech. Rep. OGC 09-025r1 and ISO/DIS 19142, Version 2.0.0 (2010)
16. Want, R., Hopper, A., Falcão, V., Gibbons, J.: The active badge location system. ACM Trans. Inf. Syst. 10, 91–102 (1992)
17. Ward, A., Jones, A., Hopper, A.: A new location technique for the active office. IEEE Personal Communications 4(5), 42–47 (1997)
18. Woodman, O., Harle, R.: Pedestrian localisation for indoor environments. In: Proceedings of the 10th International Conference on Ubiquitous Computing, Ser. UbiComp 2008, pp. 114–123. ACM, New York (2008)
19. Woodman, O., Harle, R.: RF-Based Initialisation for Inertial Pedestrian Tracking. In: Tokuda, H., Beigl, M., Friday, A., Brush, A.J.B., Tobe, Y. (eds.) Pervasive 2009. LNCS, vol. 5538, pp. 238–255. Springer, Heidelberg (2009)

Semantic Geotagging: A Location-Based Hypermedia Approach to Creating Situational Awareness

Ray Bareiss, Martin Griss, Steven Rosenberg, and Yu Zhang

Carnegie Mellon University, Silicon Valley Campus,
Moffett Field, California 04035, USA
{ray.bareiss,martin.griss,steven.rosenberg,
ian.zhang}@sv.cmu.edu

Abstract. As emergency first responders and commanders increasingly use mobile phones, tablets, and social media to communicate, coordinate, and manage information during disasters, we see a need and opportunity to provide a mobile device-appropriate semantic layer to a geographically-based common operating picture. The challenge is to provide a simple, usable structure for a rapidly growing body of information to simplify the development of situational awareness in an unfolding disaster. We use a hyperlinked structure based on the ASK model to organize information in a readily accessible form. In this paper we describe our initial design and experience with an Android-based prototype, supported by a Ruby on Rails-based repository service. Our prototype allows the incorporation, aggregation, assessment, and redistribution of dynamic human-generated and sensor-derived information.

Keywords: mobile applications, emergency response, social media, crowd sourcing, mobile collaboration.

1   Introduction

There is an increased urgency among all levels of government in improving disaster management and coordination. Recent disasters have demonstrated the difficulties in mounting fast, coordinated, and successful responses. While many things could be improved, it is clear that there are especially serious problems in acquiring, managing, and disseminating the large body of information required to develop accurate and trustworthy situational awareness.

Disaster Response Teams must share a common situational awareness to prioritize their activities, to work effectively, and to coordinate with other teams. In both the disaster management and other communities, this is ideally provided by a Common Operating Picture (COP), see, e.g., [1]. A natural framework for this COP is a geographical information system in which key elements, such as people, places, resources and events, are situated and tagged with accompanying content, usually status information. We are working with an open architecture, web-based COP, shown in Figure 1. The content of these geospatial elements is then updated as new information flows in.

J.Y. Zhang et al. (Eds.): MobiCASE 2011, LNICST 95, pp. 100–114, 2012.

Fig. 1. Web-based Common Operating Picture

Traditionally, disaster response follows a command-and-control model embodying primarily hierarchical information flows, filtered manually by incident commanders and other experts. Situational awareness grows as information flows upward from lower levels and is aggregated and organized by the higher levels; conversely it flows down from commanders to front-line responders on a need-to-know basis. Today the confluence of powerful smart phones and other mobile devices, ambient and mobile sensors, fast and ubiquitous networking, social media, and cloud-based services can and often do provide increasing volumes of on-line information (often "real time") about breaking events. These new technologies increasingly permit the "crowd sourcing" of information, from volunteers and local residents as well as professional responders, potentially generating broad situational awareness more quickly than hierarchical processing but with increased opportunity for error, disorganization, and overload. Mobile, context-aware applications are increasingly proposed and used for disaster response [2, 3] and for sensing people and things nearby in the environment [4].

The increasing use of smart phones by responders and citizens empowers humans as sensors: They take pictures, annotate, send SMS and Twitter messages, and post Facebook messages; many events are geotagged and can be displayed on maps using appropriate icons. The challenge is to provide a simple, usable structure for a potentially large, diverse, and rapidly growing body of information in order to simplify the development of situational awareness in an unfolding disaster.

Furthermore, any such organizational mechanism must be easy to use in the mobile, hurried, small screen environment, and customizable to the context, such as the roles and tasks performed by different responders at different times during a disaster response.

2   The Need for a Structured Record of Emergency Messages

The goal of our work has been to develop a prototype system to support the collaborative construction of situational awareness by distributed, mobile responders, providing a better situational awareness of a complex disaster in less time than traditional hierarchical "processing" would require.

A large-scale disaster, such as the recent pipeline explosion and resulting fire in San Bruno, California, can result in literally thousands of messages among emergency responders. (The number might go up by an order of magnitude were messages from the public -- via phone, text, Twitter, et cetera -- included.) Professional responders currently send messages primarily via voice radio, but are increasing using message-based packet radio, SMS, and even Twitter. Many of these messages may have attached images and can be geotagged. The message stream has a transitory quality. If a responder misses a message or if its content is not relevant at the time it is received, the message is essentially lost to the responder. The only information repository typically available is a linear recording of radio transmissions or the text message stream.

The challenge is not one of information scarcity but of information overload. For example, of the many, many on-line responses during the recent San Bruno, California disaster, only a small fraction were useful to first responders in dealing with their immediate situations. An easily browsable repository of messages and information would enable emergency responders to quickly find the few most immediately relevant messages among the thousands. The challenge is to define an organizational structure that can be easily applied when new messages are generated and that is at the same time useful for browsing a large corpus of messages.

Our solution, used in our prototype system, is to add semantically linked annotations to the COP. We use geotagging to associate messages (and images, cf. [5]) with locations in the COP's map-based geospatial interface. This provides a situationally relevant context for related messages. A small set of typed links with well-defined semantics then associates messages with incidents, and related messages with each other. For example, an emergency dispatcher might create a new incident based on a citizen's report of a fire; a police patrol might link an initial situation description and upload a geotagged picture; a fire unit might link an assessment to the initial description; still another fire unit might link another assessment which augments the first based on new observations; an incident commander might provide advice for dealing with the situation; et cetera.

It might be informative to compare this approach to two simpler alternatives: GeoTwitter [6] and GeoChat [7]. GeoTwitter provides only location-based indexing of tweets, and a user can easily be overwhelmed by a large number of tweets in a limited geographical space (Figures 2a and 2b). GeoChat indexes online, multi-way conversations (i.e., chats) geographically.

The strictly temporal nature of a chat makes it easy to miss things, and, like a Twitter stream, it is difficult to search, given the likely high similarity of messages within a chat. Ushahidi (http://www.ushahidi.com), which combines aspects of these two approaches, is an open source system currently gaining traction in the disaster response community.

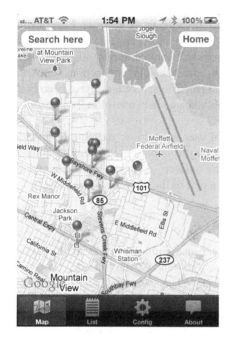

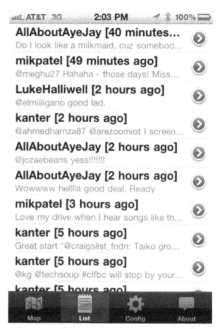

Fig. 2a. The GeoTwitter Interface (1/2)   **Fig. 2b.** The GeoTwitter Interface (2/2)

Other researchers have also addressed the use of geotagged information in disaster response. The increasing role of geotagged images and text in spatial decision making is covered in [8], and motivates approaches such as integrating geotagged citizen input from smartphones and desktops into GIS systems [9]; as these authors suggest, it is not a trivial task to automatically merge (incompatible) information into an existing GIS framework. In [10] the implications of user-generated spatial content, especially using GPS-enabled smartphones, and crowdsourcing to add geotagged annotations, extensions and mashups to base maps (such as GeoWeb) are evaluated. While this is an excellent way to quickly generate and distribute dynamic map-based information, the torrent of potentially unreliable information can increase uncertainty and add to confusion, and may in fact inhibit useful communication. Details on the use of geotagged information in the Haiti response and recovery can be found in [11]; issues of information accuracy, reliability and provenance, and incompatible duplication of effort are surfaced. Maiyo [12] stresses the importance of real-time collaborative disaster management tools, to better allow the integration of different types of mapping data from diverse sources.

3   A Cognitively Inspired Approach to Organizational Memory

In the 1990's, researchers at Northwestern University's Institute for the Learning Sciences developed an effective approach to organizing large-scale hypermedia systems, called ASK Systems [13, 14, 15]. This family of hypermedia systems uses a theory of conversational coherence [16] to provide a limited variety of typed links between content elements that correspond to the sensible connections between utterances that arise in a coherent conversation. Over 20 such systems have been built in domains as wide-ranging as military planning, management consulting, engineering design, and public water supply issues.

An ASK system must provide three types of user interaction: zooming to provide initial access (beginning a conversation), browsing to explore a sub-area of content (requesting information via a question-and-answer dialog), and responding (contributing new information that will remain a part of the conversational record).

3.1   Zooming into the Body of Information

Given that disasters, such as fires and gas leaks, cause problems in specific locations, a map-based interface provides a natural way for a responder, who is used
to reading maps, to indicate an area of interest. When a responder arrives on the scene, he or she sees a map of the local area with icons indicating incidents of various predefined types, e.g., a fire or a gas leak (Figure 3).

This standard geospatial layout, also used in a COP, provides the first level of context for relevant information. Semantic Geotagging provides additional layers that organize related relevant information in conversational threads associated with the incident. The following system description shows how a responder can quickly find and drill down on aspects of an incident of immediate interest to him or her.

Touching an icon displays a pop-up summary of the incident (e.g., "Interior fire, Building 23, Moffett Field). Touching the summary displays a more detailed description and categories of information about the incident (Figure 4):

- Situation Description: A living document that provides an overview of the situation via a series of messages to which a responder contributes when he or she learns more about the incident
- Problem Report: A message that reports a responder has been unable to complete an assigned task because of unforeseen circumstances, lack of necessary personnel or equipment, et cetera.

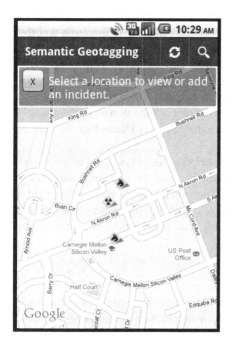

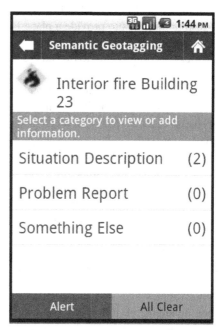

Fig. 3. The Top-Level Interface

Fig. 4. Top-Level Information about an Incident

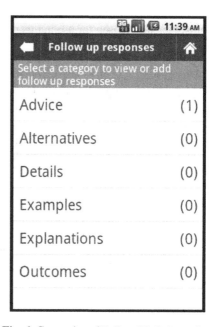

Fig. 5. Situation Description Messages

Fig. 6. Categories of Follow-Up Information

- Something Else: A catch-all category included in the current prototype for testing purposes to provide a place for test subjects to enter information that they do not believe belongs in one of the other categories. (We hope to remove this category and possibly to extend the list of categories as a result of testing.)

The screen also provides an Alert button, which enables a responder to broadcast a high-priority message to all responders in the area (e.g., "man down" or "evacuate"), and an All Clear button, which enables a responder to notify others that the incident has been resolved.

Touching a category, such as Situation Description, displays a list of previously entered messages, providing top-level information about an incident time-stamped and in reverse chronological order (Figure 5). The annotation +N more to the right of a message indicates the number of follow-up messages that responders have entered. Touching the message displays it full-screen and also provides access to the categorized list of follow-ups.

3.2   Browsing Follow Up Responses

A top-level message, such as the initial description of a building fire, can result in tens if not hundreds of follow-up messages from a number of responders. The ASK approach to organizing a hypermedia organizational memory uniquely balances power and simplicity. Follow-up messages are categorized into one of six categories, each of which might be thought of as corresponding to a general type of follow-up question that a listener in a conversation might ask in response to presentation of a piece of information. Several variant category schemes have been used in previous systems; the ones chosen for use in this prototype are (Figure 6):

- Advice: What do you recommend doing (or not doing) in this situation?
- Alternatives: Are there alternative explanations, pieces of advice, et cetera?
- Details: Can you provide more details about the information I've just received?
- Examples: Can you provide a specific example of the generality I've just read (or heard)?
- Explanations: Can you explain what you've reported, recommended, et cetera?
- Outcomes: What happened (or might happen) as a result of the situation I've just read (or heard)?

Note that although the categories remain consistent (and consistently placed within the interface), the meanings of the categories may shift slightly according to the contextualizing piece of information with which they are associated. For example, as noted above, Alternatives might be thought of as a request for an alternative explanation, alternative advice, an alternative example, or an alternative possible outcome.

To view a particular category of follow-up information, the user selects the category by touching it. (Note that the number in parentheses indicates the number of follow-up pieces of information of that type that have been entered.) Follow-ups can have follow-ups which can have deeper follow-ups, et cetera, enabling a user to explore as deeply as he or she feels to be necessary. Note that all users may not take the same path through the information. Instead, the questions raised in a particular user's mind in response to a piece of information determines the next category of information requested and viewed. Back and Home buttons enable the user to "back out" of a particular thread of conversation.

3.3   Responding to a Message

A user is not restricted to viewing information entered by others. At any time, he or she can contribute information to the conversation. When responding, the categories enumerated above take on the semantics of conversational connectives, the bridges that people often use when responding to utterances by others:

- Advice: Here's some advice for dealing with that.
- Alternatives: I disagree with your explanation, advice, et cetera, and here's my alternative.
- Details: I can tell you more about that.
- Examples: Here's an example of what you (or I) just said.
- Explanations: I can explain the phenomenon just reported.
- Outcomes: Here's what happened (or is likely to happen).

A user begins his or her response by selecting one of these categories and then goes on to enter a response. The current prototype requires the user to type the response, but we recognize that this is likely to be unworkable in an emergency situation (Figure 7). Our ultimate goal is to enable the user to dictate a response (much like emergency responders use their radios today) and to use speech-to-text technology to produce a text-based version for default display to future users.

3.4   Summary

The features described in the preceding section show how first responders can quickly home in on exactly the information of relevance to them at that time and location. Further, they have the capability to augment it, on the spot, if desired. This additional information becomes immediately available to everyone – responders in the field and chain-of-command at the emergency operations center. Of course, if it were simply broadcast to everyone, we would have recreated a situation of information overload. By providing a simple system for placing new information in the appropriate geographical context and conversational thread, we leverage the benefits of today's always connected, mobile environment for gathering information with the advantage of the semantic geotagging system for ensuring responders can easily find relevant information.

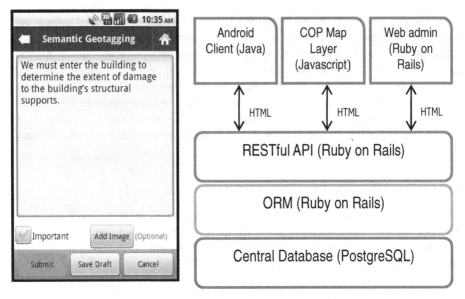

Fig. 7. The Current Information
Entry Screen

Fig. 8. The System Architecture

4   An Example of the System in Action

Mike, a fire department battalion chief, arrives at Building 23 of Moffett Field with his engine company. They see smoke but no visible fire. Mike pulls out his Android phone running the Semantic Geotagging application. A fire icon, superimposed on Building 23, is centered in the map interface of his phone. (His location has been determined via his phone's GPS.) Mike touches the fire icon to select it and then selects Situation Description from the list of top-level categories of information about the fire. Two messages have already been entered by NASA Protective Services (NPS); after skimming them Mike does his own size-up (see, e.g., [17]).

Mike then returns to the two messages that have been input. He scans the first one, an initial posting that lacks detail, and then the second. He sees that someone has entered follow-up messages to the second situation description message, so he navigates to view them. In particular, he sees that someone has entered Advice on dealing with the situation, and he reads that. The advice doesn't jibe with his experience, so Mike enters Alternative advice, linked to the first advice message.

Mike and his crew go into the building. He sees that the structural integrity of the main staircase is potentially a problem, so he adds a message to that effect to the Building 23 fire Situation Description (at the top level, not as a follow-up to an existing message).

Later, while taking a break and walking around the Moffett Field parade ground, he smells gas near Building 19. He sees that no one has entered information about this incident, so he enters this new event into the system. He begins by touching the location on the screen to create the new incident. He is prompted to choose a type of incident that generates a corresponding map icon, and he enters basic information – the building number and the nature of the problem. He also enters a sparse initial Situation Description and takes a picture to aid others in identifying the building (cf. [5]); the picture is automatically associated with his description. Finally, he enters a Problem Report because his crew is not well-equipped to handle this sort of emergency. This new situation will be immediately visible both at the emergency operations center and to any other responders interested in the status of this location (i.e., immediately updated situation awareness is available). Of course, determining an appropriate response is still the responsibility of the chain of command.

5   Prototype Implementation

The system employs a multi-client/server architecture (Figure 8). The primary client is a native Android application written in Java, using the Android framework. There are two versions: One with an interface optimized for Motorola Droid phones and the other with an interface optimized for the Samsung Galaxy tablet. The latter interface is resized, and its buttons are enlarged, but the text size is the same as the phone interface to display more content while minimizing the need for scrolling during use. Other clients include a web map-based application that we developed for administration and testing and the Golden Gate Safety Network's Common Operating Picture (also web based). All clients employ a Google map layer. The clients contain all of the "business logic" of the system and handle all interactions with users.

The server is implemented in Ruby on Rails. Use of the model-view-controller design pattern facilitates support for diverse clients. The server provides an object relational mapping (ORM) layer to interact with a PostgreSQL database. A set of representational state transfer (RESTful) API's are implemented on top of the ORM to expose different functionalities to the various clients (see, e.g., http://en.wikipedia.org/wiki/Representational_State_Transfer). The server is written to enable several people to update the evolving content, and each will immediately see updates made by others.

6   Preliminary Usability Testing

After developing a first version of the prototype, the authors conducted a streamlined cognitive walkthrough [18]. We made a number of relatively simple changes to the first version of the interface as a result. (These changes are incorporated in the screens presented earlier in this paper.)

We went on to conduct preliminary, low-ceremony usability testing (see, e.g., [19]). Our testing walks a subject through a generalized version of the scenario, presented in the example section of this paper (e.g., "Access the advice someone has entered as a follow-up. You disagree with the advice. How would you enter a message communicating your disagreement?"). We also ask a number of general questions to elicit the subject's overall impressions of ease of use, missing functionality, and the utility of such an application. We have conducted three individual user tests to date with retired and active-duty firefighters. They were not trained in the use of the application before undertaking the test.

All subjects understood the purpose of the application and generally found it to be easy to navigate. As noted earlier, all commented, nearly immediately, that voice input is a must for a fielded version of the application.

To date, we have discovered one fundamental usability issue: All subjects struggled with the idea of categorizing follow-up information entered in response to existing information – at least as the categorization process is afforded by the current interface. For example, in our testing scenario, they are asked to enter an alternative to existing advice with which they disagree; all subjects wanted to simply enter alternative advice as new advice at the same level as the advice with which they disagreed rather than linking their new advice to the existing advice explicitly as an alternative, thus creating the sort of "conversational thread" via which we envision organizing information.

Two possibilities exist for dealing with this issue: The first is to leave the interface as is and to train users to categorize follow-up information appropriately. The second is to make the process of information entry more explicitly procedural, so that a user must go through the steps (via three corresponding screens) of indicating the desire to respond to an existing piece of information, categorizing the response (e.g., as an alternative), and finally entering the follow-up. Since we believe it is unrealistic to insist on training all emergency responders in the process of information categorization and entry for our application, we have decided to implement and usability test the second alternative. We have suspended testing until this change has been made and plan to test three to seven additional users after doing so.

Our testing, to date, has also uncovered a few less fundamental things:

- On-screen instructions, which are white text on a gray background, are not adequately prominent; we will change the background and text colors before further testing.
- Not all categories of follow-up information seem useful in this emergency response context. The system originally had a Big Picture category that was removed after the cognitive walkthrough. Similarly, subjects have not seen the utility of an Examples category; that one will be removed as well before usability testing proceeds.
- A user needs to be able to ask a question as well as to enter information. The user should then be informed when the question is answered, and the answer should be added to the database. This will be added as a future enhancement.
- The map interface should be pre-populated with all units in the area. We have deferred work on this because of the technical issues involved in automatically compiling this information.
- Purpose-directed (or perhaps role-dependent) views of the database would be useful, especially when responders are engaged in a time-critical task. This complex potential enhancement is discussed in the ongoing work section below.

Additional enhancements are also discussed in the ongoing work section.

7 Ongoing Work

We are planning four threads of ongoing work: adding new functionality, expanding testing, integrating new sources of information, and envisioning new uses for the technology.

7.1 New Work

The most ambitious new functionality, as noted earlier, is a speech-to-text capability that will enable emergency responders to dictate messages instead of the current, rather impractical, alternative of typing them on the small screen of a smart phone. Because of the imperfect reliability of speech-to-text translation (we might realistically expect an accuracy ranging from 70-90% for continuous speech compared to 96-98% accuracy for speech transcription by humans, see, e.g., [20]), we also plan to store the original audio input for reference when the computer-produced text is unsatisfactory.

Another ambitious function might be called a "purpose-directed view." When a responder is planning a complex, time-critical task, there is large potential benefit to compiling and presenting just the information he or she needs at that moment rather than requiring him or her to browse to acquire the information (e.g., "Here's what you need to know as you get ready to enter the building."). Similarly, an incident commander seeking overall situational awareness would benefit from access to a digest of the most important recent messages and/or messages entered by particular responders.

In the heat of an emergency, a responder might not always remember to check for new or updated information. Pushing messages (or notifications) of certain types or from certain people would ensure that critical messages are seen when they are sent. Such a capability might be implemented as a subscription mechanism to allow different responders to select the messages and message senders most relevant to their responsibilities.

Several organizations have standard formats for various types of information, e.g., a firefighter's size-up or report of units on the scene. We plan to add standardized, but customizable, forms to facilitate the entry of such information.

While we believe a mobile application, such as the one described herein, is a useful tool for emergency response, it tends to provide a personal and local view of a disaster, so it is not optimal for providing incident commanders with a big-picture view of a large-scale disaster. We plan to integrate our application with the Golden Gate Safety Network Common Operating Picture [1] to enable an incident commander to see such a big picture and also to interact with responders using the same structured hypermedia capability as the mobile application provides.

The current Semantic Geotagging system produces a "forest" of trees of conversational threads. There are, however, potential connections across threads and even across trees, which if made available would provide access to potentially useful information that is otherwise likely to be missed. Previous research (e.g., [21, 22]) suggests that fully automated crosslinking is impractical but that it is possible to propose reasonable links that a human user can examine for suitability. We plan to revisit these techniques in light of advances in artificial intelligence research and to prototype one or more approaches for crosslinking.

7.2   Expanded Testing

While our cognitive walkthroughs and usability testing have been useful in identifying and addressing basic interaction design issues, we have not yet tested the application in an authentic usage context. Such a context would likely involve multiple, geographically separated responders addressing different aspects of a complex incident. We plan to increase the realism of our testing, first by engaging multiple users in scenario-based "tabletop" exercises and eventually by deploying the system for experimental use in "real-world" disaster preparedness exercises (see, e.g., [23]).

7.3   New Information Sources

Finally, we recognize that professional responders typically do not have all of the information relevant to emergency response. Members of the public can often supply much useful information, especially in the early stages of an incident or when professional resources are stretched thin. That said, professional responders cannot unconditionally accept public-provided information because such information might be inaccurate or even intentionally misleading. We are planning an interview-based approach to formulate a set of heuristic rules for determining which public-provided information is likely to be trustworthy. Rather than giving members of the public access to this application, however, we plan to add a new interface layer, which will display filtered, geotagged messages from social media tools, such as Twitter, when it is activated.

7.4   New Uses

We believe that the applicability of an application of this sort goes far beyond emergency response, and we are considering additional uses. One intriguing possibility is to use Semantic Geotagging as a platform for citizen participatory journalism, providing a simple tool for both access and updates to a large corpus of evolving news.

8   Conclusion

A system of this type will be most useful in a major disaster, but it is also likely to be most difficult to get responders to use it in such a situation. In particular, rank-and-file responders, such as front-line firefighters, are, to quote one of our test subjects, "a bunch of adrenalin junkies who are going 100 miles per hour. It will be hard to get them to slow down to enter information," although they might ultimately be consumers of such information. Command personnel might be more receptive to using such a system; in a fire, these include the incident commander, battalion chiefs, and safety officers. These responders are likely to be older and less tech-savvy than younger ones, so ease of use and absolute reliability are paramount. It is thus imperative that the system be thoroughly tested before even experimental deployment and thoroughly proven in exercises before attempting use in an actual emergency.

Of course, focusing on senior personnel as users is counter to our initial goal of "democratizing" the development of situational awareness as an alternative to the currently prevalent command-and-control model of information collection, curation, and dissemination. Perhaps change in the direction we envision will begin with providing all responders the opportunity to contribute to situational awareness even if most do not take advantage of it; perhaps a simplified information entry interface will be required. We will continue to explore this issue as the Semantic Geotagging project progresses.

Acknowledgments. This work was funded, in part, by a grant from Carnegie Mellon University's Cylab under grant DAAD19-02-1-0389 from the Army Research Office. The views and conclusions contained here are those of the authors and should not be interpreted as necessarily representing the official policies or endorsements, either expressed or implied, of ARO, CMU, the U.S. Government or any of its agencies. The authors would like to thank Jeannie Stamberger, Sean Lanthier, and a number of firefighters for their contributions to this work. We would also like to thank the anonymous reviewers for their careful reviews and advice.

References

1. Golden Gate Safety Network Common Operating Picture,
   http://comopview.org/ggsn
2. Luqman, F.B., Griss, M.L.: Leveraging Mobile Context for Effective Collaboration and Task Management in Disaster Response. In: Proc. ISCRAM, Portugal (2011)
3. Luqman, F.B., Griss, M.L.: Overseer: A Mobile Context-Aware Collaboration and Task Management System for Disaster Response. In: The 8th International Conference on Creating, UC San Diego, CA, USA (2010)
4. Cheng, H.T., Buthpitiya, S., Sun, F.T., Griss, M.L.: OmniSense: A Collaborative Sensing Framework for User Context Recognition Using Mobile Phones. ACM HotMobile (2010)
5. GeoCAM Share Project at NASA Ames, http://geocamshare.org/
6. GeoTwitter, http://geotwitter.org
7. GeoChat, http://instedd.org/technologies/geochat/
8. Rinner, C., Kebler, C., Andrulis, S.: The use of Web 2.0 concepts to support deliberation in spatial decision making. Computers, Environment and Urban System 32, 386–395 (2008)
9. Niko, D.L., Hwang, H., Lee, Y., Kim, C.: Integrating User-Generated Content and Spatial Data into Web GIS for Disaster History. In: Lee, R. (ed.) Computers,Networks, Systems, and Industrial Engineering 2011. SCI, vol. 365, pp. 245–255. Springer, Heidelberg (2011)
10. Roche, R., Propeck-Zimmerman, E., Mericskay, B.: GeoWeb and crisis management: issues and perspectives of volunteered geographic information. GeoJournal (June 2011)

11. Zook, M., Graham, M., Shelton, T., Gorman, S.: Volunteered Geographic Information and Crowdsourcing Disaster Relief: A Case Study of the Haitian Earthquake. World Medical and Health Policy V2, 7–27 (2010)
12. Maiyo, L.: Collaborative Post-Disaster Damage Mapping via Geo Web Services. MSc Thesis, International Institute for Geo-Information Science and Earth Observation (ITC), The Netherlands (2009)
13. Bareiss, R., Osgood, R.: Applying AI Models to the Design of Exploratory Hypermedia Systems. In: Proceedings of Hypertext 1993, pp. 94–105 (1993)
14. Ferguson, W., Bareiss, R., Birnbaum, L., Osgood, R.: ASK Systems: An Approach to the Realization of Story-Based Teachers. Journal of the Learning Sciences 2(1), 95–134 (1992)
15. Johnson, C., Birnbaum, L., Bareiss, R., Hinrichs, T.: War Stories: Harnessing Organizational Memories to Support Task Performance. ACM Intelligence 11(1), 16–31 (2000)
16. Schank, R.: Rules and Topics in Conversation. Cognitive Science 1(4), 421–441 (1977)
17. Anonymous, Fire Point Size-Up,
    http://www.fireengineering.com/index/articles/display/96802/
    articles/fire-engineering/volume-154/issue-2/features/
    five-point-size-up.html
18. Spencer, R.: The Streamlined Cognitive Walkthrough Method: Working Around Social Constraints Encountered in a Software Development Company. CHI Letters 2(1), 353–359 (2000)
19. Krug, S.: Rocket Surgery Made Easy: The Do-It-Yourself Guide to Finding and Fixing Usability Problems. New Riders Press, Berkeley (2010)
20. NIST, The History of Automatic Speech Recognition Evaluations. National Institute of Standards and Technology, NIST,
    http://www.itl.nist.gov/iad/mig/publications/ASRhistory/
    index.html
21. Cleary, C., Bareiss, R.: Practical Methods for Automating Linking in Structured Hypermedia Systems. In: Proceedings of Hypertext 1996, pp. 31–41 (1996)
22. Osgood, R., Bareiss, R.: Automated Index Generation for Constructing Large-Scale Conversational Hypermedia Systems. In: Proceedings of AAAI 1993, pp. 309–314 (1993)
23. Golden Guardian (2011),
    http://www.oes.ca.gov/WebPage/oeswebsite.nsf/Content/
    AEC4591D507E40F3882576480064882D?OpenDocument

ProbIN: Probabilistic Infrastructureless Navigation

Le T. Nguyen and Ying Zhang

Carnegie Mellon University,
NASA Research Park Building 23,
Moffett Field, CA 95035, USA
{le.nguyen,joy.zhang}@sv.cmu.edu

1 Introduction

With the increasing popularity of smart phones, knowing the accurate position of a user has become critical to many context-aware applications. In outdoor environments, standardized Global Positioning System (GPS) is often used. However, for indoor environments such as airports, hospitals or shopping malls GPS signals are usually unavailable or unreliable. Most of the existing indoor positioning solutions try to address this problem by utilizing existing infrastructures such as Wi-Fi access points or Bluetooth beacons.

In cases when the infrastructure is not available, self-contained systems provide a more flexible solution. These systems use sensors such as accelerometers, gyroscopes and magnetometers. In order to derive a user's current location, the movement of the user is tracked by the continuous logging of sensor readings. Since this technique does not rely on an external infrastructure, theoretically it can be used in any environment. The main drawback of self-contained positioning approaches is error accumulation. Since the sensors utilized are noisy by nature, the error of position estimation grows with time and distance traveled. Moreover, the noise portion in sensor measurements is significantly higher when the phone is held in the hand versus mounting it on certain parts of the body. Positioning in the hand accelerates the accumulation of error and causes a substantial decrease of estimation accuracy.

The purpose of our work is to deliver a system providing positioning and navigation functionality for consumer mobile devices in GPS-challenging environments. In the demo we will focus on a novel probabilistic approach of self-contained positioning providing a user's current location. In order to overcome the problem with noisy sensor readings of consumer mobile devices, a statistical model well-known in the field of the statistical machine translation (SMT) is utilized for positioning purposes.

In our work, the positioning problem is framed as a noisy-channel problem, where we try to recover the actual user's position from the distorted sensor inputs. To recover the user's position, we use a statistical model to map the sensor readings directly to the displacement. This is fundamentally different from state-of-the-art dead reckoning approaches. In these approaches the sensor readings are interpreted by their actual physical meanings, i.e., the accelerometer

J.Y. Zhang et al. (Eds.): MobiCASE 2011, LNICST 95, pp. 115–117, 2012.

readings are considered as being the actual acceleration of the device. Thus, theoretically based on the laws of physics the travelled displacement can be obtained by double integrating the acceleration.

In ProbIN the sensor readings are interpreted as observed "signals" which are directly mapped to the corresponding displacement based on a statistical model. The statistical model is trained by using SMT techniques adjusted for positioning purposes. During the training phase, ProbIN builds statistical models from the user's data. These models capture the user's walking patterns and adapts to the sensor errors of the mobile device. Thus, although the sensors on the mobile devices are noisy, ProbIN can still estimate the user's current position at a much higher accuracy rate than the state-of-the-art dead reckoning approaches.

2   ProbIN

Probabilistic Infrastructureless Navigation (ProbIN) is a system providing the positioning and navigation functionality for GPS-challenging environment. In the demo, we will focus on the positioning part of ProbIN, which allows tracking of a person.

The ProbIN is intended for daily applications such as assisting the user in the shopping malls or at the airports. Therefore, it needs to fulfill the three essential requirements:

1. *Scalability*: ProbIN delivers positioning functionality even without an existing external infrastructure.
2. *Affordability*: ProbIN can be run on consumer mobile devices with relatively low-quality sensors.
3. *Usability*: The user should be able to hold the devices in the hand or in a pocket without degrading delivered functionality.

In order to fulfill the first requirement ProbIN essentially utilizes the inertial sensors. As such, a self-contained positioning system can be delivered, which does not rely on any external infrastructure. ProbIN can be also improved by utilizing a magnetometer and/or digital maps in order to achieve higher positioning accuracy. The advantage for this case is that the system will remain self-contained. A viable extension would be the integration of modules utilizing external infrastructures such as GPS or a Wi-Fi network. These modules would be activated only when an infrastructure is available.

Due to the second and the third requirements, a novel approach of positioning needs to developed in order to address high error rates of the sensors. It is known that when utilizing low-cost sensors measurements are typically very inaccurate, especially when the sensors are not mounted to the user's body. In this case, the traditional physics-based positioning performs badly, since an error in the sensor reading causes an error in the estimated displacement. ProbIN addresses this issue by learning a mapping between the sensor readings and the actual true displacements based on training data. Thus, when the ProbIN is deployed, even a noisy sensor reading can be mapped to the correct displacement. The problem of minimizing the error rate is thereby transformed into a machine learning problem. In the demo, we will present a solution to this problem by utilizing machine learning techniques well-known to the field of the statistical machine translation (SMT).

As mentioned above, ProbIN utilizes a machine learning technique that is divided into training and testing phases. First, the sensor readings with corresponding true displacements are collected in the training phase. The relationship between the measurements and the displacements are used for creating a statistical model. Then in the testing phase, the statistical model is employed for mapping the sensor readings of the tracked person into a trajectory. The result of the testing phase is typically used for evaluating the approach.

3 Demo

For the demo we will be using an iPhone 4 for collecting sensor readings and a laptop for displaying user's trajectory. Since sensor readings are periodically sent to the server, we need a reliable Wifi connection. We will let attendees try out our positioning system. Therefore, we would prefer having our booth in a bigger room so that the users can walk around in order to test the positioning functionality. Our demonstration will not interference with other demonstrations. Other people being in the room can be seen as obstacles, which will help us to demonstrate the robustness of the system.

Micro-interactions
with NFC-Enabled Mobile Phones

Ben Dodson and Monica S. Lam

Computer Science Department,
Stanford University,
CA 94305
{bjdodson,lam}@cs.stanford.edu

Abstract. This paper coins the term *micro-interactions* to refer to the class of small exchanges between devices that occur almost instantaneously. For example, a mobile payment using near-field communication (NFC) is a micro-interaction. The arrival of NFC on smart phones makes possible a wide array of applications using micro-interactions, from sharing photos between a phone and a TV to checking a car into a valet parking service by touching two phones.

This paper addresses the challenge of how to create intuitive, frictionless micro-interactions that require no pre-configuration for a large class of applications. We deliver a consistent *tap-and-share* interface for many forms of micro-interactions through several concepts. We propose *interaction manifests* as universal descriptors of multi-party, cross-platform applications. Zero-click overheads are made possible by automatically using the foreground application as the context for the micro-interactions. We extend the concept of *connection handovers* to allow NFC-enabled applications to run unmodified on devices lacking NFC. We also show how these abstractions make it easy to create a variety of applications. All the application and library code is available as open source.

We demonstrate that by focusing on micro-interactions, our mobile phones can provide a single focal point that enables sharing of our digital identity, assets, applications, and personality with friends (with their mobile phones) as well as the larger-screen PCs and TVs all around us.

1 Introduction

The smart phone, being powerful, personal, always with us, always-online, is changing our everyday life. It will eventually hold the key to our identities, access rights to digital assets, personal communications, photos, media, etc. In a sense, the smart phone is an extension of our digital self. As such, there are many applications where we wish to share our digital personality on the phone with other people's phones around us, as well as with our surrounding devices. In many cases, we are sharing very small amounts of information, such as a phone number. People would not bother automating such interactions unless the overhead is kept to a minimum. We refer to such interactions as *micro-interactions*; they will not be used unless they are as frictionless as micropayments.

J.Y. Zhang et al. (Eds.): MobiCASE 2011, LNICST 95, pp. 118–136, 2012.
© Institute for Computer Sciences, Social Informatics and Telecommunications Engineering 2012

1.1   Near-Field Communication

Micropayment is poised to be widely enabled on the smart phone. It is implemented using Near-Field Communication (NFC). NFC is a radio technology that supports transactions at distances of a few centimeters. During a transaction, one party can be completely inactive, drawing power inductively from the active party. Even the active party draws little power and can be left on all the time with minimal effect on the phone's overall power draw. Also, the nearness of NFC transactions creates the possibility of using proximity as context and triggering an appropriate action almost instantaneously.

NFC, in the form factor of a credit card, has been used widely in Japan, Hong Kong, and other parts of the world for many years: for public transportation, vending machines, and convenience stores. Standards have also been created for "smart posters" [5]; posters, signs, and magazine pages can possess cheap, embedded data tags that contain information such as details of museum exhibits, transportation schedules, discount coupons, movie clips, or links to e-commerce sites. A third important use of NFC is for making long-lasting connections between electronic devices—simply touching the devices together will configure them to connect over a longer-range protocol such as Bluetooth or Wi-Fi.

Availability of NFC on smart phones presents an exciting opportunity. The ubiquity of mobile phones means that most consumers in the future will have access to this technology. The programmability means that many applications can be developed to handle the context of an NFC interaction. NFC allows our phones to easily communicate directly, without requiring a third-party server. The effortless connection of NFC opens up many opportunities for phones to enhance our physical social encounters.

1.2   Micro-interactions on the Phone

The concept of device-to-device micro-interactions has been explored by many researchers [10,14,19,26]. This paper explores specifically the new opportunities of micro-interactions as offered by the smart phone. How do we *frictionlessly* share the digital personality we have acquired on the phone with devices around us? How do we *frictionlessly* invite others to participate in applications we are running currently on our phone?

Consider sending a text message from a mobile phone. We may find ourselves near computers with keyboards and wish we could type on the keyboard instead of on the phone. Writing an SMS is a short-lived task, and so any setup (such as Bluetooth pairing) or added complexity will affect our willingness to adopt such a workflow. The tear-down must also be trivial— we do not want to permanently pair our PC's keyboard with the phone.

As an example, we have developed an application called TapBoard based on the ideas we present in this paper. With TapBoard, the user simply touches the phone with an NFC tag on the keyboard of a PC (a micro-interaction), the PC will bring up a webpage with a simple text box, as shown in Fig. 1. Any text typed in the text box shows up on the phone instantaneously. Closing

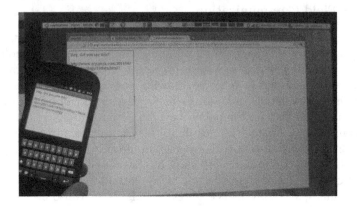

Fig. 1. Using TapBoard to enter mobile text

the webpage disassociates the phone from the PC. The NFC tag on the PC simply contains the information that enables the phone to connect to the PC, e.g. through Bluetooth, without user intervention.

Critically, the interaction occurs without requiring even a keypress. The UI is presented on the PC without the user searching for an application to launch, and the application does not hijack the user's PC usage in a permanent way. Even slightly increasing the difficulty of running the application such as accessing it from the application list or delays in loading the program may result in an experience that doesn't justify the gain in usability.

1.3   Contributions

This paper makes the following contributions:

1. We present a large number of scenarios where micro-interactions on the phone can be used in our daily life. We show that there are three major kinds of peer-to-peer micro-interactions: phone to phone, phone to another interactive device like a PC, phone to a passive device like a TV.
2. While inspired by NFC, the usage of micro-interactions we envision goes well beyond what can be implemented directly with NFC. We are able to deliver a consistent "tap and share" interface for many forms of micro-interactions with several novel concepts. *Interaction manifests* and the *Junction application platform* enable the sharing of not just data but decentralized multi-party applications across different platforms. Zero-click overheads are made possible by automatically using the foreground application as the context for the micro-interaction. Finally, *connection handovers* allow sharing across devices without NFC radios and for supporting continued interactions beyond the first touch.
3. All the abstractions presented in this paper are embodied in the publicly available Junction application framework and several libraries (EasyNFC,

LegacyNFC, and DesktopNFC). We have written a wide collection of applications (data sharing, keyboard sharing, remote presentation, and a multi-party poker game) using the libraries. Our experience suggests that the abstractions are powerful in simplifying the development of micro-interactions.

2 Uses of P2P Micro-interactions

Although micro-interactions are simplifying only small tasks, their wide applicability can have a major impact on our daily life. We imagine in the future, a child will instinctively touch his phone with different devices if he wants to share whatever he is doing to that device. Let us first describe some everyday scenarios with micro-interactions, then show how they can be organized as three major use cases.

2.1 Scenarios

We illustrate with scenarios below how pervasive micro-interactions can become, at home, in the work place, and when we are out and about. Several of the following scenarios are reminiscent of Mark Weiser's vision of ubiquitous computing, made possible by the NFC-equipped smart phones of today [25].

At Home. Consider the mundane task of turning on the alarm on the phone before turning in every night. With micro-interactions, we can simply put the phone on our bedside table and it enters into "night mode," silencing our non-critical notifications such as when we receive emails.

A digital photo frame can now be set by simply touching the frame with a phone. If the phone is showing a picture, that picture gets on the frame; if the phone is showing a contact, our contact gets permission to remotely set photos on that frame.

In the living room, our phone turns into a digital remote by touching the phone to the remote. We can then change channels with the phone by browsing or searching or even using voice control. We can also browse for multimedia files on our phone and send them to the TV by touching the remote again, and use our online services like Netflix and Amazon to stream purchased content to our TV.

We can track our workout routine on our phone, to see a graphical representation of our progress. Bringing our phone near a scale picks up our weight and other vitals (kept privately on our device!), and touching our phone to our sports watch transfers the duration of our last run.

At the Office. On our way to the office, we touch our phone to our car's center console to personalize the driving experience. It synchronizes our downloaded music and favorite radio stations and adjusts the car seat to our preference. We can also set our navigation device's destination by opening our phone's appointment book and again touching it to the console.

Suppose next we visit a company. To get a guest badge, we open the invitation from our host on our phone and touch it to the kiosk at the receptionist's desk to share who we are and with whom we are meeting. As we wait to meet our host, an email comes in that requires a lengthy reply. There is a guest computer nearby, and we touch our phone to it to borrow its keyboard.

If we are giving a presentation at a meeting, we touch our phone to the conference room's projector to bring up our presentation. The phone acts as a controller for the talk. Touching our phone to other computers in the room brings up the presentation on those devices as well. We can also touch our phone to attendees' phones in the room to give them a copy of our slides.

Out and about. Suppose we want to use valet parking at a restaurant. We hand over the keys to our car, and touch a kiosk to get a digital version of our valet ticket. We send the kiosk a picture of our face so they can recognize us when we return. We "check in" at the restaurant by touching our phone to the hostess's station. When we're done eating, we pay for the lunch using our phone, and the receipt is automatically stored in our device. Our phone knows if we are on a business trip, and automatically forwards the receipt for reimbursement. Heading back, we say "get the car" to our phone, and the valet is notified that we're on our way back, so the car is ready when we return.

Suppose next we wish to go to a party on public transportation. We touch our phone to a sign at the bus stop to get the schedule of when the next bus is coming. If the wait is too long, one click lets us call a cab. At the party, we touch our phone to a sticker at the door to check in. We can see a list of everyone else who's checked in and get their contact information. There's also a TV playing music and showing photos. Because we've checked in, we can choose music to play from our personal collection. And until we "check out", the photos we capture are sent to the running slideshow instantly.

2.2   Kinds of Micro-interactions

All the micro-interactions described above can be categorized according to the relationships of the interacting parties.

Multi-party (e.g. phone to phone). The interacting devices belong to different individuals; either or both of the parties may wish to initiate an interaction. A user may want to share the document or application he is viewing or running with a friend. He can simply touch his friend's phone to share that context. Or, a user may wish to interact with a person and then decide on the information shared later. Upon tapping the phones together, either or both users can then launch an interaction based on a menu of possibilities then displayed, filtered to show applications that support peer-to-peer. The flexibility of either choosing the applications or the participants first allows the users to interact naturally depending on the context. Finally, we like to emphasize that it is not necessary for the receiving party to have pre-installed the code for the interaction. We can download the code on the fly, requiring no intervention other than possibly an approval to download; this reduces the friction of interaction and helps the software go viral.

Self Across Interactive Devices (e.g. phone to a PC). We now consider interactions running on multiple devices, each with their own input and output capabilities, but controlled by the same person. This kind of interaction is growing with the smart phones playing a more significant role in our life. We are spending more time and storing more information on the phone, but the phone is limited in its processing, input and output capabilities.

In this use case, it is the same person who decides on the interaction of interest. He may wish to have the PC assist with a task on the phone (e.g. to borrow the use of the PC keyboard for text entry), or to have the phone assist the PC (e.g. to ask the password manager on the phone to log the user into a web page using a challenge-response protocol). In either case, the user performs the same action by touching the PC with the phone, the contexts of the devices will be shared. The device with a sharable context is the initiator. Because the same person is controlling both ends, confirmations to accept invitations are unnecessary. The mode of operation is the same regardless of whether the user owns the PC since no setup is necessary.

We also envision in the future that we may wish to pair the phone with the PC for the entire duration the PC is used. Micro-interactions lead to long-lasting sessions, in which resources can be used across each device. Such usage patterns have been explored previously, for example using platform composition [14].

Remote Control (e.g. phone to a TV or a car). This last use case refers to the control of other devices through a phone. Just like all the other cases, the micro-interaction may be initiated on either device. The user may wish to enlist another device to perform a task running on the phone. An example would be displaying a photo on the TV. Here, the phone is the initiator. Or, the device we wish to control may provide the context. For example, a driver may simply tap his phone on the car, the car will provide the context and request the driver's preference of music selection and seat setting. A device like a TV may have many possible modes of interactions, so it may wish to display a menu so that the user can pick the interaction of interest.

3   Protocols for Micro-interactions

Simple interactions must be made as frictionless as possible, otherwise users will simply not be bothered. Take for example the simple task of running a collaborative whiteboard between two phones. First, the application must be available on both devices. If someone wants to run the whiteboard with another person, but the application is not yet installed, the friction involved in finding and downloading the application may overwhelm the benefits of running it. Second, the two users must join each other in a shared whiteboard session. Again, any investment beyond a few seconds in setting up the session may be too much for the users.

We would like to enable a "tap to share" experience for such collaborative applications. To minimize the setup overhead, we introduce protocols to address each of these aspects in collaboration:

- "first packet" delivery, to establish device communication
- code discovery and execution, and
- long-lasting multi-party runtime.

The micro-interaction enabled by combining these ideas is fast and intuitive: To run a whiteboard with a friend, the user simply launches the whiteboard program, while his friend turns on his device. They touch phones and the friend's phone tells him that he does not have the whiteboard application, prompting him to install it. He confirms, the application downloads and launches, joining the first user for an interactive session. If the friend already has the whiteboard application installed, the interactive session comes up in a couple of seconds, faster than it takes to even select the program from the list of available applications.

3.1 NDEF Exchange as "First-Packet" Delivery

Our user interactions are inspired by the NFC communication pattern as implemented in the Android OS's Gingerbread release [7]. Here, the P2P model restricts users to the exchange of an NDEF message in each direction. To ensure a fast interaction, application data is made available to the underlying operating system in advance of two devices interacting physically, and messages are reacted to with an asynchronous callback. An NDEF exchange can be contrasted to the HTTP or OBEX protocols, which provide a request/response interaction model. The lack of response during the NDEF exchange is especially important for NFC as we can program both active devices such as phones and passive devices such as stickers in a uniform way.

The NDEF data format is well-suited for this style of interaction. Each message is a compact representation of some well-defined payload. The type may be well known, such as a URI or MIME type, or of a type specially designed for some application.

3.2 Interaction Manifest for Cross-Platform Code Discovery

We define a simple data format called an *interaction manifest* that specifies the application to be run on the remote device. Our goal is to support platforms of any type (phone, PC, TV, etc.), thus the interaction manifest is defined as a MIME type consisting of *one or more* platform-specific application specifications. Each entry includes:

- A platform identifier, such as "Android", "iOS", or "Web".
- A platform-specific application reference, uniquely identifying programs that are both installed on the phone or available online.

– An instance-specific application argument.
– An optional device modality, to support different application code for different device types.

The interpretation of an interaction manifest depends on the state of the remote device. If the remote device has a foreground application, it gets priority access to the interaction manifest. In the interaction manifest received comes from the same application, it acts according to the application argument provided. If it comes from a different application, it may still be able to understand the message if the applications are compatible. If there is no foreground application, or if the foreground application does not understand the message, the operating system handles the application manifest by launching the specified application. If the application is not already installed, the application for the appropriate platform will first be downloaded, with user confirmation.

For the whiteboard example, the application creates an application manifest that specifies where the source of the whiteboard application is located; the application manifest is presented to the remote device via NFC whenever two phones touch. Upon receiving the manifest, the remote operating system will launch the whiteboard application, after code download when necessary, if it is not already running.

3.3   Junction for Long-Lasting Application Sessions

Having the phones run the same application is the first step, how are they joined to the same session? For this, we use the Junction platform.

We have developed a platform called Junction as a way of maintaining a real-time application session across devices [8]. Junction applications can be contrasted to server-client programs. Under the server-client model, all devices connect to a central server, which manages the application's runtime and assets. Instead, Junction moves all application logic onto the end-devices.

Junction makes use of a communication hub called a switchboard. The switchboard does nothing but route messages to the devices in an application session. The session can be thought of as a chatroom in which all participants see all messages, and the server does nothing other than route messages to clients.

A session is represented uniquely with a URI. The URI encodes a unique session identifier as well as the switchboard's address. This URI acts as a capability for joining the application session, and is the application argument we use in the interaction manifest.

Junction is an abstraction and supports many implementations. For example, a session may be run through an XMPP chat server, locally over TCP/IP, or across phones using Bluetooth. Here, one phone acts as a hub, routing messages to other phones over Bluetooth sockets. Using Bluetooth, an application is run entirely locally, without any additional infrastructure.

4   Context Sharing

Tapping two programmable devices together creates a *symmetric* relationship, as each may try to provoke a response on the other device. This is very different from the familiar request-and-respond protocol where there is only one initiator. In this section, we discuss how two phones interact upon touching each other, with the assumption that both phones are NFC-enabled. We will relax this assumption in the next section as we show how to add NFC capabilities to legacy devices like PCs and TVs.

4.1   Context-Rich Interactions

We say that a device is *context-rich* if it is running a foreground application that wishes to share its context with a remote device. Otherwise, the device is *context-bare*. Because of the small display size, a smart phone has only one foreground application, which is the application whose interface is occupying the screen real estate. On a PC, the application with the cursor is the foreground application. The foreground application on the context-rich device registers an interaction manifest with the operating system, which is presented to the remote device whenever the phones touch.

The most straightforward combination is when a context-rich device touches a context-bare device, the former simply shares its context with the latter. In our earlier example, the phone that initiated the whiteboard application is the context-rich device. Touching it with a context-bare phone simply passes the whiteboard's interaction manifest to the latter. Consider, as a second example, a secure login application on the PC that uses the phone for challenge-response authentication. When the login application is in the foreground, the PC is context-rich, presenting to the phone an interaction manifest for authentication. The phone can then invoke its login application by simply tapping it to the PC.

If two context-rich devices come in contact, the respective interaction manifests are sent to the foreground applications, which may decide independently whether or not a received message is of interest, ignoring it otherwise. As an example, consider a device running a jukebox application (exposing its interaction manifest), and another browsing media files (exposing a file or link). The interaction results in the media file being sent to the jukebox, which opens the content, and a reference to the jukebox application made available to the browsing device, which ignores the message.

As a special case, consider two context-rich devices running the same application. We can easily establish a connection between the two devices for a long-lasting session, run over Bluetooth, Junction, or some other means. Each application indicates the connection information over which it can be reached. Because the exchange is symmetric, the devices must decide on which single session to use. They can come to an agreement by following a protocol based on the information they both have as a result of the exchange. For example, they can each generate a random number and agree to use the address given by the device who generated the smaller value, as outlined in the Connection Handover framework [5].

4.2 Context-Bare Interactions

When two context-bare devices touch, each device defaults to sharing its *handover addresses* and device type (e.g. TV, PC, phone). The handover address provides an address the device can be contacted subsequently. It also uniquely identifies the device and can be used as a contextual cue. A device, upon receiving a handover address, may wish to present on its screen a menu of applications relevant to the device type of the second party. For example, we are likely to play a phone-to-phone game with another phone, but not with a TV. Most applications on our phone are not designed for multi-party use, and so even a basic filtering algorithm provides a meaningful context-aware application menu. We can also suggest recently used applications between us and the remote device, associating applications with either the device type or identity, which has been shown to be a useful contextual cue [21].

Whether or not to require user confirmation during an interaction depends on the device and situation. For example, direct input to applications running on a TV is cumbersome, and so our applications and multimedia run on a TV without confirmation. If security is of concern, the device can maintain a whitelist of devices that are allowed to open content. The "auto-answering" of our TV can make the difference between a compelling and unappealing end-user experience.

4.3 Labeling Arbitrary Objects with Contexts

We can also write out a context on an NFC tag and label any object or location with that tag. Consider the example we described earlier where we wish to set our phone to "night mode" when we go to bed. We can do so by launching the night mode application and writing the context that launches the application on an NFC tag by simply touching the phone to the tag. We then stick the tag on our nightstand, allowing us to simply place our phone over the tag to turn on night mode.

5   Connection Handover

As we discussed above, there are many compelling reasons for connecting our phone to other programmable devices like the PC, TV, and even the car. We wish to enable the "tap and run" experience of NFC without requiring the expense and effort of integrating an NFC radio into each device. We can easily add micro-interaction capabilities to existing networked devices with the help of a passive NFC tag, which can be purchased for about $1 a piece or for 20 cents in bulk. Furthermore, two devices without NFC radios can also share easily with the assistance of an active NFC device. Moreover, an application written to use NFC can support connection handover with non-NFC equipped devices without modification.

5.1   Handover Service

We add the NDEF exchange protocol to devices lacking NFC by running a simple listening service on the device. The service can be run on a PC, TV, or phone, with the exchange occurring over a Bluetooth or TCP/IP socket. The data exchanged between applications is the same as what would be exchanged over NFC.

Similar to HTTP redirects on the web, supporting connection handover requests does not require any changes in the application. The underlying platform detects the handover message, follows the handover protocol, and passes on the NDEF message to the application.

Bluetooth and TCP/IP can be interacted with at greater distances than NFC, so we must focus on the security and privacy of the handover exchange (although NFC too requires security considerations [6]). A first step is to deactivate the service when not in use. On a mobile phone, we turn off the service when the phone's screen is off, which also helps conserve battery. To prevent eavesdropping, we use public key cryptography to secure the message exchange. We can also use a whitelist to limit the devices that are allowed to interact with a service to prevent unwanted access.

5.2   Labeling the Devices

We associate a passive NFC tag with a supporting device. The tag can be affixed to the device, as we have done with a Nexus One phone in Fig. 2(a), or placed in a representative location, such as on a television remote control.

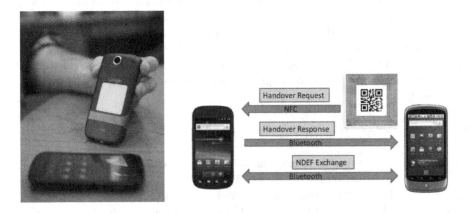

Fig. 2. The NDEF exchange handover protocol for devices lacking an NFC radio. (a), a connection handover sticker on a Nexus One. (b), the NDEF exchange handover protocol.

The tag stores the connection information for the NDEF exchange service, which must somehow be written. In our desktop and mobile applications, a link allows the user to retrieve a QR code encoding the service details. Our application allows another device with an NFC radio and a camera to scan the QR code, convert the contents to NDEF, and write it to the tag.

5.3   Protocol

When an active NFC device scans a passive tag, it typically sends the contents to the foreground application. However, if the tag is an NDEF exchange handover request, the platform preempts the normal workflow, running the NDEF exchange handover protocol depicted in Fig. 2(b). The device establishes a connection over TCP/IP or Bluetooth, initiating the bidirectional NDEF exchange and handling the newly received NDEF message as if it had come directly from a tag or active device.

5.4   Information Transfer

We have seen how we can use a phone with NFC to interact with non-NFC devices. Using this technique, we can use our phone as a means of passing data between two devices lacking NFC, for example sending a multimedia file from a PC to a TV. We simply "pick up" the content from the first device with a touch, and "drop" it to a target device with a second touch. This is an intuitive way to transfer anonymous content [2]. The user does not need to start any application prior to "picking up" the content–in our system, the default handler of NDEF messages can be used to copy and paste content across devices.

For large files, we do not have to transfer the content to the phone when copying across devices. We simply transfer a pointer to the content and let the receiving device download it directly over Bluetooth, HTTP, or some other protocol.

We can also use the NDEF exchange protocol across devices without any NFC involvement and without modifying application code. We can write out the interaction manifest in a QR code, which can then scanned by a remote device. Since scanning a QR code can be cumbersome, our application also allows a user to recall previously used endpoints quickly.

6   Implementation

To explore the development and user experience of micro-interactions, we have developed an NFC abstraction layer for Android, an NDEF exchange handover service for Android and PC, and several applications.

6.1   NDEF Exchange Handover Request

Our NDEF exchange handover request was designed using the guidelines of the NFC Forum's Connection Handover specification [5], a general-purpose framework for setting up connections that run beyond the NFC radio. We use the static request mechanism of the profile.

6.2   EasyNFC Library for Android

We have developed a library for NFC interactions on top of Android's core implementation, called EasyNFC. The library supports the NDEF exchange handover
here described. To enable connection handover, the developer must request Internet or Bluetooth permission in their application, but the handover is invisible
otherwise. EasyNFC also lets developers create a Bluetooth socket between devices easily. A developer simply implements the OnBluetoothConnected interface,
with a callback triggered after establishing a Bluetooth connection.

6.3   LegacyNFC Service for Android

The LegacyNFC application provides basic NDEF exchange functionality for
Android phones that do not have an NFC radio. The application consists of
a background service that runs whenever the screen is turned on. It listens
over Bluetooth or TCP/IP for an NDEF exchange initiated by a peer, and also
prepares local NDEF messages from applications, set using Android's system of
Intents.

LegacyNFC can display the device's NDEF exchange endpoint information as
a QR code. The QR code can be used to send messages immediately or stored
by a remote phone for later use. The endpoint information can also be written
to an NFC tag, supporting the fast NFC micro-interaction we discussed. An
NFC-enabled phone can touch this sticker and initiate an NDEF exchange using
the specified endpoint information.

When the user is running an application that uses the EasyNFC library, an
icon appears in their notification bar. This UI element is created by LegacyNFC,
requiring no extra work for the application developer. It allows the user to share
their current application with other devices using NDEF exchange. The user
can share the application via "QuickTap", following a stored NDEF exchange
address, or by scanning a QR code. We envision other contextually-driven means
of device selection.

6.4   DesktopNFC Service for PCs and TVs

DesktopNFC is similar in nature to LegacyNFC, but is designed for use on
PCs and TVs. The implementation is written in Java, and can support NDEF
exchanges over both TCP/IP and Bluetooth. DesktopNFC has a console that
allows basic functionality such as posting a URL or small file for use in an
exchange. The daemon reacts to received NDEF messages automatically for
content types deemed "safe", such as URLs and M3U playlist files. Otherwise,
the user is prompted to manually handle the message. DesktopNFC can be run
on a settop box attached to a TV. It interacts with a web browser running full
screen, so content consumes the device when received.

7   Applications

We have implemented a collection of different applications to explore the different use cases presented in this paper.

7.1   TapBoard

As discussed earlier, TapBoard allows a PC's keyboard to be used to enter text on a mobile phone (Fig. 1). Touching the phone to a PC opens a text box that is shared across devices. Using a PC's keyboard not only allows for faster typing, but also lets users copy and paste text from the PC to a phone with ease. This application relies on a connection handover since the PC does not have NFC natively and Junction for maintaining the long-lasting session. Since there is no remote software to install as the PC software is contained in a web page, we simply share a URL rather than an interaction manifest.

7.2   PocketSlides

A previously explored theme of micro-interactions is for a slideshow setup with minimal effort [13]. PocketSlides is our implementation that runs between a phone and a display. A user opens the presentation on her phone and sends this context to the display, as shown in Fig. 3. The display is written in HTML and listens for controls using Junction. When the display opens, the phone turns into a remote control to manage the display. The slideshow can be opened on any number of displays, with synchronized visualization. As with TapBoard, we share the display as a URL directly.

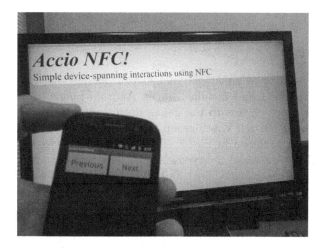

Fig. 3. A PocketSlides slideshow run between a phone and a display

7.3   Hot Potato

Hot Potato is our mobile application for sharing multimedia over NDEF exchange. We hook into Android's "send" intent to allow the sharing of files and links from existing applications. For large files, we use a handover to HTTP or Bluetooth rather than relying on NFC. With Hot Potato, we can send files to other friends' mobile devices, open multimedia directly on a TV, or quickly send a file to a PC.

Hot Potato also has a "copy and paste" feature that supports picking up a file from one device and sending it to another. For large files, we can copy and paste a reference to the file, and transfer the data over a direct link. Fig. 4 shows how we can display a picture on our phone to a TV by touching an NFC-tagged remote control.

Fig. 4. Pushing multimedia to a remote display after touching a phone to a TV remote control

7.4   weHold'Em

WeHold'Em is a game of poker played between phones and a TV. The game is built using Junction and installed on an Android phone. Touching phones together invites more players to the game, downloading the code if necessary. Touching the phone to a TV brings up the display, showing poker chips and community cards, as shown in Fig. 5. The TV's code is written in Javascript and HTML. Here, we make heavy use of the interaction manifest to specify where to download the mobile client and the software to run on the TV.

7.5   Musubi Exchange

Musubi is a social network run between phones. With a tap, users can exchange personas, including name, picture, contact information, as well as a public key for communication. The contacts enable the participants to engage in further

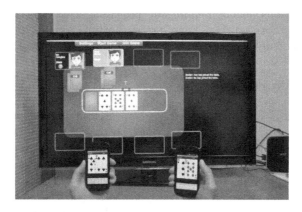

Fig. 5. A game of poker played between phones and a TV

Application	Description	Primitives
TapBoard	Use a desktop's keyboard to enter text on a mobile phone, entered in a simple text box application.	Phone-to-PC context transfer; Junction for long-lasting P2P sessions.
PocketSlides	A slideshow presentation controlled by a mobile phone and displayed on a TV or projector.	Slideshow persisted on phone; Junction for long-lasting sessions.
Hot Potato	Send files, links, and text from a phone to another phone, pc, or TV using NDEF exchange.	Android hooks via "send" intent; auto-answer on TV devices; handover for large files.
weHold'Em	A game of poker played between mobile phones and a TV. Phones are used as player controllers and the TV is a communal display.	Interaction manifest for cross-device and cross-platform support; Junction for long-lasting session.
Musubi Exchange	Touch phones to exchange profile information for a social network, including name, contact information, and public key.	Interaction manifest for viral bootstrapping.

Fig. 6. Applications featuring micro-interactions

activities such as sharing photos or running applications such as a collaborative whiteboard or playlist. Musubi's exchange uses the interaction manifest with the hopes of making the application experience more viral.

7.6   Summary

While many of these applications described above are not new, they were all built using the framework described in this paper. As such, we demonstrate that the framework is general enough to support a wide variety of applications. Each primitive is reused in several applications. Furthermore, our development experience suggests that it is relatively easy to develop such applications.

These applications do not require any pre-configuration, unlike other technologies like Bluetooth pairing. There are no buttons to click or words to type in, except occasionally the user has to approve a software download.

8   Related Work

The proliferation of our digital devices has drawn much attention to how we can use these devices in concert [12]. Many technologies have been created to support cross-device interactions, offering different solutions at each level of the stack [18]. Research has also shown that users frequently employ cross-device habits, and that the amount of configuration involved can drastically affect the usability of the system [3]. Data privacy is also a source of concern for many, which our applications embody using NFC and Junction in their runtimes.

Devices can be composed in a number of ways. For example, platform composition allows devices to share resources at the platform level [14], activity-based computing revolves applications around high-level tasks [1,4], and devices can be organized around a single owner [15]. Our focus on micro-interactions creates ad-hoc compositions in an instant, with context inferred from the interactions themselves.

The difficulties associated with pairing devices has been the focus of much research [9,17,20,23]. Micro-interactions require a pairing and service discovery process that is essentially instantaneous. The popular Bump service for the Android and iPhone platforms connects two users by mapping accelerometer readings and other environmental data on a cloud-based service [22]. All data is exchanged through this service. A major benefit of our NFC and NDEF exchange handover techniques is the interactions run purely locally, avoiding privacy concerns and also providing a faster, more robust user experience. Bump also must be run in the foreground, taking over the phone's UI, while NFC runs in the background, "behind the screen."

Using RFID and QR codes as a way to bridge the physical and digital worlds has been explored at length, and in particular, using a phone as the point of interaction [11,13,24]. In particular, the Elope system uses an RFID tag to set up a connection and also initiate an action associated with that tag. Instead, we use the tag as a contextual cue for determining which application to invoke, and combine it with the context derived from the phone itself.

9   Conclusions

As smart phones are fast becoming a part of our digital self, we believe that micro-interactions on our smart phones will have a significantly impact on our daily life. This paper shows how we can provide a consistent "tap-and-share" interface beyond what is natively supported by NFC.

This paper presents three useful ideas for developing micro-interactions. First, we propose interaction manifest as a universal descriptor of a multi-party application that can be run across multiple platforms. This concise descriptor can be embedded in an NDEF message, which can be transmitted either with NFC or other medium to enable remote participation. The Junction application platform facilitates the development of decentralized multi-party applications, by providing support for invitations, download of software, as well as a messaging service through local or remote switchboards. Finally, the concept of connection handover for NDEF exchange allows NFC-enabled applications to run on devices lacking NFC, unmodified. Our experience shows that these primitives make writing compelling micro-interactions easy and the resulting applications are simple and intuitive to use.

It is exciting that NFC is now available on the latest smart phones for which a healthy ecosystem of third-party applications already exists. We believe that the abstractions contributed by this paper will help promote the development of useful micro-interactions in the market place, and we have made all of the software discussed available as ppen source to help reach that goal. With the prediction that one in five smartphones worldwide will be NFC capable by 2014 [16], the vision of having many consumers using micro-interactions regularly, without even thinking about it, may soon become a reality.

Acknowledgments. We would like to thank Aemon Cannon, Chanh Nguyen, T. J. Purtell, and Ian Vo for their help in developing the applications described in this paper. This research is supported in part by the NSF POMI (Programmable Open Mobile Internet) 2020 Expedition Grant 0832820, NSF grant CCF-0964173, Stanford Clean Slate Program, and Stanford MobiSocial Computing Laboratory.

References

1. Bardram, E.: Activity-based computing: support for mobility and collaboration in ubiquitous computing. Personal Ubiquitous Comput. 9, 312–322 (2005)
2. Richard, A.: Bolt. "put-that-there:" voice and gesture at the graphics interface. In: Proceedings of the 7th Annual Conference on Computer Graphics and Interactive Techniques, SIGGRAPH 1980, pp. 262–270. ACM, New York (1980)
3. Dearman, D., Pierce, J.S.: It's on my other computer!: computing with multiple devices. In: Proceeding of the Twenty-Sixth Annual SIGCHI Conference on Human Factors in Computing Systems, CHI 2008, pp. 767–776. ACM, New York (2008)
4. Keith Edwards, W., Newman, M.W., Sedivy, J.Z., Smith, T.F.: Experiences with recombinant computing: Exploring ad hoc interoperability in evolving digital networks. ACM Trans. Comput.-Hum. Interact. 16(1), 1–44 (2009)
5. NFC Forum. Nfc forum technical specifications (2010), http://www.nfc-forum.org/specs/spec_list
6. Francis, L., Hancke, G., Mayes, K., Markantonakis, K.: Practical NFC Peer-to-Peer Relay Attack Using Mobile Phones. In: Ors Yalcin, S.B. (ed.) RFIDSec 2010. LNCS, vol. 6370, pp. 35–49. Springer, Heidelberg (2010)
7. Google. Near field communication (2011), http://developer.android.com/guide/topics/nfc/index.html#p2p
8. Junction, http://openjunction.org

9. Mayrhofer, R., Gellersen, H.: Shake well before use: Intuitive and secure pairing of mobile devices. IEEE Transactions on Mobile Computing 8, 792–806 (2009)

10. Olsen, D.R., Travis Nielsen, S., Parslow, D.: Join and capture: A model for nomadic interaction. In: Proceedings of 14th Annual ACM Symposium on User Interface Software and Technology, pp. 131–140. Press (2001)

11. O'Neill, E., Thompson, P., Garzonis, S., Warr, A.: Reach Out and Touch: Using NFC and 2D Barcodes for Service Discovery and Interaction with Mobile Devices. In: LaMarca, A., Langheinrich, M., Truong, K.N. (eds.) Pervasive 2007. LNCS, vol. 4480, pp. 19–36. Springer, Heidelberg (2007)

12. Oulasvirta, A., Sumari, L.: Mobile kits and laptop trays: managing multiple devices in mobile information work. In: Proceedings of the SIGCHI Conference on Human Factors in Computing Systems, CHI 2007, pp. 1127–1136. ACM, New York (2007)

13. Pering, T., Ballagas, R., Want, R.: Spontaneous marriages of mobile devices and interactive spaces. Commun. ACM 48(9), 53–59 (2005)

14. Pering, T., Want, R., Rosario, B., Sud, S., Lyons, K.: Enabling Pervasive Collaboration with Platform Composition. In: Tokuda, H., Beigl, M., Friday, A., Brush, A.J.B., Tobe, Y. (eds.) Pervasive 2009. LNCS, vol. 5538, pp. 184–201. Springer, Heidelberg (2009)

15. Pierce, J.S., Nichols, J.: An infrastructure for extending applications' user experiences across multiple personal devices. In: Proceedings of the 21st Annual ACM Symposium on User Interface Software and Technology, UIST 2008, pp. 101–110. ACM, New York (2008)

16. Juniper Research. 1 in 5 Smartphones will have NFC by 2014 (2011), http://www.msnbc.msn.com/id/42584660/ns/business-press_releases/

17. Saxena, N., Uddin, M.B., Voris, J.: Universal device pairing using an auxiliary device. In: Proceedings of the 4th Symposium on Usable Privacy and Security, SOUPS 2008, pp. 56–67. ACM, New York (2008)

18. Schilit, B.N., Sengupta, U.: Device ensembles. Computer 37, 56–64 (2004)

19. Schmidt, D., Chehimi, F., Rukzio, E., Gellersen, H.: Phonetouch: a technique for direct phone interaction on surfaces. In: Proceedings of the 23rd Annual ACM Symposium on User Interface Software and Technology, UIST 2010, pp. 13–16. ACM, New York (2010)

20. Stajano, F., Anderson, R.J.: The Resurrecting Duckling: Security Issues for Ad-Hoc Wireless Networks. In: Malcolm, J.A., Christianson, B., Crispo, B., Roe, M. (eds.) Security Protocols. LNCS, vol. 1796, pp. 172–182. Springer, Heidelberg (2000)

21. Tang, J.C., Lin, J., Pierce, J., Whittaker, S., Drews, C.: Recent shortcuts: using recent interactions to support shared activities. In: Proceedings of the SIGCHI Conference on Human Factors in Computing Systems, CHI 2007, pp. 1263–1272. ACM, New York (2007)

22. Bump Technologies, http://bu.mp

23. Uzun, E., Karvonen, K., Asokan, N.: Usability analysis of secure pairing methods. Technical report. In Usable Security, USEC (2007)

24. Want, R., Fishkin, K.P., Gujar, A., Harrison, B.L.: Bridging physical and virtual worlds with electronic tags (1999)

25. Weiser, M.: The computer for the 21st century. Scientific American 265(3), 66–75 (1991)

26. Wilson, A.D., Sarin, R.: Bluetable: connecting wireless mobile devices on interactive surfaces using vision-based handshaking. In: Proceedings of Graphics Interface, GI 2007, pp. 119–125. ACM, New York (2007)

Architecture and Evaluation of a User-Centric NFC-Enabled Ticketing System for Small Events*

Serge Chaumette[1], Damien Dubernet[1], Jonathan Ouoba[1],
Erkki Siira[2], and Tuomo Tuikka[2]

[1] LaBRI, University of Bordeaux, France
{serge.chaumette,damien.dubernet,jonathan.ouoba}@labri.fr
[2] VTT, Finland
{erkki.siira,tuomo.tuikka}@vtt.fi

Abstract. Small events are events with a limited number of attendees and limited financial means for the organizers. They represent an uncovered niche in the e-ticketing field. Our contribution, which is mainly practical, consists in proposing a solution to address this issue. We introduce an offline approach that uses Near Field Communication-enabled (NFC-enabled) mobile phones in a e-ticketing system dedicated to the management of these small events. In other words, we present an architecture which does not make use of an Internet connection during the ticket validation phase and that requires no infrastructure. Based on this architecture, we evaluate a prototype that we developed in terms of user experience, security, economical aspects and speed of use in order to show its relevance. Starting from a scenario with four use cases, we focus on the *ticket issuance* and the *ticket presentation* phases.

Keywords: Small Events, E-Ticketing, NFC, Mobile Phone, Peer-to-Peer.

1 Introduction

1.1 NFC Presentation

NFC (Near Field Communication) is an emerging technology that takes its roots in Radio Frequency Identification (RFID). It is a wireless communication tool that offers a range of about 10 centimeters. One of the most important driver for NFC is the mobile phone industry, many notable manufacturers integrating it within their devices [3] [4]. NFC offers three modes of operation: reader/writer, peer-to-peer and card emulation. The reader/writer mode makes it possible for NFC devices to interact with passive NFC tags ; the peer-to-peer (P2P) mode supports direct communication between NFC devices ; the card emulation mode allows a NFC device to act as if it were a smart card.

---

* This work is funded by the Smart Urban Spaces [1] (SUS) ITEA2 [2] project.

J.Y. Zhang et al. (Eds.): MobiCASE 2011, LNICST 95, pp. 137–151, 2012.
© Institute for Computer Sciences, Social Informatics and Telecommunications Engineering 2012

NFC devices offer support for an embedded smart card chip that is called a secure element [5]. In this mode the data (application, information to transfer, etc.) is stored in the secure element. Most of the time, with NFC-enabled mobile phones, the procedures to store data in the secure element and to update them are delegated to an external infrastructure named the Trusted Service Manager (TSM). The TSM is the entity which manages the loading, deletion and personalization of applications on the secure element of a mobile phone through a mobile operator network. Therefore the management of applications stored in a secure element can be complex to operate (especially for small structures).

The most advanced peer-to-peer communication protocol for NFC is LLCP (Logical Link Control Protocol) which makes asynchronous communication between devices possible. Peer-to-peer communication is always between two peers and multicast is not possible. Communication between devices is not secured by LLCP, but security may be achieved by other layer protocols [6].

NFC has found a domain of application in the transport area as public operators within cities are very keen on deploying NFC-based systems [7]. The deployment of NFC-based systems increases the possible passengers flow and reduces the wear of the smart cards as there is only need to touch the reader to validate a ticket. Therefore, one of the first implementations of NFC based ticketing appeared in public transportation systems being furthermore given that there is an existing infrastructure for smart card based ticketing. For example RMV, the local Frankfurt (Germany) public transportation company, has implemented a NFC transport ticketing pilot [7] using the card emulation mode. The domain of events, especially for e-ticketing management, is also more and more concerned by the NFC technology.

1.2   E-Ticketing

The use of electronic tickets (e-tickets) has become more and more common. In the event management field, ticketing has gone electronic in some stages of the chain. Generally, it reduces the costs for the service provider while accelerating the tickets issuance and validation processes. In some cases, it also improves the overall system security. From the user point of view, e-tickets are more convenient to use than standard paper tickets.

Event ticketing is a big industry [8] [9] concentrated in the hands of just a few players. Consequently, only large events, those that generate the most revenues, can use the service of ticketing companies, which charge significant fees.

The emergence of NFC associated with the use of mobile devices offers new opportunities in the e-ticketing field. As customers begin to use ticketing with NFC in public transportation, the event ticketing must aim at becoming compatible with NFC [10] because of all the advantages it brings in terms of user experience (quick and easy validation of tickets). With the release of new smartphones endowed with NFC, it is evident that big players are ready (if it is not already done) to make necessary investments in terms of infrastructures in this business sector. However, in this rising ecosystem, the small events organizers, with their limited financial means, are a little deprived in front of the costs of such investments.

1.3   Small Events Concepts

We have interviewed representatives of two major Finnish cities about categorization of events. Due to the lack of official categorization within the cultural domain, an internal size based categorization was defined where small events were up to 500 participants, medium sized events 500-3000 participants and big events over 3000. For cities the most natural way to categorize events was by the nature of their organizer. Public-owned and non-profit organizations are treated differently than commercial organizations. One of the cities questioned event organizers. The biggest complaint was that ticketing is too expensive to arrange when the amount of tickets to be sold is small. The fees of nationwide ticketing companies are scaled to be in line with events of high cost tickets, like stadium-size concerts. Consequently, another pragmatic approach in the events categorization was to consider the financial means: if an event does not have the ability to use the service of ticketing companies, then it is considered a small event.

Events organizers mentioned other problems. As they support diversified point of sales, it is difficult to monitor the sells as a whole. Moreover, they wanted to have the capability to contact the ticket buyers. A direct channel for promoting and possibly informing buyers about changes in the event was identified as one of the most desired features. It is then evident that small structures need an adapted lightweight solution to manage an event ticketing system.

1.4   Contributions

The NFC Forum, as a consortium of different stakeholders in the field of NFC technology, believes that the cost of providing event ticketing systems, in terms of card issuance and management, can be driven down by using NFC-based systems [11]. The need of moving the e-ticketing systems for events to the NFC-enabled mobile devices field is evident [12] and we believe that it is relevant to build a lightweight system to manage a NFC-enabled event ticketing system with mobile phones. This system aims at setting up an affordable solution that lowers the costs of e-ticketing particularly for the small events organizers. There is also a need for evaluating such a system to present its pros and cons, and also to show its relevance for small events organizers. Therefore, in this paper, we propose a description of a solution that requires no Internet connection at the ticket validation step (offline approach), present the implemented prototype and evaluate it in terms of security, speed of use, user experience and economical aspect. As a starting point, we lean on a four-phase event ticketing scenario and focus on the ticket issuance and the ticket validation processes which are key points in most e-ticketing architectures.

In this paper we focus on three main points: the presentation of the architecture we designed ; the description of the novel application (a combination of some state-of-the-practice technologies) derived from the architecture ; the analysis of the solution on real mobile devices to validate its efficiency and to point out the field deployment issues.

This study is part of the work on the Event ticketing with NFC-enabled mobile phones that takes place in the framework of the Smart Urban Spaces (SUS) project. It brings a preliminary solution to the problem of building an e-ticketing system dedicated to small events. In this context VTT (the Technical Research Centre of Finland) and the LaBRI (the Computer Science Research Laboratory of Bordeaux, France) are collaborating to achieve a better definition and deployment of this new service.

2   NFC-Enabled Event e-Ticketing

2.1   General Overview

For simplicity concerns, the terms 'ticket' and 'e-ticket' are used interchangeably in the rest of this paper.

A e-ticketing system can be described as a token-based authentication platform that involves 3 main entities : an Issuer, a User, and a Verifier [13]. Figure 1 presents the commonly used architecture. A NFC-enabled e-ticketing system using mobile devices will follow the same approach. The e-ticket represents the token which circulates between the different entities and can be defined as a collection of data items that gathers various information for a particular event. The data contained in the ticket can be divided in three main parts: the ticket ID, the event ID and the ticket details (price, seat number, date, time, type of ticket, etc.). Most of the time the ticket ID and the event ID are mandatory fields. The ticket details are optional and highly depend on the type of event. For instance, the type of ticket can allow to make a distinction between single tickets, serial tickets, season tickets or discount tickets for example. Event e-tickets can also contain a digital signature generated by the ticket issuer so that their authenticity can be verified (figure 2).

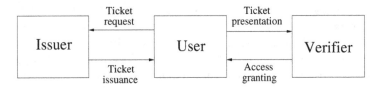

Fig. 1. Common e-ticketing architecture

Ticket ID	Event ID	Ticket info
Signature		

Fig. 2. E-ticket data model

2.2   Existing Solutions

There are many companies that work in the field of e-ticketing but the number of e-ticketing initiatives that rely on the use of NFC is very limited. Furthermore, these initiatives, although demonstrating the added value of NFC in ticketing services, either need significant infrastructure deployment at the event site or are not mobile phone oriented.

An interesting solution is the Tapango system [14] which is an electronic voucher system based on NFC smart cards used as e-Wallets. The system aims at reducing the use of paper tickets and was implemented by the Artesis´ research lab. With Tapango, the users first buy tickets via a web interface, then at the event location they synchronize their e-Wallet (by introducing their card in a reader connected to the Internet) to 'physically' acquire the tickets and finally they present the NFC card at the entrance of the event to get access. The use of NFC-enabled mobile devices is presented as a step to come in the evolution of the system. In the SmartTouch project [15], a pilot related to event ticketing in the theater of the city of Oulu (Finland) was deployed [16]. The users were able to receive tickets on their NFC-enabled phones via a specific equipment in a point of sale at the theater. The control of the tickets was achieved using another NFC-enabled mobile phone. Despite the fact that the ticket validation was relatively slow (using the peer-to-peer NFC mode) because of the phone brand, the users showed a real interest.

2.3   Need of Small Event System and Requirements

From the previous section, we can conclude that the existing solutions require the deployment of specific pieces of equipments or a steady Internet connection at the event entrance what leads to big investments (and thus only make sense for big events). Consequently, there is a lack of suitable proposition that could meet small event organizers needs and requirements. As mentioned in the introduction, the reason for using NFC is to facilitate all the event ticketing processes. It is then a question of defining a system which is flexible enough to be adapted to different types of events while answering the e-ticketing constraints in the specific context of small events. Such an approach has its limitations and benefits we want to identify. The designed system must as much as possible reduce the deployment costs (at the event location and for the tickets issuance) and rely on the assumption (which is a futuristic view for the moment) that the attendees own a NFC-enabled phone. Furthermore, the system must offer the possibility to monitor the level of sales and to send (when necessary) updated information concerning the events to the customers.

3   Presentation of the Solution

3.1   Scenario, Use Cases and Architecture

Assume that Adam wants to go to a private rock concert. He starts the application on his mobile handset which connects to the events portal where he has an account linked to his email address. From the portal, he receives a list of proposals by querying for available tickets in the rock shows category. He previews a multimedia presentation of the events he could be interested in before deciding rather to buy a ticket or not. Once he has made a decision, he selects the proper concert and enters the payment details and validates the transaction. When the payment is done, he can then download the ticket which is stored in his phone. In the case information related to the show is updated, Adam is informed via email box. The day of the show, he goes to the venue and at the entrance he presents the corresponding ticket by taping his phone on another NFC-enabled mobile handset (operated by the person responsible for the tickets validation). The ticket is transferred to the validator handset where its validity is checked by mean of a mobile application. Finally Adam is granted access to the concert. From the previous scenario four use cases can be identified: selection of an event, event description visualization, event tickets issuance, and ticket validation at the event site. These cases (see figure 3) represent the steps to follow in our solution to attend an event using a mobile phone. It is to be noted that the system follows an offline approach the concept of which was presented in Suikkanen and Reddmann work [17] ; it means that the validation phase is achieved without the use of an Internet connection (thus eliminating the need of an infrastructure at the event site). Moreover, as presented by the scenario, the system only targets single events.

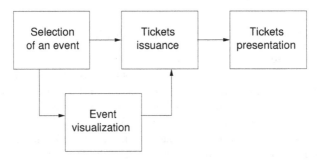

Fig. 3. Small event ticketing scenario with use cases

It is important to mention we assume that the events organizers have at their disposal a web interface where they can enter all the relevant details about their events (show description, payment options, etc.) so that it can be published. This interface also has to allow them to monitor the tickets that have been sold and to send updated information about their events.

The involved entities and their interactions as well as the processes we want to focus on are presented figure 4 and described in more details in subsection 3.2.

3.2   Processes Description

Issuance Process. The interactions during the issuance process (figure 5) involve two entities: the Client Application and the Events Portal.

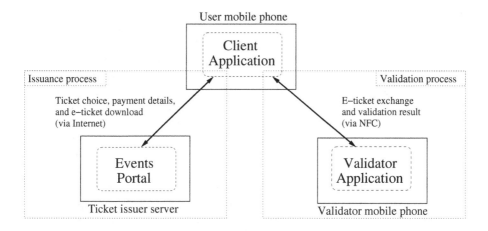

Fig. 4. Small event ticketing system architecture

The Events Portal can take the shape of a website and must present the list of events, allow the selection of the chosen event and support payment. The Events Portal is also responsible for generating the digital ticket, once the payment is done, by gathering the different pieces of information (at least the ticket ID and the event ID) and formatting them properly. Additionally, a signature with a private key must be applied to the ticket, so that its integrity can be checked at the event venue, the corresponding public key being provided to the Validator Application. A specific public/private key pair corresponds to one event. Once the ticket has been built, a link to download it must be provided. The Events Portal must also be linked to an online payment platform to ensure the security of the purchase (if the event is not free).

Concerning the Client Application, it connects to the Events Portal by Internet and displays its interface. Users can then buy a ticket and, when the purchase is validated, the digital ticket is stored by the application in the phone memory. They are other storage locations for the ticket, for instance in a secure element of the mobile phone, but that would require an infrastructure (with the use of a TSM). It would thus not meet some of the small event organizers needs.

Validation Process. The validation process (figure 6) involves two entities: the Client Application and the Validator Application.

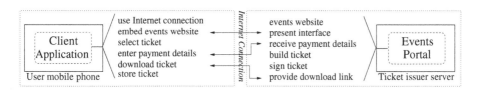

Fig. 5. Issuance process entities

First, the Validator Application must be able to receive data (a signed digital ticket in our case) sent from another mobile phone via an NFC connection. Moreover, it has to contain the mechanisms to check the signature of a ticket (using a public key) to make sure of its integrity and validity. The procedure is made possible by the fact that the Validator Application is provided, beforehand, with the public key (the corresponding private key being used to sign the event tickets). This can be done, prior to the day of the control, by connecting to a secure web interface part of the Events Portal or the Events Portal can simply send the key via SMS to the Validator Application. Finally, to avoid re-use of a ticket, a system to keep track of the presented tickets must be part of the Validator Application.

Concerning the Client Application, it allows the user to list the ticket he bought and to select the ticket he wishes to present at an event gate. The Client Application also manages the direct communication by mean of a NFC connection of the mobile phone with the validator mobile handset. This is made possible because the digital ticket is not stored in a secure element. Beforehand, the digital ticket is properly formatted so it can be easily sent to the validator device.

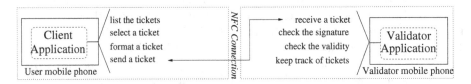

Fig. 6. Validation process entities

3.3 Technological and Equipment Choice

Our system requires, for the client and the validator, the use of NFC-enabled mobile phones that support NFC peer-to-peer mode (for direct communication between the phones). The client mobile phone must also be able to connect to Internet to download the purchased tickets. Android which is one of the major platform at the moment is supported by phones that correspond to the required specifications. We then decided to target Android which offers NFC APIs (in its 2.3.4 version) and provides a support (even though limited) for NFC peer-to-peer mode. A first lightweight prototype has been developed to analyze and to validate some aspects of the proposed architecture for a small event NFC-enabled e-ticketing system.

4 Prototype Description

4.1 Overview

As can be seen figure 7, the prototype we developed is composed of three main application blocks. The client application allows the end-user to download tickets

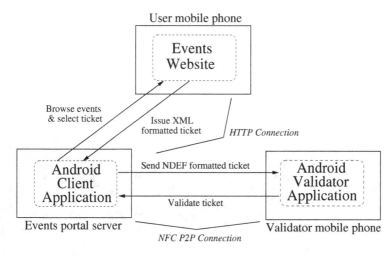

Fig. 7. Prototype Architecture

on his handset and to present them at the event entrance. The issuer application is responsible for presenting future events and issuing valid tickets. Finally, the validator application verifies the presented tickets and grants users access to the event. The mobile used for the development of this prototype is Samsung Nexus S. In this prototype, a ticket consists of a XML file that contains information about the event (ticket ID, event name, event location, etc).

4.2   Client Application

The client application provides a user-friendly interface that allows the user to easily interact with the ticket issuer (figure 8): this means browsing through a list of events as well as downloading tickets to the mobile handset. Additionally, the application offers a ticket management interface with simple actions (i.e view the ticket details, remove it or send it via NFC peer-to-peer mode to another device). Note that for the time being, the Nexus S only supports a limited version of the NFC peer-to-peer mode. It is not possible to establish a connection and have a bidirectional communication channel between two handsets. Instead, one device creates a virtual tag and behaves as a passive target allowing the second device to read it just like any other tag. Consequently, in our prototype, the ticket is embedded in a NDEF formatted message in order to be sent to the validator application. NDEF stands for NFC Data Exchange Format and is the standard format for exchanging data between a NFC handset and a NFC tag [18].

4.3   Issuer Application

In our prototype, the ticket issuer is essentially implemented through a website. It exposes a static list of events and allows client applications to download tickets through a HTTP connection. At the moment, no ticket payment platform, database or secure connection (HTTPS) is integrated.

4.4 Validator Application

The validator application retrieves the ticket from a client application through a NFC peer-to-peer link and verifies its validity. It offers a basic interface as shown in figure 8. Upon successful verification the visitor is granted access to the event. For efficiency purpose and to enhance the user experience it is essential for the validation to be performed as quickly as possible.

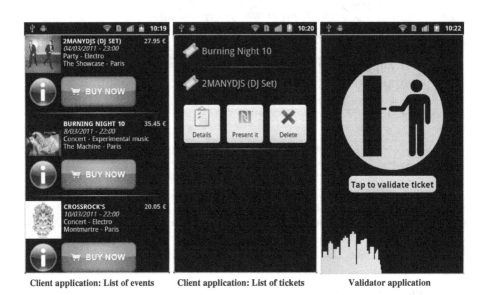

Client application: List of events   Client application: List of tickets   Validator application

Fig. 8. Prototype Screenshots

5   Tests and Evaluation of the Solution

5.1   Security

In this section, we discuss the security of our approach. It is clear that this will require (see section 6) further investigation including a formal validation.

During the issuance process the security mechanisms deployed to secure the payment procedure (which we will later integrate) and the e-ticket download are the usual ones [19] . The security analysis described thus targets the validation phase. To achieve this verification, the user taps his phone on the validator phone and a direct communication between the two devices is established.

The security of the proposed e-ticketing system mainly relies on the e-ticket signature, the recording of the tickets presented at the entrance and the trust granted to the person responsible for the validation (which must be easily recognizable as a member of the organization team, see the relay attack below). To summarize, these elements make it possible to ensure that only valid tickets can pass the validation (forgery prevention), that two identical tickets cannot be used to get access to the same event and that the validation is performed with an authorized phone. Since our approach makes use of the NFC peer-to-peer mode, the question of security is directly related to this technology. The NFC threat model contains some attack scenario such as eavesdropping, man-in-the-middle, relay, skimming, data corruption or phishing [20] [21]. All these scenarios are not to be taken into account in our context.

The phishing attack for instance, most of the time, concerns NFC tags reading systems [20] and the man-in-the-middle attack is really difficult to set up in a real NFC-based environment [21]. Concerning the relay threat, it was demonstrated that it is feasible [22]. In this kind of attack, the exchanges between two authorized entities are relayed so each entity believes it communicates with the other one. However, in our context it is the user who initiates the validation and he necessarily stands next to the person (easily recognizable as an authorized person) manipulating the validator handset. This type of attack is thus impossible. For the eavesdropping threat, we can also consider that if a user selects too early the e-ticket to be validated and then makes it ready to be transferred (using the NFC peer-to-peer mode), an attacker with the appropriate equipment could retrieve the ticket information by capturing the data to be transmitted [23]. This threat can be reduced by making sure to be in front of the validator before selecting the ticket to be presented. It will obviously increase the waiting time at the entrance, which can be a system limitation. We can also consider that the attacker can eavesdrop the transmitted data when the user taps his phone on the validator phone. However, it will be useless because an e-ticket can only be validated once since the system keeps the id of the tickets.

Another point is that the ticket is stored in the phone memory (and not in a secure element) which allows for more flexibility since the user can easily manage the tickets (i.e send it to another device, erase it, etc). A drawback is that a ticket can be duplicated. However, a validator will spot duplicate tickets and only grant access the first time the ticket is presented. This requires that one single validator is used which is most often the case for small events.

Globally, the balance between the equipment needed to perform some of the listed attacks (a passive antenna connected to an oscilloscope for instance in the eavesdropping scenario or more specialized equipment [24]) and the cost of a ticket for small events pleads in favor of a reduced number of real threats. Also, according to the properties of the NFC technology (among which very short-range communications), associated with the listing of presented tickets, the fact that the tickets are signed and the collaboration of the users, the confidentiality and the authenticity can be ensured. Some improvements are possible, for instance to perform a mutual authentication between the involved entities during the validation process to make sure of the identity of the person who presents the e-ticket, or even to better preserve confidentiality (as it is possible to eavesdrop the data transmission). Still, compromises have to be done between improvement of the system which could require the deployment of an infrastructure and the small events objective among which simplicity of deployment.

Even if the system can be enhanced, it nevertheless offers reasonable security level for small events in a lightweight system (which is the main requirement).

5.2   Validation Speed

In many e-ticketing systems, speed of validation is a crucial point. For instance Transport for London expects the validation time of an Oyster card not to exceed 500 milliseconds [25], otherwise the user experience would not be smooth and the flow of passengers would be slowed down at busy stations. In a ticketing system for small events the user flow is significantly less important but we still consider fast validation to be an important requirement. In our case, the validation time is measured, for technical feasibility reasons, from the moment the peer-to-peer target (the virtual tag) is discovered until the ticket signature is verified. With the current Android API we have reached a validation time of 400 milliseconds. The size of the ticket which is used is relatively small, it only encloses the ticket ID, the event ID and a 1024 bits digital signature. Larger tickets (i.e. tickets containing more details about the event) are longer to transfer and will thus increase the validation time. In some cases, we noticed that the Android handsets take more time than usual to establish a peer-to-peer connection bringing the validation time to more than 1 second. The reason for that delay is still to be explored.

5.3   User Experience

The use of a completely paperless NFC-enabled e-ticketing system enhances the overall user experience as demonstrated by the work of Ghiron, Sposato, Medaglia and Moroni [26] (even if it was in the transportation domain). The *Virtual Ticketing application* they developed and tested was a prototype where virtual tickets are stored in a secure element embedded within a mobile equipment. In a general way, by purchasing tickets online, the users avoid queuing at specific points of sale. Furthermore, the tickets do not need to be printed and, on top of that, the validation is done by simply taping a phone on a reader.

One of the main drawbacks of our system is that the user must select among his tickets the one he wishes to present, what can slightly reduce user-friendliness. Indeed, the way the NFC peer-to-peer mode works in the Android APIs (a virtual tag must be generated as described in 4.2) leads us to implement a solution where the user chooses in his list of tickets the one to be validated so the right ticket can be verified during the validation phase.

To get more relevant feedback for the user experience analysis (particularly for the client application), we performed basic tests with 15 persons (through a questionnaire to attribute a note on 100) with the 10-items of the system usability scale by John Brooke [27]. This system, which is meant to evaluate the usability of a system from a user point of view, has been proven valuable and robust [28] and is used by some companies member of the Smart Urban Spaces consortium. The testers were also able to make comments at the end of each test which was monitored by a member of our group. The sample of 15 people gathers men and women between 20 and 30 years old with various professional background (computer science oriented or not). We proposed a simple two-points scenario to the testers: we suppose that you need to buy two tickets for two different concerts, launch the application and try to buy the tickets ; we suppose now that we are the day of one the concerts, try to select one of the tickets you bought and to present it for validation (by taping the phone on the validator phone). By taking into account the questionnaire of each user, we obtained an average of 77 out of 100. This result provides a first idea of the potential of the application, and we received many remarks regarding the user interface. Another considerable point is that most of the people were not used to the way to tap the phone on the validator phone.

Despite the fact that many improvements can be brought to the user interface of the client application, the test results allow us to say that the user experience reaches an acceptable level.

5.4   Economical Aspects

The relevance of the proposed model can be analyzed through its underlying business model. In the SUS project, a model for the management of e-ticketing systems has emerged. The goal of the SUS consortium is to implement service prototypes that could ease the everyday life of citizens. In this context, the cities will most likely be keen to design, develop and maintain, with the help of external resources (like specialized companies), a platform for small events organizers such as the Events Portal described in our solution. The events organizers will be able to subscribe to the platform (to publish the details of their event and launch the sale) and the cities will sign the necessary agreements with them regarding the income generated by the purchase of the tickets. In the case a city has a special culture promotion policy, the platform can also be used to allow free tickets download. Obviously this business model, although viable, is strongly connected to the policy of cities in terms of ICT and to their associated investments.

6   Future Work

We will, within the framework of the Smart Urban Spaces European project, deploy pilots targeting small events (such as private concerts or small art exhibitions) in collaboration with the cities that are members of the consortium. These cities wish to set up a flexible and cheap ticketing system as the organizers of this kind of events cannot afford the deployment of expensive equipments. At the moment, some French and Finnish cities are potential candidate.

Another step in our work will be to study the scalability of the presented system (to manage larger events) and to enhance its security level by improving the countermeasures against possible attacks (for instance for a Denial of Service). Another step in our research is to focus on a e-ticket standard description completely dedicated to events and the associated storage procedures inside mobile phones. As far as we know, there is no event e-ticket standard and it would thus be relevant to make contributions in this area. Another point will be to work on interoperability.

7 Conclusion

In this paper we have presented a NFC-enabled approach to deal with e-ticketing issues in the context of small events. Starting from a definition of the concept of small event, the relevance of such a system has been shown and a business model with the involvement of the authorities of cities has been described. Even if some more points need to be discussed and defined, the prototype that we have developed demonstrates the feasibility of the proposed solution. The evaluation that we have conducted shows that it offers a reasonable level of performance. The pilot phase, which will be developed in cooperation with the interested cities, will allow to obtain more indications to improve the system and prepare a real large scale deployment.

Acknowledgement. The work presented here is carried out within the framework of Smart Urban Spaces, an ITEA2 European project, the goal of which is to define new e-services for cities. The proposed services mainly take advantage of specific technologies, in particular NFC, in order to ease the everyday life of European citizens. Several use cases are concerned for instance daycare organization, transportation or cultural events management. We would like to thank all the partners of the Smart Urban Spaces project with whom we have been working and we have discussed the topics described in this paper.

References

1. Smart urban spaces website (July 2011), http://www.smarturbanspaces.org
2. Itea2 website (September 2010), http://www.itea2.org/
3. Android 2.3.3 platform (February 2011),
   http://android-developers.blogspot.com/2011/02/
   android-233-platform-new-nfc.html
4. Samsung galaxy s ii (March 2011),
   http://www.samsung.com/global/microsite/galaxys2/html/feature.html
5. Reveilhac, M., Pasquet, M.: Promising secure element alternatives for NFC technology. In: Proceedings of the 2009 First International Workshop on Near Field Communication, Hagenberg, Austria, pp. 75–80 (2009)
6. Logical link control protocol, NFC Forum, Tech. Rep. technical specification 1.0 (December 2010)
7. Preuss, P., Reddmann, D., Weigt, F.: RMV-HandyTicket für NFC-Handys. In: Tuikka, T., Isomursu, M. (eds.) Touch the Future with a Smart Touch, Espoo, Finland, no. 2492 - Research notes, pp. 89–90 (2009)
8. Livenation financial reports: 2008 annual report (September 2010),
   http://phx.corporate-ir.net/External.File?
   item=UGFyZW50SUQ9OTYxMHxDaG1sZElEPS0xfFR5cGU9Mw==&t=1
9. Mpaa 2009 theatrical market statistics (September 2010),
   http://www.mpaa.org/Resources/091af5d6-faf7-4f58-9a8e-405466c1c5e5.pdf
10. M-ticketing whitepaper, GSMA, Tech. Rep. version 1.0 (February 2011)
11. The keys to truly interoperable communications, NFC Forum, Tech. Rep. (2007)

12. Near field communication in the real world - turning the NFC promise into profitable, everyday applications, Innovision Research and Technology, Tech. Rep. (2007)

13. Sadeghi, A.-R., Visconti, I., Wachsmann, C.: User privacy in transport systems based on RFID e-tickets. In: PiLBA (2008)

14. Neefs, J., Schrooyen, F., Doggen, J., Renckens, K.: Paper ticketing vs. electronic ticketing based on off-line system 'tapango'. In: Proceedings of the 2010 Second International Workshop on Near Field Communication, Monaco, pp. 3–8 (2010)

15. Smarttouch (February 2011),
    http://ttuki.vtt.fi/smarttouch/www/?info=intro

16. Rouru-Kuivala, O.: Vision: Touching the Future, Ticketing. In: Tuikka, T., Isomursu, M. (eds.) Touch the Future with a Smart Touch, Espoo, Finland, no. Research notes 2492, pp. 171–173 (2009)

17. Suikkanen, J., Reddmann, D.: Vision: Touching the Future, Ticketing. In: Tuikka, T., Isomursu, M. (eds.) Touch the Future with a Smart Touch, Espoo, Finland, no. 2492 - Research notes, pp. 233–235 (2009)

18. NFC data exchange format (NDEF), NFC Forum, Tech. Rep. technical specification 1.0 (July 2006)

19. Kraft, T.A., Kakar, R.: E-commerce security. In: Proceedings of the Conference on Information Systems Applied Research, Washington DC, USA (2009)

20. Madlmayr, G., Langer, J., Kantner, C., Scharinger, J.: NFC devices: Security and privacy. In: Proceedings of ARES (2008)

21. Haselsteiner, E., Breitfuss, K.: Security in Near Field Communication, NFC (2006)

22. Francis, L., Hancke, G., Mayes, K., Markantonakis, K.: Practical NFC Peer-to-Peer Relay Attack Using Mobile Phones. In: Ors Yalcin, S.B. (ed.) RFIDSec 2010. LNCS, vol. 6370, pp. 35–49. Springer, Heidelberg (2010)

23. Siitonen, K.H., Frode, M.S.: Eavesdropping near field communication. In: Proceedings of the 2nd Norwegian Security Conference, Trondheim, Norway, pp. 57–68 (2009)

24. Hancke, G.P.: Practical eavesdropping and skimming attacks on high-frequency RFID tokens. Journal of Computer Security 19(2), 259–288 (2011)

25. Transport for london (December 2010),
    http://www.nfctimes.com/news/transport-london-calls-faster-nfc-sims

26. Ghiron, S.L., Sposato, S., Medaglia, C.M., Moroni, A.: NFC ticketing: A prototype and usability test of an NFC-based virtual ticketing application. In: Proceedings of the 2009 First International Workshop on Near Field Communication, Hagenberg, Austria, pp. 45–50 (2009)

27. Brooke, J.: SUS: A quick and dirty usability scale. In: Usability Evaluation in Industry, London, England (1996)

28. Bangor, A., Kortum, P.T., Miller, J.T.: An empirical evaluation of the system usability scale. Int. J. Hum. Comput. Interaction, 574–594 (2008)

Decentralized Mobile Search and Retrieval Using SMS and HTTP to Support Social Change

Isaí Michel Lombera, Yung-Ting Chuang, L.E. Moser, and P.M. Melliar-Smith

Department of Electrical and Computer Engineering,
University of California, Santa Barbara,
Santa Barbara, CA 93106 USA
{imichel,ytchuang,moser,pmms}@ece.ucsb.edu

Abstract. Recent events have demonstrated the utility of mobile devices to coordinate mass gatherings and organize protests in support of social change and the cause of democracy. However, a common attack against the social networking abilities of mobile phone wielding protesters has been government action to censor centralized search and social networking sites. This paper describes a decentralized search and retrieval system, named iTrust, that provides greater resistance against the vulnerabilities inherent in centralized services. In particular, it describes the iTrust with SMS interface and the iTrust SMS-HTTP bridge, which enable any SMS-capable mobile phone to communicate with other nodes in the iTrust network. It also describes an Android mobile phone interface that builds on the basic SMS capabilities of a mobile phone and that offers a user-friendly way of accessing the iTrust with SMS implementation. Finally, the paper presents an evaluation of the iTrust search and retrieval system.

Keywords: decentralized search and retrieval, HTTP, iTrust, mobile search and retrieval, SMS.

1 Introduction

As mobile phones have become pervasive in day-to-day life, mobile applications have transcended from basic communication and entertainment services into enablers of societal and political transformation. Recently, social networks such as Twitter and Facebook, as well as search services such as Google and Bing, have been used to help coordinate mass uprisings and revolutions in the world. Unfortunately, centralized systems, whether controlled by a government or a business, are reliant on one or a few nodes that can be easily subverted or censored. If a service provider does not cooperate with such censoring entities, access to the service might be denied entirely. In Egypt and Syria, the Facebook group meeting service was used to help organize protest meeting places and times. In both countries, the government disabled the Internet to hinder the organization of those meetings.

J.Y. Zhang et al. (Eds.): MobiCASE 2011, LNICST 95, pp. 152–171, 2012.

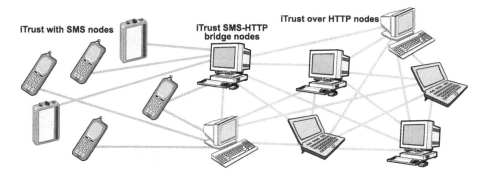

Fig. 1. The iTrust network, showing the iTrust with SMS nodes, the iTrust SMS-HTTP bridge nodes, and the iTrust over HTTP nodes

A decentralized search and retrieval system where multiple nodes, or peers, in the system share queries, metadata, and documents can better withstand temporary or sustained network blocking and shutdowns. Peers can re-route network traffic away from non-operational or non-responsive nodes and can, in some cases, fetch a document from one of several alternative sources.

The iTrust system is a distributed search and retrieval system that does not rely on a centralized search engine, such as Google, Yahoo! or Bing; thus, it is resistant to censorship by central administrators. Our previous implementation of iTrust is based on the HyperText Transfer Protocol (HTTP), and is most appropriate for desktop or laptop computers on the Internet. However, most participants in demonstrations probably use mobile phones to organize their activities. In many countries of the world, mobile phones are the only computing platform generally available; consequently, it is appropriate to provide the iTrust system on mobile phones.

Thus, we have extended the iTrust search and retrieval system based on HTTP, so that it does not rely only on the Internet but can also utilize the cellular telephony network. In particular, we have extended the iTrust system to allow users of mobile phones to connect to iTrust via the Short Message Service (SMS), so that they can benefit from the decentralized search and retrieval service that iTrust provides. Our objective is not to supplant HTTP but instead to have SMS work along side it, to increase accessibility during the dynamic environment of a demonstration or protest. Figure 1 illustrates the extended iTrust network.

In this paper, first we briefly describe the design of the iTrust search and retrieval system that uses HTTP over the Internet. Next, we describe the implementation of iTrust with SMS, focusing on the iTrust SMS-HTTP bridge that allows any hardware-capable iTrust over HTTP node to act as a relay of queries that originate from an SMS-capable mobile phone. We also describe how information is fetched and transmitted over the iTrust SMS-HTTP bridge to the querying mobile phone. This description is followed by a typical use case of iTrust with SMS by a mobile phone and also a description of a custom Android application that enables users to make queries and receive query results. Next, we present an evaluation of iTrust and, then, we present related work. Finally, we summarize our current work and discuss future work to create an even more robust iTrust network.

2   Mobile Search and SMS

Mobile search is fundamentally different from desktop search, due to the form factor, the limited bandwidth, and the battery life of the mobile device. Sohn *et al.* [1] address human factors in their study of mobile information needs.

In desktop search, users can use a simple search interface to enter keyword queries. The accuracy of the results is generally satisfactory if the desired results are within the first 10 URLs returned. If not, the user can interactively refine his/her queries in subsequent search rounds.

In mobile search, it is expensive and tedious for a user to explore even the two most relevant pages returned by a traditional centralized search engine. Moreover, in mobile search, the information sought tends to focus on narrower topics, and the queries often are shorter, *e.g.*, requests for phone numbers, addresses, times, directions, *etc.*

Kamvar *et al.* [2] have found that most mobile search users have a specific topic in mind, use the search service for a short period of time, and do not engage in exploration. In a subsequent study [3], they found that the diversity of search topics for low-end mobile phone searches is much less than that for desktop searches.

The Short Message Service (SMS) works on low-end mobile phones and is available worldwide. Global SMS traffic is expected to reach 8.7 trillion messages by 2015, up from 5 trillion messages in 2010 [4]. To quote Giselle Tsirulnik, senior editor at Mobile Commerce Daily, "SMS is cheap, it is reliable, it is universal, and it has unrivaled utility as a bearer for communications, information and services." In developing countries, SMS is the most ubiquitous protocol for information exchange after human voice.

In SMS-based search, the query and the response are limited to 140 bytes each. Moreover, the user has to specify a query and obtain a response in one round of search. An iTrust SMS request (query) consists of a list of keywords, which are typically less than 140 bytes. An iTrust SMS response simply returns the requested information if it is small (less than 140 bytes). If the requested information or document is larger, it is fragmented into multi-part SMS messages. Alternatively, the iTrust SMS response can return a URL, which is typically less than 140 bytes.

3   Design of iTrust

The iTrust search and retrieval system uses HTTP over the Internet and involves no centralized mechanisms and no centralized control. We refer to the nodes that participate in an iTrust network as the *participating nodes* or the *membership.* Multiple iTrust networks may exist at any point in time, and a node may participate in several different iTrust networks at the same time.

In an iTrust network, some nodes, the *source nodes*, produce information, and make that information available to other participating nodes. The source nodes produce metadata that describes their information, and distribute that metadata to a subset of participating nodes that are chosen at random, as shown in Figure 2. The metadata are distinct from the information that they describe, and include a list of keywords and the URL of the source of the information.

Other nodes, the *requesting nodes*, request and retrieve information. Such nodes generate requests (queries) that refer to the metadata, and distribute the requests to a subset of the participating nodes that are chosen at random, as shown in Figure 3.

The participating nodes compare the metadata in the requests that they receive with the metadata that they hold. If such a node finds a match, which we call an *encounter*, the matching node returns the URL of the associated information to the requesting node. The requesting node then uses the URL to retrieve the information from the source node, as shown in Figure 4.

Distribution of the metadata and the requests to relatively few nodes suffices to achieve a high probability that a match occurs. Moreover, the strategy is robust. Even if some of the randomly chosen nodes are subverted or non-operational, the probability of a match is high, as shown in Section 6. Moreover, it is not easy for a small group of nodes to subvert the iTrust mechanisms to censor, filter or subvert information.

4   Implementation of iTrust

The iTrust with SMS system enables any node (laptop, desktop, server) to act as a bridge between an SMS-capable mobile device and an iTrust over HTTP node. The only requirement for an iTrust with SMS node is having a hardware interface for receiving and transmitting SMS messages; a simple and inexpensive cellular modem suffices. Note that only a single hardware interface is required for sending and receiving SMS messages. (Not all iTrust nodes need to be SMS-capable.) The result is that an existing iTrust network can remain unchanged, only the iTrust SMS-HTTP bridge node must be software updated.

To explain the iTrust with SMS-HTTP bridge, we trace the path taken by an SMS request (query) message sent to the iTrust network and the path taken by an SMS response (result) message sent from the iTrust network.

Figure 5 provides a system block diagram that shows the communication path taken by SMS request and response messages. Specifically, it shows the three main components of the iTrust implementation with the SMS-HTTP bridge: the cellular network, an iTrust with SMS node, and an iTrust over HTTP node. The blocks (numbered threads or spools) show only the APIs relevant to the discussion of iTrust with SMS. Each block actually has many more APIs for the iTrust over HTTP implementation. Additionally, thread blocks are numbered to explain the examples. In a typical iTrust network, multiple threads can be running for each iTrust node.

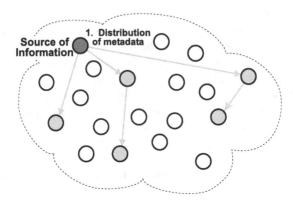

Fig. 2. A source node distributes metadata, describing its information, to randomly selected nodes in the network

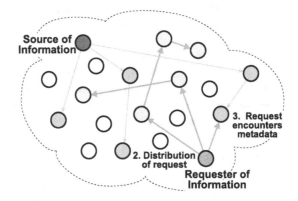

Fig. 3. A requesting node distributes its request to randomly selected nodes in the network. One of the nodes has both the metadata and the request and, thus, an encounter occurs.

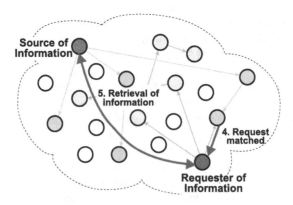

Fig. 4. A node matches the metadata and the request and reports the match to the requester, which then retrieves the information from the source node

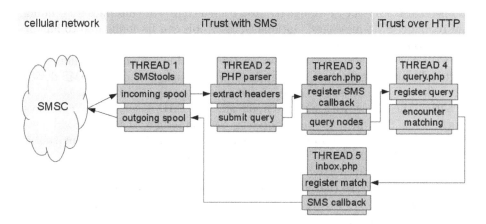

Fig. 5. The iTrust system block diagram showing the cellular network, the iTrust with SMS component, and the iTrust over HTTP component

4.1   Cellular Network

The cellular network, for the purposes of this discussion, is modeled simply by the Short Message Service Center (SMSC), which the mobile phone service providers use to relay SMS messages. In the next section, we expand the SMSC concept slightly to include mobile phones to enable presentation of the user interface for iTrust with SMS.

Briefly, the SMSC is a store-and-forward entity in the network of the mobile phone service provider. When a user sends an SMS message, the message is stored in the SMSC and, when possible, it is forwarded to the intended destination. If the destination is unavailable, the message is spooled for later transmission.

For the iTrust network, there is no distinction between a single SMSC or multiple SMSCs that handle SMS relaying. iTrust does not require any service provider agreements or integration with existing mobile networks; it simply uses a *cell phone number* like any mobile device seen by the SMSC.

4.2   iTrust with SMS

First and foremost, iTrust with SMS is an extension of the iTrust over HTTP implementation; SMS capabilities are added to the API and the iTrust HTTP implementation remains intact and operational. Thus, an iTrust with SMS node can interact with both an Internet node and a cellular network node. The iTrust SMS-HTTP bridge allows SMS-enabled mobile phones in the cellular network to interact with iTrust over HTTP nodes on the Internet.

In addition to the custom code written for the iTrust SMS-HTTP bridge, the open-source SMStools package is used to handle incoming and outgoing spooling of SMS messages. SMStools offers several advanced features that are easily leveraged by iTrust including SMS message formatting, header automation, and message validation.

The iTrust SMS-HTTP bridge requires a single hardware interface for sending and receiving SMS messages. Optionally, SMStools can be configured to handle multiple cellular modems from multiple cellular network providers and can spool the SMS messages accordingly. However, the typical iTrust configuration uses a single cellular modem to act as both the incoming and the outgoing SMS device and to have SMStools spool both incoming and outgoing SMS messages.

Within the iTrust with SMS component, THREAD 1 consists of SMStools which spools both incoming and outgoing SMS messages. Incoming SMS messages are registered with an event handler that triggers a command-line (*not* a Web server) PHP script in THREAD 2. Outgoing SMS messages are sent by writing a properly formatted plain text file and placing it in a specific SMStools monitored directory, so that an SMS response message is created and sent to the querying mobile device. Outgoing SMS messages are further explained below in the THREAD 5 functionality description.

The SMS message parser in THREAD 2 performs simple text processing to extract headers such as the sender's cell phone number and query. The extracted data are then packaged into an HTTP GET statement and submitted as a query to THREAD 3.

Particularly in THREAD 3, iTrust with SMS functionality is tightly integrated with existing iTrust over HTTP functionality; however, it remains distinct from pure iTrust over HTTP nodes. Along with query text and timestamp information, the sender's callback cell phone number is registered to enable results sent to the SMS-HTTP bridge node to be relayed back to the mobile phone. The bridge node then queries the nodes in the iTrust network as if the query originated directly from the bridge node (not as an SMS-relayed query). The cell phone number itself is not included in the query package; only the SMS-HTTP bridge node is aware of this cell phone number. Thus, the bridge node masquerades as an iTrust over HTTP node performing a routine search.

Nodes in the iTrust network execute the routines in THREAD 4 when queried for results. First, the query is registered so that any duplicate relayed queries are ignored and then an encounter (match), if any, causes a response message containing a result to be sent back to the querying node. THREAD 4 exhibits typical iTrust over HTTP behavior, no SMS information or awareness is required from a node running this thread.

The *SMS callback* routine in THREAD 3 is perhaps the most extensive part of the iTrust with SMS component. It has the dual function of pulling the source information and packaging that information appropriately before handing off the message to SMStools for spooling.

In THREAD 5, first, the resource is automatically fetched from the source node and temporarily stored on the bridge node for further processing. Second, the document (if it is less than 140 bytes) is formatted for SMS and the callback cell phone number of the original SMS querying user is added. Third, the message is written to an SMStools monitored directory, which further appends relevant message fields (*i.e.*, SMSC information, text formatting, *etc.*) before spooling the message for delivery (THREAD 1). Finally, the message is sent to the SMSC for delivery to the user's mobile device.

4.3   iTrust over HTTP

The iTrust over HTTP implementation runs on laptop, desktop or server nodes on the Internet and perhaps also on mobile phones on the Internet. There might be hundreds or thousands of iTrust over HTTP nodes in a typical iTrust network. The primary goal of each iTrust over HTTP node is to match a query it receives with a local resource and to respond with a URL for that resource, if an encounter or hit occurs. Each iTrust over HTTP node relays the query to its own membership list as specified by the local node administrator's preferences and/or load balancing services built into iTrust. The exact method of query relaying and load balancing is outside the scope of this paper. Only a few APIs related to encounters are discussed here.

When a query arrives at a node, the query is registered in THREAD 4 using the *register query* routine. If it has been seen previously, processing stops as repeating an old query is not useful. If the query is indeed new, the query text is compared against a database consisting of metadata and URLs of the corresponding resources in THREAD 4 using the *encounter matching* routine. If the query keywords match locally stored metadata, the node responds to the requesting node with the URL. Note that, in this case, the requesting node is the iTrust SMS-HTTP bridge node. It is *not* the SMS mobile phone node.

4.4   A Typical SMS Request/Response Path

A typical path along which SMS request and response messages travel from the mobile phone and back again is described below.

Sending the Request. A user sends an SMS request (query) message from his/her mobile phone with a simple text query. After being relayed by the SMSC, the SMS message enters the iTrust SMS-HTTP bridge node through a cellular hardware interface (such as a cellular modem) and is held in the incoming spool (THREAD 1). A new message in the incoming spool triggers an event handler (THREAD 2), which then loads a PHP script to process the spool and extract the user's cell phone number and text query. The cell phone number is registered for callback purposes (THREAD 3), and the query enters the iTrust network exactly as if it were originated by an iTrust over HTTP node. The query is relayed through the iTrust network until an encounter occurs (THREAD 4).

Receiving the Response. A response message is sent from an iTrust over HTTP node to the iTrust SMS-HTTP bridge node (THREAD 5). After normal processing by iTrust, the resource is fetched and placed in local storage. The locally stored resource (or a URL for the locally stored resource, if the resource is large) is further processed into an SMS message, placed into the outgoing spool, and relayed to the SMSC (THREAD 1). The user receives a new SMS message, sent from the iTrust SMS-HTTP bridge node.

4.5   API Function Call Swapping and Race Conditions

In Figure 5, in the iTrust with SMS component under THREAD 3, there are two APIs: *register SMS callback* and *query nodes*. The iTrust over HTTP nodes (where a *register SMS callback* is simply a register query callback) have the order of these two calls swapped for performance reasons. In practice, querying a node before registering the query leads to better performance in the Apache prefork model. This model inherently prevents the occurrence of a race condition, because the query is registered long before another node responds with a result. This behavior holds true particularly for threads numbering in the several thousands; however, in practice, even a self-query on a single node does not result in a race condition.

The iTrust SMS-HTTP bridge node has a stricter requirement. An iTrust with SMS node must *always* register the SMS callback cell phone number before querying another iTrust node. Otherwise, an iTrust node that is not SMS-capable might respond to a query before the callback cell phone number is registered. In this case, the particular response is not relayed to the mobile phone; future responses, that arrive after the SMS callback cell phone number has been registered, will be relayed.

Simply swapping the order to that shown in Figure 5 prevents a race condition from occurring.

5   iTrust with SMS User Interface

The addition of iTrust with SMS to iTrust over HTTP required not only an additional bridge mechanism on the iTrust nodes, but also a new interface to allow the mobile phone user to interact with the iTrust network. While iTrust over HTTP requires the use of a Web browser to search and retrieve documents, iTrust with SMS needs a more user-friendly mobile phone interface that conforms to the expectations of the user for a typical Instant Messaging (IM) service. For iTrust with SMS, we compare a generic SMS Instant Messaging interface with a custom-built Android interface for iTrust with SMS.

As an example, consider an ad hoc protest demonstration scheduling service that periodically distributes meeting locations and times to iTrust nodes. For each demonstration, there exists a file that includes basic information such as meeting location and time. A query from one iTrust node begins a search among other participating nodes in the iTrust network, and an encounter returns the demonstration named file that includes the meeting information. In particular, we consider the case that a user searches for demonstration information related to *Tahrir Square* in Cairo, Egypt.

5.1   iTrust with SMS Using the Generic IM Interface

The interface for iTrust with SMS is minimalistic in both function and use, compared to the Web interface for iTrust over HTTP. Requests (queries) are

Fig. 6. iTrust with SMS, using a generic Instant Messaging interface

simply SMS messages that are sent to the cell phone number of the iTrust SMS-HTTP bridge node; similarly, responses are SMS messages containing document data sent back to the user. There is no user hardware requirement apart from having an SMS-capable mobile phone; the SMS message may be sent to a dumb phone or a smart phone, with the user experience remaining consistent. Because the primary focus of a user of iTrust with SMS is simply to make a query, there is no interface for modifying the membership, adding resources, or configuring user parameters, as in the iTrust over HTTP Web interface.

Figure 6 shows an image of a typical iTrust with SMS interaction between a mobile user and an iTrust node. This particular screen shot uses the standard built-in SMS application bundled with Android (specifically, Android version 2.1); however, apart from aesthetics, the interaction is the same for iOS, webOS, Symbian, *etc.* Note that the only information required to interact with an iTrust node, apart from the query, is the cell phone number of the iTrust node (which is partially obscured). This particular Instant Messaging interface presents all SMS messages between the same callers in a single scrolling conversational type format. In this example, the display shows the user query *Tahrir Square* message sent to the iTrust node. A response message is sent back from the iTrust node to the user approximately one minute later (as shown in the last message); this result (or hit) is the data that correspond to the user's search keywords.

Note that the data itself are returned to the SMS user without reference to the URL, document file name, or address of the source node of the document. This

Fig. 7. iTrust with SMS, searching with the custom Android interface

presentation is consistent with the iTrust with SMS functionality, which requires that the SMS-HTTP bridge node itself must fetch the document, package it in an SMS-compatible format, and send back the SMS result. In contrast, the iTrust over HTTP interface simply presents a list of hits and does not fetch the document data automatically.

This simple and direct interaction makes it easy to carry on a conversation of sorts with the iTrust node by simply asking questions (submitting queries) and reading answers (hit data).

5.2   iTrust with SMS Using the Custom Android Interface

The custom Android application for interacting with an iTrust with SMS node is a hybrid of the generic SMS Instant Messaging interface and the iTrust over HTTP interface. Figures 7 and 8 show the submission of a query from the SMS-capable mobile phone and the returned result from the iTrust SMS-HTTP bridge node, respectively. The custom Android interface for iTrust over SMS enhances the generic SMS Instant Messaging interface in that it provides: familiarity for users accustomed to iTrust over HTTP, preset cell phone numbers to iTrust SMS-HTTP bridge nodes, and a framework for handling non-textual result data.

Figure 7 shows the entry of a query into a text editing area that is similar to that in the iTrust over HTTP search interface. Above the query is the pre-entered cell phone number of the iTrust SMS-HTTP bridge node. Although this

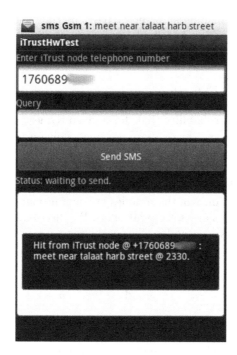

Fig. 8. iTrust with SMS, viewing a hit with the custom Android interface

is a minimal enhancement to the generic SMS interface, the rapid and transient nature of most SMS interactions favors features that reduce extraneous information not related to the SMS message itself. Additionally, once the query is sent, the query text area is cleared, so that the user can easily begin entry of another search query.

Figure 8 shows the result data returned from the iTrust SMS-HTTP bridge node; the result is the same as that for the generic SMS interface result. The resultant data are displayed in text format; however, alternate formats can be handled by the built-in framework. For example, a Portable Document Format (PDF) file sent over SMS would be *offloaded* or *handed off* to Android presumably to be opened by a PDF reader application available on the mobile phone. In this case, the user would be responsible for having access to a separate reader application appropriate to the file type. The iTrust system searches and retrieves all files, regardless of format (so long as the metadata are properly generated); however, the user is responsible for appropriate decoding.

6   Evaluation of iTrust

To evaluate iTrust, we consider the probability of a match, and also the number of messages required to achieve a match, using both analysis and simulation based on our implementation of iTrust. We assume that all of the participating nodes have the same membership set of participating nodes. In addition, we assume that communication is reliable and that all of the participating nodes have enough memory to store the source files and the metadata.

6.1 Probability of a Match

First, we consider the probability that, for a given request, a match (encounter) occurs, *i.e.*, that there are one or more nodes at which a match occurs for that request.

Analysis. We consider an iTrust network with a membership of n participating nodes, where a proportion x of the n nodes are operational (and, thus, a proportion $1 - x$ of the n nodes are not operational). We distribute the metadata to m nodes and the requests to r nodes. The probability p that a node has a match is given by:

$$p = 1 - \left(\frac{n - mx}{n} \frac{n - 1 - mx}{n - 1} \cdots \frac{n - r + 1 - mx}{n - r + 1} \right). \tag{1}$$

Equation (1) holds for $n \geq mx + r$. If $mx + r > n$, then $p = 1$.

Figures 9, 10 and 11 show the probability p of a match obtained from Equation (1) with $n = 250$ nodes where $x = 100\%$, 80% and 60% of the participating nodes are operational, respectively, as a function of $m = r$. As we see from the graphs, the probability p of a match increases, and approaches 1, as $m = r$ increases.

Simulation. Using our implementation of iTrust, we performed simulation experiments to validate the analytical results for the probability of a match obtained from Equation (1).

Before we run our simulation program, we delete all resources and data from the node. Next, the program adds the nodes to the membership. Once the nodes are added to the membership, we supply the number n of nodes for distribution of metadata and requests, and the proportion x of operational nodes, to the simulation program. Next, we call the source nodes to upload files and the program then creates the corresponding metadata. Then, the program randomly selects m nodes for metadata distribution and distributes the metadata to those nodes. Then, the program randomly selects r nodes for request distribution and distributes the requests to those nodes. If one or more nodes returns a response, there is a match and the simulation program returns 1; otherwise, there is no match and the simulation program returns 0.

We repeated the same process 100 times for the source nodes and correspondingly for the requesting nodes, and plot the mean results in our simulation graphs. We collected simulation data for 250 participating nodes when 100%, 80% and 60% of the nodes are operational.

Figures 9, 10 and 11 show the simulation results with 250 nodes where 100%, 80% and 60% of the participating nodes are operational, respectively, as a function of $m = r$. As we see from these graphs, the simulation results are very close

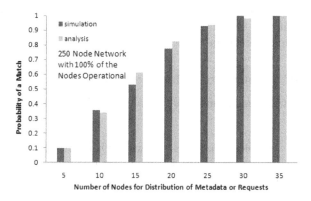

Fig. 9. Match probability vs. number of nodes for distribution of metadata or requests in a network with 250 nodes where 100% of the nodes are operational

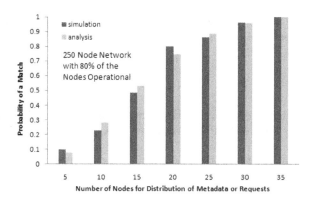

Fig. 10. Match probability vs. number of nodes for distribution of metadata or requests in a network with 250 nodes where 80% of the nodes are operational

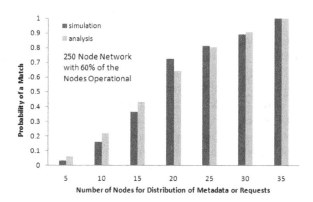

Fig. 11. Match probability vs. number of nodes for distribution of metadata or requests in a network with 250 nodes where 60% of the nodes are operational

to the analytical results calculated from Equation (1). As these results indicate, iTrust retains significant utility even in the case where a substantial proportion of the nodes are non-operational.

6.2   Number of Messages to Achieve a Match

Next, we consider the mean number of messages required to achieve a match for a given request.

Analysis. Again, we consider an iTrust network with a membership of n participating nodes, where the proportion of participating nodes that are operational is x. We distribute the metadata to m nodes and the requests to r nodes. The probability p of exactly k matches is given by:

$$p(k) = \frac{\left(\frac{mx}{k}\frac{mx-1}{k-1}\cdots\frac{mx-k+1}{1}\right)\left(\frac{n-mx}{r-k}\frac{n-mx-1}{r-k-1}\cdots\frac{n-mx-r+k+1}{1}\right)}{\left(\frac{n}{r}\frac{n-1}{r-1}\cdots\frac{n-r+1}{1}\right)}. \tag{2}$$

for $mx + r \leq n$ and $k \leq \min\{mx, r\}$.

The mean number y of messages required to achieve a match is given by:

$$y = 2 + r + \sum_{k=1}^{\min\{mx,r\}} kp(k). \tag{3}$$

The terms on the right side of Equation (3) represent: 1 request from the mobile phone to an iTrust SMS-HTTP bridge node, r requests from the iTrust SMS-HTTP bridge node to iTrust over HTTP nodes, k responses reporting matches from the iTrust over HTTP nodes to the iTrust SMS-HTTP bridge node, and 1 response from the iTrust SMS-HTTP bridge node to the mobile phone.

Figures 12, 13 and 14 show the number of messages obtained from Equations (2) and (3) with $n = 250$ nodes where $x = 100\%$, 80% and 60% of the participating nodes are operational, respectively, as a function of $m = r$. As we see from the graphs, the number of required messages increases as the probability p of a match increases (and as $m = r$ increases), but is bounded by $2 + 2r$.

Simulation. Using our implementation of iTrust, we performed simulation experiments to validate the analytical results for the mean number of messages to achieve a match obtained from Equations (2) and (3). The simulation experiments were performed as described previously in Section 6.1.

Figures 12, 13, and 14 show the simulation results with 250 nodes where 100%, 80% and 60% of the participating nodes are operational, respectively, as a function of $m = r$. As we see from these graphs, the simulation results are very close to the analytical results calculated from Equations (2) and (3).

Figures 9, 10 and 11 and Figures 12, 13 and 14 show the benefit-cost tradeoffs between the probability of achieving a match and the number of messages required to achieve a match. Note that the number of messages required to achieve a match is much greater than for centralized search engines, but is much less than for flooding strategies.

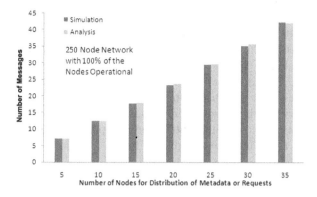

Fig. 12. Number of messages vs. number of nodes for distribution of metadata or requests in a network with 250 nodes where 100% of the nodes are operational

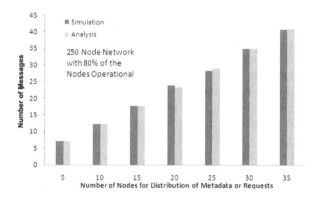

Fig. 13. Number of messages vs. number of nodes for distribution of metadata or requests in a network with 250 nodes where 80% of the nodes are operational

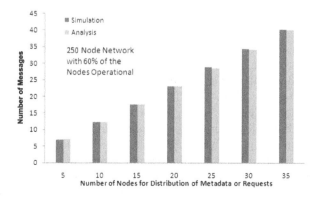

Fig. 14. Number of messages vs. number of nodes for distribution of metadata or requests in a network with 250 nodes where 60% of the nodes are operational

7 Related Work

Existing services for mobile Web search, including AOL Mobile [5], Google SMS [6], Windows Live Mobile [7] and Yahoo! OneSearch [8], are based on conventional centralized search engines. However, the results obtained from those systems are often not meaningful or not consistent for queries related to arbitrary topics. The reason is that they use a limited set of pre-defined topics, and either special keywords within the search query (*e.g.*, "directions" to obtain directions) or a specialized parser to determine the intended topic (*e.g.*, "INTC" for a stock quote). Moreover, the centralized search engines are subject to censorship, filtering and subversion.

Other mobile search systems, based on centralized search engines, have been developed. The SMSFind system [9,10] utilizes existing conventional centralized search engines at the back-end. SMSFind does not use pre-defined topics but, rather, allows the user to enter an explicit contextual hint about the search topic. SMSFind uses information retrieval techniques to extract an appropriate condensed 140-byte snippet as the final SMS search response, which iTrust does not do. The 7DS system [11] supports information sharing among peers that are not necessarily connected to the Internet. The 7DS system uses a multi-hop flooding algorithm together with multicasting of queries, which is not trustworthy. In contrast to these systems, iTrust does not use a centralized search engine and does *not* use flooding, which is too expensive in message cost.

Bender *et al.* [12] recognize the need for decentralized peer-to-peer Web search because "existing Web search is more or less exclusively under the control of centralized search engines." Mischke and Stiller [13], Risson and Moors [14], and Tsoumakos and Roussopoulos [15] provide comparisons of distributed search methods for peer-to-peer networks. The structured approach requires the nodes to be organized in an overlay network based on distributed hash tables (DHTs), trees, rings, *etc.*, which is efficient but is vulnerable to manipulation by untrustworthy administrators. The unstructured approach uses randomization, and requires the nodes to find each other by exchanging messages over existing links. The iTrust system uses the unstructured approach, which is less vulnerable to manipulation.

The distributed mobile search service of Lindemann and Waldhorst [16] broadcasts query results locally and forwards them over several hops. It is based on a passive distributed index that comprises, on each mobile device, a local index cache, containing keywords and corresponding document identifiers, where all received query results are cached. The iTrust system also maintains a distributed index, with metadata keywords and corresponding URLs stored on the iTrust nodes. However, iTrust distributes the metadata and the corresponding URLs first, rather than on receipt of the query results, which results in iTrust's having a lower message cost than their distributed mobile search service.

The Mobile Agent Peer-To-Peer (MAP2P) system [17] supports mobile devices in a Gnutella file-sharing network using mobile agents. The mobile agent (rather than the mobile device) attaches itself to the peer-to-peer network, and acts as a proxy for the mobile device. In some respects, the MAP2P mobile agent is similar to the iTrust SMS-HTTP bridge node, but iTrust has a lower message cost than Gnutella and, thus, MAP2P.

Systems for social networks exploit the trust that members have in each other, and route information and requests based on their relationships. Gummadi *et al.* [18] investigate the integration of social network search with Web search. They conclude that such integration can lead to more timely and efficient search experiences. Tiago *et al.* [19] describe a system for mobile search in social networks based on the Drupal content site management system. Their system is based on the network of social links formed from the mobile phone's address book. Yang *et al.* [20] propose a search mechanism for unstructured peer-to-peer networks based on interest groups, formed by nodes that share similar interests. iTrust likewise allows users interested in a particular topic or cause to form a social network, so that they can share information among themselves. Currently, we are investigating whether such interest groups can be protected against manipulation by subversive participants.

Several peer-to-peer information sharing systems are concerned with trust. Quasar [21] is a probabilistic information sharing system for social networks with many social groups. The objective of Quasar is to protect the users' sensitive information, which is different from the trust objective of iTrust. OneSwarm [22] is a peer-to-peer system that allows information to be shared either publicly or anonymously, using a combination of trusted and untrusted peers. OneSwarm aims to protect the users' privacy, which iTrust does not aim to do. Rather, the trust objective of iTrust is to support free flow of information and prevent censorship, filtering and subversion of information. It might be advantageous to integrate ideas from Quasar or OneSwarm into a future version of iTrust.

8   Conclusions and Future Work

The iTrust with SMS system consists of SMS-capable mobile phones that communicate with iTrust SMS-HTTP bridge nodes that act as relays for search and retrieval requests over the iTrust network. An SMS-capable mobile phone can interact with any number of inter-connected iTrust over HTTP nodes. The iTrust network can be queried from any SMS-capable mobile phone for search and retrieval of basic information. In our implementation, an Android mobile phone application provides a custom interface to facilitate quick searches.

While the iTrust SMS-HTTP bridge provides search and retrieval access to the iTrust network for SMS-capable mobile phones, the iTrust with SMS node lacks the full capabilities of an iTrust over HTTP node. Notably, large documents cannot be easily and efficiently uploaded from, or downloaded to, the mobile phone, and they are hard to read on the small screen of the mobile phone. Of importance to many mobile phone users is the ability to upload and download images, video or audio recordings directly from their mobile phones. For these reasons, we plan to develop an iTrust over SMS application that transforms an SMS-enabled mobile phone into an effective and fully functional peer in the iTrust network.

We also plan to add mobile ad-hoc Wi-Fi capabilities to create a mesh network of local peer-to-peer iTrust nodes. Thus, iTrust mobile users will be immune from even government shutdown of cellular towers, and will be fully autonomous to search and retrieve documents from peers in the local Wi-Fi network. These additions to the iTrust network will strengthen the availability of search and the robustness of retrieval to enable movements of social change.

Acknowledgment. This research was supported in part by U.S. National Science Foundation grant number NSF CNS 10-16193.

References

1. Sohn, T., Li, K.A., Griswold, W.G., Hollan, J.D.: A Diary Study of Mobile Information Needs. In: 26th ACM SIGCHI Conference on Human Factors in Computing Systems, Florence, Italy, pp. 433–442. ACM Press, New York (2008)
2. Kamvar, M., Baluja, S.: A Large Scale Study of Wireless Search Behavior: Google Mobile Search. In: 24th ACM SIGCHI Conference on Human Factors in Computing Systems, Montreal, Quebec, Canada, April 2006, pp. 701–709. ACM Press, New York (2006)
3. Kamvar, M., Kellar, M., Patel, R., Xu, Y.: Computers and iPhones and Mobile Phones, Oh My!: A Log-Based Comparison of Search Users on Different Devices. In: 18th International Conference on the World Wide Web, Madrid, Spain, pp. 801–810. ACM Press, New York (2009)
4. Tsirulnik, G.: Global SMS Traffic to Reach 8.7 Trillion by 2015: Study. In: Mobile Commerce Daily, February 3 (2011), http://www.mobilecommercedaily.com/2011/02/03/global-sms-traffic-to-reach-8-7-trillion-by-2015
5. AOL Mobile, http://www.aolmobile.com
6. Google SMS, http://www.google.com/sms
7. Windows Live Mobile, http://home.mobile.live.com
8. Yahoo! OneSearch, http://mobile.yahoo.com/onesearch
9. Chen, J., Linn, B., Subramanian, L.: SMS-Based Contextual Web Search. In: 2009 ACM SIGCOMM MobiHeld Workshop, pp. 19–24. ACM Press, New York (2009)
10. Chen, J., Subramanian, L., Brewer, E.: SMS-Based Web Search for Low-End Mobile Devices. In: 16th ACM MobiCom International Conference on Mobile Computing and Networking, Chicago, IL, pp. 125–136. ACM Press, New York (2010)
11. Papadopouli, M., Schulzrinne, H.: Effects of Power Conservation, Wireless Coverage and Cooperation on Data Dissemination among Mobile Devices. In: ACM Symposium on Mobile Ad Hoc Networking and Computing, Long Beach, CA, pp. 117–127. ACM Press, New York (2001)
12. Bender, M., Michel, S., Triantafillou, P., Weikum, G., Zimmer, C.: P2P Content Search: Give the Web Back to the People. In: 5th International Workshop on Peer-to-Peer Systems, Santa Barbara, CA (February 2006)
13. Mischke, J., Stiller, B.: A Methodology for the Design of Distributed Search in P2P Middleware. IEEE Network 18(1), 30–37 (2004)
14. Risson, J., Moors, T.: Survey of Research towards Robust Peer-to-Peer Networks: Search Methods. Technical Report UNSW-EE-P2P-1-1, University of New South Wales (September 2007), RFC 4981, http://tools.ietf.org/html/rfc4981

15. Tsoumakos, D., Roussopoulos, N.: A Comparison of Peer-to-Peer Search Methods. In: Sixth International Workshop on the Web and Databases, San Diego, CA, pp. 61–66 (June 2003)

16. Lindemann, C., Waldhorst, O.P.: A Distributed Search Service for Peer-to-Peer File Sharing in Mobile Applications. In: 2nd International Conference on Peer-to-Peer Computing, Linkoping, Sweden, pp. 73–80. IEEE CS Press, Los Alamitos (2002)

17. Hu, H., Thai, B., Seneviratne, A.: Supporting Mobile Devices in Gnutella File Sharing Network with Mobile Agents. In: 8th IEEE Symposium on Computers and Communications, Kemer-Antalya, Turkey. IEEE CS Press, Los Alamitos (2003)

18. Gummadi, K.P., Mislove, A., Druschel, P.: Exploiting Social Networks for Internet Search. In: 5th ACM SIGCOMM Workshop on Hot Topics in Networks, Irvine, CA, pp. 79–84. ACM Press, New York (2006)

19. Tiago, P., Kotiainen, N., Vapa, M., Kokkinen, H., Nurminen, J.K.: Mobile Search – Social Network Search Using Mobile Devices. In: 5th IEEE Consumer Communications and Networking Conference, Las Vegas, NV, pp. 1201–1205. IEEE CS Press, Los Alamitos (2008)

20. Yang, J., Zhong, Y., Zhang, S.: An Efficient Interest-Group-Based Search Mechanism in Unstructured Peer-to-Peer Networks. In: 2003 International Conference on Computer Networks and Mobile Computing, Shanghai, China, pp. 247–252. IEEE CS Press, Los Alamitos (2003)

21. Wong, B., Guha, S.: Quasar: A Probabilistic Publish-Subscribe System for Social Networks. In: 7th International Workshop on Peer-to-Peer Systems, Tampa Bay, FL (February 2008)

22. Isdal, T., Piatek, M., Krishnamurthy, A., Anderson, T.: Privacy Preserving P2P Data Sharing with OneSwarm. In: 2010 ACM SIGCOMM Special Interest Group on Data Communication Conference, New Delhi, India, pp. 111–122. ACM Press, New York (2010)

Mobilewalla: A Mobile Application Search Engine

Anindya Datta, Kaushik Dutta, Sangar Kajanan, and Nargin Pervin

College of Computing, National University of Singapore, Singapore
{datta,dutta,skajanan,nargis}@comp.nus.edu.sg

Abstract. With the popularity of mobile apps on mobile devices based on iOS, Android, Blackberry and Windows Phone operating systems, the number of mobile apps in each of the respective native app stores are increasing in leaps and bounds. Currently there are almost 700,000 mobile apps across these four major native app stores. Due to such enormous number of apps, both the constituents in the app ecosytem, consumers and app developers, face problems in terms of 'app discovery'. For consumers, it is a daunting task to discover the apps they like and need among the huge number of available apps. Likewise, for developers, making it possible for users to discover their apps in the large number of available apps is a challenge. To address these issues, Mobilewalla(MW), provides an independent unbiased search engine for mobile apps with semantic search capabilities. It has also developed an objective scoring mechanism based on user and developer involvement with an app. The scoring mechanism enables MW to provide a number of other ways to discover apps - such as dynamically maintained 'hot' lists and 'fast rising' lists. In this paper, we describe the challenges of developing the MW platform and how these challenges have been mitigated. Lastly, we demonstrate some of the key functionalities of MW.

Keywords: Mobile App, Search Engine, Semantic Similarity.

1 Introduction

Consumer software applications that run on smartphones (popularly known as mobile apps, or, simply, apps) represent the fastest growing consumer product segment in the annals of human merchandising [1,2]. The absolute number of apps currently in existence, as well as their rates of growth, are remarkable. At the time of writing this paper, there are 404126, 274555, 30784, 19796 apps available in Apple, Android, Blackberry and Windows platforms respectively. Since December, 2010, the app growth rates for the Apple and Android platforms are nearly 4% and 7% on monthly basis respectively.

This scenario creates a number of problems for the two key constituencies in the app ecosystem, the consumers and the developers. For consumers, there are simply too many apps and far too much fragmentation in these apps (e.g., a large

J.Y. Zhang et al. (Eds.): MobiCASE 2011, LNICST 95, pp. 172–187, 2012.

number of categories). The analogy we often use to describe the confusion faced by a mobile app consumer is to imagine a customer walking into a grocery store, needing only a few items, and finding that all aisles and category labels have been eliminated, and every product has been thrown into a pile on the floor. It is a similarly daunting task for a consumer to navigate native app stores [3,4] and discover apps they need and like, as has been widely discussed in media forums in the recent past [5,6].

For application developers, the situation is far worse. There are almost 700,000 mobile apps between Apple and Android alone and most smartphone owners only can only identify a handful - this is a nightmare scenario for developers whose success is contingent upon getting their apps "found" by consumers. "How will my apps be discovered?" is the number one question in the mind of app developers. This issue, known as the "app discovery" problem, has received wide attention in the media as well [7,8].

Clearly, a key requirement to address the above issues is an effective system of discovering and searching mobile applications - in essence, a "search engine" for apps. The reader might point out that each of the native app markets (e.g., the iTunes appstore and the Android market) offer search capabilities. However, as has been widely discussed [9,10], the native app stores are commercially driven and search results are highly influenced by what the store wants the consumer to see, rather than being solely focused on producing relevant output. Moreover, as has also been widely reported, app store designs are confusing along many dimensions, such as having multiple display lists where individual apps are often listed in conflicting orders. For example, at the time of writing this paper 'mSpot Music' was the first featured app in the Android market [3]. This app is in category 'Music & Audio'. Investigating further in the 'Music & Audio' category of the Android market, we found 'mSpot Music' is not even in top 200 apps in that category.

In response, there is intense interest in creating independent unbiased search systems for mobile apps. One of the earliest entrants in this space is Mobilewalla (MW) (www.mobilewalla.com). MW is a full fledged app search engine employing semantic search capabilities. In addition to supporting basic keyword search, MW also features a number of other ways to discover apps - such as dynamically maintained "hot" lists and "fast rising" lists. One of MW's major contributions is the creation of an unbiased scoring system for apps based on the Mobilewalla Score (MWS). MWS has rapidly become the defacto standard of rating apps and has been recently featured in a number of "top app" lists, the most prominent being the New York Times Box Scores [11].

In this paper we describe Mobilewalla platform. In Section 2, we describe the architecture and approach. In Section 4, we explain the functionality of Mobilewalla platform with some screen shots. In Section 5, we discuss some of the other app search platforms and compare those with Mobilewalla system. Lastly in Section 6, we conclude the paper.

2   Overview

As articulated previously, Mobilewalla has been developed as a search, discovery and analytics system for mobile apps. The Mobilewalla consists of three independent components.

1. A data collection (DC) component, which collects data from native app stores (iStore [4], Android Market [3], Blackberry App World [12] and Windows Mobile Marketplace [13]).
2. The Computational Backend (CB), which cleans and processes data collected by the DC.
3. A GUI component, which displays data that has been collected in step 1 and computed in step 2.

All of these components were created to address a number of challenges, which we outline below.

1. Developing automated extraction mechanisms, or *crawlers* that work on dynamic web sites.
2. As soon as we started playing around with the data available in the native app stores, we realized that there were a lot of issues with the data, such as incompatible categorizations across different stores and mischaracterization of app content by developers. A key goal was to develop automated *data cleaning* methods that presented "clean" data to the user.
3. Allowing real-time search of vast app content
4. Computing "similarity" between, and across, mobile apps
5. Finally, a key usability goal was to find effective mechanisms to present a vast amount of multi-media information to the user, which in turn would result in effective searching of apps and the discovery of apps relevant to the user's requirements.

Below, we describe the high level architecture of the complete Mobilewalla system, and elaborate on the solution methodologies employed to overcome the above challenges.

3   Architecture

Figure 1 shows the architecture of the Mobilewalla platform. The Data Collector (DC) component gathers information from the native app stores, extracts data and stores it in the Mobilewalla database (MDB). The Computational Backend (CB) interacts with the MDB to perform computations which enable users to search and discover apps efficiently. Finally, the GUI component interacts with the application server to retrieve the data from MDB and present it to users.

3.1   Data Collector (DC)

The essence of the DC component is an automated extraction system, or a *crawler*, that fetches useful data out of the native app stores and writes it to the MDB. We first describe the crawler and then discuss the MDB.

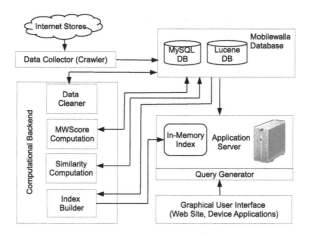

Fig. 1. Architecture of Mobilewalla

Designing crawlers for app stores is not easy, as the app stores are not based on a uniform structure of data representation. Rather, each app store has its own format. Therefore, we have developed four different crawlers, one for each of the four native app stores - (i) iStore [4], (ii) Android Market [3], (iii) Blackberry App World [12] and (iv) Windows Mobile Marketplace [13]. Typical crawlers [14,15,16], that are widely available as open source software components, have been developed to fetch information from generic internet sites. These crawlers work on the assumption that web content is available in static HTML pages and do not work on dynamically generated content created with technology such as AJAX, Silverlight and Flash ActionScript. It turns out that the native app stores are built using such kind of dynamic web technologies. These technologies are based on scripting languages, which create component based web pages on the fly. Let us consider the example of AJAX, arguably the most prevalent dynamic web development framework. AJAX is dependent on a scripting language called Javascript, which allows dynamic update of parts of a web page. This makes it difficult to download and parse the complete web page as is usually done in standard crawlers. Consider the example of the Google search engine. Google can crawl static content such as that can be found in HTML pages, PDF and Word documents. Google is unable to crawl an AJAX based web site such as Kayak.com. For a AJAX based web application, the response from the web server comes in the form of JSON and not in the form of HTML. To crawl and extract information from a AJAX based web site, one needs to parse JSON responses.

Complicating matters further, each app store has its own JSON response format. To handle this, we have developed ways to parse these individual JSON responses to extract app specific details based on the JQuery library. Consequently, we have had to develop individual store specific crawlers that encapsulate the knowledge of the JSON format for each individual store. Understanding the JSON format for each store and developing "personalized" parser routines has proven to be a non-trivial task.

Having described our idea behind our automated extraction mechanism, we now focus on the specific data item that we extract. These are shown in Table 1.

Table 1. Data Captured by Crawler

Static Data	App Name	Dynamic Data	Comment
	App Description		Rating
	Release Date		Version
	Platform		Rank in Store
	Price		Times Downloaded
	Screen Shot		
	Icon		
	Category		
	Seller/Developer Name		
	URL		
	Language		
	Size of an App (MB)		

Our extracted information consists of both static and dynamic data elements as shown in Table 1. This data is extracted and stored in the Mobilewalla database (MDB) described below in Section 3.2.

The static data is downloaded and stored in the database only once. If any changes occurs to this data the updated information is downloaded again and the old data is replaced with this new information. For example, an app might have its description updated. In this case, the old description is overwritten in the database with the new description.

Dynamic data, which typically changes frequently, is fetched by the crawler on a continuous basis. For dynamic information the old data is never deleted or replaced. Rather, all dynamic data is time stamped and retained in the database. As an example, consider the user rating of an application, an important dynamic data item. Whenever there is a change in an application's ratings in its native app store, the new rating is stored along with a date stamp. Similarly, any new comment, if discovered, are appended to the database in the same manner.

When a new app is encountered, the crawler downloads all data related to this app. The crawler then runs regularly to track data about this app. How frequently the crawler will revisit a particular app is determined dynamically. Let us assume, T_a denotes the interval at which the crawler will revisit a particular app a. Initially $T_a = 3$ hours. If in the next iteration the crawler does not find any update for the app a, the next revisit will happen at $n \times T_a$ period, i.e. T_a will be updated as $T_a^{new} = n \times T_a^{old}$, where n is a positive number. If even in the subsequent visit, the crawler does not find any new update or new dynamic data, then T_a will be updated again. At maximum value of $T_a = T_a^{max}$, the value of T_a is no more updated. We set $T_a^{max} = 48$ hours, i.e. at every 2 days the crawler will revisit each app irrespective of whether there is any update or not for that particular app. Such an approach ensures two aspects of the crawler. (i) The crawler need not visit all the apps in a store at every iteration, which reduces the total time the crawler takes at every run. In our environment, this enables the crawler to run at every 3 hours. For highly dynamic and popular apps, this in turn guarantees that the crawler will quickly (within 3 hours) identify the new data and put into our system. (ii) For less dynamic apps, the crawler will identify the new data within a maximum 2 days. This system creates a balance between dynamism of the app and the scalability of the crawler system.

In many instances, existing apps get deleted from its native stores. In these circumstances, the crawler will fail to download any data from the store. We keep a note of how many consecutive times the crawler is failing to download the information related to a particular app. If the count crosses a threshold, we assume that the app has been deleted from the store and mark it as inactive in our database.

3.2   The Mobilewalla Database

Having described the crawler system, we now delve into the Mobilewalla database (MDB), which is the store-house of the crawler extracted information. The MDB has a structured relational component created on top of MySQL DBMS [17] and an unstructured data store based on Lucene text search engine [18].

MySQL Database. The relational MySQL database of MDB primarily contains structured data captured by the DC such as Version Number, Release Date and Price along with the unstructured textual data such as title, description and comments. The database schema reflects the information captured in Table 1. Other than few global tables, each native app store has its own set of tables, that contains the data captured by DC from that store only.

One of the challenges encountered in Mobilewalla was how to enable users to browse apps by categories such as Finance, Entertainment or Life Style. Native app stores designate categories for each app; however these store specified categories have a number of issues. (1) Developers tend to wrongly categorize apps based on where it would attract most users rather than the category to which the app naturally belongs based on its content. This often results in gross miscategorization of apps. For instance, the android app 'Men and women of passion video' is in the category 'Health & Fitness' in the Android market, whereas this app is an adult video app, and should have been appropriately categorized under 'Media & Video'. Natives stores themselves often do not perform extensive verification of such errors. One of our goals in Mobilewalla was to remove these miscategorizations as far as possible. (2) Another major issue is the lack of uniform categorization across the stores. For instance, 'Skype' is under 'Communication' category in Android market, whereas it is under 'Social Networking' category in iStore. Our goal in Mobilewalla was to present apps based on a uniform ontology.

To address this issue, we have developed a unique categorization scheme across multiple stores, called global categories. The information about these global categories are kept in separate global tables. We have developed an automatic categorization scheme, which is based on the Wikipedia ontology [19]. At a high level, we use the title and the description of an app to identify the keywords for an app. These keywords are matched with the keywords for Wikipedia categories to categorize the app in a global category defined in global tables.

Lucene. A key requirement in Mobilewalla was to support free form keyword search. We use the Lucene text search engine to fulfill this requirement. In particular we create an inverted index out of the textual content attached to each app (including the description and the title). Subsequently we support search based on this index.

We should point out however that a straight forward implementation on top of Lucene was not possible. The reasons are,

1. The Lucene query processor awards equal weights to every keywords in a document. This does not work for us, as we have developed certain proprietary rules about the importance of different keywords. (e.g., keywords in title should have higher weights than keywords in the description) To handle this we modified Lucene such that variable weights could be attached to keywords.
2. Lucene does not perform stemming, i.e. if a user searches for the word "swimming" the apps related to the keyword "swim" will not be returned by Lucene. We incorporated stemming and lemmatization to transfrom a word to its base form. The stemming uses simple word transformation to modify a word to its base form, e.g. "going" to "go". The lemmatizer uses the word's parts of speech (POS) and a valid dictionary to identify the original form. Our lemmatizer is based on the OpenNLP [20] parser and the Wordnet dictionary. We used both the original word and the transformed base form of the word to index the app in the Lucene database.

3.3   Computational Backend (CB)

The Computational Backend (CB) components operates on the base data present in the MDB to perform a set of secondary computation; it first *cleans* the data and then produces a set of *proprietary metrics*.

Data Cleaning. The raw data captured by the crawler has been primarily entered by the developers who typically make a number of (often intentional) errors. The data cleaning component of the CB attempts to fix these errors by following tasks.

Categorization - We discussed the issues related to store categories before. As discussed, we can't rely on the store and developer provided categories. So we needed to develop our own automatic categorization system. A key task of the CB is to perform the Wikipedia based categorization described before.

Duplicate App Removal - Often app developers submit an app in a store and for the next version the app developers do not update the already existing app, rather they create a new entry in the system. This creates duplicate entry of the same app in the store. In iPhone stores we found that about 10,000 such apps exist. We have developed an automatic identification method of the duplicate apps based on comparing core app attributes such as app title, description and developer name.

Deleted or Inactive App - Many apps in native stores turn out to be orphaned or defunct. These apps, after release, have not had any version upgrades or platform upgrades, likely because the developer abandoned the app. We have developed a heuristic based solution to identify these defunct apps based on inactivity periods and platform compatabilities.

Mobilewalla Score (MWS). One of the values Mobilewalla provides to the end user is providing a unique and uniform scoring mechanism of apps across categories and platforms. Unlike existing app search engines, where app rankings are based on highly subjective and often commercial considerations, in Mobilewalla we wanted to rate and rank apps based on uniform unbiased criterion. This is achieved through the Mobilewalla Score (MWS). The MWS of an app is based on several objective parameters that denote how users and developers are engaged with the app. Some of the factors used to compute the MWS are (1) the current and historical ratings of the app in its native store, (2) the frequency of releases, (3) the duration that the app is active in the store since its first release, (4) number of users who rated the app, (5) number of users who provided comments on this app, (6) the current and historical rank of the app in its native store, (7) the number of apps in the category the app belongs to, and (8) the past history of the developer in producing apps. The system computes the MWS every night and posts it in the database. We keep track of the historical value of MWSs for each app.

The current and historical value of MWS are used to create a number of popular lists of Mobilewalla.

Hot Apps - This is the list of apps with the highest MWS at current time.

Fast Movers - This is the list of the apps for which the change of the MWS is the highest. This measures the velocity in the MWS for each app and report top apps with the rate of change.

All Time Greats - This is the list of the apps which have the highest average MWS over last 3 months.

Similarity Computation. Mobilewalla enables users to find apps similar to a particular app and compare the similar apps on characteristics such as MWS and price (much like the "if you like this you might also like" feature in Amazon). We compute a measure of similarity between two apps based on the semantic similarity across several parameters, such as description, title and comments received from users. The semantic similarity computation of these features are done using hypernym, hyponym and synonym relationships in Wordnet [21]. Based on the importance in describing features of an app, the similarity measurement across each of these parameters is given different weight in the final similarity measurement. For example, the similarity on title is given more weight, than the similarity on description. The similarity on comment is given the least weight.

For each app, we identify the similar apps that cross a threshold on similarity measurement with respect to that app.

In-memory Index and Index Builder. One of the objectives of the Mobilewalla application is to enable complex search in the database in real time. For this, the in-memory index contains materialized views of the database containing following items - (1) The inverted index of the Lucene data and (2) Index of the app on the basis of app parameters, such as price, release date, and developer name. These indexes are pre-built nightly, and reduce the complex join operations that require querying the database against some of the user queries.

3.4 Query Generator

The query generator module receives user provided query keywords for searching the app database. The query generator transforms this user query across several dimensions to generate more than one query. The result of the query generator is a series of queries ordered in priority. These queries are executed in Lucene's in-memory index to identify the app. If the prior queries result in a threshold number of relevant apps from the Lucene in-memory index, the later queries are not executed.

The query generator expands the query in following different ways.

Stemming and Lemmatization - The words in the user query will be stemmed and lemmatized to create original base form of the query words. Additional queries will be generated using these base forms. For example, a user query "swimming" will create a second query "swim".

Formulation of AND and OR Query - First we do "AND" query for the user given keywords. If the "AND" query does not return sufficient result, we expand the query using "OR" across the user given keywords. For example, if user given query is "Racing Bicycle", then the two queries "Racing AND Bicycle" and "Racing OR Bicycle" are formed. If the query "Racing AND Bicycle" returns less than a threshold number of results (in Mobilewalla implementation that threshold value is 20), the OR query "Racing OR Bicycle" is executed. This "AND" and "OR" combination is also applied on the original base form of the user give query keywords.

Query Expansion - If the user given query does not return a threshold number of results, we expand the query using synonyms and hyponyms of the query keywords. For example, a query "Bollywood Movie" will be expanded into "Bollywood Cinema" and "Bollywood Picture", because "Cinema" and "Picture" are the synonym and hyponym of the word "Movie".

4   Screen Shots and Descriptions

The Mobilewalla architecture is flexibly implemented using a JSON interface. The application server provides a set of JSON APIs that can be invoked by any client over HTTP. Currently, the clients supported include iOS devices (i.e., iPhone/iPod/IPad), Android devices and desktop web applications. All these clients communicate with the Mobilewalla server application using the same JSON API set, but differ in the user interface offered to the end user. We will now proceed to demonstrate some of the important functionalities of the Mobilewalla application by using desktop web application as an example (the user may interact with this application at www.mobilewalla.com).

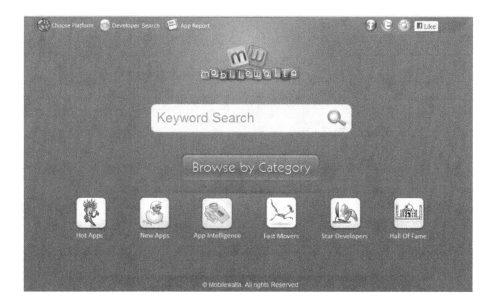

Fig. 2. Main Menu Page

When the user arrives at the Mobilewalla application, the first step is to choose a platform of interest, i.e., the user must specify which smartphone platform is of interest to the user – iPhone/iPod, iPad, Android, Blackberry or Microsoft (the user may also choose a "don't care" option, marked as "All" in Mobilewalla). Once a platform is chosen the user will be directed to the main "splash page" shown in Fig 2. In the screenshot shown in Fig 2, the platform chosen appears on the extreme right of the top menu bar (iPhone/iPod in this case). This means that all apps presented to the user will correspond to the iPhone/iPod platform until this is explicitly changed, by selecting the "Choose Platform" widget present on the extreme left of the top menu bar.

From this screen, the user may choose to navigate the app world in a number of ways. The first, and the most common method of interaction is by entering a search query in the keyword input box. Let's assume the user enters the search term "earth photo". Mobilewalla returns a set of apps that fit the user's interest as shown in Fig 3 – in this view Mobilewalla provides not only the app name, but also a number of other core features such as author and price. One notable feature of this view are the *relevance* and *Mobilewalla meter* (*MW Meter*) indicators present in each app box. Relevance indicates the quality of "fit" of that app with respect to the input seach query, whereas *MW Meter* is an encapsulation of the "goodness" of the app as measured by Mobilewalla (this is based on the Mobilewalla Score metric described earlier). Also, while not shown in the screenshot, we also segment the apps by Free and Paid and allow a number of options to sort the result set (the user may view these by visiting mobilewalla.com).

Fig. 3. Keyword Search Results Page

The user may choose any app from the app-list view just described and delve into its details. Let us assume the user chooses the Google Earth app. In this case she will be presented with the detail view of this app, shown in Fig 4. In this view, Mobilewalla displays details such as the app description and screenshots and also allows the user to view a number of other interesting artifacts related to this app, such as "Apps by Author" (other apps created by the author of the app detail being viewed), "Mobilewalla Score"(the Mobilewalla score history related to this app over the past 14 days), "Comments", and "Similar Apps" (similar to the "if you like this, you might also like" feature in Amazon).

The above two paragraphs describes how a user might interact with Mobilewalla by performing a keyword search and then drilling down on the results. However, keyword search is just one of many ways that the user can navigate Mobilewalla. He might also choose to view apps by categories, or choose one of the many "pre-defined" list options such as "Hot Apps", "Fast Movers" and "New Apps". Choosing the "Browse my category" option reveals a number of category icons from which the use may navigate the app world – Fig 5 shows the results of choosing the "Maps & Navigation" category.

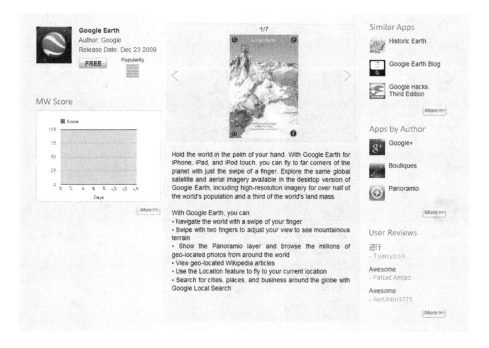

Fig. 4. App Details Page

Similarly choosing "Hot Apps" displays the list of the top 1000 apps ordered by their Mobilewalla Scores, while "Fast Rising" apps are those whose Mobilewalls scores have demonstrated the steepest ascent, i.e., apps getting hot the fastest. "New Apps" are those that are less than a month old. In every case a number of sort options are available that allow users to manipulate the result set along various dimensions.

While Mobilewalla has a number of other interesting features, it is infeasible to describe them in this paper due to length restrictions. We invite the user to visit the site.

5   Related Work

Mobilewalla is one of the earliest entrants in the app search and discovery space. In this section, we describe few alternatives available for app search.

Appolicious Inc, associated with Yahoo Inc [22], is a web application to help users easily find mobile applications that are useful and interesting to them. The Appolicious recommendation engine determines what apps you have, what apps your friends and the rest of the community have, and uses individual app ratings and reviews to suggest new apps for your use. Unlike Appolicious, Mobilewalla depends on its own developed scoring mechanism. Users can search for an app in the Mobilewalla system using keywords, which is based on its own index mechanism. Mobilewalla also identifies similar apps based on content than the usage,

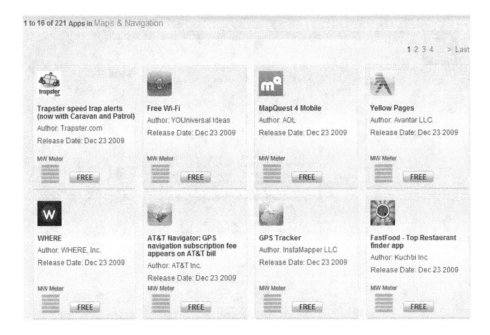

Fig. 5. Category Search Results Page

as is the case in Appolicious. The most important attraction of Mobilewalla [23] is the availability of different kind of Search functions which are 'keyword based search', 'category search' and 'developer search' based on the semantics and topics. Because of this uniqueness, through Mobilewalla one can find a much larger variety of apps.

Chomp is an app search engine [24], where the search primarily occurs based on string search. Mobilewalla, on the other hand, searches apps based on their semantic content. For example, Mobilewalla includes semantically related words in search terms. It also identifies words in app title and description that are semantically more meaningful than others. As a result, the search outputs are vastly different. For example, the search term "ESPN Cricket" in Android platform returned only one app "Sports Eye - Lite" in Chomp, whereas in Mobilewalla it returned total 486 apps with "zeendaTV Cricket", "Cricbuzz Cricket Scores and News", "ESPN Mobile" and "Cricket Mania" as the first few apps in the result list. Also, unlike Mobilewalla, which is applicable in iPhone/iPod/iPad, Blackberry, Android and Windows platform, Chomp's search is limited only to Apple and Android app stores. Chomp's trending search option is based on existing popularity of the app. Whereas Mobilewalla's trending search results are based on Mobilewalla's unique scoring mechanism, which uses other parameters indicating both the developer's and user's engagement.

AppBrain is a website [25] to search Android apps available specifically in the Google Android market, whereas MobileWalla [23] covers all the major smart phone platforms (Windows, Blackberry, Android and Apple). The main core feature of Mobilewalla system is its search functionality. It has semantic enabled keyword, category and developer based search functionalities. Keyword search in Mobilewalla is implemented in a way to find the semantically meaningful apps but not purely based on exact string match like most of the currently available app search engines like AppBrain do.

uQuery.com [26] is a mobile app search platform based on social media Facebook.com. Users can search and find applications on the iTunes App store based on what apps friends in Facebook are using. The key difference between Mobilewalla and uQuery is in the search mechanism. Mobilewalla relies on its own metrics which is combination of both the usage and the developer's engagement with an app, whereas uQuery relies on usage by friends in Facebook. The Mobilewalla's keyword based search engine is much more extensive than uQuery. Mobilewalla's keyword search can handle semantically related keywords, keywords appearing in title, description and user comments. Mobilewalla's similar app search mechanism is based on semantic similarity of apps, rather than the usage.

In summary, the key difference between the Mobilewalla and existing app search platforms is in two fronts. First, Mobilewalla depends on the semantic description of apps to enable search based on keywords and similar apps. Second, Mobilewalla ranks the app based on a scoring mechanism that incorporate both the user and the developer's involvement with the app. As discussed above, the existing search platforms consider only the user's aspect; like Mobilewalla developer's involvement with the app and the developer's history is not considered.

6   Conclusion

With the skyrocketing popularity of mobile apps on mobile devices based on iOS, Android, Blackberry and Windows Phone operating systems, the number of mobile apps is increasing in leaps and bounds. Currently there are over 700,000 mobile apps across these four major native app stores. Due to such enormous number of apps, both the constituents in the app ecosytem, consumers and app developers, face problems in terms of 'app discovery'. For consumers, it is a daunting task to discover the apps they like and need among the huge number of available apps. Likewise, for developers, getting their apps discovered in the pool of an enormous number of apps is a challenge. To address these issues, Mobilewalla provides an independent unbiased search engine for mobile apps with semantic search capabilities. It has also developed an objective app rating and scoring mechanism based on user and developer involvement with an app. Such scoring mechanism enables MW to provide a number of other ways to discover apps - such as dynamically maintained 'hot' lists and 'fast rising' lists. In this paper, we describe the challenges of developing the MW platform and how these challenges have been mitigated. Lastly, we demonstrate some of the key functionalities of MW.

Acknowledgment. We acknowledge the engineering work done by Ji Cheng and Sameer Samarth for Mobilewalla.com web site, iPhone app and Android app.

References

1. Android market grows a staggering 861.5 per cent
2. Mobile apps market to reach $38 billion revenue by 2015,
   `http://news.brothersoft.com/mobile-apps-market-to-reach-`
   `38-billion-revenue-by-2015-6089.html` (visited on May 13, 2011)
3. Android market, `https://market.android.com/` (visited on May 13, 2011)
4. Apple app store, `http://www.istoreus.com/home.html` (visited on May 13, 2011)
5. Why native app stores like itunes and android marketplace are bad for mobile developers, `http://www.businessinsider.com/why-native-app-stores-like-itunes-and-andoid-marketplace_are-bad-business-for-mobile-developers-2011-5` (visited on May 13, 2011)
6. Would you like to try android apps before buying?,
   `http://www.labnol.org/internet/android-apps-try-before-buying/19422/`
   (visited on May 13, 2011)
7. Appsfire scores $3.6m as app discovery demands grow,
   `http://gigaom.com/2011/05/30/appsfire-scores-3-6m-as-app-discovery-demands-grow/` (visited on May 13, 2011)
8. The mobile app discovery problem,
   `http://news.cnet.com/8301-30684_3-20011241-265.html`
   (visited on May 13, 2011)
9. Google finally applies its own search technology to apps,
   `http://www.zdnet.com/blog/mobile-gadgeteer/google-finally-applies-its-own-search-technology-to-apps/3332?tag=mantle_skin;content`
   (visited on May 13, 2011)
10. App search engine competition heating up,
    `http://www.zdnet.com/blog/mobile-gadgeteer/`
    `app-search-engine-competition-heating-up/3785` (visited on May 13, 2011)
11. Popular demand: App wars, `http://www.nytimes.com/interactive/2011/05/16/business/media/16most.html?ref=media` (visited on May 13, 2011)
12. Blackberry app world, `http://us.blackberry.com/apps-software/appworld/` (visited on May 13, 2011)
13. Windows, `http://marketplace.windowsphone.com/Default.aspx` (visited on May 13, 2011)
14. Heydon, A., Najork, M.: Mercator: A scalable, extensible web crawler. World Wide Web 2, 219–229 (1999), `http://dx.doi.org/10.1023/A:1019213109274`, doi:10.1023/A:1019213109274
15. Boldi, P., Codenotti, B., Santini, M., Vigna, S.: Ubicrawler: a scalable fully distributed web crawler. Software: Practice and Experience 34(8), 711–726 (2004), `http://dx.doi.org/10.1002/spe.587`
16. Hsieh, J.M., Gribble, S.D., Levy, H.M.: The architecture and implementation of an extensible web crawler. In: Proceedings of the 7th USENIX Conference on Networked Systems Design and Implementation, Ser. NSDI 2010, p. 22. USENIX Association, Berkeley (2010),
    `http://portal.acm.org/citation.cfm?id=1855711.1855733`
17. Mysql, `http://www.mysql.com/` (visited on May 13, 2011)
18. Lucene, `http://lucene.apache.org/` (visited on May 13, 2011)
19. Suchanek, F.M., Kasneci, G., Weikum, G.: Yago: A large ontology from wikipedia and wordnet. Web Semantics: Science, Services and Agents on the World Wide Web 6(3), 203–217 (2008), World Wide Web Conference 2007 Semantic Web Track, `http://www.sciencedirect.com/science/article/pii/S1570826808000437`

20. Opennlp, `http://incubator.apache.org/opennlp/` (visited on May 13, 2011)
21. Princeton University, About wordnet, `http://wordnet.princeton.edu` (visited on May 17, 2011)
22. Find mobile apps you will love, `http://www.appolicious.com/` (visited on May 17, 2011)
23. Helping you navigate the app world, `http://www.mobilewalla.com/` (visited on May 13, 2011)
24. The appstore search engine, `http://www.chomp.com/` (visited on May 17, 2011)
25. Find the best android apps, `http://www.appbrain.com/` (visited on May 17, 2011)
26. The appstore search engine, `http://www.uquery.com/` (visited on May 17, 2011)

Native to HTML5: A Real-World Mobile Application Case Study

Rachel Gawley, Jonathan Barr, and Michael Barr

JamPot Technologies Limited, Mobile Computing Research Department,
405 Holywood Road, Belfast, UK
{rachel.gawley,jonathan.barr,michael.barr}@jampot.ie

Abstract. HTML5 is capable of producing media-rich and interactive webpages that function more like desktop applications than webpages. Increasing mobile browser support for the standard has enabled the development of mobile web applications as an alternative to native applications. This paper presents a project, which recreated a cross-compiled native application in HTML5. The experience provides an insight into developing mobile web applications and identifies some of the limitations associated with using HTML5 on mobile devices.

Keywords: HTML5, mobile applications, cross-platform.

1 Introduction

By the end of 2010 there were approximately 5.3 billion mobile subscriptions [1], which was equivalent to 77% of the world population. The sale of mobile phones is increasing with smartphones showing the biggest increase. In Q1 2011, smartphone sales were 85% greater than Q1 2010 [2]. The prevalence of the smartphone, especially in the developed world [1], is creating a culture where a mobile phone becomes an integral part of the user's life as it is also a media player, pocket gaming console, business tool, means to connect to the Internet and even a substitute laptop.

Mobile applications (apps) are also becoming an increasingly common feature in daily life with 43% of American mobile phone users having apps on their phone [3]. In the last 3 years, there have been over 350,000 applications developed [4]. These applications have been downloaded over 10.9 billion times in 2010 and it is predicted that the number of downloads will be 76.9 billion in 2014 [5]. Nevertheless, Gartner analysts [2] noted that

"Every time a user downloads a native app to their smartphone or puts their data into a platform's cloud service, they are committing to a particular ecosystem and reducing the chances of switching to a new platform"

This is an issue for both the end-user and mobile application developers. Ideally, end-users should have the same applications and associated assets available to them regardless of operating system/device. Consequently, application developers are increasingly required to redevelop the same application for different mobile

J.Y. Zhang et al. (Eds.): MobiCASE 2011, LNICST 95, pp. 188–206, 2012.

platforms. This is not a trivial task as the skill sets required differ between the various mobile runtime environments.

The ultimate application development goal is to write an application once and deploy it to every screen. This includes desktop devices, tablets, mobile devices and even smart televisions [6]. No complete solution exists [7]. Nevertheless, there are mechanisms that enable the 'write once and deploy to multiple platforms' approach. This is referred to as cross-platform development and often produces cross-compiled code. The most common cross-platform approaches are:

- *Appcelerator Titanium* [8] – a native app builder for iOS and Android using web technologies, for example, HTML, CSS, JavaScript, PHP, Ruby, etc.
- *Mono* [9] – a software development kit that enables the deployment of .Net applications to Unix, Mac OSX, Windows (desktop and phone), iOS and Android as native applications.
- *Phone Gap* [10] – a hybrid app building platform that enables the creation of mobile applications for iOS, Android, BlackBerry, Windows and HP using standard web technologies, i.e. HTML, CSS and JavaScript.
- *Adobe Flash* [11] – an application-building environment used to produce native apps for iOS, Android, BlackBerry Playbook, Windows, Unix and Mac OSX.
- *Corona* [12] – a mobile development platform that enables the creation of native iOS and Android apps.
- *Unity3D* [13] – a development environment that enables the production of 3D game applications for Windows, Mac OSX, iOS, Android and games consoles.

Using a cross-platform approach can decrease development time as a mobile application is written once and deployed to multiple platforms as opposed to developing an individual application for each environment. The cross-platform approach can be used to produce applications that will be accepted into the various mobile applications stores, for example, Apple store, Android Market, Amazon Appstore for Android, BlackBerry App World, etc. Unfortunately, the app stores could, at any time, change their terms and conditions and no longer allow cross-compiled applications. In April 2010, Apple changed their developer agreement to only accept applications written in Objective C, C or C++ into their app store [14]. Any approach that creates final iOS machine code from other programming languages, for example, Adobe Flash, MonoTouch, etc. were no longer accepted. Apple, once again, changed their developer license agreement in September 2010, which relaxed the restriction on development tools used to create iOS applications [15]. Currently, cross-compiled applications are accepted into all major mobile application stores and therefore provide an excellent means of creating and distributing multi-platform mobile applications. However, the issue of app stores controlling the acceptance and distribution of mobile applications raises the question

"Whether the future of mobile applications is on the app store or with an alternative means of implementing and distributing cross-platform apps?"

The development of HTML5 and browser support for the evolving standards has created an environment suitable for developing cross-platform mobile and desktop applications that do not need an app store for distribution. Accessing applications via a browser is naturally cross-platform with desktop, tablets, laptops, mobiles, games consoles and even some televisions providing access to the Internet via a browser. However, HTML5 is an emerging technology as standards are currently being discussed [16]. Each browser uses an underlying layout engine (for example, WebKit, Gecko, Trident, etc.), which all have differing means of processing the HTML5 tags. This discrepancy between layout engines makes it more challenging to provide one solution for all screens. It has been shown that HTML5 provides many features required for media and content rich mobile applications [7]. The potential to write once and distribute everywhere, without an app store, means that HTML5 is a viable alternative to native mobile application development.

The aim of the project, described here, is to provide an insight into the practicalities and issues surrounding HTML5 mobile application development. This is achieved by replicating an existing native application created using cross-platform techniques in HTML5. This paper is structured to address the issues associated with creating an HTML5 mobile application and is organized as follows: section 2 describes the background to the project, including the specification of the existing mobile application; section 3 describes the techniques used to create the online HTML5 application; section 4 discusses the issues relating to going offline; section 5 presents a potential solution to the issue of creating a dynamic offline HTML5 application; section 6 compares the HTML5 app to the native application created using cross-platform techniques; section 7 presents and discusses some open issues relating to the future of HTML5 mobile applications; section 8 provides a brief conclusion.

2   Background

As part of a previous research project, a mobile application, 'SoundBoom', was created using cross-platform technologies similar to those mentioned in the introduction. The cross-platform techniques used in the development are proprietary to JamPot Technologies Limited and beyond the scope of this paper. However, the resulting application provides an excellent benchmark to compare other cross-platform techniques such as HTML5.

2.1   SoundBoom Requirements

SoundBoom was created as part of a project aimed at utilising cross-platform technologies to produce a media-rich application that also provides a compelling user experience. To provide a valuable insight, the resulting mobile application had to satisfy four high-level requirements:

- Contain media-rich content
- Utilise device capabilities
- Deliver dynamic content
- Provide the user with the ability to customise the application

2.2   Existing SoundBoom Application

The SoundBoom application was created, using cross-platform technologies, to meet the requirements documented in section 2.1 by providing:

1. A traditional soundboard that plays sounds when image icons are clicked, shown in Fig. 1.
2. A means of creating a custom soundboard using the device capabilities (camera, microphone and asset library).
3. The ability to save a custom soundboard to the cloud via web services.
4. The option to download a custom soundboard from the cloud thus providing dynamic content.

The resulting SoundBoom application was submitted to and is available on the following app stores: iTunes [17], BlackBerry App World [18], Android Market [19], Amazon [20] and Intel AppUp [21].   The application has also been deployed internally on the following platforms: MeeGo [22], Samsung Smart TV [6], WeTab [23], Mac OS X [24], Windows (XP, Vista, 7) [25].

Fig. 1. Screenshot of SoundBoom Application

2.3   HTML5 SoundBoom Specification

The success of SoundBoom provided an ideal foundation to investigate HTML5 as an alternative approach to cross-platform mobile application development. The aim of the project, described in this paper, is to replicate the SoundBoom mobile application in HTML5. Unfortunately, HTML5 mobile applications cannot access device capabilities such as the camera or microphone. It is possible to use a small native application such as photopicker [26], which is launched from the browser, to provide access to the device camera and upload images to a server. As this solution requires a native application that is downloaded from an app store it cannot be utilised for the purposes of this project; it was decided that no native applications or techniques could be used in the solution.   The creation of custom soundboards relies heavily on interacting with the device capabilities and, given the current state of HTML5, it would be difficult to recreate accurately the custom soundboard creation functionality. Therefore, the decision was made to create a read-only HTML5 SoundBoom application as version 1.0.

Version 1.0 will provide an interactive farmyard soundboard, which will play sounds when icons are clicked.   The application will also provide a means to download custom soundboards, which have been previously created by the original SoundBoom application available on the app stores.   Producing a read-only HTML5 version of SoundBoom is not a trivial task as the application is both media-rich and can be populated with dynamic content. The application will stretch some of the key features of the current HTML5 specification to its limits.

2.4   HTML5 as a Runtime Environment

HTML5 is the latest revision of HTML (HyperText Markup Language) and is still currently under development by both W3C [16] and WHATWG [27].   One of the main philosophies behind the development of HTML5 is to enable easier creation of web applications [28]. A web application looks and feels more like a desktop application, for example, a photo-editing tool, mapping utility, etc. Web applications often rely heavily on JavaScript or third-party plug-ins, for example, Adobe Flash [11], Microsoft Silverlight [29], etc. to embed media or enable users to interact with elements of the webpage. With the introduction of HTML5 standards, the traditional browser is evolving towards a runtime environment rather than just a means of rendering HTML.

HTML5 was not specifically created for a mobile environment but smartphones have evolved and most have sophisticated mobile browsers many of which are capable of parsing HTML5. This coupled with the following features make HTML5 mobile application development possible:

- Offline viewing – local storage and the application cache provide a means to store assets and information locally on the device and thus continual connectivity is not required.
- Rich media – <canvas>, <video> and <audio> tags provide a means of adding rich media content without additional third-party plug-ins.

The main problem associated with using HTML5 for mobile applications is the varying levels of browser support. Opera, BlackBerry and the iOS 4.2+ mobile browsers provide the best HTML5 support [30]. An additional issue is capturing and responding to touches on the screen as HTML normally responds to mouse-clicks rather than touch-events. Nevertheless, the current specification of HTML5 and mobile browser support is sufficient to create a read-only version of SoundBoom.

3   SoundBoom HTML5 Application

The aim of the project is to reproduce a read-only version of SoundBoom in HTML5 without any third-party plug-ins. Additional functionality will be provided via the well-known cross-browser JavaScript library, jQuery [31], and CSS3 [32].

The first stage of the project was to create the static part of the application. The term 'static' refers to the HTML pages of the application that utilise assets that are known on the first download/access of the application, even though the assets may be dynamic in when and how they are used in the application. The static part of SoundBoom is the farmyard soundboard, which consists of a background image and 12 images, each associated with an audio file. When an icon is clicked the associated audio file is played. The key features of the static application are:

- Image display
- Orientation specific layout
- Audio playback

3.1   Image Display

The <*canvas*> tag provides a 2D graphical area, which can have graphics, lines, text and animations, added in it. The canvas is particularly useful when creating detailed animations and is therefore suitable for game applications. It is very important to only use the canvas when another existing element will not suffice [33]. This is true for SoundBoom; the canvas element is not required as the image icons can be displayed with traditional <*img*> tag. The application needs to accommodate different screen sizes and in particular smaller screen sizes associated with mobiles. This is achieved using media queries in CSS3, shown overleaf, which enables style customisation based on the user's display [32]. The icons sizes are usually 150px, however, on small screens the size is halved to 75px.

The media query detects screens with a width less than 700px and sets the width of all the divs with class 'SBImage' to 75px. Each image icon is wrapped inside a div with the class 'SBImage'. The min-device-pixel-ratio is used to detect browsers on mobile devices, for example Safari on iOS, and scale the images accordingly.

CSS code to reduce image size

```
@media only screen and (max-width: 700px)
{
    .SBImage
    {
       width:75px;
       height:75px;
    }
}


@media only screen and (-webkit-min-device-pixel-ratio:
1.5), only screen and (-o-min-device-pixel-ratio: 3/2),
only screen and (min-device-pixel-ratio: 1.5)
{
    .SBImage
    {
       width:75px;
       height:75px;
    }
}
```

3.2   Orientation Specific Layout

Traditional webpages and web apps designed for desktop devices have a constant orientation, whereas smartphones are often designed to be used in either portrait or landscape. Therefore, HTML5 mobile applications need to accommodate the change in orientation and its impact on the layout of the application. This can be achieved using the *window.onorientationchanged* event, which is supported by WebKit, the layout engine used by the default browsers on iOS, BlackBerry and Android devices. The JavaScript function, *updateOrientation*, presented overleaf, is called both *onload* and *onorientationchanged*. The function changes the style of the application according to the orientation. When the orientation is 0 or 180, a portrait style is used and when the orientation is -90 or 90 a landscape style is used. Changing the style based on the orientation allows the best use of space in the application. Unfortunately, only WebKit supports the *onorientationchanged* event and orientation value, which means that other mobile browsers, mainly Opera mobile, will not be able to detect the event and change orientation.

Function to update layout to match orientation of device

```
function updateOrientation()
{
    switch(window.orientation)
    {
        case 0:$(".imgSB").removeClass("landscape").
        addClass("portrait");
        break;

        case -90:$(".imgSB").removeClass("portrait").
        addClass("landscape");
        break;
        case 90: $(".imgSB").removeClass("portrait").
        addClass("landscape");
        break;

        case 180:$(".imgSB").removeClass("landscape").
        addClass("portrait");
        break;

        default:$(".imgSB").removeClass("portrait").
        addClass("landscape");
        break;
    }
}
```

When this code was created the BlackBerry PlayBook had not been released. It was only when the application was tested on a PlayBook that a problem was discovered. The default orientation of the PlayBook is landscape opposed to portrait. Consequently, the orientation of 0 and 180 is actually considered to be landscape and not portrait causing the layout to be switched. A simple solution to this, shown below, is used to determine orientation based on width and height. If the width is greater than the height the device is in the landscape position and vice versa.

Function to update layout based on width and height

```
function updateOrientation(){
    var width = window.innerWidth;
    var height = window.innerHeight;

    if (width >= height)
        $(".imgSB").removeClass("portrait").
        addClass("landscape");
    else
        $(".imgSB").removeClass("landscape").
        addClass("portrait");}
```

3.3   Audio Playback

The HTML5 specification originally included an audio codec recommendation; however, Apple and Nokia objected and the codec requirement was dropped from the specification [33]. Consequently, each HTML5 engine uses different codecs and supports different audio files. The most commonly supported audio file types are MP3 and Ogg. MP3 is supported by WebKit based browsers and Internet Explorer, whereas, Ogg is supported by Mozilla. Ideally, both MP3 and Ogg formats would be supported in an application to ensure cross-platform compatibility. For the purposes of this project, it was decided to support MP3 format for the following reasons:

- MP3 files are smaller than Ogg files which makes downloading multiple audio files a better user experience.
- The default browsers on iOS, Android and BlackBerry devices support MP3. Opera mobile browser and Internet Explorer 9 also support the MP3 format.
- MP3 files are used in the native SoundBoom applications.

There is potential to update the application to accommodate other audio files when the HTML5 audio specification is standardised. The *<audio>* tag introduced in HTML5 enables audio files to be played in the browser without additional plug-ins. The code used in the SoundBoom application is shown below. The function plays a sound file from its relative location, which is stored in the *arrAudio* array. The JavaScript function has an integer, *soundPosition*, as a parameter, which indicates the position in the array of the audio file location. The *playSound* function is invoked from an *onclick* event associated with an image icon.

JavaScript to load and play audio files

```
function playSound(soundPosition)
{
    var audioclip;
    if (Modernizr.audio && (Modernizr.audio.mp3 != ""))
    {
        audioclip = arrAudio[soundFile]
        audioclip.load();
        audioclip.play();
    }
    else
        alert("Your browser does not support audio");
}
```

The JavaScript library Modernizr [34] is used to detect browser capabilities and thus provide a custom solution specific to the browser. The Modernizr script detects whether the browser supports the *<audio>* tag and is capable of playing MP3s. Only if these features are supported is an attempt to play the clip made, otherwise an alert is displayed.

4   Going Offline

Offline support is a key feature of the HTML5 specification that supports mobile application development. Offline support enables the download and storage of key assets to ensure the application will remain functional when a connection is not available [16].

4.1   Manifest and Application Cache

The manifest file associated with the HTML page lists the assets to be downloaded and stored locally in the application cache. The file is referenced in the *<HTML>* tag using *manifest="/name.manifest"*. The MIME type of the manifest file must be *'text/cache-manifest'*. The manifest file must begin with *'CACHE MANIFEST'* and include an UTF-8 encoded, line-separated list of assets. The SoundBoom manifest is shown below; for the sake of brevity, only some of the audio and image files are listed.

SoundBoom manifest listing

```
CACHE MANIFEST
# revision 47
CACHE:
js/soundboom.js
js/libs/jquery-1.6.2.min.js
js/libs/modernizr-1.7.min.js
img/h/barn.jpg
img/h/cat.jpg
img/h/cow.jpg
img/h/dog.jpg
...
error.htm
index.htm
sounds/cat.mp3
sounds/cow.mp3
sounds/dog.mp3
sounds/donkey.mp3
...
css/style.css?v=1
NETWORK:
js/blank.js
```

Comment lines in a manifest file start with #. The manifest, listed above, has a comment line with a revision number. Including a revision number comment provides a simple but effective means of ensuring application updates are propagated to devices. The offline cache will only be updated when the manifest changes and not when the files listed change. Within the manifest the inclusion of a revision number, and its subsequent increment when any of the files change, ensures the changes are downloaded when the application is accessed. The files listed under the

'CACHE:' heading are required for the application to work offline and will be downloaded and stored locally. All images, sounds, style sheets, scripts and HTML pages required for the application to run successfully offline are listed in the CACHE. The items listed under the *'NETWORK:'* heading are never cached; a network connection is required to access the files.

4.2   Offline Audio

Unfortunately, audio file caching is not well supported in HTML5 at present. It was observed that audio files listed in the CACHE were not downloaded. One potential solution is to use Base64 encoding to convert the audio file to an ASCII string format, which is stored in an XML file. XML files can be cached if they are listed in the manifest. This offline audio solution only works in desktop browsers, as mobile browsers on iOS and android devices do not support playing Base64-encoded audio. Mobile devices using the HTML5 application cannot play audio when offline.

The best overall solution is to play MP3 audio files when a connection is available and play Base64 audio strings when offline. This at least provides an offline desktop solution. The function [35], shown below, provides a means of determining the connectivity status, which is needed to implement the aforementioned solution.

Function to determine connectivity status

```
function checkNetworkStatus()
{
    if(navigator.onLine)
    {
      $.ajaxSetup({
        async: true,
        cache: false,
        dataType: "json",
        error: function (req, status, ex)
        {
          console.log("Error: " + ex);
          online = false;
        },
        success: function (data, status, req)
        {
          online = true;
        },
        timeout: 5000,
        type: "GET",
        url: "js/blank.js"});
        $.ajax();
    }
    else
      online = false;
}
```

There is a JavaScript function *navigator.onLine* that returns false if there is no Internet connection; however, it is unreliable and often returns true when it a connection is not available. Therefore, this alternative method of determining connectivity is used in the final solution. The JavaScript function *checkNetworkStatus* attempts to return a JSON object stored in the blank.js file. As blank.js is listed in the NETWORK section of the manifest it will not be cached. Therefore, if the JSON in the JavaScript file can be accessed it can be inferred that the device is online.

5   Dynamic Content: Cloud Interaction

A key feature of the original SoundBoom, shown in Fig. 2, is the ability to create user-generated soundboards, upload the assets of the soundboards to the cloud, which can then be downloaded to other devices and platforms running SoundBoom.

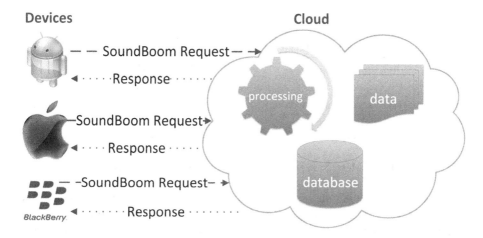

Fig. 2. SoundBoom cloud interaction on multiple devices

Version 1.0 of HTML5 SoundBoom is read-only; and enables users to download custom soundboards and their associated assets. Fig. 3 is a message sequence chart of the interaction between the original SoundBoom application and the cloud as a means of generating dynamic content. A user enters a PIN into the application and selects to load the soundboard associated with the unique PIN. A request is sent to the cloud; if there exists a custom soundboard associated with the PIN the details of the assets (absolute URLs) are returned to the application. A connection is required to make the request and download the assets. Once the assets have been downloaded they are stored for offline access within the application. Only when another custom soundboard is downloaded will the assets be replaced.

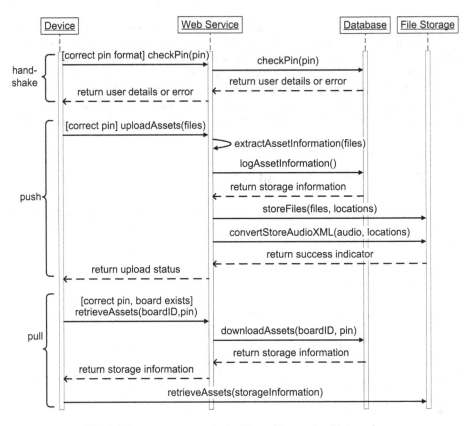

Fig. 3. Message sequence chart of SoundBoom cloud interaction

The key to replicating the original SoundBoom is storing locally the assets of the soundboard for offline viewing. The issues relating to going offline have been discussed in section 4 but caching dynamic content has not been addressed. The problem with caching dynamic content is the fact that the assets are not known when the page is accessed and are not present in the manifest file when the page is loaded. A means of dynamically adding to the application cache after the page has loaded would be a good solution to the dynamic caching issue. The Mozilla browser has suggested the *moz-add* function to add files to the application cache; unfortunately, this is experimental and not part of the official specification.

There is no reliable means of dynamically adding to the manifest at run-time on the client-side, therefore, the problem must be solved on the server side (cloud). The solution implemented in the HTML5 SoundBoom application is shown in the message sequence chart in Fig. 4. When a user accesses the cloud with their unique PIN, a new manifest file is created on the cloud listing all the assets of the custom soundboard associated with the PIN. A new HTML file of the custom soundboard is also created and includes a link to the aforementioned manifest file. Both the HTML and manifest files are named using GUIDs to prevent users accessing the soundboards by guessing the naming convention.

The GUID is linked to a unique instance of a custom soundboard. If the unique soundboard has been accessed previously, the HTML and manifest files will already exist on the cloud and will not be recreated thus reducing the stress on the cloud. On successful competition of the request, the cloud responds with the location of the new HTML file, which is then loaded into the browser. When the page loads, the dynamic content is cached due to the listings provided in the new manifest file.

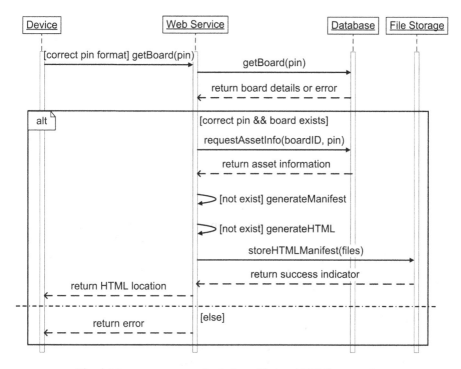

Fig. 4. Message sequence chart of manifest and HTML generation

6   Cross-Platform vs. HTML5

The aim of the project is to provide insight into developing cross-platform mobile applications in HTML5. The SoundBoom application had been developed previously using cross-platform approaches. The result is an application that was coded once, cross-compiled and runs natively on different platforms. Replicating SoundBoom in HTML5 provides an insight into using HTML5 as a means of developing mobile applications. Eight key features were used to compare the two development approaches: development time; cloud interaction; user-interface; media content (audio); multi-platform performance; offline performance; ease of distribution; ease of updating.   One mark is awarded to the approach that satisfies the feature the best and zero to the other. If both approaches performed equally they are both awarded one mark. Table 1 presents the results and the overall total for each approach.

Table 1. Cross-compiled native applications vs. HTML5 applications

Comparison Feature	Native	HTML5
Development time	1	1
Cloud interaction	1	1
User-interface	1	1
Media content (audio)	1	1
Multi-platform performance	1	0
Offline performance	1	0
Ease of distribution	0	1
Ease of updating	0	1
Total	**6**	**6**

The cross-compiled native application and the HTML5 application have a total score of six. The development time for both approaches was approximately the same; the cloud services for the original SoundBoom were reused in the HTML5 version and this was taken into consideration when scoring development time. Interaction with the cloud was easily achieved with cross-platform techniques and HTML5. CSS3 and JavaScript facilitated the creation of a HTML5 interface that replicated the original SoundBoom design. Both approaches had the same issue of finding an audio format that provides a solution for all devices.

The application developed using the cross-platform approach worked consistently on all devices/platforms tested. The HTML5 approach worked on many platforms (iOS, Android, BlackBerry PlayBook, Windows and Mac OSX), however, it did not function consistently across all platforms due to variation in browsers. Once the custom assets were downloaded to the cross-platform SoundBoom there were always available even without connectivity. The HTML5 SoundBoom does not provide a truly offline application as audio files cannot be cached and Base64 encoded audio strings, which can be cached, cannot be played on mobile browsers.

HTML5 applications are very easy to distribute – the page is uploaded on to a server and is instantaneously available to any device with a browser. Cross-compiled applications need to be submitted to many app stores. It is only once the application has been accepted by a store that is available to the public. There is no guarantee that the application will be accepted and the process can take up to three weeks to complete. Similarly, updating requires the resubmission of the application to each store and the update will take time to process. Updating the HTML5 application requires updating files on a server and changing the manifest file. The update is available everywhere instantaneously and will automatically download the next time the user accesses the application when connected to the Internet.

In general, both approaches are comparable in development time, cloud interactivity, user-interface building and the ability to include media. Focusing on where the two approaches differ (one approach is identified as providing a better solution) is essential to providing insight into HTML5. The main areas where the approaches differ are: cross-platform performance; offline performance; distribution and updating of the application.

7   HTML5 Analysis

The SoundBoom mobile application was replicated in HTML5. The results indicated that HTML5 is a valid means of creating cross-platform mobile applications but there are limitations that need addressed. The main issues with HTML5 identified from the SoundBoom project are:

- Consistent cross-platform performance
- Consistent offline performance

These issues can be attributed to the fact that HTML5 is an evolving standard with differing runtime environments provided by browsers. HTML5 is more easily distributed when compared to native applications and this should be viewed as a positive feature. As it differs from the traditional app store approach a different business model is required. It is worth noting that the ease of distribution will affect the protection of Intellectual Property.

7.1   The Evolving Standard

HTML5 is an evolving standard under development by both WHATWG and W3C. The current state of WHATWG is in 'Draft Standard' and W3C is in 'Working Draft'. The specification of HTML5 is an on-going process; it will be many years before reaching the final W3C recommendation state. Even though the specification of HTML5 is not stable, all the major web browsers have committed to support it.

Browsers do not have a rigid specification to follow and therefore browser layout engines differ in their support for HTML5 tags. The differing browser layout engines make it difficult to provide a solution that works consistently across all devices. The HTML5 SoundBoom application targeted the WebKit implementation of HTML5 as it is the layout engine most frequently used by mobile devices.

The debate surrounding HTML5 has also caused previously included specifications to be dropped. For example, audio codecs that were supported were dropped and currently there is no codec specification in HTML5. Also, the delay in deciding on a specification has forced vendors to make a choice without knowing whether or not their solution will become part of HTML5 specification. For example, Safari, Chrome and Opera all use Web SQL [37] as a means of storing data that can be queried. In November 2010, W3C indicated that the specification was "no longer in active maintenance" and that the Indexed Data API is now supported. Three of the main browsers use a HTML5 database implementation that is no longer in the W3C specification. Developers will continue to use this functionality as long as browsers support it. These kinds of situations will continue to cause differences between browser support for HTML5 thus hindering the adoption of HTML5 for mobile application development.

7.2   HTML5 Mobile Application Business Model

HTML5 applications do not require an app store for distribution. The applications can be freely distributed on the Internet and just as easily updated. The ease of distribution is a positive aspect of HTML5 mobile applications but has far-reaching consequences. Distributing mobile applications via an app store simplifies the process of receiving payment and distributing the product. The app creator sets the price, adds a description, details, etc. and the app store does the rest. The app store even provides a target audience interested in mobile applications. Even though the commercialisation mechanisms have been provided by the app store the key to success is getting people to purchase the app.

The HTML5 mobile application distribution model and therefore business model is completely different. HTML5 applications are easily distributed on the web – anyone with an Internet connection can access an HTML5 application. Bypassing the app store and connecting directly to the consumer requires the app developer to assume the billing responsibility for their app. Of course, an ecommerce system could be built around HTML5 applications to require payment to access the application. However, the open-source nature of HTML5 would mean that it would be difficult to protect the code and stop it being copied and distributed freely. One alternative approach could be to embrace the easy distribution by making the application free and adopting a different business model. Another approach would provide free access to the app and require the user to subscribe to a paid service to unlock full functionality. For example, SoundBoom allowed the user to download a custom soundboard via a unique PIN. A user could pay a set fee or subscription and be provided with a PIN to access the customisation/download functionality. An ecommerce system to manage payment/subscription could be easily implemented.

8   Conclusion

The aim of the project, presented here, was to recreate a cross-compiled native application in HTML5. The resulting HTML5 application included much of the functionality of the original. The solution also included a method to download and cache dynamic content. However, there were two features the HTML5 application could not provide: playing audio offline on mobile devices; accessing device capabilities. The latter was not even attempted in this project due to lack of HTML5 support. For HTML5 to provide a real alternative to native application development these issues need to be addressed either by W3C and WHATWG or the browser vendors.

References

1. ITU press release,
   http://www.itu.int/net/pressoffice/press_releases/2010/39.aspx
2. Gartner press release, http://www.gartner.com/it/page.jsp?id=1689814
3. The Rise of Apps Culture, http://pewinternet.org/Reports/2010/The-Rise-of-Apps-Culture/Overview.aspx
4. Mobile App Internet Recasts The Software And Service Landscape,
   http://www.forrester.com/rb/Research/mobile_app_internet_recasts_software_and_services/q/id/58179/t/2
5. IDC study, http://www.idc.com/research/viewdocsynopsis.jsp?containerId=225668
6. Samsung Smart TV, http://www.samsung.com/uk/smarttv/
7. Melamed, T., Clayton, B.: A Comparative Evaluation of HTML5 as a Pervasive Media Platform. In: Phan, T., Montanari, R., Zerfos, P. (eds.) MobiCASE 2009. LNICST, vol. 35, pp. 307–325. Springer, Heidelberg (2010)
8. Appcelerator Titanium, http://www.appcelerator.com/
9. Mono, http://www.mono-project.com/Main_Page
10. Phone Gap, http://www.phonegap.com/
11. Adobe Flash Player, http://www.adobe.com/products/flashplayer/
12. Corona, http://www.anscamobile.com/
13. Unity 3D, http://unity3d.com/
14. New iPhone Developer Agreement,
    http://daringfireball.net/2010/04/iphone_agreement_bans_flash_compiler
15. Statement by Apple on App Store Review Guidelines,
    http://www.apple.com/pr/library/2010/09/09Statement-by-Apple-on-App-Store-Review-Guidelines.html
16. HTML5 Working Draft, http://www.w3.org/TR/html5/
17. SoundBoom iTunes,
    http://itunes.apple.com/gb/app/soundboom/id429903896?mt=8
18. SoundBoom BlackBerry App World, http://appworld.blackberry.com/webstore/content/38624?lang=en
19. SoundBoom Android Market, https://play.google.com/store/apps/details?id=air.ie.jampot.SoundBoomPro&feature=search_result#?t=W251bGwsMSwxLDEsImFpci5pZS5qYW1wb3QuU291bmRCb29tUHJvIl0
20. SoundBoom Amazon, http://www.amazon.com/JamPot-Technologies-Ltd-SoundBoom/dp/B004X6GU56/ref=sr_1_1?ie=UTF8&s=mobile-apps&qid=1303284579&sr=1-1
21. SoundBoom Intel AppUp,
    http://www.appup.com/applications/applications-SoundBoom
22. MeeGo, https://www.meego.com/
23. WeTab, http://wetab.mobi/en/
24. Mac OSX, http://www.apple.com/macosx/
25. Microsoft Windows, http://windows.microsoft.com/en-US/windows/home
26. iPhone Photo Picker, http://code.google.com/p/iphone-photo-picker/
27. WHATWG, http://www.whatwg.org/
28. Lawson, B., Sharp, R.: Introducing HTML5. New riders (2010)

29. Silverlight, http://www.microsoft.com/silverlight/
30. The HTML5 Test, http://html5test.com/results.html
31. jQuery, http://jquery.com/
32. CSS3, http://www.css3.info/
33. Lubbers, P., Albers, B., Salim, D.: Pro HTML5 Programming. Apress (2010)
34. Modernizr, http://www.modernizr.com/
35. Detecting offline status in HTML5,
    http://ednortonengineeringsociety.blogspot.com/2010/10/
    detecting-offline-status-in-html-5.html
36. Mobile Browser Stats for (January 2011),
    http://www.quirksmode.org/blog/archives/2011/02/
    mobile_browser_5.html
37. Web SQL Database, http://www.w3.org/TR/webdatabase/

A Framework for the Development of Mobile Social Software on Android

Robert Lübke, Daniel Schuster, and Alexander Schill

Computer Networks Group, Technische Universität Dresden, Dresden, Germany
{robert.luebke,daniel.schuster,alexander.schill}@tu-dresden.de

Abstract. Nowadays, social aspects can be found in more and more mobile applications. Analyzing the domain of mobile social software and especially the offered features shows much similarity in the different apps. A framework that supports often used functionalities can facilitate and speed up the development of new innovative mobile applications. This paper presents the Mobilis framework, which aims to extensively support the developers of mobile social software. It provides often used features and offers the functionality in a service environment, that can easily be integrated into new mobile applications.

Keywords: social software, mobile computing, framework, social network, group formation, collaboration, XMPP, Android.

1 Introduction

In the last years social networks have gained a huge popularity. Nowadays they connect millions of internet users with each other. Facebook Places[1], Foursquare[2] and Gowalla[3] are well-known examples of apps that combine social networking and pervasive computing and thereby form the trend of *pervasive social computing*. While many social platforms are accessible via apps for mobile devices, they do not unfold their full potential until the connected users can interact and collaborate with each other in a way that is adapted to the current situation and technical infrastructure. With collaborative features users interact with each other in a target-oriented way to reach a common goal and they coordinate each other with their mobile devices. Such collaborative social apps can be applied in the private and the business sector. However, the development of those collaborative services is quite expensive. There are various other features of mobile social software that should also not be designed and implemented from scratch in every new app.

This paper presents the Mobilis framework, that aims to overcome this issue by extensively supporting the developers of mobile social software. It consists of client and server components and basic XML-based communication mechanisms

---

[1] http://www.facebook.com/places
[2] http://www.foursquare.com
[3] http://www.gowalla.com

J.Y. Zhang et al. (Eds.): MobiCASE 2011, LNICST 95, pp. 207–225, 2012.
© Institute for Computer Sciences, Social Informatics and Telecommunications Engineering 2012

between those components. It provides features, that are often used in mobile social applications. The functionality is offered as parts of a service environment, which can be easily integrated into new mobile applications. These services do for instance cover (location-based) group formation, user context management, integration of social networks, collaborative editing of documents and media sharing. Furthermore it provides an infrastructure for easy communication within social networks. To our knowledge until now there is no other system supporting the developers of mobile social software with these needed special functions, neither in research nor in commerce.

After giving an overview about the domain of mobile social software and discussing related work, we define the requirements of the framework for mobile social software. We further discuss possible technologies to use in this service environment. The Mobilis platform itself is presented in the following sections. At the end the results are evaluated by showing apps that were developed using the Mobilis framework.

2   Background and Related Work

Mobile social software is a class of applications for mobile devices with the main goal to allow and support the social interaction in a community of mobile users. Mobile social software enables communication, coordination and collaboration within social networks.

There is a large number of applications in this domain. Hence there are multiple attempts to create classifications and taxonomies, in which the mobile social apps can be arranged.

According to [1] there are three social network models: *intimate, crowd* and *hybrid*. In intimate social networks the users interact with people they have close personal connections to, for example friends and family. In crowd networks on the other hand the interaction is among users who are unknown to each other. A good example for these networks is the auction platform eBay[4]. Hybrid networks combine aspects of both social network models. In systems such as Flickr[5] the user can benefit from personal connections, but one can also use content generated by the user crowd.

In [2] mobile social software is classified depending on the social context. The authors consider four dimensions of social context: *spatial, temporal, inference* and *people* (STIP). The spatial dimension defines how relevant the geographical distance of the users is. In the temporal dimension the authors differ between short-, mid- and long-term social interactions. The inference dimension describes how the social context of the user is inferred. Finally the people dimension represents the kind of the counterpart the users interacts with. These can be individuals, groups or anonymous communities. All systems are analyzed according to these dimensions and given a characteristic STIP vector.

---

[4] http://www.ebay.com
[5] http://www.flickr.com

One can also classify the applications according to their main functionality. Many apps allow the sending of media or simple text messages like Twitter[6]. Other systems notify the user if a friend or a special event is in the vicinity. Examples for these proximity-based services are VENETA [3], WhozThat [4] and PeopleTones [5]. Urbiflock [6] and Socialaware [7] are systems that exploit location context to establish user groups. Geotagging apps like Google Buzz[7] form another class. One can also find many dating apps, for example MeetMoi[8]. There are also Mobile Social Games and apps with gaming features like Foursquare and Gowalla.

In summary, many mobile social applications often show similar or even identical functionalities like communication, media sharing, grouping and collaborating. The notion of location also plays an important role in most applications. These features should not be designed and implemented from scratch in every new mobile app. Hence there is the need for a framework supporting these often used functions.

Different existing frameworks and middleware layers like SAMOA [8], MobiSoc [9] and MobiClique [10] facilitate the development of new applications. These systems have the main goal to divide the user community into multiple social networks. For this purpose user and location profiles are applied and matched with each other to detect interesting persons and places for the user. All of the mentioned frameworks and middleware layers cover the details of social networking while app developers can concentrate on their application logic. But in essence they do not support the mentioned typical functions that are used within a social network. Therefore we want to discuss the requirements, the conceptual design, implementation details and evaluation aspects of the mobile social software framework Mobilis, that provides exactly this often used functionality.

3   Requirements

The previous section showed that mobile social software often has the same or similar features. Therefore a framework providing these features would be useful. In this section the required features are analyzed.

The framework should support simple communication mechanisms for all involved entities (*FR-1*). Especially the users of the applications must be able to exchange text messages. Furthermore all communication partners should be able to exchange and fetch presence information (*FR-1.1*). Every user can set his own presence status (available, busy, do not disturb, etc.) and propagate it to a presence server. Additionally, groups of users must be able to communicate in multi-user chat rooms (*FR-1.2*).

Context information of the user (current location, friends, used device, etc.) play an important role in the area of mobile social software, for example to make

---

[6] http://www.twitter.com
[7] http://www.google.com/buzz
[8] http://www.meetmoi.com

applications adaptable. Therefore the framework should determine and manage the different kinds of context information. The collected data can also be shared with authorized entities similar to a notification service in a publish/subscribe scenario (*FR-2*).

It is a common feature of mobile social software to use existing social networks like Facebook or Foursquare. The framework should support developers with the integration into own applications (*FR-3*).

The framework should offer file sharing functionality (*FR-4*), because this is often used within social networks. Mainly photos and videos are shared with friends. Therefore the framework should also support the more special sharing of media. Those media files can be tagged with meta information (recording time and location, author) that help searching in large collections.

Another main component in social networks is the formation of groups with users of similar interests. The claimed group management (*FR-5*) includes creating and deleting of groups but also the management of members and joinings. There is a special kind of grouping in the context of mobile social software. It is called location-based group formation and it allows the users to see and join special groups only at certain places.

The framework should support a matching mechanism (*FR-6*), that can be used based on proximity, interests, preferences and activities. Proximity detection informs the user about possible actions in his near surrounding. An application that matches locations of entities could for instance raise an alarm if one of the user's friends is near or if a near restaurant has a special offer. Another example is a trading function based on matching of requests and offers. It could for instance be used in a shopping application, that allows to offer and search for products in a social network.

Real-time collaboration within social networks gains more and more importance. One reasonable collaborative function is the shared editing of documents or other shared state. The framework should support simultaneous editing of XML-based documents by multiple users (*FR-7*). Thus, developers of mobile social apps can utilize this function for easily managing any structured multi-user objects like game state, a shared playlist or shared task list. The mentioned features were already implemented in some of the systems we surveyed (yet without using a shared editing service).

All of the above mentioned functions shall be implemented as reusable services. So the service paradigm should be realized (*FR-8*). As in common service-oriented architectures the functionality is encapsulated and should be accessible via well-defined interfaces (*FR-8.1*). The usage of these services has to be independent from the underlying implementation (*FR-8.2*). Furthermore, such a service environment needs to have mechanisms for service discovery (*FR-8.3*), the different entities can use to find the functionality they are looking for. Additionally the framework should support different versions of the various services (*FR-8.4*).

Table 1 once more summarizes all the mentioned functional requirements we derived from our survey of current mobile social apps. It represents a good core

Table 1. Requirements

Identifier	Description
FR-1	Communication
FR-1.1	Management of presence information
FR-1.2	Multi-user chat
FR-2	User context management
FR-3	Integration of existing social networks
FR-4	File and media sharing
FR-5	Group management (based on location)
FR-6	Matching mechanism
FR-7	Shared editing
FR-8	Realize service paradigm
FR-8.1	Encapsulate functionality; well-defined interfaces
FR-8.2	Transparency to underlying implementation
FR-8.3	Service discovery
FR-8.4	Support of different service versions

of services covering most of the commonly used functionality in the mobile social apps we surveyed. As such a list can never be complete in terms of covering every reusable functionality, an open, extendable approach is needed for the architecture of the platform. In the following, we first survey appropriate technologies for this purpose before defining our architecture.

4   Technologies

This section presents details about the technologies used to realize the service environment of the framework. Many existing solutions use proprietary protocols. While this may be an efficient solution, they mostly depend on a special mobile platform. Thus, interoperability is not given and the degree of reusability is low. Therefore a fundamental requirement is to use standardized solutions. The technology should also have an active community adapting it to recent developments.

One possible solution is to implement the functionality in web services and to let client and server communicate via *SOAP*. However, SOAP can not meet the main requirement of easy communication among all clients (see *FR-1*).

The *Session Initiation Protocol* (SIP) meets the stated demands. Especially the mechanisms of the registrar servers and the location service make SIP a convenient protocol for mobile environments. SIP is appropriate for the given use case, but unfortunately most providers block all SIP messages in their networks to avoid VoIP traffic. It would be counterproductive to apply a protocol, that can not be used in all mobile communications networks, as a basis for innovative mobile apps. Furthermore SIP has a big overhead due to the protocol headers in every message.

The eXtensible Messaging and Presence Protocol (XMPP) [11] is an XML-based protocol collection for the exchange of messages and presence information, that also meets the requirements of the service environment of the framework. Originally the project was called Jabber which was developed from 1998 to 2000. In 2002 Jabber was standardized by the Internet Engineering Task Force (IETF) under the name XMPP.

One of the strengths of XMPP is security, because the core standard includes multiple mechanisms for encryption and authentication. For example one can use the *Simple Authentication Security Layer* (SASL) to authenticate and *Transport Layer Security* (TLS) for encryption.

Each XMPP entity has its own XMPP address, that can be used to contact this entity. It is also called XMPP-ID, Jabber ID oder JID. A JID is composed similarly to an email address, because it has the form `username@XMPP-server`. Of course the user has to possess a registered account at the specified XMPP server. XMPP also supports multiple simultaneous connections over one account. A special resource identifier is used to differentiate between the connections. It is appended to the *bare JID*. The resulting form `username@XMPP-server/resource` is also called *full JID*.

At first an XMPP client has to log in at his XMPP server. After establishing a TCP connection with two XML streams – one for each communication direction – information can be exchanged via well-defined XML stanzas. There are three different kinds of XML stanzas in the XMPP standard.

The *message stanza* can be compared to a push mechanism. Mostly it is used for instant messaging among the users as it can contain text messages. But it can also be used for notifications about special events.

The *presence stanza* contains presence information about XMPP users. This is realized with a publish/subscribe mechanism, i.e., multiple entities can receive status updates about the entity they are subscribed to. These status updates are sent to all subscribers like in a broadcast. A presence stanza can also contain priorities besides the textual description of the status (available, do-not-disturb, away, etc.).

The *info/query stanza* can be used to realize simple request/response services within the XMPP architecture. Like in a remote procedure call, one entity can send a request to another entity, that processes this request and then sends back a result or an error message. Therefore an IQ stanza has one of the following four types: `GET` to request information, `SET` to determine values, `RESULT` to return the outcome of a request or `ERROR` to report on maloperation. The XML structure of an IQ with all necessary elements and attributes is shown in Figure 1. It has an `iq`-element as its root. Beside the `type` every IQ has an identifier (`id`), a sender (`from`) and a recipient (`to`). Below the root element one can find the child element with the namespace (`xmlns`). The part consisting of the child element and all its children is also called payload of the IQ.

Another major strength of XMPP is its extensibility. All three stanza types can be extended regarding various aspects. One can define and use own protocol extensions, but there are also over 200 existing XMPP Extension Protocols

```
<iq id="abc123" type="get"
    from="client@xmpp/MyCar"
    to="NavigationSystem@xmpp/RouteCalculation">
    <query xmlns="example.com#services/RouteCalculation">
        <target-location>
            <longitude>13.766044</longitude>
            <latitude>51.036649</latitude>
            <altitude>45</altitude>
        </target-location>
        <target-name>
            Potsdamer Platz 1, Berlin, Germany
        </target-name>
    </query>
</iq>
```

Fig. 1. Example of an Info/Query (IQ) stanza

(XEP) that were developed and later standardized by the XMPP community. Some of the most useful ones for mobile social apps are multi-user chat, service discovery, and publish/subscribe, which will shortly be introduced in the following.

XEP-0045 [12] defines the XMPP extension protocol for multi-user chat. Like every other XMPP entity, a multi-user chat room has its own XMPP address. The participants have to register with the chat room, to take part in the conversation. Group messages are sent directly to the chat room JID and then forwarded to all participants. The Service Discovery extension XEP-0030 [13] covers finding information about special entities in the XMPP network, for example supported protocols, features, extensions and offered services. This XEP is very important in service environments like the one that should be developed for the mobile social software framework. XEP-0060 [14] defines the functionality of a generic publish/subscribe service, that can be employed in various use cases. One user publishes a certain piece of information and a notification about that event is sent to all authorized subscribers. XEP-0060 also defines how the subscription of such information updates and the authorization is done.

There are still other XEPs that could be interesting in mobile social software, especially those extensions, that define a certain payload format to exchange information about the user, for example his location [15], his mood [16] or the music he is currently listening to [17]. It was already pointed out before, that file sharing, which is covered by XEP-0096 [18], is an important feature in social networks, too.

In summary, XMPP suits well as a technology for the service environment of the mobile social software framework. Especially the IQ mechanism enabling simple request/response services will be used in the framework. XMPP also supports easy communication between the entities (see *FR-1*). XMPP is based on XML and therefore platform independent. Many of the mentioned standard extensions are applicable in mobile social software. The XMPP standard includes security aspects that have even more importance in mobile environments.

The disadvantage of high overhead is due to platform independent coding in XML format. So it is not a special disadvantage of XMPP but one of all platform independent service environments. Extensions for XML stream compression [19] help to overcome this issue.

5   The Mobilis Platform

This section gives a detailed overview about the Mobilis platform - a framework for mobile social software. After describing the general architecture, some of the main components are discussed in detail.

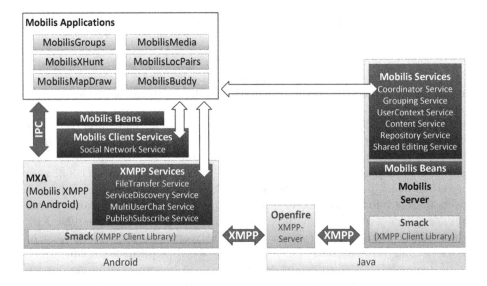

Fig. 2. General architecture of the Mobilis platform

5.1   General Architecture

The general architecture of the Mobilis platform is shown in Figure 2. The MobilisServer offers various services, the so-called Mobilis Services, to the client applications. These services have their own XMPP addresses and can be called via XMPP messages. The communication is based on the XMPP client library Smack[9]. It facilitates sending and receiving of XMPP packets within Java applications. We use Openfire[10] as XMPP server, but every other XMPP server could also be employed as we do not extend the XMPP server implementation itself.

To assure the communication on the client side several adjustments had to be made to Smack to use it within Android applications. Therefore the functionality

---

[9] http://www.igniterealtime.org/projects/smack/
[10] http://www.igniterealtime.org/projects/openfire/

of Smack is encapsulated in the application MXA (Mobilis XMPP on Android). This application provides an AIDL (Android interface definition language) interface to the services of MXA. In this way MXA can be used by the different Mobilis applications to communicate via XMPP with the MobilisServer.

Beside the basic communication, MXA provides additional XMPP Services. These services realize certain XMPP extensions. One service enables file transfers within the XMPP architecture, another provides administrative functionality for multi-user chats. It is also possible to use XMPP service discovery and a publish/subscribe mechanism.

The component Mobilis Beans is a collection of structures that help to create the custom XMPP messages, which are exchanged between the MobilisServer and the clients. Therefore the Mobilis Beans contain the custom protocols and define how to use the services of the MobilisServer from the Mobilis application's point of view.

Developers of Android applications can find special services in the Android Library Mobilis Client Services. These services are components that are often used in mobile collaborative and social software. One of these services is the Social Network Service, that facilitates the integration of existing external social networks into own applications.

5.2   Mobilis Client Services

Developers of Android applications can find special services in the Android Library *Mobilis Client Services*. These services are components that are often used in mobile collaborative and social software.

At the moment one can see that existing social networks more and more link with each other. Therefore it should be possible for new social applications to integrate existing networks. Furthermore new social apps suffer from small user numbers. A real networking among the users is not possible until a critical mass of participants is reached.

For these reasons the integration of existing external social networks into own applications is the main task of the Mobilis Client Services and especially of the Social Network Service. This service encapsulates the application programming interfaces (API) of different social networks and provides the developers with this functionality conveniently at one central place. The general architecture of the Mobilis Client Services is illustrated in Figure 3.

The Social Network Service is implemented as an Android Service, that provides its functionality via an AIDL interface. It manages multiple *Social Network Manager* components, which encapsulate the respective API functions.

At the moment the supported systems are *Foursquare, Gowalla* and *Qype*[11]. Foursquare and Gowalla are mobile social networking applications with gaming characteristics. Users tell the system where they currently reside by checking in at special locations. This is rewarded with points or bonus items. The most frequently visiting user becomes the virtual mayor of a place. Both APIs support

---

[11] http://www.qype.com

vicinity search within the recorded locations, that can also be integrated into own applications. Qype is a recommendation system, in which the users can evaluate companies, locations, services etc. Adapters for other services like Facebook or Twitter can be added accordingly.

Applications have to authorize before they can use the APIs of the different social networks. Most systems use $OAuth$[12] for this purpose. With this protocol a user can authorize an application to access data on the social network system, without revealing the user credentials. The OAuth component of the Social Network Service manages this authorization process.

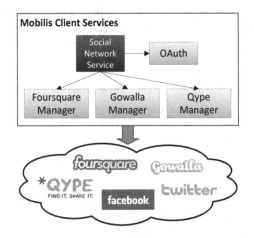

Fig. 3. Concept of the Mobilis Client Services

5.3   XMPP Services

Several adjustments to the XMPP library Smack have to be made to use it within Android applications. Therefore the functionality of Smack is encapsulated in the application MXA (Mobilis XMPP on Android). This application provides an AIDL interface to its services that can be used by the different Mobilis applications to communicate via XMPP with the MobilisServer.

Beside the basic XMPP communication function MXA supports some special XMPP extensions, that are listed in Figure 4. One of these extensions is the multi-user chat, that is specified in [12]. With the help of the *MultiUserChat Service*, one can use the basic functions like joining and leaving such a chat room, reacting on invitations, retrieving detailed information about a chat room and sending group messages. But it also supports various administrative functions like creating a new chat room, inviting users and kicking participants.

The *FileTransfer Service* enables file sharing within the XMPP network. It is based on XEP-0096 SI FileTransfer [18]. Users can send files and manage the incoming file tranfers.

---

[12] http://oauth.net/

The *ServiceDiscovery Service* realizes XEP-0030 that is specified in [13]. An application can find out more information about other XMPP entities with this service. That covers supported protocols, features and extensions of the respective XMPP entity. The service is used within the Mobilis platform to find all services that are currently running on a MobilisServer.

The *PublishSubscribe Service* realizes parts of XEP-0060. This extension specifies the basic functionality of a generic publish/subscribe mechanism. The PubSub Service supports subscription and cancellation of information updates.

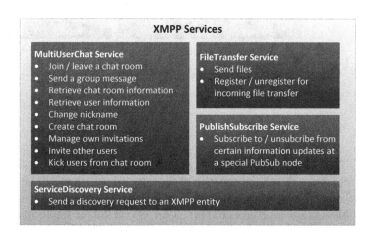

Fig. 4. Functionalities of the XMPP services

5.4   Mobilis Services

The MobilisServer offers various services to the client applications. These so called Mobilis Services are the main component of the Mobilis service environment. Figure 5 illustrates the different layers the services can be divided into.

Client applications can get information about all active and supported services on a MobilisServer with the help of the *Coordinator Service*. This is done with an own XMPP protocol extension that is based on XEP-0030 (Service Discovery). It extends this XEP for instance with version numbers for the services. The Coordinator also allows to start new service instances. The client application only has to send the corresponding IQ stanza with the namespace of the required service and the Coordinator starts a new instance.

The generic and reusable services are the basis of the MobilisServer. The most important services are presented in the following:

User Context Service. The User Context Service manages all kind of context information of the users. Context covers all information that can be used to characterize the situation of a certain entity. Mostly these entities are people, but one can also think of places or other objects that can be relevant for the interaction of user and application [20]. The physical context for instance includes

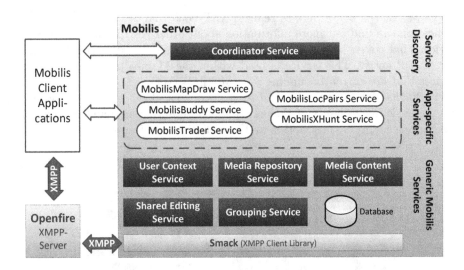

Fig. 5. Service layers of a MobilisServer

temperature, light and sound intensity of the user's surroundings. Examples of technical context are the characteristics of the network (bandwidth, latency) the user is connected to and also information about the mobile device he is using. Every user also has a personal context. This covers for example his address, phone number, calendar and his favorite payment method. Furthermore one can define the user's social context. This includes information about friends, family and groups of the user.

The User Context Service is designed to support all these different kinds of context information. It manages a so called context tree for every user. The nodes of this tree contain related pieces of context information about the user, for example his location, the music he is listening to or his mood. The nodes consist of simple key/value pairs. Additionally one can find the date of the last time the node was updated and the date it expires. After expiration of validity all data of the node is deleted. This assures a secure handling of possibly confidential context data.

The User Context Service is based on a publish/subscribe mechanism. The user decides which information to publish by sending it to the service. He also has to authorize all entities that should be able to access his data. All subscribers of a special node of the context tree are notified in real time if the data was updated.

Grouping Service. The Grouping Service implements the functionality for the management of user groups, but it also includes location and time. This idea is called location-based group formation and discussed in detail in [21]. Groups are a very important feature in social software. Users with the same interests can find each other, discuss the group's topic, share photos, etc. But groups do mostly have spatial and temporal aspects like a special place and time of a meeting. Applying this idea in mobile social networks links the physical and the virtual world by creating incentives to be at a certain place at a certain time.

Repository and Content Service. Media sharing is also an often used feature in social software. Mostly photos are exchanged among friends. The Repository Service and the Content Service realize this within the Mobilis platform. It furthermore specializes in sharing of photos with tagged geographical information. Users can for example search photos by location, time and author.

Collaborative Editing Service. This service enables the shared and simultaneous editing of data by multiple users at different locations. This is also called Collaborative Editing or Shared Editing. The aim is to let all participants of a collaborative editing session see each other's changes in a document in real time. Possible conflicts during editing are detected and resolved. The Collaborative Editing Service supports any XML formatted document.

Application-specific services can be found in the layer above the generic services. These parts are not reusable because they do only serve special applications, but they can access and reuse functionality of the *Generic Mobilis Services*. They mediate between mobile apps and the generic services. Client applications can either directly contact and use the Generic Mobilis Services, or they can have an own App-specific Service that includes additional application logic. Examples for App-specific services are XHunt and LocPairs service. These are the server components of two location-based games that have been implemented with Mobilis (further details in section 6). The MobilisBuddy Service realizes proximity detection.

All services on a MobilisServer have their own XMPP address. That allows client applications to contact and use the services' functionality. Each service therefore has its own connection to the XMPP server. The discussed splitting of functionality into different services enables the deployment in distributed scenarios. Each service can run on its own machine without any further adjustments.

5.5   Mobilis Beans

It was already discussed in detail that the communication within the Mobilis platform uses XMPP and especially the IQ stanzas. Developers of new applications should not always implement the creation and parsing of IQ stanzas on their own. This is the task of the *Mobilis Beans* component, that contains various structures for the creation of XMPP stanzas, which are exchanged between client and server. Here one can find the particular parts of the protocols, that define how to use the services of the framework. Developers of applications can use the Mobilis Beans to start requests to the services.

The main advantage is the reuse of the Mobilis Beans in all server and client components. Both parts of a Mobilis application reference the Mobilis Beans project and use parts of it for the communication among each other. This furthermore assures the same stanza syntax on both sides.

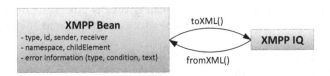

Fig. 6. Overview of important attributes and methods of Mobilis Beans

Each Bean represents a certain XMPP IQ stanza. It contains methods for the conversion into an XMPP IQ to send it, but there are also methods to parse incoming IQs into the correspondent Bean (see Figure 6). Furthermore it contains typical attributes of an IQ, for instance sender, receiver, namespace and child element. If it represents an IQ of type `Error`, it also carries detailed information about the occurred malfunction.

5.6 Web-Based Access

Mobilis does not only provide access to its services for native Android apps but also for web browsers. A web gateway to the Mobilis service environment enables access from PCs and Notebooks, but it also opens up other mobile platforms like iOS or Windows Phone. With new APIs introduced with HTML5 web applications can use more device functions. Furthermore new versions of JavaScript engines with increased performance allow designing impressive user interfaces for the web browser - even on mobile devices.

Using XMPP as communication protocol for the service environment of Mobilis leads to two major problems concerning the web-based access. First, the Hypertext Transfer Protocol (HTTP) is inadequate for bidirectional real-time communictation between client and server. Second, there are no APIs for native XMPP communication in the web browser. The first problem will be solved by the WebSocket API of HTML5 in the near future. But it is not appropriate to use this technology at the moment because of open security issues and the insufficient support by most of the web browsers.

Therefore we reuse existing established technologies to emulate the semantics of a long-living bidirectional connection. One of these technologies is *Bidirectional-streams Over Synchronous HTTP* (BOSH) that is specified in XEP-0124 [22]. It uses synchronous HTTP request/response pairs and no frequent polling to realize the bidirectional connection. The Connection Manager, that is part of the web server, administrates the long-living connection by establishing and releasing it.

A solution to the second problem is given in XEP-0206 [23] with the title *XMPP Over BOSH*. With this extension XMPP stanzas can be transfered as child elements of the `<body>` element via BOSH. In the web browser a Javascript BOSH Client can extract and process the payload information. Combining this idea with the long polling paradigm of XEP-0124 enables bidirectional XMPP real time communication over HTTP.

With this mechanism the presented Mobilis Services (see section 5.4) can be used by client-side web applications that are based on JavaScript. A convenient level of abstraction is given, because the Mobilis JavaScript client library hides all the details of connection management and exchanging XMPP stanzas. It also has a plugin interface and can thereby be extended with further functionality.

6   Evaluation

The previous sections highlighted conceptional aspects and implementation details of the Mobilis platform. This section focuses on the evaluation of the framework especially concerning the functional requirements defined in 3. The easiest way to prove that Mobilis meets the stated requirements is to show applications that use exactly this functionality. Various mobile apps have been developed with Mobilis and there is always at least one demonstration app for each framework service. Some of these apps should be discussed in the following.

MobilisMapDraw demonstrates the server-side Collaborative Editing Service. The graphical user interface of the mobile app shows a drawing area that can be overlaid with a geographical map. The user can join a collaborative drawing session or start a new one. Within the session all participants can draw simultaneously on the map or the shared whiteboard as illustrated in Figure 7 on the left. Use cases of shared drawing can be found in various scenarios, for example in a tourism scenario to manage a trip within a group of participants.

MobilisMedia enables the exchange of multimedia content. More precisely it allows users to store their geotagged photos in repositories. The content of these repositories can be browsed by location, time and author name. The photos are arranged on a map as it can be seen in Figure 7 in the middle. Additionally it is possible to send photos directly to friends without the usage of server repositories.

The basic idea of *MobilisXHunt* is the transformation of the board game *Scotland Yard* by Ravensburger into the reality. It is a game for two to six players. One player is the wanted Mister X and the others are the agents looking for him. The position of Mister X is unknown to the agents but will be published regularly, for example in every third round. In the original game every player has various tickets (taxi, ferry, bus, tram) to move on the board game. The game ends once an agent is on the same station as Mister X or if Mister X could not get caught within a predefined number of rounds. In MobilisXHunt the players are provided with smartphones (with built in GPS receivers) and go on the hunt for Mister X in a real city using real transportation means to get from one station to the next. The user interface of MobilisXHunt is shown in Figure 7 on the right.

MobilisLocPairs is a transformation of the famous children's game Pairs. It can be played inside of buildings which are tagged with special bar codes (QR codes). Behind each code hides one card with a picture. By scanning these codes, the players can see these pictures on their smartphones. The game is also turn-based like the original Pairs but it must be played in teams of two players. Each round has a predefined maximum time (e.g. 60s). In this time the

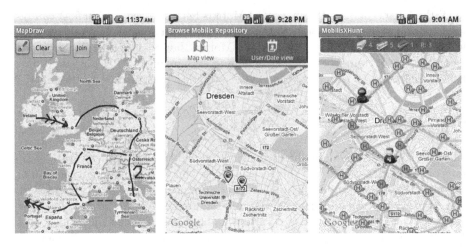

Fig. 7. Screenshots of MobilisMapDraw (left), MobilisMedia (middle) and MobilisX-Hunt (right)

first teammate virtually turns a card by scanning the first bar code. The second teammate then has the task to find the corresponding card / bar code. The aim of the game is to find as much pairs as possible. There is also a special benefit in the game. In every bar code scanning process the smartphone measures the signal strength to all visible WiFi access points and saves this information in a fingerprint which is then sent to a central server. These fingerprints can later be used to improve the indoor positioning in the building where the game took place.

MobilisGroups is a mobile application for location-based group formation, that uses the server-side Grouping Service of the Mobilis framework. The management of user groups as it is known from common social networks is enriched by temporal and spatial aspects. Most of the groups (e.g. associations, communities of interest, sports clubs) and events (e.g. concerts, parties, BarCamps) are located at a special place, for example where the head office is located or meetings take place. These groups sometimes also have an allocated time period, that for example defines when an event happens. The idea of MobilisGroups is to extend the group management of common social networks with these temporal and spatial values as restrictions. To join or even to see certain groups the user has to be at a certain place at a certain time. The user interface of MobilisGroups is shown in Figure 8. The main component is the map view showing all visible groups in the surroundings of the user. Furthermore the user can administrate own groups, see a list of his friends and browse through the groups they are subscribed to. Every group also has a multi-user chat room that can be used by all members.

MobilisContext is a prototype app with the main goal to demonstrate the functionality of the server-side User Context Service. In the tabs of the application's main view one can see the different types of context information that

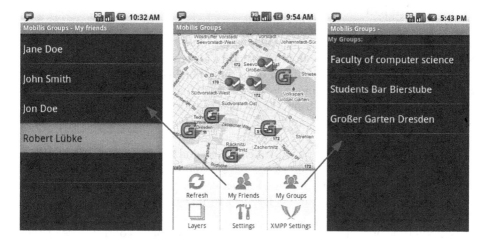

Fig. 8. Screenshots of MobilisGroups

can be shared: the mood of the user (based on XEP-107 [16]), the music he is actually listening to (based on XEP-0118 [17]) and his current location (based on XEP-0080 [15]). Besides these standardized context formats it is also possible to publish and subscribe to generic context information updates. If a user subscribes to another user's context updates, an authorization request is sent to the given XMPP-ID of the user.

MobilisBuddy realizes location-based search for friends on mobile devices. The start screen of MobilisBuddy is a normal map view on which the user can see his own position. In the menu one can organize different XMPP and Facebook accounts. These accounts are used to fetch the user's buddy lists. If one of the user's Facebook friends or XMPP buddies also uses MobilisBuddy and if this friend is located within a special visibility radius (e.g. 500m) of the user, then both receive a notification. So MobilisBuddy is a mobile application for proximity detection and proximity alerts. Within the radius both users can see each other's live location updates. That makes spontaneous meetings very easy. If one user leaves the visibility radius, one can see a gray flag on the user's last known location. This improves the privacy, because only nearby friends can receive live location updates.

This section showed that the framework functionality is used in real apps. We also wanted to point out that the developed apps come from various areas and therefore cover a wide range of use cases. Most of the presented mobile apps are prototypes of student theses or the results of practical courses for mobile app development. All student developers had enough time to get familiar with the Mobilis framework and it's functionalities. The detailed investigation of the learning curve remains an open issue.

In a survey with 35 students who were developing mobile apps we wanted to evaluate the benefit for the developers. The majority (56,25%) of the mobile app projects included features that are offered by the Mobilis framework. The concrete benefit (e.g. in time and LOC) will be explored in future surveys.

7   Conclusion

The main idea of this paper is to provide a reusable framework for mobile social software. It contributes with an infrastructure for easy communication, collaboration, grouping, media sharing and other functionalities that are often used in mobile social networks. A unique feature is that major parts of the framework can be used independently from the mobile platform. The evaluation section showed the variety of mobile applications that were already implemented with the Mobilis framework.

The protocols, the prototype implementations and the framework components are freely available on our Sourceforge page[13] and can be reused by other applications. We are constantly refining and extending the framework and want to encourage the community to use it for their own research projects.

Acknowledgment. The authors want to thank the many contributors of the Mobilis platform for their conceptual and implementation work. The thesis of Nikolas Jansen served as a very good basis for section 5.6. Daniel Esser and the anonymous reviewers helped to improve this article with their feedback.

References

1. Heyer, C.: Mobile Social Software. Phd thesis, The University of Queensland (April 2008)
2. Endler, M., Skyrme, A., Schuster, D., Springer, T.: Defining Situated Social Context for Pervasive Social Computing. In: Second IEEE Workshop on Pervasive Collaboration and Social Networking (PerCol), Seattle, USA (March 2011)
3. Arb, M., Bader, M., Kuhn, M., Wattenhofer, R.: VENETA: Serverless Friend-of-Friend Detection in Mobile Social Networking. In: 4th IEEE International Conference on Wireless and Mobile Computing, Networking and Communications (WiMob), Avignon, France (2008)
4. Beach, A., Gartrell, M., Akkala, S., Elston, J., Kelley, J., Nishimoto, K., Ray, B., Razgulin, S., Sundaresan, K., Surendar, B., Terada, M., Han, R.: WhozThat? Evolving an ecosystem for context-aware mobile social networks. IEEE Network 22, 50–55 (2008)
5. Li, K.A., Sohn, T.Y., Huang, S., Griswold, W.G.: Peopletones: a system for the detection and notification of buddy proximity on mobile phones. In: MobiSys 2008: Proceeding of the 6th International Conference on Mobile Systems, Applications, and Services, Breckenridge, CO, USA (2008)
6. Carreton, A.L., Harnie, D., Boix, E.G., Scholliers, C., Van Cutsem, T., De Meuter, W.: Urbiflock: An experiment in Dynamic Group Management in Pervasive Social Applications. In: First International Workshop on Communication, Collaboration and Social Networking in Pervasive Computing Environments (PerCol), Mannheim, Germany (2010)
7. Gartrell, C.M.: SocialAware: Context-Aware Multimedia Presentation via Mobile Social Networks. Master Thesis, University of Colorado, Department of Computer Science (2008)

---

[13] http://mobilisplatform.sourceforge.net/

8. Bottazzi, D., Montanari, R., Toninelli, A.: Context-Aware Middleware for Anytime, Anywhere Social Networks. IEEE Intelligent Systems 22, 23–32 (2007)
9. Gupta, A., Kalra, A., Boston, D., Borcea, C.: MobiSoC: a middleware for mobile social computing applications. Mobile Networks and Applications 14, 35–52 (2009)
10. Pietiläinen, A.-K., Oliver, E., LeBrun, J., Varghese, G., Diot, C.: MobiClique: middleware for mobile social networking. In: WOSN 2009: Proceedings of the 2nd ACM Workshop on Online Social Networks, Barcelona, Spain (2009)
11. XMPP Standards Foundation (June 2011)
12. Saint Andre, P.: XEP-0045: Multi-User Chat. tech. rep., XMPP Standards Foundation (July 2008)
13. Hildebrand, J., Millard, P., Eatmon, R., Saint Andre, P.: XEP-0030: Service Discovery. tech. rep., XMPP Standards Foundation (June 2008)
14. Millard, P., Saint-Andre, P., Meijer, R.: XEP-0060: Publish-Subscribe. tech. rep., XMPP Standards Foundation (July 2010)
15. Saint Andre, P., Hildebrand, J.: XEP-0080: User Location. tech. rep., XMPP Standards Foundation (September 2009)
16. Saint Andre, P., Meijer, R.: XEP-0107: User Mood. tech. rep., XMPP Standards Foundation (October 2008)
17. Saint Andre, P.: XEP-0118: User Tune. tech. rep., XMPP Standards Foundation (January 2008)
18. Muldowney, T., Miller, M., Eatmon, R.: XEP-0096: SI File Transfer. tech. rep., XMPP Standards Foundation (April 2004)
19. Hildebrand, J., Saint Andre, P.: XEP-0138: Stream Compression. tech. rep., XMPP Standards Foundation (May 2009)
20. Dey, A.K.: Understanding and Using Context. Personal Ubiquitous Comput. 5, 4–7 (2001)
21. Lübke, R., Schuster, D., Schill, A.: MobilisGroups: Location-based Group Formation in Mobile Social Networks. In: 2011 IEEE International Conference on Pervasive Computing and Communications Workshops (PERCOM Workshops), pp. 502–507 (March 2011)
22. Paterson, I., Smith, D., Saint Andre, P., Moffitt, J.: XEP-0124: Bidirectional-streams Over Synchronous HTTP (BOSH). tech. rep., XMPP Standards Foundation (July 2010)
23. Paterson, I., Saint Andre, P.: XEP-0206: XMPP Over BOSH. tech. rep., XMPP Standards Foundation (July 2010)

A Toolkit for Usability Testing
of Mobile Applications

Xiaoxiao Ma, Bo Yan, Guanling Chen, Chunhui Zhang,
Ke Huang, and Jill Drury

Computer Science Department, University of Massachusetts Lowell,
1 University Avenue, Lowell, Massachusetts, 01854
{xma,byan,glchen,czhang,khuang,jdrury}@cs.uml.edu

Abstract. The usability of mobile applications is critical for their adoption particularly because of the relatively small screen and awkward (sometimes virtual) keyboard, despite the recent advances of smartphones. Traditional laboratory-based usability testing is often tedious, expensive, and does not reflect real use cases. In this paper, we propose a toolkit that embeds into mobile applications the ability to automatically collect user interface (UI) events as the user interacts with the applications. The events are fine-grained and useful for quantified usability analysis. We have implemented the toolkit on Android devices and we evaluated the toolkit with a real deployed Android application by comparing event analysis (state-machine based) with traditional laboratory testing (expert based). The results show that our toolkit is effective at capturing detailed UI events for accurate usability analysis.

Keywords: Toolkit, Usability Testing, Mobile Application, Automated, Logging method.

1 Introduction

Led by the rapid growth of the smartphone market, mobile Internet usage in the US is expected to approach 100% penetration and to reach 50% total usage by 2013 [1]. The usability of the mobile applications, however, remains a thorny issue. A recent study shows that the task completion rate using mobile Web ranges from 38% to 75% on different phones [2]. The average success rate was only 59%, substantially lower than the roughly 80% success rate when testing websites on a regular PC today. Another study shows that 73% of users experienced the slow-to-load problem when using the mobile Web, and 48% of users found mobile Web applications difficult to read and use [3].

In this paper, we focus on the usability testing of mobile applications, particularly native (instead of Web based) applications. We envision a system that can automatically collect user interface (UI) events as the user interacts with the mobile application. The collected UI data will then be uploaded to a remote server for either automated or manual usability analysis. This kind of system can complement traditional laboratory testing, and we believe it will be particularly

J.Y. Zhang et al. (Eds.): MobiCASE 2011, LNICST 95, pp. 226–245, 2012.
© Institute for Computer Sciences, Social Informatics and Telecommunications Engineering 2012

useful to deploy for field-based usability testing. For many mobile application developers, it is often too costly to conduct extensive laboratory-based usability testing and we anticipate that the system described in this paper will be an indispensable toolkit for low-cost usability analysis. We have implemented an Android-based automatic usability toolkit. To use our usability testing system, the Android developer needs to modify the application source code by inserting statements calling our library, which captures UI events and uploads them to a central server. We have designed the system to minimize the amount of required code modification and the impact of event-uploading overhead. To evaluate this system, we conducted a traditional laboratory-based usability testing on a home-built Android application, and compared it with state-machine based usability analysis using collected UI events. The results show that our usability toolkit can effectively capture most of the usability problems, some of which were not even discovered by traditional laboratory testing.

In the rest of this paper, we first discuss related work in Section 2. Section 3 describes the details of the design and implementation of our toolkit. Then we discuss the user study and present the usability analysis results in Sections 4 and 5, respectively. Last we talk about some potential issues in Section 6 and conclude in Section 7.

2 Related Work

Many studies have been done with event logging methods, which are compared to traditional laboratory testing methods in terms of usability problems identified. Tullis et al. [4] presented results that showed high correlations between laboratory and remote tests for task completion data and time-on-task data. The most critical usability issues with web sites were identified by both techniques, although each technique also uniquely uncovered other issues [5]. Another study by West and Lehman [6] was conducted to evaluate a method for usability testing with an automated data collection system. They found it to be an effective alternative to a laboratory-based test [5], but these studies were conducted on desktop machines instead of mobile devices.

Waterson et al. [7] conducted a remote usability study on mobile devices. They asked participants to find some information on a web site with wireless Internet-enabled digital assistants. Half of the participants ran the test in a traditional laboratory set-up while the other half performed the task with an observer present, but with an event logging tool to collect clickstream data remotely. They revealed that the event logging and analysis tool can easily gather many of the content-related usability issues, but had difficulty in capturing device-related usability problems. However, their study focused on the mobile websites rather than the mobile applications.

There have been few usability tools developed especially for mobile applications. Flurry Analytics[1] was developed to provide accurate, real time data to developers about how consumers use their mobile applications, as well as how

---

[1] http://www.flurry.com/

applications are performing across different handsets. Application developers receive anonymous, aggregated usage and performance data, as well as the use of robust reporting and analysis tools. However, this tool focuses on statistical information instead of identifying usability problems.

3   Design and Implementation

In this section, we first provide an overview of the Android UI framework, which forms the foundation for our event logging system. Then we discuss the details of its implementation and how it can be integrated with Android applications.

3.1   Android UI Framework

To set up the event logging system and integrate it with developers' applications, we need to have a comprehensive understanding on Android system's UI components, as well as how these components communicate with users' interaction. So here we give a brief introduction of this knowledge. The user interface of an Android application consists of *Activity* classes (terms with itatic font indicates they are classes of Android Library; we use this convention throughout this paper, unless specially stated). Each screen in an Android application is a Java class that extends the Activity class, and activities use *Views* to form graphical user interfaces that display information and respond to user actions. An activity itself can be considered to be the root View for a screen and it is composed of smaller Views, which are interaction components like controls or widgets. Also, there might be other components attached to an activity, such as *Dialogs* or *Menus*, which are usually small windows that may appear in front of an activity. The top-most window in the foreground (View, Dialog or Menu) will always intercept and handle user inputs, whether it occupies a full or only partial screen.

To allow an application to react to user events such as a key press, screen touch and button click, developers have to utilize either event handlers or event listeners to accept user inputs and respond to them. An event handler is usually implemented by overriding some callback function while an event listener is a programming interface that contains a single callback method. As both event handlers and event listeners are constructed through calling underlying Android callback functions and they have the same functionality, for convenience we will use the term "Event Listener" to stand for both of them in the rest of this paper.

Usually an Event Listener is only attached to the window that registers it, and it will "consume" the events captured by it. This means if a button registers an *onClickListener* and then is clicked, the Event Listener of the button would intercept and handle the click, while the screen activity that owns the button has no idea that there was ever a click. Hence, if we want to log every single movement of users' interaction, for each Event Listener that handles an user input, we need to trace into the innermost level of the window that possesses it, and acquire our desired information that is intercepted by it.

3.2   Event Logging System

For usability studies of websites, it is possible to build an instrumented Web browser which allows the users' interactions with the websites to be automatically logged in a fashion that is transparent to the website developer. On the other hand, this is not feasible for Android applications because the UI interactions cannot be automatically captured. Application developers must get involved in modifying the source code and capturing UI events explicitly. To minimize developers' effort, we provide an event logging toolkit that takes care of most of the work of event capturing, formatting and packing, and transmission.

Our event logging system works as follows. The developers make small modifications to the source code of their applications adding API calls and recompiling the source code with the Software Development Kit (SDK) we provide. The SDK contains the APIs for each Event Listener and the developers call the corresponding API in their own listener code. The functionality of the Application Programming Interface (API) is to log ongoing user interaction events, its timestamp and properties of the relevant windows. For example, by inserting one statement in a View's *onClickListener*, the library can retrieve information such as the View's identifier, size, owner activity, and so on.

The recompiled applications now can automatically record the users' UI events, and transmit the captured interaction data periodically to a central server. These events are then used for usability analysis by the evaluators. Instead of transmitting the events immediately to the remote server, the logger runs in the background as a service and puts the captured events in a memory queue. When the number of events accumulates to a predetermined amount, they are transferred to our remote server through the 3G or WiFi network. If there is no available network at the time of transmission, these events will be stored on the device's Secure Digital(SD) card or hard disk sequentially according to their availability. In every event uploading cycle, these two places will be examined, and all existing data stored there will be transmitted if the network allows. The event transmitter creates a new thread for the transporting module so that this process is separated from the UI process.

The remote receiver module simply provides a relational database, as all the UI events are saved into different tables depending on their type. Usability analysis can then be conducted either manually or automatically (see Section 5).

3.3   The Logger Implementation

Android has many Event Listeners, and one listener can be attached to a View, a Dialog or a Menu. As Views, Dialogs and Menus have different appearances and functionalities, they have different sets of listeners. For instance, clicking on a Menu may trigger *onMenuItemClickListener* while clicking on a View may trigger *onViewClickListener*, though both of the interactions are click events. Moreover, even if two subclasses inherit from the same parent, they may not have the same sets of listeners. Take View for example, the subclass *AbsListView* nests the interface component *onScrollListener*, which will handle the user's scrolling on this view. In comparison, most subclasses of View do not support scroll events (they discard these events) if they do not implement *onScrollListener*. Indeed, the View class hierarchy is quite complex, as it has 8 direct subclasses and dozens of indirect subclasses. To assure we log user interaction events as completely as possible, we performed a thorough survey of the class hierarchy of View, Dialog and Menu, and only extracted those listeners that are related to user interaction. We then consolidated the listeners in the following ways.

View Events. Some listeners differ in their names or adhering classes, but they take care of the same user interaction, e.g. *onOptionItemSelectedListener, onMenuItemClickListener* and *onMenuItemSelectedListener* may all be responsible for selecting one item in an Option Menu. More interestingly, the three listeners can be registered at the same time, which means that they can all be triggered upon one click. Since we are interested in the user's interaction type rather than listeners' name, we decided to combine these sorts of similar listeners into one event type to avoid redundancy. Some listeners were distinguished by the type of user event they can handle but take identical parameters, such as the View's *onClickListener* and *onLongClickListener*, which deal with View's short click and long click events, respectively. For the simplicity of the logging library and back-end database design, we treated them as the same events as well, but differentiated them by adding a flag parameter. Thus the View's events were consolidated into *view click, view key press, view scroll* and *AdapterView item click* (note the terms for event types are also italicized). An *AdapterView* is a View whose children are determined by an *Adapter* object acting as a bridge between the *AdapterView* and its underlying data, e.g. an *ArrayAdapter* allows an array of objects to reside in the *AdapterView*.

Dialog and Menu. Events triggered by Dialog and Menu are harder to capture. Dialogs and Menus are usually managed by their adhering activities, and they may not have an identifier (anonymous). Thus in order to locate which Dialog or Menu was fired, we need to infer it from the users' action sequence, by looking at which activity, through which action a Dialog or Menu, was initiated and how a Dialog or Menu was dismissed. It is not difficult to record the initiation event, but some attention needs to be paid to the dismiss event. Dialog has an *onDismissListener* but we cannot rely on it because it does not provide any information about how a Dialog was dismissed. Even worse, no matter how a dialog disappeared, this listener would always be triggered. For instance, if a user presses the OK button in a dialog, Android will first call Dialog's *onClickListener*, and then call *onDismissListener* as the dialog will disappear after the action. This will cause a double counting problem because the single event fires two listeners. Fortunately, we found that if a dialog was not dismissed by hitting the BACK key on the hard keyboard, at least one of the Dialog's *onClickListener* methods will be called, and it tells us which button was clicked that caused the dialog to be dismissed.

We have a different solution for Menu's dismiss event. An *onOptionMenu-Closed* or *onContextMenuClosed* method will be toggled when a menu is closed, depending on the menu type. We can monitor *onMenuItemSelectedListener* to judge whether a menu was closed by selecting an item or by other means. Overall, we included *dialog key press* and *dialog button clicked* events for Dialog and *menu item select* and *menu close* events for Menu to our logging library.

System Keys. Android devices have BACK, MENU, HOME and SEARCH hard keys, and we name them system keys collectively as these keys function for all applications in general. Since an Android application is composed of activities, we can override *onKeyDown* listener in each activity to intercept these system keys. However, Android disabled HOME key interception to preserve its system's running state. If the developers can intercept all key events, they can easily make the system malfunction, such as preventing users from quitting their applications by intercepting the HOME key press. Thus, we have to find other ways to detect that a user clicked the HOME key. Through a class named *ActivityManager*, we can acquire the currently running tasks as well as the top activity of each task. Then we can override each activity's *onStop* method to check if its top activity equals to *com.android.launcher*, which is the activity name of the Android home screen, to decide if the activity is stopped by clicking the HOME button.

Unhandled Events. We believe that the above effort can already help us to record those events whose listeners were registered by the developers. This, however, is not enough. We want to collect a comprehensive set of the user's interaction behaviors, but the developers will most likely only register listeners in which they are interested. Suppose a developer does not register an *onKeyDownListener* method in one activity, and a user tried to click a button that belongs to this activity. If, for some reason, this user missed clicking on the button but happened to click on the activity itself (recall an activity is also a view), the application will still run well because that activity will discard this mis-click by default. The developers may not care about this kind of event, but these events can be important to discover usability issues. For example, if we detected many clicks around the button, we can infer that the button is hard to click for some reason. Thus we would like to capture such events as much as possible, and we name them unhandled events in general.

In summary, the events we captured were classified by their adhering class and are listed in the Table 1. For different events, we obtained different attributes according to their own available properties. From an event that occurred in a View, we can retrieve its ID, width, height and its parent class etc., while for events that happened in a menu or dialog, they may not have such information. But for whatever window, we tried to retrieve as many event attributes as possible.

3.4   Code Revision

The extent of the revision that needs to be done in the developers' code greatly depends on the hierarchical organization of the source code. Thus here we only

Table 1. Event Type Summary

	Event Type
View	click, key press, adapter item click, scroll
Dialog	key press, button click
Menu	item select, close
Other	unhandled motion event, unhandled key event, home key click, system key click, preference click

discuss the best and the worst cases in terms of the code modification workload. In the best case, all activities in an application extend from a single root activity, so the developer just needs to insert one event recording statement (by calling our API) into the *onTouchEvent, onKeyUp, onStop* methods of that root activity. Meanwhile, the event listeners were implemented uniformly rather than redefined in each View/Dialog/Menu, so that only one recording statement in the implemented View/Dialog/Menu event listeners needs to be inserted.

In the worst case, the activities in the application have no hierarchical structure at all and the event listeners were implemented separately from each View/Dialog/Menu. Then the developers have to insert the recording statement into the *onTouchEvent, onKeyUp, onStop* methods in each of their activities, and insert the recording statement into each View/Dialog/Menu Event Listener.

In both cases, we require that the application classes extend the application class of our own library so that our library can make use of the static memory space allocated to the application.

There are two additional challenges. First, the Android framework has already implemented some event listeners by default, such as the *onKeyDownListener* for an edit box. In this way, an edit box can accept key presses even without developers registering this listener explicitly. For such cases, we have to override the related listeners and register them so as not to miss recording the user's input. Second, the hierarchical relationship between classes can be troublesome for counting the user's interaction events accurately. While usually the user's interaction in one window will not be passed to its parent, the developers can call the super method to allow this to happen. If we add the logging function in both super and subclasses, one event that happened in the subclass may be recorded twice. Thus to avoid this double counting problem, we have to examine the application's class hierarchy and check whether at some point the developers called the super method.

In the future, we plan to provide a tool that can automatically inspect an application's source code and make appropriate changes for event logging, without the developers' involvement.

3.5   Events Not Captured

So far, our logging system is able to capture all the events that the developers have already set to listen as well as those unhandled events at the activity level. But there still remain some events that are not being captured. First, we cannot log events that occurred in Android native activities, such as the Android Settings. We do not, however, really need these events as the goal of our system is to identify usability issues of the third-party applications, rather than the Android native screens. Second, we have not found any feasible way to trace keystrokes on the Android soft keyboard. Finally, we did not capture the unhandled events occurring in child Views, Dialogs and Menus of an activity. Although this is doable by registering listeners in each View/Dialog/Menu, we do not think it deserves so much effort (which involves changing source code) compared to its usefulness and potential event logging overhead.

Despite missing these events, the current system can already capture a comprehensive set of interaction events that can be used for usability analysis, as demonstrated in the next section.

4   User Studies

We conducted a user study to evaluate whether the proposed event logging toolkit is effective and helpful in identifying usability problems. One Android application called AppJoy [8], which has been deployed to the Google Market, was used as our subject application. It was developed by our group; we have the source code so it is convenient for us to integrate it with our logging library. We recruited participants to use this application and asked them to execute certain tasks assigned by us. Afterwards, we examined the logged events for usability analysis.

4.1   AppJoy Overview

The explosive growth of the mobile application market has made it a significant challenge for users to find interesting applications in crowded App Stores. While the application stores allow the users to search for applications by keywords or browse top applications in different categories, it is still difficult for the users to find interesting applications that they like. In light of this problem, existing industry solutions often use users' application download history or their ratings on some applications to predict users' preferences, such as Amazon's book recommendations. However, "downloading" is actually a weak indicator of users' fondness for an application, particularly if the application is free and users just want to try it out. Using application ratings, on the other hand, suffers from tedious manual input and potential data sparsity problems.

AppJoy makes personalized application recommendations by analyzing users' statistical usage of their installed applications. It can also allow users to browse popular applications according to their location, and track their application usage.

4.2   Participant Briefing

Participants were recruited through posters. We recruited 12 participants in total, all of them were undergraduate or graduate students of our school. We asked the participants to fill in a demographic information survey before the study. The questions included gender, major, own cellphone platform, familiarity with Android platform and previous experience in usability testing, and so on.

Among the participants, 7 were from the Computer Science department while 5 were not, 7 were male and the other 5 were female. All of them were between 20 and 35 years old. 2 participants owned an Android phone, 3 participants owned an iPhone and 7 participants did not have a smartphone. One iPhone user and one non-smartphone user also used an Android phone before, so in addition to the two participants who owned an Android phone, we had 4 Android phone users, but none of them were Android developers. 4 participants had previous experience with usability tests. None of the participants had used AppJoy before.

4.3   AppJoy Tasks

All participants were given the same Android device – Motorola Droid with Android version 2.2.2. AppJoy was preloaded onto the device and the device was connected to a university WiFi network. Every participant was assigned the following tasks one by one in the same order:

1. Browse recommended applications in AppJoy and "dislike" the first application the user is not interested in.
2. Browse the newest applications in AppJoy and install the first one whose rating is greater than 4 stars and the number of downloads is greater than 50,000.
3. Clear search history in AppJoy settings.
4. Search applications used by people in Boston, and point out the first application that was installed on this device.
5. Use AppJoy to uninstall the application that has been installed in task 2.
6. In AppJoy, look up the usage time of AppJoy.

As we did not code a special function to indicate the completion of a task, we used Android's SCREEN_ON and SCREEN_OFF broadcasting events as the separator between tasks during the test. Participants were asked to give the device back to one of the evaluators after completing each task, and the evaluator turned off and turned on the screen twice and reset the application to its homepage before the next task.

5   Evaluation Results

In this section we answer the question of whether the UI events collected via the Android UI framework can indeed be used for usability analysis. The laboratory-based usability testing method known as formal usability testing is one of the most widely used approaches by usability practitioners for performing usability analysis [9,10]. Thus we performed a laboratory-based usability test and compared it to a quantified state-machine based analysis using the collected events.

When the participants were executing tasks, we asked them to "think aloud" [11] and had several evaluators sitting beside them to take notes. At the same

Table 2. Usability Problems Identified by Laboratory Testing

	AppJoy Problem	Android Convention
Cosmetic	5	2
Minor	4	2
Major	4	2
Catastrophe	1	0

time, all of the user's interaction events with the AppJoy were simultaneously logged and the data was transmitted to our server. In this way, we were able to get a fair comparison for the two different methods, since they were compared using the same participants, the same Android device, at the same time, within the same testing environment and the same user behaviors.

During the test, we lost two participants' data due to the misconfiguration of the event logging system. So when comparing the two methods, we only considered information collected from the remaining 10 participants. The two people we lost data from were participant 4 and 5, one of them is male and the other is female. Neither of them majored in computer science and neither of them had prior Android experience. When presenting the evaluation in this section, we do use all 12 participants' data except for the comparison results.

5.1 Traditional Laboratory-Based Usability Testing Results

When the participants were executing tasks, we asked them to "think aloud" and had 3 evaluators taking notes beside them. The evaluators were all very familiar with AppJoy and one of them is the lead developer. In order to get a better understanding of wrong moves the participants made when executing specific tasks, we talked with them about the difficulties they encountered during the test, and what caused their confusion. We found that these conversations with participants were indeed valuable for us to judge the exact cause of a usability problem. After the experiment was over, the evaluators discussed and consolidated usability problems identified based on their notes, the participants' survey and their verbal feedback. Then we rated the severity of each usability problem according to Nielsen's severity rating criteria [12], and summarized them in Table 2.

Some of the problems were apparently caused by the AppJoy design, which we call AppJoy problems. Some of the other issues could not be categorized as AppJoy problems because AppJoy just leveraged some components of the Android framework that caused the user confusion. For instance, some participants did not know how to view the notifications on Android, as they tapped on the notification bar instead of dragging. Also, there was one participant who said that he/she did not know how to scroll the view on the screen, and he/she moved his/her finger in the opposite direction. For these problems, we say that they were generated by the users' unfamiliarity with some of the Android conventions.

In addition, we have two problems not included in Table 2. One problem was that the participants had trouble finding the AppJoy setting. The reason for this problem was unclear, and we could not arbitrarily say whether this was because the participants did not know that pressing the Menu button can trigger application settings as an Android convention or they did not believe that the Menu is the right place to find the AppJoy settings. Although the confusion was mostly from the Non-Android participants, one Android participant also spent a lot of effort before getting to the right place. The other problem was that the participants frequently touched the AppJoy's caption bar by tapping, dragging or scrolling. This problem is not negligible as 5 participants had this issue in 6 tasks. However, we cannot simply blame either AppJoy or Android for this as we do not see that any application or the Android framework itself defined the functionality of the caption bar. Thus we left the two problems described above uncategorized.

5.2 Event Logging Method Result

Hilbert and Redmiles described the sequence comparison technique as the process of comparing a target sequence against source sequences and producing measures of correspondence [13]. Here we leveraged the Finite State Machine (FSM) approach as our sequence comparison method for data collected from the event logging toolkit. We believe that FSM can maximumly make use of these data because the experiment was task-based: we can identify the *baseline* (correct) sequence for each task; and we have the participants' entire clickstreams so we can examine how users' interaction sequences deviated from the baseline sequence.

First we draw finite state machines with a baseline sequence for each task. These state machines only involve indispensable steps from the AppJoy home page to the destination state of task completion. Each step here is a state in the finite state machines, and the user actions are represented as transition functions between states. Figure 1 shows the baseline finite state machine for task 1, and Table 3 lists the associated activities corresponding to the states, and the user actions corresponding to the transition functions. As we can see, there are four states in this state machine with state 0 being the initial state and state 3 being the final state. Because this state machine represents the baseline sequence, we name the states in the state machine as fundamental states. Events e1, e3, e5 are the three imperative actions to complete this task, while e2 and e4, though not required, are also considered to be "correct" actions. Recall the task was asking the participants to dislike one application they were not interested in, so the participants may freely browse the applications by scrolling in the activity, or by checking the detailed information of an application and then going back. Events e2 and e4 correspond to these two actions, respectively.

Clearly not all participants will follow this baseline sequence, and they may enter many activities or states that are not shown in Figure 1. We call those states mistake states. We analyzed these mistake states and counted two kinds of behaviors that can, to some extent, indicate participants' confusion. One is

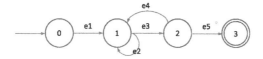

Fig. 1. Task 1 Baseline State Machine

Table 3. States and Transitions for Baseline State Machine of Task 1

	Activity		Event
a0	Home Page	e1	Click *My Recommendations*
a1	My Recommendation	e2	Scroll in *My Recommendations*
a2	Application Detail	e3	Click in an Application
a3	Dislike Dialog	e4	Click *Back* Button
		e5	Click *Dislike* Button

backtracking (sometimes called "regressive behavior" by usability evaluators), and the other is engaging in unhandled events as we mentioned before.

Here we define backtracking as redundantly returning to the state that has already been traversed. We use "redundant" only to exclude situations where backward transitions are also considered to be appropriate responses, such as e4 in task 1. Basically if a user goes back to a state which he/she has visited before, that is backtracking, no matter whether he/she traces back from a baseline state or a mistake state. Additionally, if a user goes back from one activity to another, then immediately back to an even earlier state, we count this circumstance as two backtracking events rather than one. Usually backtracking reflects a user's confusion. When a backtracking event happens [14], it means that the user has picked the option that he/she thought to be most probably right, but apparently he/she did not reach the desired state via that option. For example, to find the usage time of AppJoy, many participants went to AppJoy settings first. After realizing there is no such information, they stepped back to the home page of AppJoy.

Similarly, unhandled events are user behaviors that occurred beyond the developers' expectations, since the developers did not even register listeners for those events. Although some events were triggered by the users' unintentional touches, most of these events reflected the users' intentional purpose. If a user performed a lot of such actions, we can infer that this user might not know where to navigate to the next step, as he/she was trying actions either randomly or exhaustively, hoping to hit something correct by chance or by systematically attempting to activate all plausible interface actions in turn. We list the number of instances that occurred for the above two behaviors by task in Table 4.

Simply from these numbers, we can infer that task 3 and task 6 were the two most difficult jobs for the participants, and tasks 1 and 2 were relatively easy. However, having only these numbers is insufficient for us to analyze usability problems; thus we examined these events more closely.

Table 4. Backtracking and Unhandled Events in Each Task

	T1	T2	T3	T4	T5	T6
Backtracking	14	13	36	35	14	70
Unhandled Motion	1	4	11	1	1	21
Unhandled Key	7	3	4	1	30	4

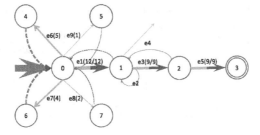

Fig. 2. Task 1 Traffic Flow Chart

Table 5. States and Transitions for All User Actions of Task 1

Activity		Event	
a4	Most Recent	e6	Click *Most Recent*
a5	My Downloads	e7	Click *My Downloads*
a6	Location-based Search	e8	Click *Location-based Search*
a7	Top-Rated	e9	Click *Top-Rated*

As we recorded the participants' every single move from one activity to another, we represent these transitions as well as the volume of these transitions graphically, in a form of traffic flow chart. We present task 1's traffic flow chart in Figure 2 and list its states and transition functions in Table 5. Note here we only show those states and transition functions that were not included in Table 3 (in other words, mistake states and transition functions).

We use the width of an edge to represent the volume of the transitions. Blue edges represent incoming flows, while green edges and orange edges represent outgoing flows to a baseline state or a mistake state accordingly. Additionally, we use dashed red edges to indicate backtracking flows. The volume of traverses along with each transition function is marked above each edge. Note that the number of correct outgoing flows from one baseline state and the number of incoming flows to the next baseline state have different implications. The former means how many times the participants made the right choices from one state, and the latter means how many situations occurred in which the participants were asked to make a choice. For example, if one participant went to some mistake state from state 1, and then returned back to state 1, the number of incoming flows to state 1 would be greater than the number of correct outgoing flows from state 0. Thus we have two figures above every baseline transition function, with the first one representing correct outgoing flows from one state and the second one representing incoming flows to the next state. Coincidently, the two figures for all baseline transitions turn out to be equal in this task.

As shown in Figure 2, the participants traversed to the home page of AppJoy 24 times, of which they went to state 1 12 times, while they went to different mistake states another 12 times. Comparatively speaking, from state 1 to state 2, among the 12 incoming flows, 9 times the participants progressed immediately to state 2, backtracking occurred two times during this stage, and one participant failed to find the next move. From state 2 to state 3, all of the 9 incoming flows traveled to the correct state. The correct flow ratios for the three stages were 50%, 75% and 100%, respectively. Clearly the users were less confused at state 2 than at state 0. We calculated the success ratio of flows in each step as a measurement for detecting usability problems, becaus this can be considered to be a measure of the users' confusion at each step. Also, the amount of flow that entered the final state is actually the number of participants who successfully completed a task. On the other hand, the number of participants who failed to complete a step is also an important indicator of usability problems. We calculated these metrics for each task and summarized them in Table 6.

Note that the step in which backtracking occurred is determined by the next baseline state rather than the current baseline state, as we think users' difficulties in locating the next baseline state is the main reason that causes backtracking in the current baseline state. For instance, the 12 backtracking events that happened during the transition between state 0 and state 1 were counted as backtracking events that occurred at state 1.

Many usability problems can be discovered by reviewing Table 6. Too much backtracking, such as the amount that occurred at step 1 of task 6, indicates that the desired information is located at a different place than anticipated by participants, or it was not visible to users. Low correct flow ratio, in our case less than 50%, is another sign of potential usability problems. For instance, the ratio of correct flows for step 1 of task 3 was only 28.6%, which is congruent with our previous discussion regarding participants having problems finding AppJoy settings. Also, if the number of participants who cannot complete a step exceeded a certain threshold, there is possibly a usability problem. For instance, 4 out of 10 participants failed to find the usage time at step 2 of task 6. Although we are unaware of the cause, we would strongly recommend that the developer of AppJoy inspect that component to show usage time clearer more clearly.

By taking a step further to examine which mistake state attracted most of the incorrect traffic, we may possibly predict the reason for that problem. If many participants went often to the same mistake state, that state must be very confusing to the participants. Hence we call that state the "most misleading state". For example, at step 3 of task 4, 18 out of the 20 incorrect flows went to the detailed page of location-based applications; obviously this is the most misleading state. We guess the underlying reason of this problem is that the users sought to find something at the summary screen of the location-based applications, but that information was not sufficiently visible.

Table 6. Traffic Flow Metrics Based on Number of Mistakes

Metrics	Step 1					
	T1	T2	T3	T4	T5	T6
No. of Backtracks (*)	12	10	29	11	11	61
Mistake State No.	4	3	12	6	4	8
Correct/Incorrect Flows	12/12	12/10	16/40	12/7	9/12	14/58
Correct Flow Ratio	50%	54.5%	28.6%	63.2%	42.9%	24.1%
Fail to Pass No.	1	0	1	1	3	0

Metrics	Step 2					
	T1	T2	T3	T4	T5	T6
No. of Backtracks	2	3	7	5	2	9
Mistake State No.	0	0	1	2	1	3
Correct/Incorrect Flows	9/3	13/3	9/7	11/6	11/2	6/8
Correct Flow Ratio	75%	81.3%	56.3%	64.7%	84.6%	42.9%
Fail to Pass No.	0	0	0	1	0	4

Metrics	Step 3					
	T1	T2	T3	T4	T5	T6
No. of Backtracks	0	0	0	19	1	N/A
Mistake State No.	0	0	0	2	0	N/A
Correct/Incorrect Flows	9/0	10/0	9/0	8/20	10/1	N/A
Correct Flow Ratio	100%	100%	100%	28.6%	90.9%	N/A
Fail to Pass No.	0	0	0	0	0	N/A

Metrics	Step 4					
	T1	T2	T3	T4	T5	T6
No. of Backtracks	N/A	N/A	0	N/A	N/A	N/A
Mistake State No.	N/A	N/A	0	N/A	N/A	N/A
Correct/Incorrect Flows	N/A	N/A	9/0	N/A	N/A	N/A
Correct Flow Ratio	N/A	N/A	100%	N/A	N/A	N/A
Fail to Pass No.	N/A	N/A	0	N/A	N/A	N/A

* No. of Backtracks = number of backtracking incidents

Table 7. Traffic Flow Metrics Based on Number of Participants Making Mistakes

Metrics	Step 1						Step 2					
	T1	T2	T3	T4	T5	T6	T1	T2	T3	T4	T5	T6
No. of Backtracks	4	6	4	2	6	8	0	0	2	1	2	3
No. to the MMS (*)	3	2	5	2	7	8	0	0	0	2	1	2

Metrics	Step 3						Step 4					
	T1	T2	T3	T4	T5	T6	T1	T2	T3	T4	T5	T6
No. of Backtracks	0	0	0	4	1	N/A	N/A	N/A	0	N/A	N/A	N/A
No. to the MMS	0	0	0	4	0	N/A	N/A	N/A	0	N/A	N/A	N/A

* MMS = Most Misleading State

An interesting phenomenon emerged in task 5. Three participants failed to progress through step 1 but surprisingly all of the participants successfully completed this task. This means that some participants avoided one fundamental state and reached the objective state through another route. We provided this information to the developer of AppJoy who confirmed that the way it was designed had some problems.

For unhandled motion events, we inspected the activities in which unhandled motion events occurred and their physical positions on the screen. Among 39 unhandled motion events across all tasks, 30 of them (76.9%) were clicks or moves at the caption bar in different activities; this was the case for all 11 events in task 3 and 17 out of 21 events in task 6. Although we didn't classify it as a usability problem, this phenomenon reflects the participants' frustration. As these behaviors happened frequently in the two tasks that participants had trouble dealing with. Maybe only when the users could not find other ways to complete a task, they touched the caption bar as a last resort. For the remaining 9 unhandled events, 8 of them were clicks or moves on blank pages between two activities; these actions were not noticed in laboratory-based usability testing. Even though we cannot conclude that lengthy loading time between two pages caused the users to perform such actions, at least this is an interesting finding that we did not expect: that such events can be captured by the event logging library. The last unhandled motion event was a mis-click on the side of one button that one participant intended to click, but this was a rare case.

For unhandled key events, we inspected the key code for each click and its related activity. Our library does not log the key code for keystrokes on the Android keyboard except for the delete key out of concern for the users' privacy. However, none of these unhandled key events were from keystrokes on the Android keyboard. Actually, only four keys were pressed: the volume down, volume up and camera focus keys on the right side of the device, and the search key below the screen (we did not classify the search key as a system key because most third party applications do not respond to this key). Except for the search key presses, other unhandled key events were not observed by the evaluators during the experiment. We speculate that these keys were probably pressed without the users' conscious purpose as these keys can be easily touched by mistake in daily usage. However, the search key presses constitute a different case, as 36 out of 49 unhandled key events are from search key presses, including all of the 30 unhandled key events in task 5. Recall that in task 5 we asked participants to uninstall the application they just installed in task 2; we can infer that in task 5, the users were trying to search the application directly with the search key because they knew the application name, but apparently AppJoy did not handle this key event. This confirms a usability problem identified in laboratory testing that AppJoy should add some mechanisms to search or at least sort the recommended applications. Furthermore, 3 search key presses were from task 3 and 3 were from task 6, yet these two tasks did not involve looking for a special application. We guess that the participants intended to search the functionalities of AppJoy setting and usage time by doing so.

The above statistics only dealt with the number of total occurrences of each event but ignored the differences between the participants. The number may be difficult to interpret if a minority of the participants made a large number

Table 8. Usability Problems Identified by Auto Logging Method

	AppJoy Problem	Android Convention
Cosmetic	0(5)	1(2)
Minor	4(4)	1(2)
Major	5(4)	1(2)
Catastrophe	1(1)	0(0)

of mistakes. In fact, if only a few people had problems with a user interface component, this component's design is probably satisfactory. To avoid the difficulties of interpretation, we calculated how many participants backtracked and how many participants entered the most misleading state in each step of a task. In this way, we can alleviate the above issue: if the backtracking number for all participants was large but the number of participants who experienced backtracking was small, it means that a few participants were confused. Similarly, only if many participants backtracked from a particular state can we conclude that the state was really misleading. The two metrics related to the number of participants are summarized in the Table 7.

Regarding backtracking, the data in Table 6 and Table 7 shows fairly uniform behavior across participants, because more backtracking across all participants corresponds to more participants navigating with backtracking. Regarding the correct flow ratio and most misleading state, while the data again shows fairly uniform behavior, there are some minor differences that can be observed. For instance, at step 3 of task 4, the number of incorrect flows was higher across all users, compared to that at step 1 of task 5, but fewer participants went to the most misleading state. This means the problem in task 5 is more general across the users, hence that problem should be considered to be more critical. In summary, we can look at the data in both of the tables to rate the severity level of usability problems.

Besides the above measurements, developers or evaluators can almost "replay" the users' behaviors if they have time to manually review the logged events. Though time-consuming, this approach can help to detect additional usability problems, even for some subtle issues that were overlooked during the laboratory-based usability testing. For example, there was a button that overlapped with recommended applications which made it hard to be seen, so that only one participant clicked that button and none of the evaluators observed this phenomenon during the experiment. But by examining the logged sequence, we noticed this event and confirmed that this was a usability problem.

5.3   Comparison Results

Finally, we summed up all usability problems identified through the event logging toolkit, and compared the number with that discovered by laboratory-based usability testing in Table 8. Note that in this comparison we excluded the two participants' data that was lost with the event logging method.

Usability problems identified by laboratory-based usability testing are shown in parentheses here for comparison. From the rest of the 10 participants, we identified exactly the same number of usability problems as from all 12 participants in laboratory-based usability testing. We can easily see that the laboratory-based testing method can identify more cosmetic problems. All 5 cosmetic usability issues observed through laboratory testing were not discovered by the event logging method. But the event logging method is effective for identifying critical usability issues, including major and catastrophic usability problems. All critical usability problems discovered through laboratory testing were found by the event logging method, and by manually reviewing the participants' behavior sequences, we found out one more major problem that was overlooked in the experiment. However, the shortcoming of the event logging method is, for most of the issues it identified, that although it can point out the location of a problem, it cannot tell the cause of that problem. This is an issue common to all event logging methods because they lack the information that can be gleaned from listening to participants' verbalized thoughts and observing participants' facial expressions and other nonverbal signals.

Compared to laboratory testing, the event logging method found fewer problems that were introduced by the users' unfamiliarity with Android conventions. We expected this because the library cannot record the users' interactions outside of AppJoy. But because the objective of this library is to find usability problems in third-party applications rather than in the Android framework itself, we do not consider this to be a big issue.

6   Discussion

We have only tested the event logging toolkit on one application, which is of course far from enough to conclude that it can be effective to help evaluators, developers and designers identify usability issues on all Android applications. We will integrate this library into more Android applications to validate its usefulness in the future. One thing to note is that our toolkit does not help applications developed without the Android UI framework, such as games based on OpenGL.

On the other hand, even after conducting just one test, we can already demonstrate that the proposed event logging toolkit can detect some subtle actions that are difficult to observe in laboratory testing, such as some quick moves and the unhandled events discussed above. Meanwhile, it can provide strong quantitative measurement and lots of statistical data describing users' interactions with the application. So it can at least complement traditional laboratory-based usability testing.

We tested the application in a WiFi network environment, which neglects possible networking problems that could happen under poor network conditions. Although we know that AppJoy sometimes has trouble connecting to the server under the 3G network, we did not identify this problem through this experiment. Hence we can see context information is needed to locate usability issues under some conditions, and this is precisely the weak point of laboratory-based usability testing. We will include context information retrieved from sensors of the Android device in the next version of the event logging toolkit. Because we can collect the users' interaction data in a real world environment, we can determine usability problems under different conditions through the toolkit. We anticipate that this approach will be a big advantage for an event logging method as it is more suitable for field-based usability testing.

7 Conclusion

It is challenging to conduct usability testing for mobile applications. In this paper, we present a UI event logging toolkit that can be embedded into Android applications. The toolkit requires minimum source code modification by the developers and automatically uploads fine-grained UI events to a central server. By testing a deployed Android application, a state-machine based sequence analysis is evaluated using the logged events and compared to traditional laboratory-based usability testing. The results show that the proposed toolkit is effectively capturing detailed interaction events, which can provide accurate and quantitative analysis of usability problems. In summary, the event logging toolkit can discover most usability problems comparable to those uncovered by the laboratory method, and also reveal some unexpected issues. In future work, we will extend the toolkit so it can be deployed for field-based journal usability testing.

Acknowledgment. This material is based upon work supported by the National Science Foundation under Grant No. 1016823. Any opinions, findings, and conclusions or recommendations expressed in this material are those of the author(s) and do not necessarily reflect the views of the National Science Foundation.

References

1. Kerr, R.: Us mobile internet usage to near 50% in 2013. Vator News (August 2009)
2. Budiu, R., Nielsen, J.: Usability of mobile websites: 85 design guidelines for improving access to web-based content and services through mobile devices. Nielsen Norman Group Research Report (July 2009)
3. Why the mobile web is disappointing end-users. Equation Research Report (October 2009)
4. Tullis, T., Fleischman, S., McNulty, M., Cianchette, C., Bergel, M.: An empirical comparison of lab and remote usability testing of web sites. In: Usability Professional Association Conference, Orlando (2002)
5. Bastien, J.M.C.: Usability testing: a review of some methodological and technical aspects of the method. Computing Research Repository 79, 18–23 (2010)
6. West, R., Lehman, K.: Automated summative usability studies: an empirical evaluation. In: Proceedings of the SIGCHI Conference on Human Factors in Computing Systems, CHI 2006, pp. 631–639. ACM, New York (2006)

7. Waterson, S., James, A.L.: In the lab and out in the wild: remote web usability testing for mobile devices. In: Conference on Human Factors in Computing Systems, pp. 296–297 (2002)

8. Yan, B., Chen, G.: Appjoy: personalized mobile application discovery. In: Proceedings of the 9th International Conference on Mobile Systems, Applications, and Services, MobiSys 2011, pp. 113–126. ACM, New York (2011), http://doi.acm.org/10.1145/1999995.2000007

9. Rosenbaum, S., Rohn, J.A., Humburg, J.: A toolkit for strategic usability: results from workshops, panels, and surveys. In: Proceedings of the ACM CHI 2000 Conference on Human Factors in Computing Systems, New York, pp. 337–344 (2000)

10. Upa 2007 salary survey, Usability Professionals' Association (2008)

11. Ericsson, K.A., Simon, H.A.: Verbal reports as data. Psychological Review 87, 215–251 (1980)

12. Nieslen, J.: Severity ratings for usability problems, in Retrieved June 4th from UseIt (2007), http://www.useit.com/papers/heuristic/severityrating.html

13. Hilbert, D.M., Redmiles, D.F.: Extracting usability information from user interface events. ACM Comput. Surv. 32, 384–421 (2000)

14. Akers, D.: Backtracking events as indicators of software usability problems. Ph.D. dissertation (2009)

A Framework for Efficient Web Services Provisioning in Mobile Environments

Khalid Elgazzar, Patrick Martin, and Hossam Hassanein

School of Computing, Queen's University, Canada
Kingston, Ontario, K7L 3N6
{elgazzar,martin,hossam}@cs.queensu.ca

Abstract. Advancements in wireless networks and mobile device capabilities enable ubiquitous access for Web resources anywhere anytime. Web service technologies enable rapid and low-cost development of networked and portable applications. The successful convergence of these technologies produces mobile Web services provisioning, where mobile devices can host and provide Web services. However, the resource constraints of mobile devices and the characteristics of wireless networks pose key challenges to mobile Web services provisioning. Several research efforts have studied the Web services provisioning from mobile devices, however, they address specific aspects in isolation which may yield inefficient Web service provisioning. This paper proposes a generic framework for efficient Web services provisioning in mobile heterogeneous environments with resource-constrained mobile devices. We demonstrate the proposed framework using a use-case scenario and a sample prototype. A preliminary provisioning prototype shows that the framework is able to provide reliable and personalized Web services while maintaining the service availability.

Keywords: mobile devices, Web services, service provisioning, mobile computing.

1 Introduction

Ubiquitous information access through mobile devices has become a typical practice in everyday life. Mobile users naturally expect that their mobile devices support "anywhere, anytime" communications and computing while on-the-move. Indeed, recent advancements in mobile device manufacturing coupled with the rapid evolution of wireless technologies offer the promise of a new prosperous era of mobile computing paradigms and seamless data access. However, the error-prone communications that characterize wireless networks and the resource limitations of mobile devices present challenges for leveraging this type of convenient access of information.

Web services, on the other hand, allow applications written in different programming languages for different platforms to interact seamlessly through standard protocols. These protocols are independent from any platform and underlying

J.Y. Zhang et al. (Eds.): MobiCASE 2011, LNICST 95, pp. 246–262, 2012.

operating system. While mobile devices span a wide range of device form factors with a variety of different capabilities and different platforms, applications that are developed for a specific mobile platform are not fully compatible, in most cases, with other mobile platforms. Web services are then a method of enabling interoperable mobile applications through standard message exchange communications.

With the ever-expanding mobile-customer base and the growing consumer interest of ubiquitous Internet access from mobile devices, people tend to use their mobile devices to access the Web and carry out their daily life. Hence, mobile Web services again become an interesting approach. The idea of providing Web services from mobile devices facilitates the integration of Web service offerings into mobile applications while putting the flexibility of managing and administrating self-offered Web services at hand. Mobile devices are typically equipped with multihoming capabilities, i.e. multiple network interfaces with different wireless technologies, which means mobile providers can select the best network interface for provisioning or switch to another interface in case of primary network failure.

Mobile web services offer the great potential of a multitude of services and opportunities; marking a shift in how everyday businesses interact and perform. Real-time access to context information would facilitate time-critical applications, such as healthcare and location-based services. Emergency disaster situations form another rich domain in which mobile Web services may play a critical role. More importantly, mobile service provisioning would expand on devices embedded on mobile devices, such as cameras or GPS units.

Several important considerations should be taken into account when designing mobile Web services to cope with both mobile and wireless environment constraints, yet provide Web services efficiently. Much effort has been put forward to investigate the efficient access of Web services by wireless mobile devices, however, less attention has been given for mobile Web service providers. Although there have been several research efforts concerning mobile services provisioning, these research efforts address a specific aspect, such as asynchronous invocation [1] or service replication [2], and are done solely in isolation of other issues. The research presented in this paper is an attempt to bring all aspects together to form a big picture of the efficient Web service provisioning from mobile devices.

This paper proposes a generic framework for efficient Web service provisioning from mobile devices. The framework aims at exploiting the features of mobile devices including their ubiquitous wireless access, multihomed interfaces, their attachment to specific context information such as user and location, and their capability to behave in an ad-hoc manner. At the same time the proposed framework tackles most of the mobile environment constraints such as intermittent connectivity and diversity of mobile device form factors. The framework, hence, satisfies the essential requirements for service provisioning in mobile wireless domains such as ubiquitous service access by supporting different wireless access technologies, persistent service availability by supporting provider/customer disconnection-handling, and adaptability for different device form factors.

The remainder of this paper is organized as follows. Section 2 outlines some of the related works. Section 3 presents the essential requirements for efficient mobile Web services provisioning. A brief overview of how mobile devices are capable of achieving ubiquitous connectivity is given in Section 4. The description of the framework components is introduced in Section 5. Section 6 presents a use-case scenario and a preliminary prototype implementation and results. Lastly, Section 7 concludes the paper and outlines future research directions.

2   Related Work

Advancements in mobile device manufacturing, in addition to wireless technologies, triggered a great interest in the research community in adopting mobile Web services. Several research efforts have studied Web services provisioning from resource-constrained providers, however, they address specific aspects in isolation which may yield inefficient provisioning.

El-Masri [3] addresses enabling hosting capabilities in mobile devices. The author presents a framework for a "Mobile Web Server" that supports Web services provisioning and Web applications from mobile devices. Mobile providers and clients communicate with the mobile Web server and each other through their respective network operators. Services that live on mobile devices are registered in a public UDDI registry and are made accessible for both mobile and Web applications through the mobile Web server.

Singh et al. [1] introduce a framework that supports asynchronous invocation of mobile Web services with the integration of telecommunication services such as SMS messaging. It supports disconnected operations and releases the client device once the service operation is invoked. Then, the SOAP response is dispatched to the terminal when it's ready via the SMS protocol.

A recent direction on reducing the overhead of services provisioning in resource-constrained providers has been explored by Hassan et al. [4]. They propose offloading some of the workload of complex services from mobile devices to the Cloud. Their framework proposes a distributed SOAP engine that runs a group of tasks on mobile devices and others on a static server. A partitioning strategy is presented to arbitrate the split of service tasks.

In an effort to cater for the constrained resources of mobile devices, Kim et al. [5] propose a lightweight framework for hosting Web services on mobile devices. The core of their work is improving service availability via service migration. The migration is initiated by the mobile service provider or in response to a context change. The migration *manager* selects the candidate new host based on a context-suitability function that comprises host capabilities and service requirements. Although the framework supports only SOAP-based Web services the main idea is still valid for REST-based Web services.

Service replication is another way to approach the service availability problem in dynamic mobile environments due to providers' mobility, battery outage, or environmental changes. A framework that supports Web service migration for achieving seamless provisioning is proposed in [5]. The migration takes place as per the provider's request or a change in the context information. Candidate hosts are chosen from neighbor devices based on a suitability function.

Sheng et al. [2] propose an on-demand replication approach to reduce the risk of Web service unavailability under large volume of service requests. Their approach deploys services, on selected idle hosts based on a multi-criteria utility function that takes into consideration service requirements. The replication model calculates the number of required replicas to maintain a predefined level of service availability.

In the case of multihomed mobile devices, Meads et al. [6] discuss Web services provisioning from devices with multiple wireless interfaces. The authors present a middleware infrastructure that relies on *Jini* surrogate architecture and supports vertical handover between Bluetooth and HTTP. The handoff mechanism between different *interconnect channels* can be initiated by the user (proactive) or in response to a context change (reactive). Enabling HTTP connections over Bluetooth channels is also investigated by Auletta et al. [7]. The authors introduced a Bluetooth Http Server Proxy (BHSP) that handles the interface between Bluetooth-enabled clients and HTTP Web server. Their implementation of this interface extends the J2ME standard class `HttpConnection` to `BtHttpConnection` class that supports the underlying communication on a Bluetooth channel transparently.

Despite current research efforts on facilitating service provisioning on mobile devices, a holistic approach that provides Web services from resource-constrained providers (i.e. mobile devices) is still lacking. Specifically, one that takes into account their specific features and limitations. In this paper, we address this void by proposing a framework for Web services provisioning from mobile devices in mobile heterogeneous environments; adopting reliability and efficiency in provisioning as core metrics. We provide a high level description of the framework components and describe the applicability of related approaches in it.

3   Requirement for Efficient Mobile Web Services Provisioning

Resource limitations of mobile devices, such as memory, computational power, battery life, and wireless network characteristics, such as intermittent connectivity and limited bandwidth pose several challenges for mobile services provisioning. An efficient service provisioning framework takes advantage of the unique features of mobile devices and reduces the impact on performance that stems from providing services from resource-constrained providers attached to wireless networks.

A successful framework should satisfy the following essential requirements:

1. Efficient provisioning must adopt existing Web service and wireless networking standards. The framework should be flexible, interoperable and independent of any underlying platform.
2. Since wireless communications are often unreliable and mobile providers may change their point of attachment to the network as they move, full support

of wireless intermittent connection-handling, and seamless handoff for both service providers and customers, are a must.

3. Availability of Web services is an important QoS parameter; especially in mobile domains where the constraints of mobile devices and unreliable wireless connections may diminish the possibility of service availability. Mobile Web services may become inaccessible, mainly due to: host battery outage, connection loss, system crash either of mobile devices or of Web service container, large number of concurrent service requests, and bandwidth limitations. To maintain a specific threshold of service availability and reliable delivery, mechanisms for service replication and asynchronous service invocation should be supported.

4. Service provisioning should enable ubiquitous access by utilizing the multi-homing feature; especially that it exists in most current mobile devices.

5. Flexible service provisioning must provide the necessary adaptation mechanisms to accommodate a variety of consumer device form factors .

6. A chief benefit of mobile services is the provisioning of personalized services, which are services tailored specifically to best fit within a particular context. Providing personalized services, hence, incorporates user preferences, device profile, and other context information in service discovery and execution.

7. Web services, generally speaking, can be designed using SOAP messaging protocol to exchange messages (SOAP-based), or conforming to the REST principles (REST-based). Although REST-based approach is lightweight and suitable for resource-constrained providers, an efficient provisioning must handle requests from both SOAP-based and REST-based Web services.

The mobile services provisioning framework proposed in this paper satisfies all the above requirements, and paves the road for a better understanding of efficient services provisioning in dynamic mobile environments.

4   Mobile Devices Ubiquitous Connectivity

Mobile devices, specifically smartphones, have become the most convenient ubiquitous computing interface due to the advancements in their capabilities and functionalities, which have gone far beyond just providing traditional telephony services. Nowadays, mobile users can access a wide range of data services and Web applications over multiple wireless technologies including 3G, WiFi, Bluetooth, and more recently ZigBee [8]. These wireless interfaces differ in their capacity, transmission range, and power consumption. Mobile devices can handover between different access technologies not only to achieve ubiquitous connectivity transparently to the running applications, but also to enhance the quality of services they receive or deliver.

Most of contemporary mobile devices are equipped with short range/low-power wireless connectivity, such as Bluetooth, to establish connectivity with one another in an ad-hoc manner. Bluetooth provides free wireless access to mobile users in the unlicensed frequency band with no cost. Bluetooth standards enable automatic discovery of mobile devices and network services in the device transmission range. Therefore, Web resources such as Web services can be provided over Bluetooth technology [6]. Communication over Bluetooth could be useful when providers and customers are within proximity of each other to reduce the cost and save battery power for both of them.

ZigBee offers greater coverage compared to Bluetooth and consumes less energy compared to WiFi, while having relatively limited data rates. ZigBee technology particularly targets applications that demand low bandwidth. Jin et al. [8] designed and developed a WiZi-Cloud system with a ZigBee interface for mobile devices to overcome some of the constraints that exist with other wireless technologies such as the short range of Bluetooth and the high energy consumption of WiFi. Their system supports seamless handover between WiFi and ZigBee technologies, easy integration with existing HW/SW, flexibility in determining which interface is appropriate to use, and efficient energy consumption.

5   Service Provisioning Framework

Mobile environments are characterized by intermittent connections and constantly changing signal quality. Mobile devices have limited-resources and change their point of attachment to the network or their access technology frequently. Our framework aims to provide seamless and reliable mobile Web services in dynamic mobile environments. Figure 1 illustrates the framework components. The framework comprises nine essential components: request/response handler, service execution engine, response representation, context manager, directory manager, performance monitor, disconnection support, publication/discovery, and user feedback manager.

5.1   Request/Response Handler

Generally speaking, users can request access to Web services or other Web contents. A Web service request could be SOAP/XML for SOAP-based Web services or HTTP request for REST-based Web services. The *Request/Response Handler* plays the role of a multiplexer, it receives users' requests and differentiates between "Web service" requests and "Web content" requests. The handler forwards the latter directly to the Web server whereas the former is sent to the service *Execution Engine* for processing. SOAP/XML service requests are handled by *SOAP Manager* before they sent down to the Web server, whereas HTTP requests for Web services are analyzed directly by a servlet which selects the appropriate class and method to respond to these requests based on the class and method annotations. The proposed *Request/Response Handler* supports HTTP and other protocols such as Bluetooth and ZigBee. If a service request is received over a Bluetooth or ZigBee channel the message will be forwarded to the *Bluetooth/ZigBee Protocol Handler*. Likewise, responses for Web service requests are treated the same except that they are put in a device-compatible form by the *Response Representation* before sending them to the requester.

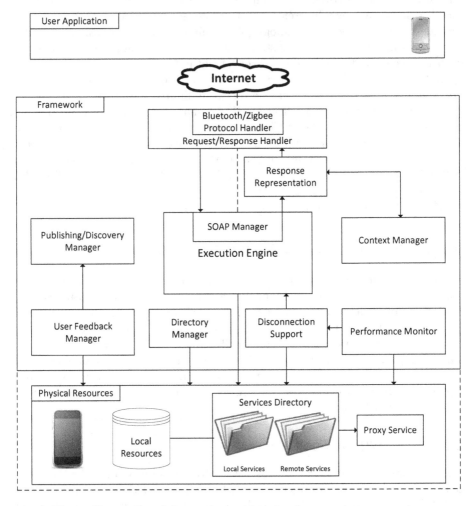

Fig. 1. Illustration of the service provisioning framework components

5.2   Bluetooth/ZigBee Protocol Handler

Most of the current mobile devices and smartphones are equipped with a sort of short range wireless connectivity interface such as WiFi and Bluetooth (Zig-Bee technology is envisioned to be embedded soon [8]). The *Bluetooth/ZigBee Protocol Handler* then provides the essential mapping between the used communication channel format (channel-specific logic [6]) and HTTP format to be accepted at the Web server interface (satisfying requirement #4). In this regard, an infrastructure that supports channel switching between Bluetooth and HTTP seamlessly while provisioning Web services from multihomed mobile devices is presented in [6]. The handler can also implement a protocol-specific proxy server to deal with a request/response at one side and forward it for processing to the Web server at the other side [7].

5.3   Execution Engine

After the *Request/Response Handler* de-serializes the XML data that is associated with the service request and converts it to a Java object, the service *Execution Engine* invokes the corresponding method for execution. The execution engine can handle both SOAP-based and RESTful Web services (requirement #7). The execution engine includes a *SOAP Manager* [5] to handle SOAP-based Web service communications and SOAP messages. In contrast, RESTful Web service requests are executed directly by the servlet container. Once the execution is done, the response is sent to the response representation, which then performs the proper response optimization to fit within the requester's device before forwarding it to the *Request/Response Handler*.

5.4   Response Representation

While most of today's mobile devices feature some sort of Web browsing capabilities, Web navigation by mobile devices has not become as convenient as it is on their desktop counterparts. However, some research efforts have been put forward to take advantage of the device profile to support device-related adaptations for Web content delivery [9]. Generally, mobile devices differ in their display features and screen capability support. Some devices have small screens with limited colors while others have relatively large displays with high resolutions and full color support. Web service responses could be sent as simple as text or rendered with graphic demonstrations and/or multimedia entities. The *Response Representation* receives the device information from the *Context Manager* and adapts the service response accordingly (requirement #5). The *Response Representation* can also take into account the available transmission rate and choose to send simple but representable format from the response to cope with the limited transmission rate despite the fact that the requester's mobile device is powerful and features a large display. From that perspective, Ortiz et al. [10] employed the Aspect-Oriented Programming and model-driven developments to develop flexible Web services that can adapt to mobile devices and produce appropriate responses according to the device capabilities.

5.5   Context Manager

The *Context Manager* collects context information about the customer's device (device profile), customer preferences (customer profile), running environment status (i.e. transmission rate, available bandwidth). The objective of collecting these contexts is to use them for Web service discovery and personalized service provisioning, which satisfies requirement #6 of our defined requirements for efficient service provisioning in mobile environments that we stated earlier. Using the device profile in Web service discovery ensures that the discovered/selected service will function properly with in the mobile device [11]. Service provisioning, especially in mobile domains, can take advantage of the knowledge about service requesters to provide services that best match with their preferences, hobbies, habits, and maybe current location [12]. The environment context can be used for service selection/ranking to ensure a reliable execution for the selected Web service given a certain environment status. For example, at the discovery time, services with multiple behaviors or a service that can adapt to the environment context [13,14] would be ranked first or given a higher priority, whereas at the running time, a switch to a service that is more appropriate within the new environment context could be performed.

5.6 Directory Manager

The *Directory Manager* is responsible for managing the services offered by mobile devices. They fall under two categories: *local services*, which are hosted and provided by the mobile device, and *remote services*, which are "active and running" services that are hosted on other mobile devices but provided by a local proxy service; or simply announced to others through local publishing mechanism/broker.

5.7 Performance Monitor

The *Performance Monitor* component aims at managing the behavior of Web services to ensure that the performance meets the requirements of Service Level Agreements (SLA). Tracking the performance of mobile Web services enables mobile providers to decide on a proper action in response. A proper action could be blocking any upcoming service requests to keep services up and running and their performance meets the requirements' threshold until more resources become available. Another option for mobile providers if they become overloaded during peak demand periods is to offload the service to the cloud or to replicate it to some idle hosts as suggested by Sheng et al. [2]. Performance monitoring reports the status of specified requirements that may include response time, latency, and bandwidth availability. Some commercial products exist that perform service monitoring using API's and can send alerts to identify and resolve performance issues based on predefined configurations.

5.8 Disconnection Support

Mobile users typically suffer from intermittent connectivity. Consuming or providing mobile Web services must efficiently handle this property of wireless communications. The traditional Web services-based communication assumes that the service consumer and the service provider maintain an active connection until a response is received by the consumer or a connection time out occurs. The *Disconnection Support* manager provides mechanisms to support disconnected consumers as well as disconnected providers, which satisfies requirement #3.

Supporting Disconnected Consumers. Reliable provisioning of Web services in mobile domains means that services should function properly during the absence of network connection. This means that the consumer could be blocked as long as the service is executing, which is not be feasible in mobile wireless networks, especially for services that could have a lengthy execution [15]. Asynchronous invocation then is a viable alternative that can be used for Web services based communication in dynamic mobile environments, where consumers may disconnect after invoking the required Web service and interaction techniques such as "Callback" and "Polling" can be used to communicate the response. *Asynchronous Service Access Protocol (ASAP)* [16] is specifically designed by OASIS targeting the service interactions in Web services that require complex processing or lengthy execution. ASAP enables services to run asynchronously (in terms of response handling) and independently from their caller. The service consumer invokes the service and the response is sent back whenever it is available or a later separate request can be made by the consumer to communicate the results of the Web service operations. ASAP enables consumers to send update messages and change previously sent parameters or information if the consumer requirements change during the service execution. The asynchronous Web service should then have the ability to update itself accordingly at runtime.

Supporting Disconnected Providers. Mobile providers similarly suffer from intermittent connections which could make their Web services temporarily inaccessible. For a reliable and seamless provisioning, mobile providers in such cases should provide users with service access alternatives to ensure continuous service availability. The issue of providers' connectivity outage can be approached in three ways, caching Web services, service replication, and using the Cloud to host the services of the disconnected providers. Caching Web services relies mainly on the existence of a proxy that can take over the service provisioning whenever the original provider experiences a network disconnection. However, this approach requires additions to WSDL specifications. The proxy may partially or fully support the service operations depending on the nature of the service and whether its operations need access to a real time data from the mobile provider or not. Furthermore, Web services are typically active entities and need access to live data most of the time, hence HTTP passive caching may not be an appropriate approach for them. Service replication then is another alternative to tackle this problem, where providers that experience frequent connection loss may deploy or replicate their services on other available nearby hosts. The deployment of replicas could be transparent to service consumers, i.e. they need not to be aware of the underlying replication [2]. The third option supports robust service provisioning, where providers may resort to hosting Web services on the Cloud not only when they experience or expect connection loss, but also when their services become inaccessible due to the large amount of invocations. Clouds usually perform elastic resource assignments, that is more resources could be acquired on demand to cope with the high volume of service requests and released when these resources are not needed anymore (resources can grow up and shrink on demand).

5.9   Publishing and Discovery Manager

Publishing is carried out by service providers to inform potential customers of the existence of Web services. Discovery is the process of finding a Web service that fulfills a particular consumer objective. There could be a mediator (service broker) that facilitates the link between service providers and consumers. Providers typically have two options to publish their services; either by registering the services with a service broker in a public service repository, using the UDDI standard, or publishing the services in a local service directory. Also, providers may publish two types of services, services that they host and provide locally (local services) and services that they know about from other providers (remote services) and both are managed by *Services Directory Manager*. Providers may also provide a proxy service for remote services. Local services typically have access to locally managed resources such as databases or real time data collectors (i.e. sensors and embedded devices). In P2P overlay networks, Web services are often published as JXTA modules, each module includes a module class, module specification, and module implementation [17]. The module class basically represents the information needed to declare the services. The module specification contains the information required for the potential consumer to access the service, whereas implementation indicates the methods (possibly across different platforms) of the advertised specifications. A high level description of a distributed publishing of Web services in P2P networks is proposed by Sun and Hao [18]. In their framework, Web services are registered on a specific peer according to their contained ontologies. In contrast, publishing and discovery in client/server based interactions follow the traditional Web service standards (i.e. UDDI).

5.10   User Feedback Manager

Service providers may dishonestly claim unrealistic QoS capabilities for their advertised services to attract interested consumers. The QoS is primarily of particular interest to distinguish services with equivalent functional properties. *User Feedback Manager* collects the perceived QoS by consumers to reflect reality and users' satisfaction, which can be then exploited to improve the service delivery and draw providers' attention to issues that concern service consumers. Although, the previous research work done on this perspective [19] targets the improvements of service discovery and ranking, the same concepts could be applied to enhance the service delivery by collecting consumers feedback. However, mechanisms that prevents or at least reduces false ratings and misleading feedback should be incorporated in collecting users' feedback for credibility.

6   The Egyptian Revolution, 2011: A Use-case Scenario

In the Egyptian revolution of 2011, people protested to get rid of a dictatorship. The call for the revolution began on social networks and people organized themselves and communicated mainly over Facebook. Some essential communications are required in such scenarios, as those calling for leaders to share some information, coordinate between groups, communicate messages to protesters or arrange for medical emergencies, etc. In such a scenario, we look at leveraging communication capabilities with mobile Web services provisioning, aiding protesters to communicate with each other at their best; especially for carrying out crucial tasks like tending to medical emergencies.

To provide medical emergency services, health professional volunteers created a fixed medical emergency facility at each gathering square in each city where the vast majority of protesters exist, as well as some mobile medical emergency units that can promptly respond to injured persons at their locations. These emergency units should be able to announce their locations to the crowds and receive injury reports from protesters. The service provisioning, at the same time, should maintain a specific level of reliability, availability, and adaptability.

According to our framework we show how to provide reliable mobile services from mobile devices in such a scenario taking advantage of mobile phones available with the protesters and the P2P overlay network that they can form together. A Web service can be developed and deployed on the mobile device of the medical emergency volunteers. The *Publication/Discovery* component registers the Web services on the local services directory and advertises the services to all peers in the transmission range, the same way Web service requests are handled in P2P overlay networks. Peers, consequently, cooperate to disseminate the service advertisement. The advertisement in this case could be as simple as a URL that could be used to access the Web service interface associated with some human readable service description. Whoever receives the advertisement originates a copy to its neighbors after reducing the Time To Live (TTL), that is associated with the advertisement, by 1. Peers stop forwarding the service advertisement if (TTL = 0). This is marginally different than the traditional service publications, where users initiate a Web service request to discover relevant services that fulfill their objectives. The TTL value controls how far a service advertisement can go.People then can access these services and submit reports of injuries to the medical emergency volunteers who would respond appropriately.

The *Disconnection Support* component provides the required mechanisms for mobile devices that lose the connectivity due to becoming temporarily out-of-range of any supporting peer, whether they forward a response or a service call. The type of support depends on whether the disconnected peer is a service provider or a service consumer. In case of service providers the support action could be a service replication to a capable connected peer [13], while in service consumer it could be integrating some telecommunication services such as SMS [1]. In both cases the asynchronous service invocation is a viable option [1]. The *Context Manager* in this scenario provides network status reports and maintains a reference for all the available network connectivity. In case the active connection goes down for any reason, a seamless switching procedure to one of available networks can be issued preserving the status of all active connections [6,7].

Our framework can also handle the heterogeneity of client device form factors by adapting the service response to cope with their capabilities. The *Response*

Representation module changes the format of the service response to best fit within the mobile device's profile parameters. If the client's mobile device supports only text mode, a simple text that represents the service response is sent to the client. Otherwise, a more appealing graphical representation is sent to capable terminals.

On January 28, 2011, the Egyptian government shut down the Internet and cellular networks to isolate protesters and prevent them from communicating. Our framework would have enabled service requests and invocation of Web service functionalities over Bluetooth or any other short range wireless connectivity (that already exist on most of mobile devices) via the *Bluetooth/ZigBee Protocol Handler*. At the same time, when better connectivity (e.g. 3G or WiFi) becomes available, the transition will be seamless and transparent with no interruption to the provisioned services [6].

Figure 2 illustrates a sample behavior of our framework and actions taken to maintain the service availability in this scenario. We assume that the mobile service provider has access and is connected to WiFi and 3G networks. In such cases, WiFi is more preferable due to the higher bandwidth availability in contrast with the 3G. The *Request/response Handler* receives the service requests from different users over different wireless channels and provides the proper protocol handling. The handled request is then forwarded to the service *Execution Engine* which invokes the appropriate method. At the same time the *Context Manager* takes advantage of HTTP sessions and collects the device profile parameters. The *Response Representation* component, which is an application specific module, receives both the device profile and the raw service response to reformat the response to best fit within the device profile. At some point of time, suppose that WiFi connectivity is lost due to the provider's mobility or any other reason. The *context Manager*, therefore, reports this network loss to the *Disconnection Support* component, which in turn replicates the service on another available candidate host as a protective action (set by the service administrator) to maintain service availability and reliable provisioning. The candidate host of the replica and it's location are out of this paper's scope, however, these issues are studied in [20,2]. We also assume that the consistency between replicas is handled by underlying Web server/system. When the service experience a large number of requests which violate the performance goals (such as a response time threshold set by the service administrator), the *Performance Monitor* reports this violation and another replica is triggered to keep the service performance within certain limits. During the performance violation interval, any upcoming requests are temporally rejected until another replica becomes up and running or the violated parameters fall down under their threshold.

6.1   Implementation

We have implemented a preliminary prototype system to test and validate our framework for the above scenario. Our prototype focuses on the reliability and adaptability issues (i.e. how to handle service availability and provide different formats of same service response to different customers).We conducted several

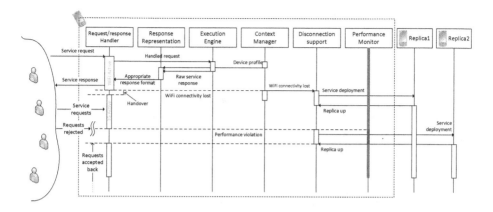

Fig. 2. A sample behavior of the mobile services provisioning framework and actions taken to maintain the service availability

experiments to demonstrate the effectiveness and reliability of the service provisioning framework, where phone-based users can mainly depend on their mobile devices to seek and receive help in emergency situations. We developed a RESTful Web service that sends the locations of field medical assistance facilities and accepts medical emergency requests. We chose the REST-based design for Web services because of its lightness and scalability. RESTful Web services typically communicate over HTTP using standard HTTP methods such as "GET" and "POST". The Web service is deployed on a mobile device using Apache Tomcat 7.0 as a servlet container.

Our prototype demonstrates three aspects: the first is how the framework supports providers who experience or expect frequent disconnection and when to maintain the service availability; the second is how the framework provides reliable Web services and responds to performance violations, and the third is how the framework handles the heterogeneity of mobile device form factors. We emulate concurrent users using Java mulithreading. The *Performance Manager* observes the average response time to maintain a certain level of QoS. When the response time exceeds the predetermined threshold, the service request handler rejects any upcoming requests to keep services alive and issues a service replication command. For the sake of simplicity we perform the service replication using the remote deployment feature that Apache Tomcat 7.0 provides.

In this prototype, service replication is performed if the *Context Manager* reports a network loss (as long as an alternative connection is available) or the threshold of the average response time exceeded. We set the response time threshold, perceived at the server side, to 80 ms (as per the SLA for example). We remark here that we are not testing the network performance, but rather evaluate how our framework responds to context changes and QoS violations to maintain a certain level of service reliability and availability. Any other set of criteria could be set.

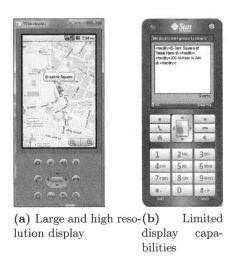

(a) Large and high reso-(b)   Limited
lution display   display   capa-
                        bilities

Fig. 3. Service response adaptation based on device profile

After successful deployment of a replica, the framework updates the service
endpoints by adding the new service access point to the alternative endpoints
in the description file, so that customers may try alternative endpoints if the
primary host does not respond, if the replication strategy allows such communication. The replication strategy [20], which regulates whether customers are
allowed to communicate with replicas directly or through the primary host, is
out of this paper's scope. However, we update the service description file with
the alternative access points to make it ready for any replication strategy.

To demonstrate how the framework adapts the service response according to
the client's device profile, we conducted an experiment to access the Web service
from different devices with different capabilities (more specifically in terms of
display size and graphics support). In this experiment, we obtain device profiles
from the emulator specifications. It worth noting here that this experiment is
application dependent and yields application specific service response formats.
Figure 3 shows different response formats for different mobile devices despite
the same response content. Figure 3a shows a map view of the locations of the
medical emergency facilities that protesters created at El-Tahrir square, Cairo.
Although, we generate the map at the client side using location information,
it may be generated at the server side and sent as an image. This response
viewed on a standard Android emulator. Figure 3b shows the same information
formatted as a simple XML string (as it is extracted from the HTTP-GET
response) viewed on the default CLDC "DefaultCldcJtwiPhone" emulator that
is embedded with Java ME SDK 3.0 [21]. This CLDC emulator has a limited
display size of 180x208px.

7   Conclusion

Mobile devices have become the most convenient interface for pervasive and ubiquitous computing as they offer "anywhere, anytime" communication and computing while on-the-move. The ever-increasing numbers of mobile customers are becoming more interested in accessing ubiquitous information from their mobile devices. Mobile Web services provisioning is an approach in which mobile devices play the role of service providers. In this paper, we introduce a holistic approach for effective Web services provisioning from mobile devices in wireless mobile environments. We present the essential requirements of efficient provisioning and propose, based on these requirements, a generic framework that takes advantage of mobile device and wireless network features and hide their limitations. The framework proposes disconnection support for mobile service providers through service replication and service consumer through asynchronous service invocation. A preliminary prototype has been developed to evaluate the proposed framework. Testing the response adaptation yields different response formats for different customers based on their device profile.

Our ongoing research will extend the prototype implementation of the proposed framework to include the efficient service discovery and maintain the service continuity during the handover process.

References

1. Singh, R., Mishra, S., Kushwaha, D.S.: An efficient asynchronous mobile web service framework. SIGSOFT Software Engineering Notes 34, 1–7 (2009)
2. Sheng, Q.Z., Maamar, Z., Yu, J., Ngu, A.H.H.: Robust Web Services Provisioning through On-Demand Replication. In: Yang, J., Ginige, A., Mayr, H.C., Kutsche, R.-D. (eds.) UNISCON 2009. LNBIP, vol. 20, pp. 4–16. Springer, Heidelberg (2009)
3. El-Masri, S.: A framework for provising mobile web services. In: The Second International Conference on Innovations in Information Technology, IIT 2005 (2005)
4. Hassan, M., Zhao, W., Yang, J.: Provisioning web services from resource constrained mobile devices. In: Proceedings of the 2010 IEEE 3rd International Conference on Cloud Computing, CLOUD 2010, pp. 490–497 (2010)
5. Kim, Y.-S., Lee, K.-H.: A lightweight framework for mobile web services. Computer Science - Research and Development 24(4), 199–209 (2009)
6. Meads, A., Roughton, A., Warren, I., Weerasinghe, T.: Mobile service provisioning middleware for multihomed devices. In: Proceedings of the 2009 IEEE International Conference on Wireless and Mobile Computing, Networking and Communications, pp. 67–72. IEEE Computer Society, Washington, DC (2009)
7. Auletta, V., Blundo, C., De Cristofaro, E.: A j2me transparent middleware to support http connections over bluetooth. In: Proceedings of the Second International Conference on Systems and Networks Communications, pp. 3–9. IEEE Computer Society, Washington, DC (2007)
8. Jin, T., Noubir, G., Sheng, B.: Wizi-cloud: Application-transparent dual zigbee-wifi radios for low power internet access. In: The 30th Conference on Computer Communications, INFOCOM 2011, Shanghai, China (2011)
9. Zhang, D.: Web content adaptation for mobile handheld devices. Commun. ACM 50, 75–79 (2007)

10. Ortiz, G., Prado, A.G.D.: Improving device-aware web services and their mobile clients through an aspect-oriented, model-driven approach. Information and Software Technology 52(10), 1080–1093 (2010)
11. Al-Masri, E., Mahmoud, Q.H.: Mobieureka: an approach for enhancing the discovery of mobile web services. Personal Ubiquitous Computing 14, 609–620 (2010)
12. García, J.M., Ruiz, D., Ruiz-Cortés, A.: A Model of User Preferences for Semantic Services Discovery and Ranking. In: Aroyo, L., Antoniou, G., Hyvönen, E., ten Teije, A., Stuckenschmidt, H., Cabral, L., Tudorache, T. (eds.) ESWC 2010, Part II. LNCS, vol. 6089, pp. 1–14. Springer, Heidelberg (2010)
13. Maamar, Z., Tata, S., Belaid, D., Boukadi, K.: Towards an approach to defining capacity-driven web service. In: International Conference on Advanced Information Networking and Applications (AINA 2009), pp. 403–410 (2009)
14. Tao, A., Yang, J.: Context aware di erentiated services development with con-gurable business processes. In: Proceedings of the 11th IEEE International Enterprise Distributed Object Computing Conference, pp. 241–252. IEEE Computer Society, Washington, DC (2007)
15. Aijaz, F., Hameed, B., Walke, B.: Towards peer-to-peer long lived mobile web services. In: Proceedings of the 4th International Conference on Innovations in Information Technology, pp. 571–575. IEEE, Dubai (2007)
16. Fuller, J., Krishnan, M., Swenson, K., Ricker, J.: Oasis asynchronous service access protocol, asap, May 18 (2005),
    http://www.oasis-open.org/committees/documents.php?wg_abbrev=asap
17. Gong, L.: Jxta: a network programming environment. IEEE Internet Computing 8, 88–95 (2001)
18. Zhen Sun, F., Gang Hao, S.: A discovery framework for semantic web services in p2p environment. In: 2010 International Conference on Electrical and Control Engineering (ICECE), pp. 44–47 (June 2010)
19. Averbakh, A., Krause, D., Skoutas, D.: Exploiting User Feedback to Improve Semantic Web Service Discovery. In: Bernstein, A., Karger, D.R., Heath, T., Feigenbaum, L., Maynard, D., Motta, E., Thirunarayan, K. (eds.) ISWC 2009. LNCS, vol. 5823, pp. 33–48. Springer, Heidelberg (2009)
20. Juszczyk, L., Lazowski, J., Dustdar, S.: Web service discovery, replication, and synchronization in ad-hoc networks. In: Proceedings of the First International Conference on Availability, Reliability and Security, pp. 847–854 (2006)
21. Java (tm) platform, micro edition software development kit 3.0 (June 2011),
    http://www.oracle.com/technetwork/java/javame/javamobile/
    download/sdk/index.html

From UAProf towards a Universal Device Description Repository

José Quiroga, Ignacio Marín, Javier Rodríguez, Diego Berrueta,
Nicanor Gutiérrez, and Antonio Campos

R&D Department, Fundación CTIC,
C/ Ada Byron, 39 – 33203 Gijón, Spain
{jose.quiroga,ignacio.marin,javier.rodriguez,
diego.berrueta,nicanor.gutierrez,
antonio.campos}@fundacionctic.org

Abstract. Techniques to create software and content that adapt to different apparatus require gathering information about device features. Traditionally, Device Description Repositories (DDRs) have provided limited descriptions, in terms of description granularity and of the amount of devices included. A Universal DDR (UDDR) would allow any software developer or content creator to have complete, up-to-date and trustworthy device descriptions for any application domain. Collaboration of all stakeholders in the adaptation business would be necessary to populate the UDDR, but without compromising the quality of the information. Device manufacturers usually publish first-hand device descriptions using UAProf. Unfortunately, UAProf documents are known to contain mistakes or inaccurate/incomplete information. This work suggests a multi-step process to manipulate UAProfs in order to correct their most common mistakes, to extend their expressiveness and to allow amendments from different contributors. More specifically, amendments are annotated with provenance information, enabling device description consumers to decide whether to trust them.

Keywords: device description repository, UAProf, CC/PP, software adaptation, content adaptation, RDF, data provenance, profile resolution.

1 Introduction

The development of software solutions for the vast heterogeneity of connected computing devices in the market is a grand challenge. Multi-device development is a great opportunity for the software industry, considering the extraordinary amount of connected devices far beyond traditional PCs. Mobile and portable devices, set-top boxes, home media players, in-vehicle devices and other embedded devices are some examples of such device diversity. For instance, mobile devices, which are an obvious case of device fragmentation, have widely spread over the last years. The International Telecommunication Union claims in the 2010 edition of their annual "Measuring the Information Society" [1] report that 67% of the population of the world was subscribed to a mobile cellular connection by the end of 2009. When compared to global penetration of fixed broadband subscriptions (7%), which have

J.Y. Zhang et al. (Eds.): MobiCASE 2011, LNICST 95, pp. 263–282, 2012.

traditionally been one of the most relevant driving forces of the software industry, the business opportunity seems to be significant.

However, writing software which adapts to multiple operating systems and device characteristics and capabilities is a very complex issue. One of the key aspects of this type of adaptive software is the availability of a database containing device descriptions. Organizations devoted to content and software creation and provisioning for multiple devices and/or software platforms keep their own databases for their internal developments –Google or Amazon, for example. Some others, as DeviceAtlas [2], publish commercial device databases for creators of adaptive software and content creators to use it. Additionally, there are open-source and/or free efforts (e,g., WURFL [3] and maDDR [4]) which intend to populate and maintain device databases in a collaborative manner. Even commercial proprietary device databases must be considered collaborative databases, as their maintainers watch the novelties regularly added to open and free device databases. The two greatest problems to populate a device database are that (P1) there is usually a delay between the release of a new device in the market and the insertion of its description in the database and that (P2) there is no annotation about the provenance of the information contained in the database. As an example of (P1), the WURFL database version dated on 12/31/2010 adds 11 devices to the previous version (12/6/2010). In between early owners of those devices might experience a lack of support for their corresponding new devices. This is an important business problem, as these users are candidates to be intensive consumers of data services. In what regards to (P2), even when a device description is added to the WURFL database, it may happen that it is an incomplete description to be refined in the future releases. Therefore, it is important to know who refines that information and how such information is obtained for the sake of trustworthiness. The balance between getting device descriptions of new device models as soon as possible and waiting for trustworthy device descriptions to be available is the principal warhorse in device databases guiding software and content adaptation. The existence of trustworthy collaborative device databases would invite an increasing amount of software developers and content creators to face the challenge of multi-device development.

Device description databases have been named as Device Description Repositories (DDRs) by the World Wide Web Consortium (W3C [5]) through their already extinct Device Independence Working Group [6]. It is important to note that DDRs include device descriptions which include information known a priori. In this way, a client device can perform a request to a server system and the server can subsequently obtain evidences about the identity of the device. These evidences can be used to query a DDR in order to find out the actual identity of the device and its software and hardware features. This process enables the adaptation of the response from the server to the client (for example, provisioning an application in the binary format accepted by the client device or some type of content, i.e. a raster image, in the format expected at the client side).

The authors of this work are developing a universal DDR to be populated and maintained in a collaborative way. Because of this, the authors have decided to name the proposed DDR as UDDR (Universal Device Description Repository). The term universal means that it intends to capture all the device features required by any type of application and content transformation. Therefore, one of the most important features for the UDDR is that its various contributors have mechanisms to include new device properties which make sense for novel application domains.

In what regards to the collaborative nature of the UDDR, access to the information that it will keep will be provided by means of an Application Programming Interface (API) which will seamlessly enforce submission of new device descriptions or properties, although this feature is out of the scope of this article. Although collaborative DDRs as WURFL have been successful, organizations tend to avoid contributing their amendments back to the DDR.

The level of granularity of the information about each device is an important issue to obtain a universal DDR. So far, DDRs have mainly focused on the description of the web browser of the device and other aspects related to the browser: supported images, sound and video formats or encryption algorithms (related to SSL and HTTPS), for instance. There is a lack of fine-grained information about the operating system, non-HTTP protocol support (RTSP, SIP and others), the presence of optional APIs (supported JSRs, for example, in the case of Java), or about technologies for connectivity (such as supported Bluetooth profiles).

In order to have a sufficient expressivity, UAProf [7] has been considered by the authors of this work as the starting point to develop a device description framework for the UDDR. The reason for this decision is that its ancestor technology (Composite Capability/Preference Profiles or CC/PP [8], which is based on RDF [9]) provides an extensible mechanism for device description which will permit the conversion of UAProf documents to UDDR-Profiles, as suggested later in this article. UDDR-profiles are individual device descriptions in the UDDR, analogous to the concept of UAProf profiles. One of the advantages of this approach is to start populating the UDDR with existing UAProf instances published by device makers. Unfortunately, UAProf was not intended to be a language to express device descriptions in a DDR but for device manufacturers to announce device characteristics to software developers and content creators.

This article is organized in sections. Section 2 provides a technological background in order to explain what UAProf is and how and why it was invented. Section 3 describes the problem suggested in the article: why device descriptions in UAProf documents are not sufficient as information items in a Universal Device Description Repository and an introduction to how they may be manipulated to obtain device descriptions useful for a UDDR. Section 4 lists and comments previous research works devoted to the improvement of the existing UAProf specification. In Section 5, the requirements expected for the UDDR-profile are actually explained. Section 6 comments the steps proposed by the authors to populate the UDDR after original UAProf documents published by device manufacturers. Section 7 describes profile resolution, the suggested mechanism to avoid ambiguity and contradiction when querying the UDDR. Section 8 details the step-by-step process to transform the UAProf description of an actual device into its UDDR-Profile description. Sections 9 and 10 present the conclusions obtained and the future work to be accomplished in order to develop the UDDR after the UDDR-Profile definition.

2   Technological Background

UAProf is a vocabulary proposed by the Open Mobile Alliance (OMA [10]) from the CC/PP specification defined by the W3C through the extinct Device Independence working group, which is expressed in RDF. UAProf profiles are created as documents expressed in the homonymous vocabulary. They are referenced by means of a URI provided by some web browsers (generally, a significant amount of mobile web browsers) in their HTTP requests. As an example, Figure 1. shows the *x-wap-profile* header contained in an HTTP Request as submitted by the web browser of a BlackBerry 9700 device.

```
user-agent: BlackBerry9700/5.0.0.423 Profile/MIDP-2.1 Configuration/CLDC-1.1 VendorID/603
accept: text/html,application/xhtml+xml,application/vnd.wap.xhtml+xml,application/vnd.wap.wr
descriptor,*/*;q=0.5
accept-charset: UTF-8,ISO-8859-1,US-ASCII,windows-1251,windows-1252,windows-1253,wind
accept-language: es
accept-encoding: gzip,deflate
x-wap-profile: "http://www.blackberry.net/go/mobile/profiles/uaprof/9700_umts/5.0.0.rdf"
x-up-subno: pkkZSkJqCY41xLnzuGPa0A==
X-Forwarded-For: 213.30.36.217
Cache-Control: max-stale=0
Connection: Keep-Alive
X-BlueCoat-Via: A98A1152CCCD4E0F
```

Fig. 1. URI associated to the UAProf which describes a BlackBerry 9700

The URI for a UAProf profile may also be found in the value of other headers in HTTP Requests, such as *Profile*, *wap-profile* or *xx-profile* (with xx being a number, usually indicated in an additional *Opt* header), depending on the choice of different device manufacturers and HTTP Proxy implementations. An example of the content of a UAProf document can be found in Figure 2.

```
<?xml version="1.0" encoding="utf-8"?>
<!--
<rdf:RDF xmlns:rdf="http://www.w3.org/1999/02/22-rdf-syntax-ns#"
    xmlns:rdfs="http://www.w3.org/2000/01/rdf-schema#"
    xmlns:prf="http://www.openmobilealliance.org/tech/profiles/UAPROF/ccppschema-20021212#"
    xmlns:mms="http://www.openmobilealliance.org/tech/profiles/MMS/ccppschema-20050301-MMS1.2#"
    xmlns:date="java:java.util.Date"
    xmlns:pss6="http://www.3gpp.org/profiles/PSS/ccppschema-PSS6#">
    <rdf:Description rdf:ID="DeviceProfile">
    <!-- Hardware Platform Description -->
    <prf:component>
        <rdf:Description rdf:ID="HardwarePlatform">
            <rdf:type rdf:resource="http://www.openmobilealliance.org/tech/profiles/UAPROF/ccppschema-200:
            <prf:BluetoothProfile>
                <rdf:Bag>
                    <rdf:li>Advanced Audio Distribution Profile</rdf:li>
                    <rdf:li>Audio/Video Remote Control Profile</rdf:li>
                    <rdf:li>Headset Profile</rdf:li>
                    <rdf:li>Handsfree Profile</rdf:li>
                    <rdf:li>Object Push Profile</rdf:li>
                    <rdf:li>Serial Port Profile</rdf:li>
                    <rdf:li>Dial-Up Networking Profile</rdf:li>
                    <rdf:li>Phone Book Access Profile</rdf:li>
                </rdf:Bag>
            </prf:BluetoothProfile>
            <prf:BitsPerPixel>16</prf:BitsPerPixel>
            <prf:ColorCapable>Yes</prf:ColorCapable>
            <prf:CPU>XScale</prf:CPU>
            <prf:InputCharSet>
                <rdf:Bag>
                    <rdf:li>ISO-8859-1</rdf:li>
                    <rdf:li>UTF-8</rdf:li>
```

Fig. 2. Part of the UAProf document which describes a BlackBerry 9700 device

It is important to note that UAProf documents contain static device descriptions. This means that they contain information that is known *a priori*, such as screen resolution, Bluetooth profiles supported or the web browser(s) installed from factory. Some examples of dynamic device information are battery charge level, or screen orientation (landscape, portrait).In the early times of mobile web development, HTTP headers were parsed in search of a URI referencing the UAProf document describing the device for a later adaptation of web content. An obvious improvement to that technique was caching UAProf documents at the web server side, thus giving birth to the first UAProf-based Device Description Repositories. The main goals of this approach were (1) reduction of device identification time by avoiding repetitive HTTP interaction to access a UAProf document already accessed before, and (2) availability of device description even when the web server containing the original UAProf document is temporarily or permanently unavailable.

3   Description of the Problem

Unfortunately, UAProf documents contain mistakes despite the fact that they are generated by device manufacturers themselves. Some mistakes are caused by mere copying-and-pasting errors when device makers release a new model which is an evolution of a previous device –proofs of the copy-and-paste technique are shown in Section 7. Some others are caused by engineers not being aware of the restrictions imposed by the CC/PP and UAProf specifications. Therefore, UAProf documents are made available without being validated against the UAProf Schema in the Appendix A of the specification.

Once that an original UAProf is cached, the obvious need to correct mistakes appears. In addition to this need, DDR maintainers might want to add new properties to the device description in UAProf and to enhance the expressivity power of device descriptions in order to overcome some of the limitations of the vocabulary and of the overall CC/PP framework, as suggested in the next sections of this document.

Both UAProf and CC/PP offer an interesting framework for device description. They have been providing device descriptions used by the software industry over the last decade. Hundreds of device models expose their software and hardware characteristics by means of a UAProf document which may be cached and then enhanced. Information enhancements or amendments are required to obtain a UDDR, as suggested by some of the requirements listed in Section 5. These requirements do not only include changes in mistaken information or adding new properties to the existing categories grouping device features. They may also include new sections in UAProf documents reorganizing the categorization of device features.

Moreover, there is an aspect in device description manipulation which is the inclusion of information about the authorship of amendments to previous content. One of the foundations of the future UDDR is its collaborative nature. Collaborative approaches in the development of a DDR are not innovative, with WURFL as the flagship. Still, one of the uncovered problems of DDRs being maintained by different contributors is to keep track of contributions provenance [11] as an estimation of the fidelity of the information contained in each device description. One of the requirements in the UDDR is to ensure that information can be updated by any contributor as soon as a new device (or device feature) is detected. Thus, device descriptions will be patched by different contributors and it is likely that not all the consumers of device descriptions will trust all the amendments. They might subscribe only to changes from trusted contributors, therefore establishing their own balance between quick availability of new descriptions and relying only on trustworthy information in the DDR.

4   Related Work

Previous research work has considered UAProf and CC/PP limitations. The first efforts in the analysis of these specifications were done by Mark Butler, at the HP Labs research group, through several white papers. [12] and [13] reflect the absence of a formal specification for profile resolution, the lack of a mechanism to allow combining profiles expressed in different vocabularies and the need for a formal definition of vocabularies –unfortunately, often indicated as comments in UAProf profiles. These problems were notified later to the W3C Device Description Working Group by means of a Position Paper [14]. Moreover a CC/PP-UAProf validation tool (DELI) [15] was created by the same author.

In [16], a CC/PP-based vocabulary is proposed in order to represent more detailed context information for content and software adaptation. One of the most relevant problems found in CC/PP is the organization of device description in two layers. This forces the use of undesired syntactic sugar to express some definitions and relationships between device properties. An example of relationship is the required existence of an attribute X in the device description when another attribute Y exists. Another relevant issue mentioned in the article is the need to provide CC/PP with a mechanism for profile resolution (which is commented later in subsection 5.7), as previously suggested by Butler.

Related to the aforementioned work, an interesting study of the limitations in CC/PP and UAProf is carried out in [17]. Its conclusions state that basing CC/PP on RDF does not seem very appropriate as it basically models a hash table with name-value pairs. The study also considers that CC/PP and UAProf describe the data structures in which device profiles are represented but they do not provide an API to access the properties contained. Finally, one of the most evident problems is the diversity in vocabularies actually used by different device makers. The authors consider that a mapping mechanism between vocabularies should be provided, as it was also previously noted by the rest of related work.

5   Requirements for UDDR-Profile

In order to use UAProf documents as the central element for a Device Description Repository, we propose a number of extensions to UAProf driven by the following requirements.

5.1   Provenance Support

All the contributions must be associated to the author of such changes. The original UAProf lacks mechanisms for tracking this information, which is essential to enable a trustworthy access to a collaborative DDR. For instance, it may be relevant to know if a contribution has been originated from the decisions of a human or from a software probe which has gathered device capabilities in an automated way.

Information providing more details about amendments to the original UAProf may also be included [16] in order to allow developers to estimate the trustworthiness. For instance: temporal information (freshness and history), accuracy, confidence in correctness and digital signature to ensure the authorship.

Using RDF named graphs [18] is the proposed mechanism to fulfill this requirement. Named graphs enable the annotation of information subsets with provenance metadata about authorship and change tracking. This approach has already been applied to other domains, such as biological data resources [19]. Although the current specification of RDF does not contemplate named graphs, the SPARQL [20] query language does, and there is ongoing work at W3C to revise RDF in this direction.   This fact leads the authors to avoid introducing all the expressivity requirements in the proposed UDDR-Profile and therefore use resolution rules which will be triggered after the SPARQL queries to the UDDR.

In order to increase the value of provenance annotations, it is convenient to re-use existing vocabularies, such as the ones listed in the W3C Provenance Incubator Group final report [21], as well as existing identifiers for entities, e.g., URIs of FOAF profiles to characterize the agents involved in the data evolution. All these mechanisms will be used in the UDDR-Profile format.

5.2   Correct Separation of UDDR-Profile Description Aspects

Sometimes, information about a generic software component (for instance, web browser) is provided in a UAProf description. Actually, a device may include more than one implementation of that software component (for instance, two or more web browsers) without its UAProf clarifying whether both of them are compliant to the description.

A specific example is the inclusion of the MIME types supported by "the web browser" when the device has two browsers installed from factory. This can be found in the UAProf description of the HTC Touch mobile phone[1], in which the coexistence of two web browsers is declared as:

> *<rdf:Description rdf:ID="BrowserUA_Opera">*
> *<rdf:Description rdf:ID="BrowserUA_pIE">*

A simple test accessing different media types from both browsers with such device indicates that some MIME types supported by the device are unevenly supported, contradicting what is stated in the *<prf:CcppAccept>* property. This is the case of the *image/svg+xml*, not included in that property, although it is supported by the Opera Mobile browser –but not by the Pocket Internet Explorer. The *<prf:CcppAccept>* property is attached to the resource *<rdf:Description rdf:ID="SoftwarePlatform">*, not to the specific instance of the browser. Consequently, UAProf lacks the ability to express these implementation details.

---

[1] http://www.htcmms.com.tw/gen/HTC_Touch_HD_T8282-1.0.xml

These limitations invite to a re-engineering of the structure of UAProf. It is likely that some attributes may need to be assigned to more specific resources. Although these changes may initially introduce an apparent redundancy due to the need to state large chunks of shared features, this drawback can be mitigated by a mechanism that permits to refine resource descriptions, as explained next.

In order to obtain a correct separation, it is necessary to eliminate expressivity restrictions in CC/PP which do not exist in RDF. CC/PP defines a hierarchical structure based on two main levels (components and attributes). It means a significant restriction over RDF, as its expressiveness is considerably reduced [16]. In practical terms, CC/PP could be seen as a kind of big table in the form key-value, where content providers are very restricted in what regards to the semantic relationships they can define.

In the UDDR-Profile format, a more comprehensive usage of the RDF model will be encouraged in order to express more complex hierarchies.

5.3   Grouping of Common Attributes

Hardware and software components from the same vendor or the same family usually share common features. It is just natural to organize the information to minimize redundancy by creating descriptions that refine or extend other descriptions. The representation of these relations and their semantics are not straightforward in RDF. We propose the use of property paths featured in the upcoming revision of SPARQL [22], to introduce basic reasoning capabilities on top of RDF datasets. For instance, variable-length property paths make it possible to formulate queries that find the value of a property that is associated to the resource directly or indirectly.

As shown in Figure 3. , there is a top level profile that defines the features of *Symbian 9.4* operative system. Then, there is another profile with the features of *Series60 5th Edition* that will extend, and override if necessary, the top level profile. At last, in the lowest level, there is a profile of the device *N97*, which extends, and override if needed, both higher level profiles.

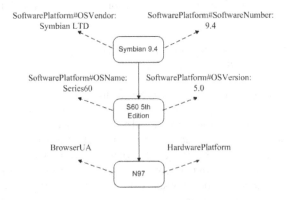

Fig. 3. Example of description hierarchy for some Symbian devices

5.4   Value Normalization

In some cases, the different values that an attribute in UAProf may take are strictly defined. This leads to incoherent device descriptions in the sense that, for instance, an attribute is valued with a string for which there is no formally specified format. As an example, the authors have reviewed the values for the attribute *BluetoothProfile* in a set of actual UAProf description files downloaded from different manufacturers' repositories. A quick read after the values accepted show that the support for the AVRCP Bluetooth profile is noted with different strings (in alphabetical order): *"audio vedio remote control"*, *"Audio Video Remote Contorl Profile"*, *"Audio Video Remote Control"*, *"Audio Video Remote Control – Target"*, *"Audio Video Remote Control Profile"*, *"audiovideoremotecontrol"*, *"AVRCP"*, etc.

Some other typical inconsistencies include the expression of the values of a same attribute by means of different types. Following the same procedure for the *BluetoothProfile* attribute, a study of the *NumberOfSoftKeys* attribute has been carried out. In addition to the expected *xsd:integer* values (0, 1, 2, 3, 4, 5, ..), a *"None"* value has been found for many Motorola devices, such as the A1600. This is due to different versions of the CC/PP schema, UAProf vocabulary and third-party schemas (such as those from the 3GPP) published over time.

For the sake of interoperability and to simplify queries to the UDDR, it becomes necessary to enforce a tighter control over the values of the attributes. Some constraints, such as type restrictions, can be defined at a syntactic level, whereas others may require defining a well-known and extensible set of entity URIs (e.g., for Bluetooth profiles). The UDDR will enforce the usage of the latest versions of schemas and vocabularies used in UAProf, defining conversion rules from previous versions to the most recent ones. Additionally, strict values for the various properties in device descriptions will be enforced, with mapping mechanisms defined after expertise –to avoid, for instance, the "string hell" in Bluetooth profile definitions.

5.5   Uniform Device Description Granularity

Distinct device descriptions of similar devices provide different granularity. For example, some Java devices include a list of the JSRs available whereas some do not. Such divergence exists even in device descriptions of device models of the same device family, as in the case of the GT B7330 Omnia PRO[2], with supported JSRs listed, and GT B7300 Lite[3], without such description detail. Even in a same UAProf document, two analogous components may provide different information granularity. For example, both web browsers in the UAProf describing the HTC Mini[4] provide information about the XHTML version supported. However, supported XHTML modules are listed for the Opera Mini but not for the Pocket Internet Explorer.

In UDDR, guidelines will guide the process to publish descriptions, so a uniform granularity baseline can be set. Moreover, the collaborative aspect of the repository evolution may help to reconcile divergences in the granularity level.

---

[2] http://wap.samsungmobile.com/uaprof/GT-B7330V_2G.xml

[3] http://wap.samsungmobile.com/uaprof/GT-B7300.xml

[4] http://www.htcmms.com.tw/gen/HTC_HD_mini_T5555-1.0.xml

5.6   Appropriate Semantic Expresiveness

Vocabulary extensibility is a key issue on using the CC/PP-UAProf stack [13], which is defined by XML/RDF namespaces. However, using multiples vocabularies causes interoperability problems. For instance, the *BrowserUA#HtmlVersion* property defined in both 2002[5] and 2007[6] versions of the CC/PP Schema will not be interpreted in the same way by a CC/PP processor.

An additional aspect to be considered is the definition of relational constraints such as cardinality (e.g. the number of values in a bag) or existence/absence of attributes within the profile [16]. This kind of restrictions makes necessary to use validation tools. An example of validation tool is the DELI validator [23] commented in section 4, but this framework presents some weakness (again [17]). Therefore, a new semantic validation is needed based on rules or query engines.

Schema and ontology languages on top of RDF, such as RDF Schema and OWL, bring in the ability to declare certain constraints. However, some of the aforementioned integrity constraints are beyond the expressiveness of these languages. Even those that are possible usually lead to consequences that are not intuitive for people trained in databases and XML. Thus, it may make sense to introduce an *ad hoc* validation tool that implements the logic behind semantic restrictions. This kind of tools is not uncommon and is often implemented by means of rule or query engines. Interestingly, the upcoming version of the SPARQL query language for RDF may be a good candidate for the task, due to the aggregated functionality and ASK queries.

Finally, UAProf documents offer many chances for improvements in the light of recent developments in Linked Data [24]. More specifically, UAProf documents, profiles and the resources they contain should be assigned HTTP-resolvable URIs. By doing so, they become extensible and linkable, and new opportunities appear for re-using shared resources.

5.7   Profile Resolution

One of the main difficulties when using CC/PP and UAProf is to carry out the resolution of profiles properly. The complexity of this issue stems from the fact that the same attributes may be defined in different source profiles. These profiles might have been created by different providers, so possible contradictions might be found. The notion of *profile resolution* in this document refers to the process of determining the correct values for each attribute in order to make up a definitive profile. Because different contributors may provide additional or overriding information, the resolution process must analyze all the available data to determine the final attribute values.

As stated in Section 4, one of the main claims of the scientific community in what regards to profile resolution is the absence of advanced formal mechanisms to automate this process. On the one hand, profiles resolution is out of the scope of the CC/PP recommendation. On the other hand, UAProf provides a mechanism to treat profile resolution. Unfortunately it presents some important drawbacks. UAProf incorporates a resolution rule associated to each attribute in the RDF schema as a

---

[5] http://www.openmobilealliance.org/tech/profiles/UAPROF/ccppsch ema-20021212

[6] http://www.openmobilealliance.org/tech/profiles/UAPROF/ccppsch ema-20070511

comment. Each attribute must take one of the following values: "locked", "override" and "append". For instance, the OSVersion attribute has been defined as "locked" in the RDF schema. It means that a profile provider would not be allowed to take advantage of an existing profile (e.g. a profile from a previous version of the device) and extend it with a new value for the OSVersion attribute.

The first limitation of this approach is that the resolution rules are expressed in the RDF schema itself. It means that, a given attribute will be associated to a concrete resolution rule regardless of the intention of the profile provider. Other important disadvantage is that data related to resolution rules is stored in the form of comments, which makes it hard to parse and process.

Our approach towards the resolution of profiles is based on two key pillars: the addition of meta-information within the profiles and the usage of advanced query mechanisms to take advantage of from the available data. The inclusion of semantic annotations, as outlined in section 5.1, allows us to resolve profiles taking into account important aspects such as the trustworthiness of amendment providers or the freshness of the provided data. In order to extract this kind of information from the profiles description, we use the SPARQL query language. By way of example, a SPARQL fragment is shown in Figure 4. to define the following query expressed in natural language: "Ask for all the XHTML versions supported by mobile web browsers, but just considering sources coming from my contacts network". Note that for this example to make sense, all "my" social information is supposed to have been externally described by using FOAF vocabulary.

```
PREFIX foaf: <http://xmlns.com/foaf/0.1/>
PREFIX dct: <http://purl.org/dc/terms/>
PREFIX ccpp:
<http://www.openmobilealliance.org/tech/profiles/UAPROF/ccppschema-20021212#>
SELECT ?browser ?xhtmlVersion ?trustedGraph ?someoneInMyNetwork
WHERE {
        ?me foaf:knows* ?someoneInMyNetwork .
        ?trustedGraph dct:creator ?someoneInMyNetwork .
        GRAPH ?trustedGraph {
                ?browser a ccpp:BrowserUA .
                ?browser ccpp:XhtmlVersion ?xhtmlVersion .
        }
}
```

Fig. 4. Provenance-based SPARQL query

5.8   Corollary

After the previous requirements, a division of the improvements suggested for the UAProf format to obtain appropriate device descriptions in the UDDR is proposed. Firstly, some improvements affect the way in which information is handled in the various versions of the CC/PP and UAProf specifications but not breaking the UAProf format. In second place, some improvements imply exploiting the RDF nature of CC/PP-UAProf, thus breaking the original format. Finally, conflict resolution needs to be performed at querying time after SPARQL sentences.

The previous sentence suggests a new division, considering the moment when information manipulation occurs. The first and second types of manipulation take place when populating the UDDR, in that specific order –improvements keeping the UAProf format first and improvements breaking that format afterwards. The third type takes place at querying time, as previously stated.

6   Populating the UDDR

This section is intended to provide a step-by-step process to obtain the UDDR-Profile device descriptions that will be managed by the UDDR after original UAProf descriptions. There is an intermediate state for document conversion called UAProf+. A UAProf+ device description is the result of using properties and values in the original UAProf profile as expected in the latest versions of the different schemas used in the UAProf specification. The authors of this work consider that this will permit a later contribution to the Open Mobile Alliance, as indicated in Section 10. To illustrate it, each step of the profile definition process will be explained, as shown in Figure 5.

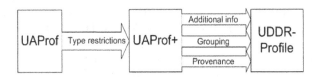

Fig. 5. Step-by-step process from UAProf to UDDR-Profile

The starting point for the UDDR profile definition is an existing UAProf document as it was referenced in the *x-wap-profile* or equivalent HTTP header sent from the mobile browser to the server. Once the original UAProf is retrieved, a new version of the document, UAProf+, will be generated by the UDDR. This new UAProf+ document will impose further type restrictions in order to guarantee an appropriate document processing avoiding inconsistencies. The next step will be the addition of custom extensions to provide more information about the device and to better group the already available data. In this way, a UDDR-Profile device description is obtained after the UAProf+ device description. Extensions will be generally obtained by carrying out a set of semiautomatic tests, although annotations by a human expert will also be allowed. Finally, device descriptions are decorated by adding provenance information, which will be used in the profile resolution process.

6.1   Obtaining UAProf Documents

The initial step to start generating profile definitions for the UDDR would be providing the system with a URI referring a UAProf profile. These URIs may be obtained from product pages of device manufacturers (as it happens in Nokia's product page), by following specialized web sites and manually providing found UAProf URIs, or by analyzing the HTTP request headers coming from the device mobile browser of tested devices and check whether any of the headers points to a UAProf document If a UAProf document already exists for the device, it will be cached and used as a basic data template to be completed in step B.

6.2   Generating UAProf+ Documents

As stated in section 5.5, one of the main difficulties when working with UAProf-CC/PP is to process type restrictions. The XSD types defined in the UAProf schemas are often not sufficiently restrictive. Moreover, distinct UAProf schemas sometimes place different restrictions on the same properties. This is the case of the *NumberOfSoftKeys* property. A *"None"* value for this property would be valid according to the 2002 version of the CC/PP schema, but invalid according to the 2007 version as shown in Figure 6. In the latter case, the expected value would be *"0"* rather than *"None"*.

```
<!---------------------------ccppschema-20021212------------------------------------>
<rdf:Description rdf:ID="NumberOfSoftKeys">
  <rdf:type rdf:resource="http://www.w3.org/1999/02/22-rdf-syntax-ns#Property"/>
  <rdfs:domain rdf:resource="#HardwarePlatform"/>
  <rdfs:comment>
    Description: Number of soft keys available on the device.
    Type:        Number
    Resolution:  Locked
    Examples:    "3", "2"
  </rdfs:comment>
</rdf:Description>

<!---------------------------ccppschema-20070511------------------------------------>
<!DOCTYPE rdf:RDF [
  <!ENTITY ns-rdf  'http://www.w3.org/1999/02/22-rdf-syntax-ns#'>
  <!ENTITY ns-rdfs 'http://www.w3.org/2000/01/rdf-schema#'>
  <!ENTITY ns-prf  'http://www.openmobilealliance.org/tech/profiles/UAPROF/ccppschema-20070511#'>
  <!ENTITY prf-dt  'http://www.openmobilealliance.org/tech/profiles/UAPROF/xmlschema-20030226#'>
  <!ENTITY xsd     'http://www.w3.org/2001/XMLSchema#'>
]>
<rdf:Description rdf:ID='NumberOfSoftKeys'>
  <rdfs:comment xml:lang='en'>
    Description: Number of soft keys available on the device.
    Examples: "3", "2"
  </rdfs:comment>
  <rdfs:label xml:lang='en'>NumberOfSoftKeys</rdfs:label>
  <rdf:type rdf:resource='&ns-rdf;Property'/>
  <rdfs:domain rdf:resource='#HardwarePlatform'/>
  <rdfs:range rdf:resource='&prf-dt;Number'/>
  <prf:ResolutionRule rdf:datatype='&prf-dt;ResolutionRule'>Locked</prf:ResolutionRule>
</rdf:Description>
```

Fig. 6. Difference between vocabulary definition restrictions in CC/PP Schema version 2002 and version 2007

UDDR will provide a schema as restrictive as possible for the UAProf property values (as stated in section 5.3). Furthermore, a mapping mechanism to convert from those values which have been defined against a less restrictive schema into the appropriate value in the UDDR schema will be provided. For instance, each appearance of *"None"* value under the *NumberOfSoftKeys* property should be transformed into a "0" value.

The resulting document format after applying these changes to the original UAProf document has been named as UAProf+.

6.3   Generating UDDR-Profile Documents

Once the UAProf+ document has been generated, the UDDR might need to modify its structure (as exposed in 5.2 and 5.3) and to add new information to the already available data. These new extensions are required due to the universal nature of the proposed DDR and to the unevenness in the granularity of data in the existing UAProf documents (as aforementioned in 5.6).

One of the extensions introduced by the UDDR is the addition of new properties over an already defined component. For instance, we might need to add a new *BrowserUserAgentString* to define all the possible User Agent strings that a given instance of the *BrowserUA* component (e.g. *BrowserUA_pIE*) might have. In order to accomplish this goal, the most recent version of the CC/PP schema (2007) has been extended. The proposed schema extension defining a new *BrowserUserAgentString* inside the *BrowserUA* component is illustrated in Figure 7.

```
<!DOCTYPE rdf:RDF [
 <!ENTITY ns-rdf 'http://www.w3.org/1999/02/22-rdf-syntax-ns#'>
 <!ENTITY ns-rdfs 'http://www.w3.org/2000/01/rdf-schema#'>
 <!ENTITY prf "http://www.openmobilealliance.org/tech/profiles/UAPROF/ccppschema-20021212#">
]>
<rdf:RDF xmlns = '&ns-rdf;'
    xmlns:rdf = '&ns-rdf;'
    xmlns:ns-rdfs='&ns-rdfs;'
    xmlns:prf="&prf;">
 <rdf:Description ns-rdf:ID="BrowserUserAgentString">
   <ns-rdfs:comment xml:lang='en'>
   Description: User-Agent header sent within the HTTP Request
   Example: "HTC_Touch_HD_T8282 Mozilla/4.0 (compatible; MSIE 6.0; Windows CE; IEMobile 7.11)"
   </ns-rdfs:comment>
   <rdf:type ns-rdf:resource="&ns-rdf;#Property"/>
   <ns-rdfs:domain ns-rdf:resource="&prf;#BrowserUA"/>
   <ns-rdfs:label xml:lang='en'>BrowserUserAgentString</ns-rdfs:label>
   <rdf:type rdf:resource='&ns-rdf;Property'/>
   <prf-dt:ResolutionRule rdf:datatype='&prf-dt;ResolutionRule'>Locked</prf-dt:ResolutionRule>
 </rdf:Description>
</rdf:RDF>
```

Fig. 7. Example of extension of an existing vocabulary

Once the extended schema has been created, it is possible to define an instance of the BrowserUA component for the Pocket Internet Explorer of the HTC Touch HD as depicted in Figure 8. :

```
<rdf:RDF xmlns:rdf="http://www.w3.org/1999/02/22-rdf-syntax-ns#"

    xmlns:prf="http://www.openmobilealliance.org/tech/profiles/UAPROF/ccppschema-20021212#"
    xmlns:prfext="http://fundacionctic.org/miCCPPSchema#">

     <rdf:Description rdf:ID="BrowserUA_pIE">
       <rdf:type rdf:resource="http://www.openmobilealliance.org/tech/profiles/UAPROF
         /ccppschema-20021212#BrowserUA" />
       <prf:BrowserName>Microsoft Pocket Internet Explorer</prf:BrowserName>
       <prf:BrowserVersion>4.0</prf:BrowserVersion>
       <prfext:BrowserUserAgentString>
        HTC_Touch_HD_T8282 Mozilla/4.0 (compatible; MSIE 6.0; Windows CE; IEMobile 7.11)
       </prfext:BrowserUserAgentString>
       <prfext:BrowserUserAgentString>
        HTC_Touch_HD_T8282 Mozilla/4.0 (compatible; MSIE 6.0; Windows CE; IEMobile 7.11)
       </prfext:BrowserUserAgentString>
       <prfext:BrowserUserAgentString>
        HTC_Touch_HD_T8282 Mozilla/4.0 (compatible; MSIE 6.0; Windows CE; IEMobile 7.11)
       </prfext:BrowserUserAgentString>
       <prfext:BrowserUserAgentString>
        HTC_Touch_HD_T8282 Mozilla/4.0 (compatible; MSIE 6.0; Windows CE; IEMobile 7.11)
       </prfext:BrowserUserAgentString>
       <prf:HtmlVersion>4.01</prf:HtmlVersion>
       <prf:XhtmlVersion>1.1</prf:XhtmlVersion>
       <prf:FramesCapable>No</prf:FramesCapable>
       <prf:PreferenceForFrames>No</prf:PreferenceForFrames>
       <prf:TablesCapable>Yes</prf:TablesCapable>
     </rdf:Description>

</rdf:RDF>
```

Fig. 8. Example of extended profile definition

Another improvement carried out in the UDDR is the re-use of data previously defined in other profiles. Analyzing the UAProf documents created by HTC, we have noticed that they include a comment after each profile document as shown in Figure 9.:

```
<!--
  Revision History
  ===================================================
  Date : 23Jul08 Modified By : Justin Chiu Copied from Quartz-1.0

  ===================================================

  End Revision History
-->
```

Fig. 9. Revision history as commented in some HTC device profiles

The comment is intended to note that the HTC Diamond UAProf document has been created based on the Quartz-1.0 by modifying some properties. After comparing these documents, we came to the conclusion that 463 lines out of 466 are completely the same in both profiles. This means that the 99.35% of the data is duplicated. The proposed mechanism to solve this issue is commented in Section 8.

Additionally, to create a Universal DDR, it is necessary to provide further information about the devices than those coming from the original UAProf document. To carry out this task, some tests must be performed. Some of the tests can be completely automatic, since a lot of information can be extracted by running predefined software programs on the devices. What is more, sometimes part of the information automatically extracted after the execution of specific software is already described in the original UAProf. However, if such a piece of information might have been defined in a generic way and it should have been associated to a specific component (as has been explained in section 5.2), so a refactoring process is needed. Unfortunately, not all the tests can be performed by a software component and they require the human expert intervention, for instance to guarantee that the quality of some audiovisual content is acceptable.

UDDR-Profiles need not only to add more information about the device capabilities, but also to include the provenance of the amendments. As stated in section 5.1, the provenance information must be represented using named graphs. This requires the usage of UAProf documents combined with graph definition files in charge of linking the provenance information with the associated profile definitions. The provenance information might annotate information about the provider (company name), the editor, date and time for the update, etc.

7   Profile Resolution

In the context of this work, the process of gathering available information pieces and assembling a coherent profile description is named "profile resolution". This process becomes necessary because the UDDR relies on many information sources, including UAProf+ profiles, but at the same time it is expected to hide the diversity and provide precise answers to the queries. The profile resolution also deals with amended information, descriptions with different degrees of granularity, and also with sources of different trustworthiness. Finally, profiles can be built by refining other profiles. The resolution process is in charge of assembling general and detailed profiles into a single view of the device description.

Some of the profile descriptions may be contradictory or ambiguous. Our approach to tackle this issue is twofold. In the first place, it is necessary to assess whether a conflict actually exists. Multiple concurring but different values of a property do not necessarily lead to a conflict, because the property may be multivalued. It is also possible that values can be merged or unified (e.g., the meaning of *VendorName = "HTC"* and *VendorName = "High Tech Corporation"* it is the actually same). However, in other situations, the conflict cannot be avoided, and consequently a mitigation method comes into effect. A number of strategies can be conceived, the simplest one being just to discard those information pieces that are in conflict. This conservative strategy, which can be applied in the absence of meta-data, sacrifices completeness for the sake of soundness. One of the goals of introducing provenance meta-data in the UDDR is to enable cleverer strategies. For instance, a more interesting approach would be to keep the most recently updated value, because it is assumed to be a fix for an erroneous value. Another strategy would rank values according to the popularity or trustworthiness of their source.

Figure 10. suggests the fact that profile resolution takes place after the population of the DDR commented in the previous section.

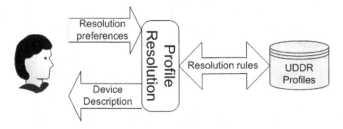

Fig. 10. Profile resolution mechanism

8   Example

In order to illustrate the populating and querying processes exposed in previous sections, a brief and concise example will be explained step-by-step. As a proof of concept, a specific device model, the HTC Touch HD (also known as Blackstone), has been chosen, and it is exemplified how to convert from its original UAProf document to the final UDDR-Profile. For the sake of brevity, the intention of the example is not to provide a full profile describing all the possible device capabilities, but to illustrate the technique to be followed in order to create a UDDR-Profile by using a reduced and comprehensive set of properties. Throughout this section some references are made to various documents, as the UAProf, UAProf+ or UDDR-Profile documents and its corresponding schemas. All the mentioned files are available online[7].

The first step to be applied is to create the UAProf+ document from the original UAProf file. To accomplish this goal, first of all those changes necessary to guarantee that the UAProf+ use the last available schemas for the distinct defined namespaces

---

[7] http://idi.fundacionctic.org/mc2011/index.html

must be performed. For instance, the *pss5:audioChannels* and *pss5:rendering ScreenSize* properties which had originally been included within the Streaming component under the pss5 namespace have been moved to the *PssCommon* component, under the last PSS namespace (pss6). Moreover, the values defined in the *pss5:pssAccept* property have been moved to the *pss6:StreamingAccept*.

The next step is to normalize the possible values for each property. For instance, the "HTC Corporation" value for the Vendor property has been converted to "HTC" as it is the notation established by convention in UDDR. Similarly, the Bluetooth profile values defined inside the *BluetoothProfile* property have been defined by using the appropriate acronym. Upon the completion of this task, the conversion from UAProf to UAProf+ can be considered as finished.

The last step to complete the populating process is the generation of the final UDDR Profile. To do that, three sub-steps are necessary:

1) Add information about the capabilities of the device. In this case, it has been decided to extend the multimedia information available for the device. A custom software tool has been developed in Windows Mobile. This software analyzes the Windows register in search of the MIME types and protocols supported by each media player pre-installed in the device. Moreover the tool is able to find out which is the default media player for each protocol. To guarantee the correctness of the information coming from the Windows register, some manual tests have been performed by a human expert.

2) Group the available information. In order to avoid data redundancy, UDDR tries to group data properly and reference other profiles when possible. For instance, the UDDR-Profile will be based on the UAProf+ descriptions, so it is not necessary to duplicate in the former all the data defined the latter. To carry out this task, a set of custom properties with a specific semantic meaning have been included. Such properties are intended to state that the subject description contains all the properties and attributes defined in the object.

3) Add provenance information. In step 1, we have added new information about the HTC Touch HD. However, in step 2, we have stated that we had also reused part of the information which was previously available in the original UAProf+ document. For the management of the UDDR it is crucial to annotate all the possible information about the provenance of the information. In this case we have created two distinct named graphs: one for the original information created by HTC and other for the information provided by the authors of this work.

Having completed the population phase, it is now possible to proceed to the querying process. Since the UDDR-Profile of the HTC Touch HD has already been defined, it is possible to query the UDDR about its properties. For instance, someone might like to ask the UDDR for the complete profile for such device by providing its URI as input evidence. Some other might want to retrieve all the possible User Agent strings for the default mobile browser of the device. Even more, and just supposing for the sake of example that we would had performed the population process over a thousand of devices, it might be interesting to ask for all the devices containing the substring "Opera" as part of the User Agent string of its mobile browser.

9   Conclusions

The main contribution of this paper is a process to obtain new device descriptions for a Universal Device Description Repository which builds on top of existing technologies, namely CC/PP and UAProf. We characterize the UDDR by means of its requirements, and we attempt to overcome the limitations found in the current alternatives. A repository without comprehensive contents would be useless, therefore we suggest a method to adapt existing (and possibly broken) UAProf profiles. UAProf+ arises as an intermediate step in such transition, and introduces a number of improvements while maintaining backward-compatibility with UAProf.

More precisely, UAProf+ aims to be fully aligned with existing schemes, and to be accepted by current conformance-checking tools such as the DELI validator. We expect UAProf+ to become the baseline of real interoperability between profile descriptions based on current practices, vocabularies and toolsets.

However, we believe that backward-compatibility must be eventually sacrificed in order to fulfill the long-term vision, particularly with respect to the requirements of provenance, adequate profile resolution and semantic precision. We argue that significant gains in these fronts can be obtained by fully exploiting the benefits of the RDF model. In other words, we propose to lift some of the XML-oriented syntactical restrictions inherited from CC/PP, as well as to introduce some refactoring in the schemes. Therefore, our final step is the UDDR, which re-uses as much as possible of its predecessor schemes, and fully leverages the RDF model in order to obtain expressivity, precision and concision. Our proposed UDDR profiles are easier to manage due to their reduced verbosity and redundancy, and can be intelligently combined taking into account provenance information. The usage of RDF becomes more idiomatic, and is aligned with the "linked data" principles. For instance, vendors, protocols or file formats are promoted from literal values to resources, a movement that enables unambiguous references and exploitation of information from external sources.

We shall not build the UDDR data sets from scratch. In addition to schema re-use, we also propose to integrate UAProf+ data in the UDDR. To this end, we introduced and exemplified a profile-extension mechanism that permits to derive UDDR profiles from UAProf+ ones (e.g., by means of the extendsProfile property). This data-extension mechanism is a custom add-on to the RDF model, and its semantics must be enforced by the UDDR, through the query evaluation engine. It is also tightly coupled to provenance tracking and profile resolution. We believe that these semantics can be implemented using SPARQL 1.1 queries.

Finally, we envisage another application of SPARQL to the implementation of advanced validation tools for UDDR profiles. The main issue here is to find the delicate balance between the permissiveness of the open-world assumption and partial descriptions on the one hand, and enforcing some essential semantic restrictions on the other one. As with other semantic web schemes, such as SKOS [25], Description Logic reasoners fall short to check all the restrictions and entailments. We propose to capture these additional restrictions as invariants expressed in SPARQL. Therefore, new UDDR profile validation tools will have to be created and made available to the industry.

10   Future Work

The authors of this article intend to further develop a formal definition for the UAProf+ format beyond the proof-of-concept suggested in this article. After that definition, a UAProf+ validator would be created in order to help device manufacturers to create interoperable device descriptions. In addition, a new version of the conversion tool from existing UAProf documents to the new UAProf+ would be developed and released. In this way, software tools might use a single language processor based on the new format to extract information from device descriptions. The success of both format and software tools (validator and legacy-UAProf conversor) will depend on their acceptance by the Open Mobile Alliance, after the corresponding submissions from the authors.

In what regards to the improvements in the current prototype of the UDDR and its population and query, a more formal model will be established and published. More specifically, the authors intend to develop the grouping mechanism to create hierarchies of device descriptions and avoid storing redundant information. The initial candidate approach to create hierarchies for different device families is the obtention of the common factor (common values for a subset of device properties) among device descriptions with the same operating system, operating system version, operating system flavor (i.e., S60 in the case of Symbian), operating system flavor version (S60 5th edition, for the previous example), etc.

References

1. Ramioul, M., Huws, U., Bollen, A.: Measuring the information society. HIVA Publication
2. DeviceAtlas: Mobile Device Detection, http://deviceatlas.com/
3. WURFL. The Wireless universal Resource FiLe, http://wurfl.sourceforge.net/
4. The maDDR Project, http://www.maddr.org/
5. The World Wide Web Consortium, http://www.w3c.org/
6. Device Independence working group. The World Wide Web Consortium, http://www.w3.org/2001/di/
7. Wireless Application Group–User Agent Profile Specification (1999)
8. Klyne, G., Reynolds, F., Woodrow, C., Ohto, H., Hjelm, J., Butler, M., Tran, L.: Composite Capability/Preference Profiles (CC/PP): Structure and vocabularies 1.0. W3C Recommendation 15 (2004)
9. Beckett, D., McBride, B.: RDF/XML Syntax Specification (Revised). W3C Recommendation. The World Wide Web Consortium, February 10 (2004)
10. Open Mobile Alliance, http://www.openmobilealliance.org/
11. Buneman, P., Khanna, S., Tan, W.-C.: Why and Where: A Characterization of Data Provenance. In: Van den Bussche, J., Vianu, V. (eds.) ICDT 2001. LNCS, vol. 1973, pp. 316–330. Springer, Heidelberg (2000)
12. Butler, M.: Some questions and answers on CC/PP and UAProf. Tech. rep., Hewlett Packard Laboratories (2002)
13. Butler, M.: CC/PP and UAProf: Issues, improvements and future directions. In: Proceedings of W3C Delivery Context Workshop, DIWS 2002 (2002)

14. Butler, M.: Input to Device Description Working Group (2005),
    `http://lists.w3.org/Archives/Public/public-ddwg/2005Aug/att-0005/ddwgPositionPaper.htm`
15. DELI: A Delivery Context Library For CC/PP and UAProf,
    `http://delicon.sourceforge.net/`
16. Indulska, J., Robinson, R., Rakotonirainy, A., Henricksen, K.: Experiences in Using CC/PP in Context-Aware Systems. In: Chen, M.-S., Chrysanthis, P.K., Sloman, M., Zaslavsky, A. (eds.) MDM 2003. LNCS, vol. 2574, pp. 247–261. Springer, Heidelberg (2003)
17. Gergic, J., et al.: Addressing On-Demand Assembly and Adaptation Using a Run-time Intentional Versioning Engine. Ph.D. thesis, Charles University in Prague, Faculty of Mathematics and Physics (2008)
18. Carroll, J.J., Bizer, C., Hayes, P., Stickler, P.: Named graphs, provenance and trust. In: Proceedings of the 14th International Conference on World Wide Web, WWW 2005, pp. 613–622. ACM, New York (2005),
    `http://doi.acm.org/10.1145/1060745.1060835`
19. Zhao, J., Miles, A., Klyne, G., Shotton, D.: Linked data and provenance in biological data webs. Briefings in Bioinformatics 10(2), 139–152 (2009),
    `http://dx.doi.org/10.1093/bib/bbn044`
20. Prud'hommeaux, E., Seaborne, A.: SPARQL query language for RDF (working draft). Tech. rep., W3C (March 2007),
    `http://www.w3.org/TR/2007/WD-rdf-sparql-query-20070326/`
21. Gil, Y., Cheney, J., Groth, P., Hartig, O., Miles, S., Moreau, L., da Silva, P.P.: Provenance XG Final Report (December 2010),
    `http://www.w3.org/2005/Incubator/prov/XGR-prov/`
22. Harris, S., Seaborne, A.: SPARQL 1.1 Query Language. W3C working draft, W3C (October 2010)
23. OMA DELI-2 UAProf Validator,
    `http://validator.openmobilealliance.org/cgi/`
24. Heath, T., Bizer, C.: Linked Data: Evolving the Web into a Global Data Space, 1st edn. Morgan & Claypool (2011), `http://linkeddatabook.com/`
25. Miles, A., Bechhofer, S.: SKOS Simple Knowledge Organization System Reference. The World Wide Web Consortium (August 2009), `http://www.w3.org/TR/skos-reference/`

Cross-Compiling Android Applications to Windows Phone 7

Oren Antebi, Markus Neubrand, and Arno Puder

San Francisco State University,
Department of Computer Science,
1600 Holloway Avenue,
San Francisco, CA 94132
{antebi,mneubran,arno}@mail.sfsu.edu

Abstract. Android is currently leading the smartphone segment in terms of market share since its introduction in 2007. Android applications are written in Java using an API designed for mobile apps. Other smartphone platforms, such as Apple's iOS or Microsoft's Windows Phone 7, differ greatly in their native application programming model. App developers who want to publish their applications for different platforms are required to re-implement the application using the respective native SDK. In this paper we describe a cross-compilation approach, whereby Android applications are cross-compiled to C# for Windows Phone 7. We describe different aspects of our cross-compiler, from byte code level cross-compilation to API mapping. A prototype of our cross-compiler called XMLVM is available under an Open Source license.

Keywords: Android, WP7, Cross-Compilation.

1 Introduction

Android is a software stack for mobile devices maintained by the members of the Open Handset Alliance (OHA) since 2007. It employs Java as a programming language as well as its own API for mobile applications. The Android API offers support for application lifecycle, device management, and UI programming. Apps are offered via the Android Market but can also be downloaded from third-party web sites. In early 2010, Microsoft released its Windows Phone 7 (WP7) platform. The programming environment is based on the .NET framework [4] and applications can be developed in C# and VisualBasic. The WP7 platform offers its own proprietary API for mobile development. Apps are made available through Microsoft's Marketplace.

Developers targeting smartphones ideally want their applications to be available on as many platforms as possible to increase the potential dissemination. Given the differences in the way applications are written for smartphones, this incurs significant effort in porting the same application to various platforms. In this paper, we introduce a cross-compilation approach, whereby an Android application can be cross-compiled to WP7. The solution we propose not only

J.Y. Zhang et al. (Eds.): MobiCASE 2011, LNICST 95, pp. 283–302, 2012.

cross-compiles on a language level, but also maps APIs between different platforms. The benefit is that only skill set for the Android platform is required and only one code base needs to be maintained for both devices. In an earlier project we have followed the same approach targeting iOS devices [9].

This paper is organized as follows: Section 2 provides an overview of Android and WP7 followed by a discussion of related work in Section 3. Section 4 presents our cross-compilation framework that can cross-compile Android applications to WP7 devices while Section 5 outlines the API mapping from Android to WP7. In Section 6, we discuss our prototype implementation of this framework as well as an application that was cross-compiled using our toolchain. Finally, Section 7 provides a conclusion and an outlook to future work.

2   Overview of Android and Windows Phone 7

Table 1 provides a comparison of the Android-based Nexus S sold by Google and Samsung's Omnia 7 which uses Microsoft's WP7. The intent of this side-by-side comparison is to show that although both smartphones are relatively similar with respect to their hardware capabilities, they differ greatly in their native application development models.

Android advocates a mobile operating system running on the Linux kernel. It was initially developed by Google and later the Open Handset Alliance. Android is not exclusively targeting smartphones, but is also available for netbooks, tablets and settop boxes. The Windows Phone 7 is a proprietary platform by Microsoft. WP7 stipulates hardware requirements that must be met in order to install Microsoft's mobile OS. Different smartphone manufacturers have licensed WP7. Targeting both platforms requires significant skill sets. Whereas Android uses Java as the development language, WP7 is based on .NET using either C# or VisualBasic. While Java and C# are relatively similar, their respective object models differ in subtle ways. C# features true generics and also supports events and delegates as part of its object model in contrast to Java.

Similar differences exist in the APIs and programming models defined by Android and WP7. To better highlight the different programming environments, the following two sections will show a simple application for both smartphones using their respective native programming language. The application allows to enter a name and upon pressing a button, the name will be echoed in a label. This application is more involved compared to a simple "Hello World", but the purpose is to provide a brief introduction to the programming abstractions employed by the respective platform and also to demonstrate the heterogeneity of smartphone application development.

2.1   Android

An Android application consists of a set of so-called *activities*. An activity is a user interaction that may have one or more input screens. An example for an activity is the selection of a contact from the internal address book. The user

Table 1. Smartphone comparison

	Nexus S	Omnia 7
OS	Linux	Windows CE
CPU	Hummingbird S5PC110, 1 GHz	Snapdragon QSD8250, 1 GHz
RAM	512 MB	512 MB
Sensors	Accelerometer, GPS, proximity, ambient light, compass.	Accelerometer, GPS, proximity, ambient light, compass.
IDE	Eclipse	VisualStudio
Dev-Language	Java	C#, VisualBasic
GUI	Android	WP7
VMs	Allowed	Only .NET
License	Open Source	Proprietary

may flip through the contact list or may use a search box. These actions are combined to form an activity. Activities have a well-defined life cycle and can be invoked from other activities (even activities from other applications). The sample application that we introduce here consists of a single activity which uses three widgets: a text input box, a label, and a button. Upon clicking the button, the name from the text input box is read and echoed with a greeting in the label. The following code is the complete implementation of the Android application:

———————————— Java (using Android API) ————————————
```
1  public class SayHello extends Activity {
2    @Override
3    public void onCreate(Bundle savedState) {
4      super.onCreate(savedState);
5      LinearLayout panel = new LinearLayout(this);
6      layout.setOrientation(LinearLayout.VERTICAL);
7      LayoutParams params =
8          new LinearLayout.LayoutParams(LayoutParams.FILL_PARENT,
9                                        LayoutParams.WRAP_CONTENT);
10     params.setMargins(10, 10, 10, 10);
11     final EditText box = new EditText(this);
12     box.setLayoutParams(params);
13     panel.addView(box);
14     final TextView label = new TextView(this);
15     label.setLayoutParams(params);
16     label.setGravity(Gravity.CENTER_HORIZONTAL);
17     panel.addView(label);
18     Button button = new Button(this);
19     button.setLayoutParams(params);
20     button.setText("Say Hello");
21     button.setOnClickListener(
22       new OnClickListener() {
23
24         @Override
```

```
25        public void onClick(View view) {
26            label.setText("Hello, " + box.getText() + "!");
27        }
28
29      });
30      panel.addView(button);
31      setContentView(panel);
32    }
33 }
```

Every Android application needs to designate a main activity whose implementation has to be derived from the base class **Activity**. The main entry point of an activity is the method **onCreate()** that also signals the creation of the activity. In case the activity was active at an earlier point in time, the saved state of the previous incarnation is passed as an argument to **onCreate()**. Inside the **onCreate()** method, a **LinearLayout** is instantiated that acts as a container and allows to automatically align its children vertically (line 5). Next, some general layout parameters are created (lines 7–10) that define padding of 10 pixels, tell that a widget's horizontal size should use up all available space of the parent (**FILL_PARENT**) and its vertical size should be the widgets natural size (**WRAP_CONTENT**). Those layout parameters are applied to all widgets created subsequently.

Three widgets are created in total: a text input box (line 11), a label (line 14), and a button (line 18). A click listener is added to the button (line 21) in the form of an instance of an anonymous class. Whenever the button is clicked, the click listener will read the name from the text input box and echo a greeting via the label. The remaining code of the "Say Hello" application defines the view hierarchy by adding the widgets to the **LinearLayout** and then setting the **LinearLayout** as the main content view (line 31).

Besides a variety of widgets, Android also allows the declarative description of user interfaces. XML files describe the layout of a user interface which not only simplifies internationalization but also allows to render the user interface on different screen resolutions.

2.2 Windows Phone 7

This sections shows how the same "Say Hello" application can be implemented for WP7. The primary languages offered by Microsoft for WP7 development are C# and VisualBasic, hence the "Say Hello" application for this device has to be written in one of those languages.

```
                              C# (using WP7 API)
1 public class SayHello : Application {
2   private TextBox box = new TextBox();
3   private TextBlock label = new TextBlock();
4   private Button button = new Button();
5
```

```
 6  public SayHello() {
 7    this.Startup += new StartupEventHandler(Main);
 8  }
 9
10  public void Main(object sender, StartupEventArgs args) {
11    label.Foreground = new SolidColorBrush(Colors.White);
12    label.Margin = new Thickness(10);
13    button.Content = "Say Hello";
14    button.Click += new RoutedEventHandler(Click);
15    button.Margin = new Thickness(10);
16    box.Margin = new Thickness(10);
17    StackPanel panel = new StackPanel();
18    panel.Children.Add(box);
19    panel.Children.Add(label);
20    panel.Children.Add(button);
21    this.RootVisual = layout;
22  }
23
24  public void Click(object sender, RoutedEventArgs args) {
25    label.Text = "Hello, " + box.Text + "!";
26  }
27 }
```

A WP7 application class needs to be derived from a base class called
Application. Its constructor adds a new event handler to the Startup property
(line 7) that will result in method Application.Main() to be invoked (line 10).
Analogous to the Android version, the three widgets of the "Say Hello" application are called TextBox, TextBlock and Button (lines 2–4). Method Main()
first sets various properties of those widgets including a 10-pixel margin and
a click listener for the button (line 14). Just as with the startup property, the
click listener is added via the overloaded += operator in C#. If the user clicks
the button, method Click() of class Application will be invoked. The vertical
alignment of the three widgets is realized in WP7 by a so-called StackPanel
(line 17).

3 Related Work

Several frameworks promise to facilitate the development of cross-platform applications. In the following we briefly discuss the approach taken by PhoneGAP,
MonoTouch, and Adobe AIR. Each framework will be classified with regards to
the mobile platforms it supports, the programming languages it offers, the API
it uses, the IDE it can be used with and finally the license under which it is
released.

PhoneGAP is an Open Source project that addresses web developers who wish
to write mobile applications. It is available for iOS, Android, BlackBerry and
the Palm Pre. Applications need to be written in JavaScript/HTML/CSS. But
instead of downloading the application from a remote web server, the JavaScript

is bundled inside a native application. E.g., for iOS devices a generic startup code written in Objective-C will instantiate a full-screen web widget via class UIWebView. Next the JavaScript that is embedded as data in the native application is injected into this web widget at runtime. Special protocol handlers allow the communication between JavaScript and the native layer. All iOS widgets are rendered using HTML/CSS mimicking the look-and-feel of their native counterparts. PhoneGAP supports a common API for sensors such as the accelerometer. Platform-specific widgets have their own API. PhoneGAP is available under the MIT Open Source license at http://phonegap.com.

Xamarin (formerly Novell) offers with MonoTouch a .NET based framework for mobile applications. MonoTouch allows iOS applications to be written in C#. The C# iOS API is mapped one-for-one from the Cocoa Touch/Objective-C API. MonoTouch is able to read so-called XIB (Xcode InterfaceBuilder) files created by Xcodes InterfaceBuilder. Applications written in C# are compiled to ARM instructions utilizing the Open Source project Mono. Since Apple does not permit the installation of a virtual machine, C# applications are compiled using AOT (Ahead-of-Time) compilation instead of JIT (Just-in-Time) execution. Xamarin recently released a .NET based framework for Android called MonoDroid that allows Android applications to be written in C#. MonoTouch and MonoDroid are available under a commercial license at http://ios.xamarin.com.

Table 2. Comparison of Cross-Platform Frameworks

	PhoneGAP	MonoTouch	Adobe AIR	XMLVM
Platforms	iOS, Android, Blackberry, Palm Pre	iOS	iOS	iOS, Android, WP7
Language	JavaScript	C#	ActionScript	Java
API	Common Sensor API	iOS-only	Graphics-only	Android API mapped to iOS, WP7
IDE	Xcode	MonoDevelop	N/A	Eclipse
License	Open Source	Commercial	Commercial	Open Source

Another cross-platform framework is the Adobe Integrated Runtime (AIR) for iOS development. Similar to MonoTouch, Adobe AIR includes an AOT compiler based on the LLVM compiler suite that translates ActionScript 3 to ARM instructions. This facilitates porting of existing Flash applications while not relying on an installation of a Flash player on the iOS device. AIR offers API based on ActionScript to the device's sensors, but does not provide access to the native iOS widgets which limits AIR applications to games. As the only framework, AIR does not depend on Apple's Xcode SDK. AIR applications can be written under Windows. AIR is available under a commercial license at http://www.adobe.com/products/air/.

Table 2 summarizes the distinguishing factors of the various cross-platform frameworks introduced in this section. XMLVM is similar in the respect that it offers one programming language (Java) for different mobile devices. It also includes an AOT compiler to translate Java to native applications in order to avoid the installation of a Java virtual machine on the target platform. In contrast to other cross-platform frameworks, XMLVM relies on the Android API for application development. Instead of creating a new API for various functionalities, XMLVM makes use of the Android API that is mapped to the target platform. Besides sensor API, XMLVM is also capable of mapping Android widgets and layout managers such the ones used in the "Say Hello" application. Both the cross-compilation on a language-level as well as the API mapping is discussed in detail in the following section.

4 Cross-Compilation Framework

In this section we introduce our language-level cross-compiler, as a backend extension of a general flexible byte code level cross-compiler. The latter is named XMLVM due to its internal representation of byte code instructions of the virtual machine via appropriate XML tags. In Section 4.1 we give an overview of the general XMLVM toolchain. In Section 4.2 we explain how XMLVM is used to translate Java byte codes to the C# programming language.

4.1 Toolchain

Our general XMLVM framework [10] only assumes familiarity with the Android software stack. Thus, Android developers may use XMLVM toolchain to cross-compile an Android application to other smartphones, even without any iOS or WP7 skills.

The choice of Android as a canonical platform was made since we believe that there is a wider skill set for the Java programming language and there are powerful tools to develop in Java. For instance, we view this as an advantage over Objective-C used for iPhone and iPad development.

Moreover, Android was specifically designed to offer applications the means to adapt to a wider range of mobile devices. Hence, we believe that it serves as a natural umbrella platform over other smartphone platforms. Furthermore, our toolchain is able to benefit from many open source tools offered for the Android software stack. We use some of these tools for our API mapping and for the transformation of Oracle's stack-based virtual machine instructions [8] to register-based byte code instruction set introduced by the Dalvik virtual machine [1] to allow generation of more efficient code in the target language.

As illustrated in Figure 1, our toolchain cross-compiles byte codes, rather than source code of high-level programming languages as done by other tools (e.g., [5]). The choice to transform byte codes has several advantages. First, byte codes are much easier to parse than Java source code. Moreover, some high-level language

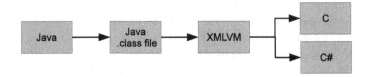

Fig. 1. XMLVM Framework

features such as generics are already reduced to low-level byte code instructions. Furthermore, the Java compiler does extensive optimizations to produce efficient byte codes.

In the following examples we focus on the register-based format of XMLVM which separates the frontend from the backends (XMLVM in Figure 1). As we illustrate in the next section, generation of high-level code in the target language, which for our backend is C#, is then a matter of a simple XSL transformation. Other backends have also been considered in earlier work, of which the most complete is the C backend used to build complex iOS applications.

4.2 Byte Code Level Cross-Compilation

To illustrate our approach, consider the following simple Java class `Account`, whose method `deposit()` adds a given amount to the `balance` of an account:

──────────────────── Account.java ────────────────────
```
1 public class Account {
2     int balance;
3     // ...
4     public void deposit(int amount) {
5         balance += amount;
6     }
7 }
```

The source code is first compiled to Java byte codes via a regular Java compiler, and fed into our XMLVM tool. The first transformation converts the stack-based byte code instructions to register-based instructions introduced by Dalvik. The conversion from a stack-based to a register-based machine has been researched extensively [2], [11]. Internally, XMLVM represents the virtual machine via the following XML document based on the `Account` class:

──────────────────── XMLVM ────────────────────
```
1 <vm:xmlvm ...>
2   <vm:class name="Account" ...>
3   <vm:field name="balance" type="int" />
4   <!-- ... -->
5   <vm:method name="deposit" ...>
6     <vm:signature>
7       <vm:parameter type="int" />
```

```
 8          <vm:return type="void" />
 9        </vm:signature>
10        <dex:code register-size="3">
11          <dex:var name="this" register="1"
12                   type="Account" />
13          <dex:var register="2" param-index="0"
14                   type="int" />
15          <dex:iget member-name="balance"
16                    vx="0" vx-type="int"
17                    vy="1" vy-type="Account" .../>
18          <dex:add-int vx="0" vy="0" vz="2" />
19          <dex:iput member-name="balance"
20                    vx="0" vx-type="int"
21                    vy="1" vy-type="Account" .../>
22          <dex:return-void />
23        </dex:code>
24      </vm:method>
25    </vm:class>
26 </vm:xmlvm>
```

On the top-level, there are tags to represent the class definition (line 2), field definitions (line 3), method definition (line 5) and its signature (line 6). The children of the tag <dex:code> (line 10) represent the byte code instructions for the method deposit(). The attribute register-size specifies the number of registers required to execute this method.

In the following we give a brief overview of the byte code instructions generated for the method deposit(). Upon entering a method, the last n registers are automatically initialized with the n actual parameters. Since the method deposit() has three registers labeled 0 to 2, register 2 is initialized (line 13) with the single actual parameter of that method (the amount). The implicit this-parameter counts as a parameter and will therefore be copied to register 1 (line 11). The byte code instructions read and write to various registers that are referred to via attributes vx, vy, and vz, where vx usually designates the register that stores the result of the operation. The first instruction <dex:iget> (*instance get*) loads the content of the field balance of the account object referenced by register 1 into register 0 (line 15). The <dex:add-int> (*add integer*) instruction (line 18) adds the integers in registers 0 (the current balance) and 2 (the actual parameter) and store the sum in register 0. This instruction performs the operation $vx = vy + vz$. The <dex:iput> (*instance put*) instruction (line 19) performs the opposite of <dex:iget>: the content of register 0 is stored in field balance of the object referenced by register 1.

Once an XML representation of a byte code program has been generated, it is possible to use XSL stylesheets [13] to cross-compile the byte code instructions to arbitrary high-level languages such as C#, by simply mimicking the register machine in the target language.

Registers can only store integers, floats, doubles, longs and object references. Shorter primitive types such as bytes and shorts are sign-extended to 32-bit integers. In order to map individual registers to C# variables, we introduce a C#-struct that imitates a C-union and reflects the different data types that registers may contain:

```C#
using global::System.Runtime.InteropServices;
namespace org.xmlvm {
    [StructLayout(LayoutKind.Explicit)]
    public struct Element {
        [FieldOffset(0)]
        public int i;
        [FieldOffset(0)]
        public float f;
        [FieldOffset(0)]
        public double d;
        [FieldOffset(0)]
        public long l;
    }
}
```

Variables representing registers are automatically generated by XSL templates during the code generation process. They are always prefixed with _r followed by the register number, and their definition is based on org.xmlvm.Element. However, variables representing registers that store object references are defined separately as System.Object, to avoid overlapping by non-object fields which is not permissible in C#.

With the help of these variables, it is possible to map the effect of individual byte code instructions to the target language using XSL templates. As an example, the following XSL template shows how the aforementioned byte code instruction <dex:add-int> is mapped to C# source code:

```XSL template
<xsl:template match="dex:add-int">
    <xsl:text>    _r</xsl:text>
    <xsl:value-of select="@vx"/>
    <xsl:text>.i = _r</xsl:text>
    <xsl:value-of select="@vy"/>
    <xsl:text>.i + _r</xsl:text>
    <xsl:value-of select="@vz"/>
    <xsl:text>.i;</xsl:text>
</xsl:template>
```

Applying all XSL templates to the XMLVM of the class Account shown earlier yields the following C# source code for the method deposit():

```
──────────────────── Generated C# for deposit() ────────────────────
1 //...
2 public virtual void deposit(int n1) {
3     org.xmlvm.Element _r0;
4     System.Object     _r1_o;
5     org.xmlvm.Element _r2;
6     //...
7     _r1_o = this;
8     _r2.i = n1;
9     _r0.i = ((Account) _r1_o).balance;
10    _r0.i = _r0.i + _r2.i;
11    ((Account) _r1_o).balance = _r0.i;
12    return;
13 }
```

In particular, note that the code in line 10 was generated by the XSL template for the <dex:add-int> instruction explained earlier.

In practice, field and method names have to be mangled to escape C# keywords (such as "out" and "internal"), to avoid clashes of method and field identifiers and to escape $s in Java identifiers. Moreover, the Java object model differs from C# [3]; a C# method will not override its parent unless it is annotated with the override modifier and its parent is annotated with virtual. Therefore, our tool identifies Java methods that override their base class methods, such as:

```
──────────────────── InvestmentAccount.java ────────────────────
1 public class InvestmentAccount extends Account {
2     public void deposit(int amount) {
3         //...
4     }
5 }
```

and annotates them internally by adding special attribute called isOverride to the <vm:method> tag. Subsequently, the stylesheet transforms this attribute into the required modifier:

```
──────────────────── Generated C# ────────────────────
1 public class InvestmentAccount: Account {
2     //...
3     public override void deposit(int n1) {
4         //...
5     }
6 }
```

Furthermore, C# does not allow covariant return types which is permissible in Java. For example, consider an InvestmentBank class that overrides an openAccount() method of a base Bank class:

———————————— Covariant return example in Java ————————————

```java
1 public class Bank {
2     //...
3     public Account openAccount() {
4         return new Account();
5     }
6 }
7
8 public class InvestmentBank extends Bank {
9     @Override
10     public InvestmentAccount openAccount() {
11         return new InvestmentAccount();
12     }
13 }
```

Since Dalvik registers are always of the type `java.lang.Object`, return types of methods can always be replaced with `System.Object` in the cross-compiled C# code:

———————————————— Generated C# ————————————————

```csharp
1 public class Bank: java.lang.Object {
2     //...
3     public virtual System.Object openAccount() {
4         global::System.Object _r0_o;
5         _r0_o = new Account();
6         //...
7         return _r0_o;
8     }
9 }
10
11 public class InvestmentBank: Bank {
12     //...
13     public override System.Object openAccount() {
14         global::System.Object _r0_o;
15         _r0_o = new InvestmentAccount();
16         //...
17         return _r0_o;
18     }
19 }
```

Besides the special cases discussed in this section, our code generation tool is fully Java compliant and is also able to handle Java exceptions and arrays (by wrapping them inside their C# counterparts), inner classes, interface fields, reflection API and native interface.

5   API Mapping

While the previous section focused on cross-compiling Java programs to C#, we discuss the mapping of the Android API to the API of the respective target platform in the following. This section is organized as follows: Section 5.1 provides an overview of the different layers used for the API mapping and discusses the functions they provide and their APIs. Section 5.2 presents the implementation details of the wrapper library layer while Section 5.3 discusses the implementation details of the other two layers: the Android Compatibility Library and the Native Adapter Library.

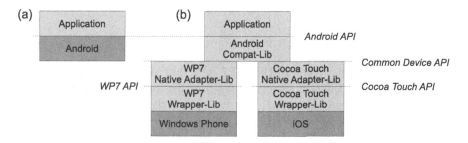

Fig. 2. (a) Classic Android Application (b) Android Application in the XMLVM layer model

5.1 Overview

Figure 2 shows a classic Android application versus the layer model of XMLVM. While a classic Android application makes direct use of the underlying native platform, the mapping of an Android application to a different platform is divided into several different layers.

The highest level of the XMLVM layer model is the *Android Compatibility Library (ACL)*. It offers the same API as the Android platform, but supports multiple underlying platforms through use of our *Common Device API*. The Android Compatibility Library contains the implementation of all parts which can be solved in a platform independent manner. Amongst others this includes APIs like layout manager, XML parsing or the Android application lifecycle. If a part needs access to native functionality it uses our Common Device API to access it.

To provide Android APIs the ACL uses parts of the Android project that is available under an Open Source license. However, Android also uses APIs which are not Android specific, but part of the standard Java SE APIs. The most common are data structures and other parts of `java.util.*`. Like Android itself we use the project Apache Harmony, an Open Source implementation of Java SE, to provide these APIs. Since Apache Harmony is itself written in Java, it is simply cross-compiled with XMLVM.

Native Adapter Libraries are responsible for adapting differences between Android's API and the API of the underlying platform and implement our specified Common Device API. The Common Device API is exposing all platform dependent native functionality needed by the ACL. Typical examples for exposed native functionality are UI widgets, like buttons or text fields, or sensor API. The adapter library hides platform specific API from the ACL and clearly separates the wrapper libraries from any Android related dependencies.

Wrapper libraries are the lowest level of the XMLVM layer model. As the supported platforms use different programming languages than the Android platform, the wrapper libraries are exposing native API in Java. C# WP7 API, or Objective-C Cocoa Touch API, is represented as a Java API, allowing Java programs to interact with native functionality. Both the ACL and Wrapper Libraries are explained in detail in the following sections.

5.2   Wrapper library

XMLVM uses the C# version of the WP7 API that gets exposed in Java as a wrapper library. C# offers a variety of features like properties, operator overloading or delegates and events, that are not directly supported by the Java object model. In order to represent these constructs, they are emulated by using POJOs with the goal in mind to represent the original C# API as closely as possible.

The following listing shows the Java version of a button from the WP7 wrapper library:

```
─────────────────────── Java: WP7 Button Wrapper ───────────────────────
1 package Compatlib.System.Windows.Controls;
2
3 @XMLVMSkeletonOnly
4 public class Button {
5   public void setContent(String content) {}
6
7   public final ClickEvent Click;
8
9   private class ClickEvent extends Event {
10     public void __add(EventHandler handler) {}
11     public void __fire(Object sender, RoutedEventArgs args) {}
12   }
13
14   //...
15 }
```

As can be seen in the listing above, the implementation of the class is left empty since its only purpose is to provide a Java API against which the developer can implement an application. C# events and delegates are emulated by the Java classes `Event` and `EventHandler`. Operator overloading is mimicked by specially named methods representing the overloaded operator, like `__add` for `+=` in the example above. Properties, like `Button.Content`, are represented by appropriate getter/setter methods. The package name of a wrapper class is the C# namespace of the class prefixed with `Compatlib` to avoid conflicts after cross-compilation.

Wrapper classes are marked with an @XMLVMSkeletonOnly annotation and are treated special by XMLVM's cross-compiler. The implementation of a method in a wrapper class is ignored and instead special comment markers are emitted. The programmer can inject manually written code between these comment markers. This code is tying the wrapper class together with the native class it wraps. The following code excerpt demonstrates this concept for the Button class.

```
──────────── C#: Cross-compiled WP7 Button Wrapper ────────────
1 using native = System.Windows.Controls;
2 namespace Compatlib.System.Windows.Controls {
3   public class Button {
4     public ClickEvent Click;
5
6     public virtual void setContent(java.lang.String n1) {
7       //XMLVM_BEGIN_WRAPPER
8       wrapped.Content = Util.toNative(n1);
9       //XMLVM_END_WRAPPER
10    }
11
12    //XMLVM_BEGIN_WRAPPER
13    public native.Button wrapped = new native.Button();
14
15    public Button {
16      wrapped.Click += ClickHandler;
17    }
18
19    public void ClickHandler(object sender, RoutedEventArgs args) {
20      Click.__fire(Util.toWrapper(sender), Util.toWrapper(args));
21    }
22    //XMLVM_END_WRAPPER
23
24    //...
25  }
26 }
```

Note that the wrapper class above is not implementing the widget itself, but only wraps the WP7 API Button class (line 13). Code between XMLVM_BEGIN_WRAPPER and XMLVM_END_WRAPPER comments is manually written C# code which gets injected on either method- or class-level during cross-compilation. The comment markers allow the manually written code to be automatically migrated if it should become necessary to regenerate the wrappers.

Communication between the native API and the wrapper library can happen in both directions. Method setContent() is an example for communication from the wrapper library to the native widget. The code above converts a java.lang.String instance to a native C# string via a helper function and sets the Content property of the wrapped button to the converted string (line 8).

Events represent communication in the opposite direction: from the native widget to the wrapper library. During construction of the wrapper we register an event handler function for the `Click` event of the wrapped button (line 16). When a native click event is received our event handler function converts the accompanying parameters to wrapper library classes. Afterwards it fires off the `Event` class in the wrapper library which emulates C# events as POJOs (line 20).

To summarize, wrapper libraries are responsible for the communication between the native layer and Java code. We achieve that by injecting hand-written C# code, responsible for this communication, into them during cross-compilation.

5.3   Android Compatibility Library (ACL) and Native Adapter Libraries (NAL)

The purpose of the ACL is to offer the Android API to an application while supporting multiple different platforms for its implementation. The codebase from the original Android sources used for the implementation is modified to use the Common Device API exposed by the Native Adapter Libraries. The Native Adapter Libraries bind the Android API to the previously discussed wrapper libraries.

In addition to the Android codebase, Harmony is used to provide the Java SE APIs. The majority of Harmony's Java SE APIs are themselves written in Java. A useful subset of this API is simply cross-compiled as well to the language of the target platform and used as part of the compatibility library. XMLVM calculates dependencies to J2SE API at compile time and automatically includes needed classes in the cross-compilation process.

On system-level, Apache Harmony uses native Java methods to access func-tionality of the underlying operating system. These methods are implemented by using native functionality of the target platform (e.g. WP7 API on WP7 or Posix API on iOS). As with wrappers, the code for the implementation of native methods gets injected during cross-compilation.

As the codebase of the Android Compatibility Library is shared between all supported platforms we try to keep all functionality that does not necessarily need access to native capabilities in this layer. For some tasks, like XML parsing, native support would exist on the supported platforms, but to keep the Common Device API as small as possible we chose to implement those parts purely in Java as well. This minimizes the effort needed to add new platforms because these APIs are automatically available through cross-compilation.

Due to the fact that XMLVM supports multiple different platforms, function-ality from the Android API must be mapped to several different native platforms. To achieve this the ACL is written platform independent and uses platform spe-cific Native Adapter Libraries that implement an API called Common Device API. Due to the fact that all Native Adapter Libraries implement the same API the actual underlying platform is completely hidden from the ACL.

The following code excerpt shows how an `android.widget.Button` is mapped to the `Button` from the WP7 wrapper library explained in the previous chapter:

```
———————————— Java: excerpts from ACL and NAL ————————————
1 // Android Compatibility Library
2 package android.widget;
3
4 public class Button {
5   private ButtonAdapter adapter;
6   // ...
7   public Button(Context c) {
8     AdapterFactory f = FactoryFinder.getAdapterFactory();
9     adapter = f.createButtonAdapter();
10  }
11
12  public void setText(String string) {
13    adapter.setText(text);
14  }
15 }
16
17 // WP7 Native Adapter Library
18 public class WP7AdapterFactory implements AdapterFactory {
19  // ...
20  public ButtonAdapter createButtonAdapter() {
21    return new WP7ButtonAdapter();
22  }
23 }
24
25 public class WP7ButtonAdapter implements ButtonAdapter {
26  Compatlib.System.Windows.Controls.Button wrapper;
27  // ...
28  public void setText(String string) {
29    wrapper.setContent(string);
30  }
31 }
32
33 // Cocoa Touch Native Adapter Library
34 public class IOSButtonAdapter implements ButtonAdapter {
35  UIButton wrapper;
36  // ...
37  public void setText(String string) {
38    wrapper.setTitle(text, UIControlState.Normal);
39  }
40 }
```

To communicate with an underlying platform the ACL uses the FactoryFinder to get an instance of an AdapterFactory (line 8). The FactoryFinder will instantiate a platform specific AdapterFactory, in case of WP7 a WP7AdapterFactory. By using the AdapterFactory to instantiate adapter classes the ACL does not know which underlying platform it uses. The AdapterFactory is implemented for every supported platform and instantiates adapter classes. Adapter classes are responsible for translating between

Android API and native API exposed by the wrapper library. In the very simple case above the `WP7ButtonAdapter` translates from the Android API method `setText` to the equivalent WP7 API method `setContent()` (line 29). The class `IOSButtonAdapter` shows the same adapter for iOS. In this case the adapter translates from the Android `setText()` method to the `setTitle()` method of the iOS `UIButton` wrapper (line 38).

Adapters are responsible for a variety of simple tasks like converting units or method names. In more complicated cases, where no equivalent of an Android class is available on the native platform, they emulate the class by using several different wrapper classes.

These abstractions give us the advantage that new platforms can be easily added by implementing the specified Common Device API. Another advantage is that all supported platforms can share code in the ACL if it is not platform-dependent. By having a clean adapter layer both other layers, wrapper libraries and the ACL, can be developed without any dependencies to each other.

6   Prototype Implementation

We have implemented a prototype based on the ideas described in this paper. We make use of Dalvik eXchange (DX) [1] and JDOM [6] to parse Java class files and build up the XMLVM files. Saxon [7] is used as the XSL engine to apply the stylesheets that are responsible for the code generation for the different backends. The implementation of the Java to C# cross-compilation is fully Java compatible including exception handling, threading, and reflection API. However, our tool does not offer the same kind of completeness for the API mapping, since Android and WP7 API are complex libraries, consisting of thousands of methods. Some UI idioms, such as Android's hardware buttons, cannot be mapped by a tool, but require platform-specific implementations to make the application look and feel native for the respective platform. Nevertheless, the currently supported API already allows for cross-compilation of complex applications, as shown in the following example.

 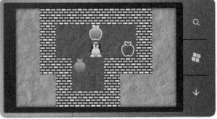

Fig. 3. Xokoban in the Android and WP7 emulator

To demonstrate the capabilities of our tool, we used our prototype to cross-compile Xokoban, an Android application previously used to showcase cross-compilation to iOS, to WP7. Xokoban is a remake of the classic Sokoban puzzle game in which the player has to push objects in a maze. Xokoban makes use of a range of Android APIs and widgets:

- 2D animation.
- Alert views, buttons, checkboxes.
- Accelerometer and swipe interface.
- Saving/loading of preferences.

By using XMLVM, the original Android application was successfully cross-compiled to WP7 as well as iOS devices without any changes. When cross-compiled to WP7, XMLVM generates a turnkey VisualStudio Windows Phone 7 project. The project generated by XMLVM contains all cross-compiled source files and other resources, like images, but no binaries. To compile the application and bundle it as a XAP, using VisualStudio is necessary.

Figure 3 shows the original Android version of Xokoban running in the Android emulator together with the cross-compiled WP7 version running in the WP7 emulator. The original version of Xokoban is available in the Android Market and a cross-compiled version for iOS can be found in the Apple App Store. The cross-compiled version for WP7 has been submitted for review to the Windows Marketplace.

7   Conclusion and Outlook

The popularity of smartphones makes them attractive platforms for mobile applications. However, while smartphones have nearly identical capabilities with respect to their hardware, they differ substantially in their programming environments. Different programming languages and different APIs lead to significant overhead when porting applications to various smartphones. We have chosen Android as the canonical platform. Our byte code level cross-compiler XMLVM can cross-compile an Android application to C# code that can be run on WP7 devices, therefore not requiring the Dalvik virtual machine on the target platform. We have demonstrated that a cross-compilation framework is feasible, thereby significantly reducing the porting effort. However there are capabilities offered by the Android API, e.g. background services or being able to replace existing system applications like the home screen or the dialer, which are not available in any similar form on WP7 or iOS as of now. This functionality cannot be cross-compiled by our prototype implementation.

In the future our goal is to support debugging of cross-compiled applications. The idea is that a Java application that was cross-compiled with XMLVM can be debugged on the device with any standard Java debugger such as the one integrated in Eclipse. In order to accomplish this, an implementation of the JWDP (Java Wire Debug Protocol) needs to be available on the target platform. We plan to use the Open Source Maxine project [12] that features a Java implementation of JWDP. With the help of the Java-to-C# cross-compiler we will cross-compile Maxine to C# to support debugging on a WP7 device. The challenge of this task will be to interface with the generated C# code to determine the memory layout (such as stack and heap) at runtime.

XMLVM is available under an Open Source license at `http://xmlvm.org`.

Acknowledgment. The work described in this paper was supported by a grant from Microsoft Research.

References

1. The Android Open Source Project. Dalvik eXchange (DX),
   `git://android.git.kernel.org/platform/dalvik.git`
2. Davis, B., Beatty, A., Casey, K., Gregg, D., Waldron, J.: The case for virtual register machines. In: IVME 2003: Proceedings of the 2003 Workshop on Interpreters, Virtual Machines and Emulators, pp. 41–49. ACM, New York (2003)
3. ECMA. C# Language Specification, 4th edn. (June 2006)
4. ECMA. Common Language Infrastructure (CLI), 4th edn. (June 2006)
5. El-Ramly, M., Eltayeb, R., Alla, H.A.: An Experiment in Automatic Conversion of Legacy Java Programs to C#. In: ACS/IEEE International Conference on Computer Systems and Applications, pp. 1037–1045 (2006)
6. JDOM. Java DOM-API (2004), `http://www.jdom.org/`
7. Kay, M.: Saxon: The XSLT and XQuery Processor,
   `http://saxon.sourceforge.net/`
8. Lindholm, T., Yellin, F.: The Java Virtual Machine Specification, 2nd edn. Addison-Wesley Pub. Co. (April 1999)
9. Puder, A.: Cross-Compiling Android Applications to the iPhone. In: PPPJ, Vienna, Austria. International Proceedings Series. ACM (2010)
10. Puder, A., Lee, J.: Towards an XML-based Byte Code Level Transformation Framework. In: 4th International Workshop on Bytecode Semantics, Verification, Analysis and Transformation. Elsevier, York, UK (2009)
11. Shi, Y., Casey, K., Anton Ertl, M., Gregg, D.: Virtual machine showdown: Stack versus registers. ACM Trans. Archit. Code Optim. 4(4), 1–36 (2008)
12. Ungar, D., Spitz, A., Ausch, A.: Constructing a metacircular Virtual machine in an exploratory programming environment. In: Companion to the 20th Annual ACM SIGPLAN Conference on Object-Oriented Programming, Systems, Languages, and Applications, OOPSLA, pp. 11–20. ACM, New York (2005)
13. W3C. XSL Transformation (1999), `http://www.w3.org/TR/xslt`

ICT Intervention to Enhance Health Services to Mothers and Children in Remote Communities in Jordan

Edward Jaser[1] and Islam Ahmad[2]

[1] Princess Sumaya University for Technology,
Khalil Al-Saket St. Al-Jubaiha P.O. Box 1438 Amman 11941 Jordan
ejaser@psut.edu.jo
[2] Royal Scientific Society,
70 Ahmad Al-Tarawneh St. Al-Jubaiha P.O. Box 1438 Amman 11941 Jordan
islam@rss.jo

Abstract. In this paper we share the experience we gained from the implementation and deployment of a proof-of-concept ICT intervention aiming at improving the health of women and children in rural and remote communities in Jordan. The intervention has a web and mobile components. The developed system serves as: (1) a tool for medical experts to disseminate awareness information; (2) a source of medical knowledge to residents of rural communities and clinics serving those communities; and (3) a tool for clinics to manage immunization of children in remote and rural areas.

Keywords: Mobile applications, Mobile pervasive applications, Mobile social networking, Health Systems.

1 Introduction

In Jordan, as in most third-world countries, quality health services are offered in capital and big cities. This is mainly because those cities offer more opportunities to medical staff to forward their careers in addition to the ease of life beside many other advantages. This leaves rural areas and remote communities deprived of specialized and experienced medical staff. It is not difficult to imagine that many medical cases will have to travel to the capital city or other big cities to obtain needed treatment; or wait till the next medical day in their region (where a consortia of medical doctors visit rural areas) to happen. This constitutes a major challenge to governments. This is also apparent even in developed countries as shown in a recent study by Lenthal et al. [1] addressing the challenges facing rural Australia as a result of decreasing numbers of nurses and midwives.

Information and Communication Technologies (ICTs) are now widely considered by developing countries as the motor of growth, the driver of efficiency and effectiveness and the tool to enhance human development. With the advancement of ICTs and the Internet, communication and web-based technologies can be exploited

J.Y. Zhang et al. (Eds.): MobiCASE 2011, LNICST 95, pp. 303–310, 2012.

to address the challenge of virtually allowing medical expertise and knowledge to become available to rural areas and remote communities. In recent years, social networking websites (such as MySpace and Facebook) have become very popular tools to connect people and allow human-human interaction regardless of physical location. Such websites easily attract users as they are discrete, connect large number of individuals and eliminate the middlemen. While most popular networking websites are social in nature, professional networking websites can also be used as a tool to tackle issues and problems in society.

Many ICT interventions have been introduced recently to address social challenges including those of rural communities [2, 3]. One very important and priority sector is health. As mentioned earlier, quality health services are specific to large communities only and adequate services or support groups are not widely available for rural areas. Health is among the top sectors that are benefiting from the opportunities that the technology offers as shown in many studies such as [4, 5].

In this paper we report the experience gained from one project concerned with enhanced health services to women and children in remote and rural communities in Jordan. This is realized through the design and implementation of a proof-of-concept medical social networking portal. The portal is complemented by other access means, such as mobile phones to maximize the outreach of information and the utility of the system. Such intervention would provide the tool for medical practitioners to interact with the public regardless of their geographical proximity. The system allows contributions from medical doctors, medical students, nurses, pharmacists and other medical personnel in Jordan to assist stakeholders (whether doctors or patients) with questions related to health. Also, it allows interaction between users (patients) themselves to form common interest support groups. The system's information channels, such as mobile phones allow access to health information to such groups in a cost effective manner.

Health issues are wide-ranging, and for a pilot project it is challenging to find the needed experts and resources to support such wide range of health issues. It was important to narrow the scope of the problem in such a way that enables us to measure the impact of the project on rural communities. We focused the application of the system to women and children health.

This paper is organized as follows. In Section 2 we look at some facts about communities in Jordan's rural and remote areas. In Section 3 we describe the detailed design of the ICT intervention. Deployment is covered in Section 4. Preliminary evaluation of the system is reported in Section 5. We conclude the paper in Section 6.

2   Jordan's Urban and Rural Communities

Jordan is a small country with an area of approximately 92,300 km2 and an estimated population of 5,723,000 people (i.e. that is a density of 62/km2). There are 12 Governorates in Jordan. According to the Statistical Yearbook of Jordan (published in 2007 by Jordan's Department of Statistics - DoS), the population is divided between urban communities (those localities of 5000+ inhabitants) and rural communities.

Almost 17% of the population are classified as rural and 83% as urban. Amman, Irbid and Zarqa are the biggest cities of Jordan and more than 62% lives in these governorates. The remaining governorates are larger in area and have higher percentage of rural communities. Fig 1 shows the status and the location of rural communities in Jordan.

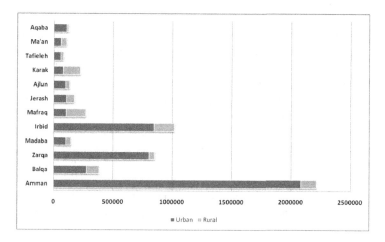

Fig. 1. Estimated Population of Jordan classified as Urban and Rural (end year 2007, Department of Statistics)

Birth rate in Jordan is average compared to the world. According to DoS, Crude child rate (per 1000) is 28; Crude death rate (per 1000) is 7; Total fertility rate for each woman is 3.7; and Population growth rate is 2.3%. Governorates are served with different types of medical centers such as Mother and Child health centers (MCH), village centers and health centers. These centers have very basic infrastructure when located in rural areas.

To understand the usage of ICT in rural communities, we designed a scoping questionnaire and distributed it to randomly selected users. The questionnaire was designed to capture personal information about the user, their background, the usage of internet, the usage of mobile phone, usage of mobile services and main health topics of interest. From analyzing the collected questionnaire (91 in totals) we report the following:

- The most usage of internet in rural Jordan are for checking the various news site, communication through e-mails and searching.
- Significant number of users in rural communities are depending on government initiatives (such as Knowledge Stations: www.ks.gov.jo) for internet access.
- It was noticed that almost 90% of surveyed users own at least one mobile phone. This is quite significant penetration rate.
- The usage of mobile phones is for the purpose of making and receiving calls as well as communication through text messages.
- Using mobile e-Government services (provided through the national SMS gateway) is still not popular among mobile users and many users are not

aware of these services. In this case, maybe the services offered under the gateway are generally more specific to urban communities.

- When asking about what are the main resources when someone would like to obtain certain medical knowledge, majority thinks that medical doctors are the most appropriate resource for medical information. Internet was a quite popular option too.
- Dietary information, diseases, alternative medicine and maternity and child care are the most searched topics for users (as shown in Fig 2).
- As for the reasons to seeking medical knowledge, the first choices were preventive care and obtaining general knowledge about medical issues (which is essential for preventive care as well).
- Who is responsible for medical awareness? The majority believed that Ministry of Health should be responsible for this task. Many also put some responsibilities on TV and Radio to provide medical awareness content to their viewers.
- How could concerned organization support medical awareness? Organizing workshops and inviting medical experts were the most popular choices.

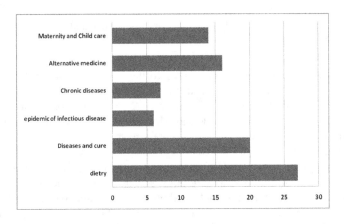

Fig. 2. Medical topics of interest. Maternity and child care is popular search subjects.

3   Designing ICT Intervention

The main aim behind the design of the pilot project was to measure the advantages and impact of ICT interventions in enhancing health care services and support health clinics and hospitals in rural and remote communities. The focus of our evaluation was on women and children health care services. During the life of the project we attempted to answer the following key research questions: (1) Could ICTs contribute to the enhancement of the general health of rural and remote communities? (2) How ICTs can be effectively exploited to improve the general health of rural and remote communities? and (3) What incentives structures could be utilized to stimulate participation in ICT-based health networks (particularly participation of doctors and health practitioners)?

3.1   Stakeholders

One of the early stages in the project was to identify the primary stakeholders who directly interact with the system. We can categorize the stakeholders as follows:

- *Medical content consumers:* individuals who use the system to obtain medical knowledge through the various channels available for the project. They can either be registered users or use the system as anonymous.
- *Medical content producers:* those who populate the database with required medical knowledge whether diagnosis, awareness ... etc. To be able to use the system, they need to be registered
- *Medical experts:* those who filter incoming information to ensure validity and consistency. They need to be registered and be granted privileges to rate any piece of incoming information.
- *Administrators:* those who will manage system users and manage existing accounts.

There are also secondary stakeholders who affect and are affected by the system: Ministry of Health (MoH), NGOs working in rural areas and e-Government portal.

3.2   Requirements

There are three main type of users, who can carry out six different types of interactions with the system: (1) guest users can browse the public information on the project and view the various content provided by the website, as well as ask anonymous questions to the medical experts; (2) registered users, in addition to having access to the same functionality as guests they can participate in the activities where only registered users are allowed to participate such as forum, adding content (for medical experts) and supervising content to check validity and correctness (for content supervisors); (3) administrator who additionally take the responsibility of user and system management activities.

   The system was developed to meet the following main requirements: (i) allowing content consumer to interact with the system and access stored knowledge and provide them with the tool to post medical questions; (ii) the system able to store information about stakeholders who would like to be contacted to receive awareness information and information about organized events; (iii) allowing content producers (medical expert) to log in to the system and maintain medical knowledge and answer questions; (iv) allowing content supervisor to log in to the system and receive notification of new material added to the system and to rate them and filter them accordingly; (v) allowing system administrator to define new users and manage existing ones as well as manage system components; and (vi) allowing clinics serving rural and remote areas to manage vaccination process of children.

3.3   System Design

Fig 3 shows the architectural design of the ICT. For the mobile module, it was designed to realize the following functionality:

- A sub module to manage the posting of medical questions (all users with mobile access). Users were allowed to either send the questions by short message (SMS) or use a dedicated application if they have a java enabled phones.
- A sub module to manage the replies to questions or blocking questions (specific to registered medical experts). This is done through SMS text.
- A sub module linked to a web page which manages the sending of awareness material to mobile users (specific to registered medical experts).
- A sub module to manage vaccination of children automatically.

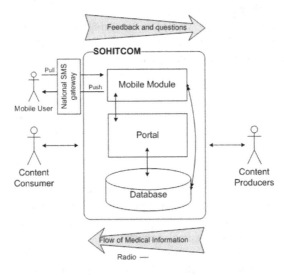

Fig. 3. Architectural Design of the System showing both the portal and the mobile modules

For the portal, it was designed to allow users to post medical questions (all users whether registered or not), post replies to questions or blocking questions (medical experts), forum discussion (all registered users), post medical content (medical experts), filter medical content (content supervisors) and user and system management (administrator).

3.4   Implementation

There have been many work reported in the literature concerned with the development of ICT4D interventions. A good example is [6] focusing on mobile applications. Our intervention was developed using the following technologies: Java Server Pages (JSP) and Java Servlet for the Dynamic Interaction with the users in the user interface; J2ME to develop mobile application; Hyper Text Mark-up Language (HTML) for the Content of the static pages in the system; JavaScript for the validation of the data entered by the users; AJAX for the smooth interaction in items (Data Swap without DB Rendering); The Tag-libs technology for the Modularity and Template adaptation in Inner and Main Pages; MySQL for database functionality; and XML for the optimized and structured data transfer.

4   Deployment

The web portal was available for users to browse content and interact with the Q&A facility. The mobile module was made available to download and install. Also the SMS engine was made available in cooperation with the national SMS gateway. We selected five clinics serving rural communities. The selection was based on needs analysis done jointly with the Ministry of Health. We provided those clinics with the minimum hardware needed for the operation: a basic netbook, a Java enabled mobile phone and internet connection. Adequate training was given to the health workers in those clinics to start using the system.

5   Evaluation

We made the necessary awareness about the availability of our intervention to concerned stakeholders and we started to collect the needed information to answer our research questions. Valuable information were collected (either by interviews or questionnaires) from various stakeholders with this regards. We discuss the analysis in terms of system functionality.

For using the system as *awareness tools*, we noticed that all stakeholders expressed their satisfaction an appreciation of it. Clinics and Medical staff were able to connect with large number of users and disseminate important advices and information effectively and efficiently (in terms of time and cost). They reported more feedback to their announcements than previous methods, including printed materials with no guarantee that it will reach the intended audience.

For the *Q&A facility*, there have been some major issues. One important issue is responsibility from issuing an online advice or answer to a question. Health worker were reluctant to participate in this module worried that they might be officially blamed for misdiagnosis or misinformation. The majority of participating medical experts believed that more work need to be done both in terms of legal infrastructure and technological infrastructure to aid online diagnosis. Another issue was financial compensation for their time spent in the system.

Perhaps the most successful module was the vaccination management system. This is specific to clinics and it allows them to register newborn babies. The system then automatically calculates the vaccination program based on MoH guidelines. The system issues automatic reminders to parents regarding the date for a specific vaccine. Also the system issues statistical information to clinics about number of needed vaccines per day to allow them to prepare those vaccines and make them available. Both users and medical experts expressed their extreme satisfaction with this module since it help tackling and important issue which is children missing vaccination (quite high in rural areas).

Overall, and in spite of the advancement in mobile applications developments and innovations, there are certain challenges: (i) Concrete evidence: we are in need of a robust analysis and evaluation tools and standards of mobile intervention in health to help designing better and effective services; (ii) Legislations: this is quite important to establish a clear policies and laws to govern ICT interventions and their deployment; (iii) Sustainability of ICT interventions, sustainability is important issue for ICT4D projects. There should be clear understanding of how to fund these projects and to continue to provide resources and (iv) Capacity building: there should be focus on building the competency of various stakeholders in terms of ICT usage. Also mobilize resources to bridge the technological gap between urban and rural communities.

6   Conclusion

In this paper we described a proof-of-concept ICT intervention to enhance health services provided to rural communities in Jordan. Evaluation from the system shows that ICT plays an important role in enhancing services and outreach for a large section of users in a cost and time efficient manner. Evaluation showed that using ICT to manage awareness and manage vaccination is useful and can help overcoming several challenges. More investigation is needed to deal with smooth and effective online communication between patient and health workers. Future work will focus on widening the evaluation to include more clinics and region in rural Jordan to reach a working system that can be adopted nationally. Also an important future work is to investigate the security of such system given the sensitive information it deals with.

Acknowledgments. The authors thank the International Development Research Center (IDRC) for funding our work through their ICT4D-ME program and the Royal Scientific Society and its staff for the implementation of the project.

References

1. Lenthall, S., Wakerman, J., Opie, T., Dunn, S., MacLeod, M., Dollard, M., Rickard, G., Knight, S.: Nursing workforce in very remote Australia, characteristics and key issues. Australian Journal of Rural Health 19, 32–37 (2011)
2. Cespedes, L.M., Martin, F.J.: Mobile Telephony in Rural Areas: The Latin American perspective. The i4d Print Magazine VII(9) (January-March 2011)
3. Liu, J.: Mobile Social Network in a Cultural Context. In: Canessa, E., Zennaro, M. (eds.) M-Science: Sensing, Computing and Dissemination, ISBN: 92-95003-43-8
4. Ping, Y., Wu, M.X., Yu, H., Xiao, G.Q.: The Challenges for the Adoption of M-Health. In: IEEE International Conference on Service Operations and Logistics, and Informatics, June 21-23, pp. 181–186 (2006)
5. Maeda, T., Okamoto, T., Fukushige, Y., Asada, T.: Mobile Application Framework for Health Care Education. In: 7th IEEE Consumer Communications and Networking Conference, January 9-12, pp. 1–2 (2010)
6. Amanquah, N., Eporwei, O.T.: Rapid application development for mobile terminals. In: International Conference on Adaptive Science & Technology, January 14-16, pp. 410–417 (2009)

Probabilistic Infrastructureless Positioning in the Pocket

Le T. Nguyen and Ying Zhang

Carnegie Mellon University,
NASA Research Park Building 23,
Moffett Field, CA 95035, USA
{le.nguyen,joy.zhang}@sv.cmu.edu

Abstract. With the increasing popularity of smart phones, knowing the accurate position of users has become critical to many context-aware applications. In this paper, we introduce a novel Probabilistic Infrastructureless Navigation (ProbIN) system for GPS-challenging environments. ProbIN uses inertial and magnetic sensors in mobile phones to derive users' current location. Instead of relying on basic laws of physics (e.g. double integral of acceleration equals to displacement) ProbIN uses a statistical model for estimating the position of users. This statistical model is built based on the user's data by applying machine learning techniques from the statistical machine translation field. Thus, ProbIN can capture the user's specific walking patterns and is, therefore, more robust against noisy sensor readings. In the evaluation of our approach we focused on the most common daily scenarios. We conducted experiments with a user walking and carrying the phone in different settings such as in the hand or in the pocket. The results of the experiments show that even though the mobile phone was not mounted to the user's body, ProbIN outperforms the state-of-the-art dead reckoning approaches.

Keywords: Inertial positioning, low-cost inertial sensors, Dead Reckoning, Bayes' theorem, Expectation Maximization.

1 Introduction

With the increasing popularity of smart phones, knowing the accurate position of a user has become critical to many context-aware applications. In outdoor environments, standardized Global Positioning System (GPS) is often used. However, for indoor environments such as airports, hospitals or shopping malls GPS signals are usually unavailable or unreliable.

Most of the existing indoor positioning solutions try to address this problem by utilizing existing infrastructures such as Wi-Fi access points or Bluetooth beacons [12]. In cases when an infrastructure is not available, self-contained systems provide a more flexible solution. These systems use sensors such as accelerometers, gyroscopes and magnetometers. In order to derive a user's current location, the movement of the user is tracked by the continuous logging of sensor readings.

J.Y. Zhang et al. (Eds.): MobiCASE 2011, LNICST 95, pp. 311–330, 2012.
© Institute for Computer Sciences, Social Informatics and Telecommunications Engineering 2012

Since this technique does not reply on an external infrastructure, theoretically it can be used in any environment. The main drawback of self-contained positioning approaches is error accumulation. Since the sensors utilized are noisy by nature, the error of position estimation grows with time and distance traveled. Moreover, the noise portion in sensor measurements is significantly higher when the phone is held in the hand versus mounting it on certain parts of the body. Positioning in the hand accelerates the accumulation of error and causes a substantial decrease of estimation accuracy.

The purpose of our work is to deliver a system providing positioning and navigation functionality for consumer mobile devices in GPS-challenging environments. The main contribution of this paper is to introduce a novel probabilistic approach of self-contained positioning providing a user's current location. In order to overcome the problem with noisy sensor readings of consumer mobile devices, a statistical model well-known in the field of the statistical machine translation (SMT) is utilized for the positioning purposes.

In our work, the positioning problem is framed as a noisy-channel problem, where we try to recover the actual user's position from the distorted sensor inputs. To recover the user's position, we use a statistical model to *map* the sensor readings directly to the displacement. This is fundamentally different from state-of-the-art dead reckoning approaches. In these approaches the sensor readings are interpreted by their actual physical meanings, i.e., the accelerometer readings are considered as being the actual acceleration of the device. Thus, theoretically based on the laws of physics the travelled displacement can be obtained by double integrating the acceleration.

In ProbIN the sensor readings are interpreted as observed "signals" which are directly mapped to the corresponding displacement based on a statistical model. The statistical model is trained by using SMT techniques adjusted for positioning purposes. During the training phase, ProbIN builds statistical models from the user's data. These models capture the user's walking patterns and adapts to the sensor errors of the mobile device. Thus, although the sensors on the mobile devices are noisy, ProbIN can still estimate a user's current position at a much higher accuracy rate than state-of-the-art dead reckoning approaches.

This paper extends our previous work [13] where there were several limitations in the way how the phone can be positioned. Since the smart phone used for the evaluation was not equipped with a gyroscope the pitch and roll angles of the device were unknown. Therefore, in the previous experiments the phone was positioned on a moving cart. While lying on the cart the pitch and roll angles remain constant. Thus, we were able to evaluate the ProbIN approach by using a phone without a gyroscope.

In this paper, we are focusing on more realistic scenarios. By utilizing iPhone 4 equipped with a gyroscope and by introducing the integration of the gyroscope readings into ProbIN we were able to achieve promising results even when the phone was not mounted on users' body. In order to evaluate the new approach we conducted experiments with a user walking and carrying the phone in different settings such as in the hand or in the pocket.

2   Related Works

Self-contained systems are also called infrastructureless systems, since they can locate a mobile user without any external infrastructure. These systems can provide finer-granular position estimation than infrastructure based systems. Thus, they can be deployed in combination with infrastructure-based systems in order to achieve higher estimation accuracy.

Infrastructureless positioning is typically based on the dead reckoning principle that describes an iterative process of position estimation. According to this principle, a user's current position is determined based on the previous estimated position and the current sensor reading. The main drawback of the dead reckoning is the error accumulation. Since sensor readings are noisy by nature, they are the main source of the error in each positioning step. Due to the dead reckoning principle error generated in one step is carry out to the next step. Thus, the accumulated error increases with time and traveled distance.

Many research projects try to minimize the estimation error by employing high-quality sensors. For example, a ring laser gyroscope [6] or high-quality IMU [14] can be utilized in order to reduce the error in the measurement of rotation rate. However, these hardware components are usually very large and expensive. Therefore, they are not appropriate for daily use.

The noise can be also partially extracted by using a Kalman filter [18] which estimates true values of the observed sensor measurements based on the parameter settings.

In many research projects [6, 2] step-based techniques are applied in order to estimate user's position. The idea is based on counting the number of steps and estimating the length of each step from the accelerometer reading. The heading information is provided by fusion of magnetometer and gyroscope readings. The best approaches were able to achieve an accumulated error of about 2% of the total distance travelled [2]. However, the conducted experiment reveals many drawbacks of these techniques. As mentioned above the heading is derived from the magnetometer and gyroscope readings. However, this heading does not always correspond to the direction of the user's movement. Let us assume that the sensors are mounted on a helmet [2]. If the user walks straight forward and will look straightforward then the estimated trajectory will be correct. However, when the user starts looking around during the walk, the estimations will be incorrect, since the heading determines the estimated trajectory direction. Therefore, in order to achieve the good results the user has to look always into the direction of the walk. Also, it is very difficult to detect side steps, walking backwards or walking up/down the stairs.

Since the step-based techniques are not very practical due to the above mentioned drawbacks an alternative solution using the basic physics seems to be more promising [3, 14, 8]. Instead of utilizing the acceleration magnitude the actual values of the acceleration in all three x-, y- and z-axis can be used. In theory the integral of acceleration over time equals to velocity. When we calculate the integral of the velocity we obtain the displacement. By summing up the calculated displacements during the walk we can estimate a user's current position.

Due to the noisy sensor readings and the integration process, each estimation of the velocity and displacement will contain some error. Since the current velocity and position is always calculated based on the previous values, the accumulated error will grow significantly over time.

By mounting the sensors on a foot, the above-mentioned issue can be partially addressed. The idea is based on the analysis of the human locomotion. During one gait cycle, each foot will go through the two basic phases: swinging in the air and stance on the ground. In the stance phase, the foot velocity is zero. Also in this phase the most accurate orientation can be calculated from the sensor readings. Therefore, by identifying the stance phase based on the sensor readings the Zero Velocity Update (ZUPT) and Zero-Attitude Rate Updates (ZARUs) can be applied [1].

Several research projects [14] reported achieving an error rate lower than 1% by utilizing the physics-based techniques. However, these results seem to be rather an exception. The average reported error rate was around 3% to 5% of the travelled distance [14, 8].

Physics-based techniques benefits from the application of ZUPT and ZARU, which can significantly prevent the accumulation of the estimation error. These techniques also do not suffer from the drawbacks of the step-based techniques, since the direction of the movement is extracted not only from magnetometer and gyroscope but also from the accelerometer, side steps, walking backwards and walking up/down the stairs can all be detected. On the other hand, all sensors need to be mounted on the foot, which in many situations is not possible or practical. When we want to utilize the sensors in mobile device, we cannot assume that the users will mount their phone on the foot every time they use the indoor navigation system.

Besides mounting sensors on the foot, sensors can also be mounted to other parts of the body such as head, waist or shank. However, by selecting these mounting options the ZUPT and ZARU cannot be applied. Therefore, for these mounting settings only the step-based techniques can be utilized.

The more loosely mounting options was investigated in [15]. The sensors were carried in a backpack or mounted on a PDA that was hold in the hand. The experiments showed that the results of the loosely mounting options are significantly worse than the ones acquired by mounting the sensors on the person's body.

3   Probabilistic Infrastructureless Navigation

Probabilistic Infrastructureless Navigation (ProbIN) is a system providing the positioning and navigation functionality for GPS-challenging environment. In this paper, we will focus on the positioning part of ProbIN, which allows tracking of a person.

ProbIN is intended for daily applications such as assisting a user in shopping malls or at airports. Therefore, it needs to fulfill three essential requirements:

1. *Scalability*: ProbIN delivers positioning functionality even without an existing external infrastructure.
2. *Affordability*: ProbIN can be run on consumer mobile devices with relatively low-quality sensors.
3. *Usability*: The user should be able to hold the devices in the hand or in a pocket without degrading delivered functionality.

In order to fulfill the first requirement ProbIN essentially utilizes the inertial sensors. As such, a self-contained positioning system can be delivered, which does not rely on any external infrastructure. ProbIN can be also improved by utilizing a magnetometer and/or digital maps in order to achieve higher positioning accuracy. The advantage for this case is that the system will remain self-contained. A viable extension would be the integration of modules utilizing external infrastructures such as GPS or a Wi-Fi network. These modules would be activated only when an infrastructure is available. The scope of this paper is to develop a system providing the positioning based on inertial sensors and extended by the magnetometer readings.

Due to the second and the third requirements, a novel approach of positioning needs to developed in order to address high error rates of the sensors. It is known that when utilizing low-cost sensors the measurements are typically very inaccurate, especially when the sensors are not mounted to the user's body. In this case, the traditional physics-based positioning performs badly, since an error in the sensor reading causes an error in the estimated displacement. ProbIN addresses this issue by learning a mapping between the sensor readings and the actual true displacements based on training data. Thus, when ProbIN is deployed, even a noisy sensor reading can be mapped to the correct displacement. The problem of minimizing the error rate is thereby transformed into a machine learning problem. In this paper, we will present a solution to this problem by utilizing machine learning techniques well-known to the field of the statistical machine translation (SMT) [4].

As mentioned above, ProbIN utilizes a machine learning technique that is divided into training and testing phases. First, the sensor readings with corresponding true displacements are collected in the training phase. The relationship between the measurements and the displacements are used for creating a statistical model. Then in the testing phase, the statistical model is employed for mapping the sensor readings of the tracked person into a trajectory. The result of the testing phase is typically used for evaluating the approach.

In the following, we will present our approach in a reverse order. First, we will introduce how a user's trajectory is estimated based on the statistical model in order to give an intuition behind ProbIN. Then we will describe the process of training the statistical model in more detail.

4   Statistical Dead Reckoning of Mapping Sensor Readings to Displacements

ProbIN's positioning is a statistical dead reckoning approach allowing erroneous sensor readings to be mapped to correct displacements. This is achieved by framing the problem as a noisy-channel problem [16] where we try to recover the actual position of a user from the distorted sensor inputs. Noisy-channel models have been widely used in fields such as Statistical Machine Translation (SMT), Automatic Speech Recognition or Optical Character Recognition.

The noisy-channel describes the communication process in which a transmitter sends a message through a noisy channel and the receiver receives a corrupted or ambiguous message. The aim is to find the original message produced by the transmitter by analyzing the message observed at the receiver.

In SMT the transmitter produces a sentence in a familiar language, let us say English. On the other end of the channel the receiver observes a sentence in a foreign language, let us say German. The aim is to find an English translation of the German sentence. This issue is addressed by applying Bayes' theorem, which utilizes both the likelihood of translating from a foreign language word to a familiar language word (*translation model*) and also a priori knowledge about the "properness" of sentences in the familiar language (*language model*). The translation model and the language model form together the *statistical model* used for finding the translation of the sentence observed by the receiver.

Similarly to SMT, ProbIN uses also a statistical model for finding the most likely trajectory for the given sequence of sensor readings. The observed sensor readings correspond to the German sentence in the above example. The aim is to find the hidden displacements of the trajectory, which correspond to the English sentence.

4.1   Quantizing Sensor Readings and Displacements

Unlike SMT where the vocabulary of a language is limited, the number of possible sensor measurements and displacements are unlimited. It is possible but too complicated to train a reliable continuous statistical model to map raw sensor readings into a displacement in the real value space. Therefore, in ProbIN we first quantize the sensor readings using the K-means clustering [11] which converts the real-valued sensor data to discrete values. Each cluster is then labeled with a *motion label m*, which will represent all sensor readings belonging to this cluster. Thus, the vocabulary size of ProbIN is limited to the number of motion labels. In that case, the statistical model can be efficiently trained for the discrete finite vocabulary space.

Figure 1 shows an example of employing the K-means clustering to quantize sensor readings into motion labels. In ProbIN each sensor reading corresponds to an acceleration and an orientation, which is derived from the gyroscope and magnetometer reading. After the clustering is processed, each sensor reading is represented by a motion label m. Thus, the sequence of t sensor readings collected during a user's movement is represented by a sequence of motion labels $M = m_1, m_2, \ldots, m_t$ where m_i denotes a motion label of the sensor reading at timestamp i.

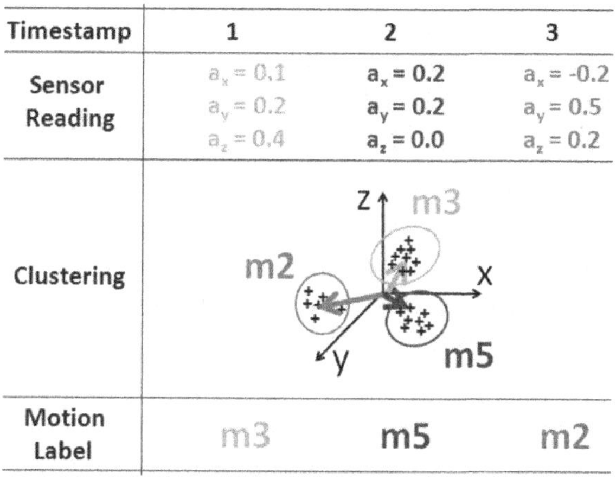

Timestamp	1	2	3
Sensor Reading	$a_x = 0.1$ $a_y = 0.2$ $a_z = 0.4$	$a_x = 0.2$ $a_y = 0.2$ $a_z = 0.0$	$a_x = -0.2$ $a_y = 0.5$ $a_z = 0.2$
Clustering			
Motion Label	m3	m5	m2

Fig. 1. Example of using k-means clustering in order to define the motion labels

The continuous space of displacements is also quantized in ProbIN. The *displacement label d* is assigned to each displacement cluster. Thus, a sequence of traveled displacements is represented by a sequence of displacement labels $D = d_1, d_2, \ldots, d_t$.

After limiting the size of vocabulary by quantizing the sensor reading space and displacement space, the statistical model can be similarly applied as in SMT. For a sequence of motion labels M, ProbIN searches for the optimal sequence of displacement labels D^* such that:

$$D^* = \arg\max_{D} P(D|M) \tag{1}$$
$$= \arg\max_{D} P(M|D) \cdot P(D)$$

To express the above idea in terms of the noisy-channel model, the receiver observes a sequence of motion labels, which might be ambiguous or noisy. The aim is to find the translation in form of a sequence of displacement labels, which was originally produced by the transmitter.

Mathematically, $\arg\max P(D|M)$ returns a sequence of displacement labels D^* that maximizes the probability $P(D|M)$. The term $P(M|D)$ is provided by the translation model and $P(D)$ is provided by the trajectory model, which corresponds to the language model in SMT. The noise channel model can be confusing here as conceptually we are trying to "translate" from motion labels (sensor readings) to displacement labels to estimate a user's position. Yet by applying the Bayes rule (to incorporate the *a priori* knowledge of the trajectory model, the translation model uses conditional probability of "translating" from displacement to motion labels.

The statistical model of ProbIN consists of two parts: the translation model and the trajectory model.

4.2   Translation Model

The *translation model* estimates the likelihood of mapping a sequence of motion label M to a sequence of displacement label D. Assuming the translation of a displacement label to its corresponding motion label is independent of other pairs, we can write:

$$P(M|D) = \prod_{i=1}^{t} P(m_i|d_i) \tag{2}$$

$P(m_i|d_i)$ is the likelihood of "translating" a displacement d_i back to the motion label m_i. This value is extracted from the training data during the training phase.

4.3   Trajectory Model

The *trajectory model* in ProbIN works similarly to the language model used in SMT. A language model estimates how likely a sequence of words is a meaningful English sentence. For example, the sentence "Tomorrow I will go shopping" should have higher language model probability than sentence "Morning I will go shopping", since the former is more likely to be a correct English sentence.

The intuition of utilizing the trajectory model in ProbIN is also based on the idea that not all trajectories are meaningful. It is obvious that some trajectories are physically impossible to achieve. For example, a trajectory with a length of 10 meters after 1 second collected from a person walking with constant speed is somehow suspicious. Moreover, when a user is walking forward, his trajectory is most likely to be a sequence of forward moving displacements rather than a sequence of forward-backward-forward-backward. The information about "meaningfulness" of the trajectories can be extracted from the training data in advance. The probability of a trajectory D is calculated as:

$$P(D) = \prod_{i=1}^{t} P(d_i|d_1^{i-1}) \tag{3}$$
$$= P(d_1) \cdot P(d_2|d_1) \cdot \ldots \cdot P(d_i|d_1, \ldots, d_{i-1})$$
$$\cdot \ldots \cdot P(d_t|d_1, d_2, \ldots, d_{t-1})$$

Under the Markov assumption that a displacement label d_i only depends on the immediate $n-1$ displacement labels in history, $P(d_i|d_1, \ldots, d_{i-1})$ can be estimated as $P(d_i|d_{i-n+1}, \ldots, d_{i-1})$. This is equivalent to the n-gram language model approached use in SMT.

4.4   Decoder

Given the input sensor readings, which are now quantized as motion labels, a so-called *decoder* applies the translation and trajectory models to search for an optimal displacement label sequence. In our work the sensor reading sequence is called *source sentence* M. First, the translation model generates different translation options D for the whole source sentence M. These translation options are called *hypotheses* as in SMT. Second, for each hypothesis the values of $P(M|D)$ and $P(D)$ are calculated based on the information from translation and trajectory models. The hypothesis with the highest probability $P(M|D) \cdot P(D)$ is selected as the optimal translation for M.

Decoding Process Figure 2 illustrates an example of the decoding process. At each timestamp, one new sensor reading is collected. The decoder generates different hypotheses for the sensor readings observed up to this point. A hypothesis is represented as a path from the root the leave of the updated *decoder tree*. To avoid the explosion of hypothesis due to combinations of different translations, we prune out hypotheses with lower probabilities. Pruning is likely to terminate some hypotheses prematurely as it is based on the incomplete information during decoding. Practice in SMT has shown that pruning is necessary and the degradation on performance is acceptable. By the end of the decoding, the optimal hypothesis with the highest probability is output as the user's estimated trajectory (shown as the red path in the Figure 2).

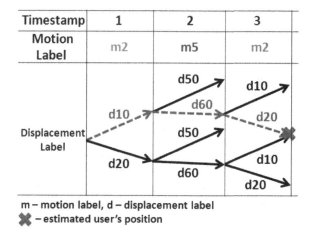

Fig. 2. Example of generated hypotheses. The red path corresponds to the hypothesis being the most probable translation for the given source sentence.

Process Optimizations As it can be observed from the above example, the complete hypothesis space is exponential to input length N and the number of translation alternatives. If each motion label can be mapped to r different displacement labels, the total number of possible trajectories is r^N for an input sequence of N sensor readings. Let us assume that each word in the sentence "Morgen gehe ich einkaufen" would have three possible translations. Thus, there are 81 $(= 3^4)$ possible hypotheses such as "Tomorrow I will go shopping", "Morning I will go shopping", "Tomorrow I go buy", "Morning I go buy", etc. In a real natural language, each word can have 10 translations (including different variations). A typical sentence size is around 10 to 15 words. In that case, the number of hypotheses can grow to 10^{15}. Therefore, it is computationally infeasible to search the complete hypothesis space for the global optimal trajectory, especially in case of high N.

On the other hand, a greedy search of keeping only one best hypothesis at time t is likely to end up in a local optimum. In order to approximate the globally optimal translation, we use a multi-stack based decoding technique [10]. The multiple stack data structure stores multiple partial hypotheses that have the highest probabilities up to time t. Thus, not the whole hypotheses space needs to be explored. On the other hand, the number of analyzed hypothesis is sufficient high for finding a translation close to the globally optimum.

The above-described optimization causes that the hypotheses stored in the stack tend to be similar to each other. Therefore, the decoder applies additionally the *hypotheses recombination* technique to merge hypotheses that have the same trajectory model endings and thus cannot be distinguished by future hypothesis expansion. For those partial hypotheses that have the same trajectory model endings, only the one with highest probability will survive [17].

5   Training the Statistical Model

In the previous section we described how the statistical model of ProbIN could be used for estimating a user's current position. This model is created in advance based on the training data set. We assume that the model can be trained based on the user's past trajectory data, in order to deliver the high accurate position estimation. Thus, each user would train his or her own model, which captures the motion patterns of the specific person. However, the initial model can be also created from the trajectory data of different persons in order to capture characteristics common for all users. Once the initial model is created, a user would be able to use the system for the positioning purposes. While the system is used, the data from a specific user can be collected in order to adapt the model to the particular person. In the following we will present the approach of creating the model based on an available training data set.

5.1   Training the Translation and Trajectory Model

In order to extract the translation model probability $P(M|D)$ we need a training data set where correspondences between motion labels and their displacement label are known. To estimate the trajectory model probability $P(D)$, we need a training data with known trajectories of a user in the form of sequences of displacement labels.

Table 1 shows an example of the training data. The training data set should contain sequences of (motion label, displacement label)-pairs. These pairs provide information about the correspondences between motion labels and their reference displacement label. To train the trajectory model, we use just the displacement part from the training data, for example, sequence (d54, d67, d45, d12, ...).

Table 1. Example of sequences of training data,which consist of (motion label, displacement label)-pairs

#	Sequence of training data
1	(m3, d54), (m2, d67) (m4, d45), (m7, d12) ...
2	(m15, d13), (m6, d45) (m10, d43), (m30, d11) ...
	$\vdots$

Based on the frequency of (motion label, displacement label)-pairs, the translation probability can be estimated through the Maximum Likelihood Estimation (MLE) [5]:

$$P_{MLE}(m|d) = \frac{count(m,d)}{count(d)}. \tag{4}$$

where count(x) returns a number of occurrences of the given x.

The maximum likelihood estimation of the n-gram trajectory model is based on the displacement label only:

$$P_{MLE}(d_i|d_{i-n+1}, d_{i-n+2}, \ldots, d_{i-1}) = \frac{count(d_{i-n+1}, d_{i-n+2}, \ldots, d_{i-1}, d_i)}{count(d_{i-n+1}, d_{i-n+2}, \ldots, d_{i-1})}$$

5.2 Expectation Maximization Algorithm

Motivation In practice, obtaining data in the format illustrated in Table 1 is infeasible. Getting the accurate displacement for each motion label would require for example high speed motion capturing devices. These devices would capture very fine-granular movements and transform them into reference displacements. Since the sampling rate of inertial sensors in mobile phones is 50-100 Hz, the motion capture device needs to record the motions at similar high sampling rate.

Since our work is intended for daily applications, we can not assume users have access to such devices to collect data for training. However, it is reasonable to assume that we can obtain less detailed reference displacement information either from GPS (Table 2) during outdoor training sessions or from user's input overlaid on floor plans. ProbIN uses this coarse-grained data to "estimate" the reference displacement for each sensor reading.

In Table 2 the data is collected during several walks. Besides the sequence of motion labels, each walk also contains information of the GPS coordinates of the starting and the ending positions for the whole walk. However, the reference displacements for each motion label cannot be collected (Figure 3). In ProbIN we apply the Expectation Maximization (EM) to estimate this reference displacement information.

Table 2. Information available for training the models

Walks	Sequence of motion labels	Start	End
Walk 1	m3, m2, m4, m7, ...	(0,0)	(4,10)
Walk 2	m15, m6, m10, m30, ...	(4,10)	(7,15)
⋮			

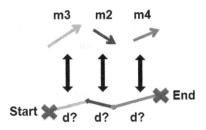

Fig. 3. Missing displacement information

EM Algorithm Expectation Maximization (EM) algorithm [7] is an iterative method for finding hidden parameters of a statistical model. In ProbIN the displacement label is considered as the hidden information. Therefore, the EM algorithm is applied in order to iteratively estimate the hidden displacements for sequences of motion labels. Each EM iteration consists of two steps: Estimation and Maximization. The goal of the *estimation* step is to estimate the hidden displacement using the current statistical model. Based on the estimation the *maximization* step updates the statistical model. In the first iteration the statistical model has not been created yet. Therefore, for the estimation we use the traditional inertial positioning technique based on the laws of physics to bootstrap the model (Figure 4).

The training input contains K instances of "walks":$W_1, W_2, \ldots, W_K$ shown in the Table 2. Each walk W_k has a sequence of motion label M_k, the reference starting position s_k and the reference ending position e_k. In the estimation step of each iteration, we use the current model to find the estimated hidden trajectory D_k for each walk W_k.

In the first iteration the trajectory is estimated by using a traditional physics-based positioning technique. First, the orientation of the phone is calculated by fusing the inertial measurements with magnetic sensor readings through a Kalman filter. This orientation is then used for rotating the raw acceleration readings from the device frame into the global frame. By applying double integral on acceleration readings in the global frame we obtain a user's estimated trajectory.

Since the phone is not mounted on a foot, the Zero Velocity Update (ZUPT) cannot be applied. This is the main concern for the traditional physics-based positioning approaches. Without being able to reset the velocity after each step

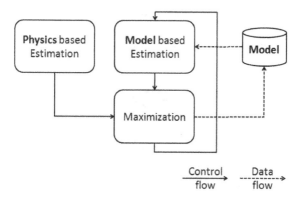

Fig. 4. The EM Algorithm starts with trajectory estimation based on the basic physics and in each iteration updates the statistical model

the error accumulates rapidly over the time. In ProbIN we address this issue by using only the walks with short distances and short time durations in the training process. Thus, the error rate of the trajectory estimates for these walks are minimal.

In the next EM iterations, the physics-based positioning is replaced by the statistical model created at the first iteration. Thus, the statistical model is used to decode the motion label sequence M_k to get the estimated trajectory D_k^*.

Most likely D_k^* is incorrect and does not end at e_k. We assume that the correct trajectory has the similar "shape" as D_k^*. Thus, we can stretch and rotate D_k^* such that it ends at e_k as shown in Figure 5. The resulting trajectory D_k' is the newly estimated trajectory for M_k in this iteration. In other words when D_k does not end up at e_k, we know this trajectory is incorrect. Since we do not know which segments caused the error, we distribute the error to each of the t segments in D_k through the stretch and rotation operations.

The stretching factor is calculated as:

$$f_{stretch} = \frac{distance(s_k, e_k)}{distance(s_k, e_k^*)} \tag{5}$$

where s_k is the starting position of walk W_k and e_k is the ending position. e_k^* is the ending position based on the estimated trajectory D_k^*. $distance(x, y)$ returns a Euclidean distance between two points.

The rotation angle is calculated as:

$$f_{rotate} = cos^{-1}\left(\frac{e_k^* \circ e_k}{\|e_k^*\| \|e_k\|}\right) \tag{6}$$

where $\circ$ represents scalar product and $\|x\|$ represents Euclidean norm.

In order to correct the estimated trajectory we correct each d_t by stretching it with the $f_{stretch}$ and rotating it by angle f_{rotate}. The trajectory calculated from the corrected d_t^{cor} should end in the position e_k.

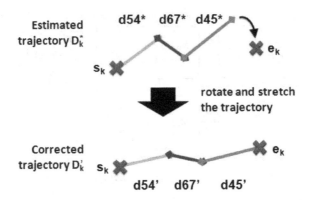

Fig. 5. Correcting the estimated trajectory

In the maximization step the translation and trajectory models are updated based on the corrected estimation of the underlining trajectories D'_k. Thus, the probability of the entire training data can be maximized. The pseudo code of the EM algorithm is described in Algorithm 1.

6   Experiments

Our approach is evaluated on the iPhone 4, the first phone on the market equipped with an additional gyroscope besides an accelerometer and a magnetometer. The gyroscope provides information about the rotation rate of the phone. This information allows our system to accurately calculate the phone's orientation even when the phone is in motion. This is necessary for the process of position estimation in ProbIN and also in any state-of-the-art physics-based positioning system.

In order to evaluate ProbIN approach we conducted experiments on a square-shaped basketball court. For training the statistical model we used sensor readings of straight walks with a length of 4 meters as shown in Figure 6(a). For testing the statistical model we use two types of trajectories. The first type has an L-shape (shown in Figure 6(b)) and the second type has a square-shape (shown in Figure 6(c)). Since each side of the basketball court was 15 meters long, the walks used for testing were 30 meters resp. 60 meters long.

We conducted experiments to evaluate whether the accuracy of the estimations are dependent on the way the user holds the phone. We collect sensor data while the phone is in one of three different settings. First, the user holds the phone in the hand in front of him as if he would be looking to the display. Second, the user is holding the phone loosely in the hand, but he is not looking at the display during the walk. Finally, the phone is carried in the pocket.

Data: Training data: a set of K *walks*: $W_1, W_2, \ldots, W_K$. $W_k = (M_k, s_k, e_k)$
iteration $\leftarrow 0$;
while *not converge* **do**
    for $k \leftarrow 1$ **to** K **do**
        (Estimation step for walk W_k) ;
        if *iteration==0* **then**
           | Use basic physics (double integral of acceleration) to estimate D_k^*
        end
        else
           | Find D_k^* for M_k given the current statistical models
        end
        if D_k^* *does not end at* e_k **then**
           | *stretch* and *rotate* D_k^* to create D_k' such that D_k' ends in e_k
        end
        else
           | $D_k' \leftarrow D_k^*$
        end
        foreach (m, d) *pairs in* (M_k, D_k') **do** increase the count of (m, d) ;
        foreach n-*gram in* D_k' **do** increase the count of the trajectory n-gram ;
    end
    (Maximization step);
    Update the translation model from counts of (m, d);
    Update the trajectory model from counts of trajectory n-grams;
    iteration++;
end

Algorithm 1: EM algorithm used to training the statistical model.

For evaluating our approach we used the relative error rate as the evaluation metric. The relative error of an estimation is calculated for 2 dimensional trajectory, i.e., the altitude is omitted in our experiment:

$$error_{rel} = \frac{error_{abs}}{trajectory_{ref}} \qquad (7)$$

The absolute error $error_{abs}$ corresponds to the distance between the user's position estimated by a positioning system e^* and the user's true position e:

$$error_{abs} = distance(e^*, e) \qquad (8)$$

The $trajectory_{ref}$ is length of the reference trajectory. Thus, the relative error grows with the increasing absolute error. However, the relative error is additionally normalized by the length of the reference trajectory in order to be able to compare the results of different experiments with different length of walks.

In the first experiment we focus on the cases when the user holds the phone in the hand in front of him or her as if she would be looking to the display. The results (shown in Table 3) are grouped based on the type of the test data: L-shape and Square-shape. We also evaluate the estimation accuracy for different speed of the walks: slow, normal and fast. In our experiments we use the traditional

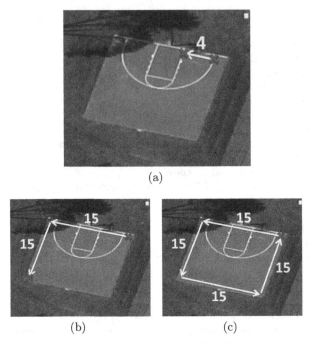

(a)

(b)   (c)

Fig. 6. Basketball court used for the experiments. The figures show the walks used for training the model (a) and evaluating ProbIN approach (b), (c)

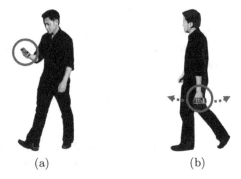

(a)   (b)

Fig. 7. The phone can be carried in the hand or in a pocket. While carrying the phone in the hand the user can be occasionally looking at the display.

physics-based positioning system (described in Section 5.2) as a baseline. The error rate of this system is displayed in the column *Physics*. The following columns contain results of the estimations using ProbIN's statistical model generated in the EM iterations 1, 2 and 3.

For training ProbIN's statistical model we used sensor data from 60 straight walks. Each walk was 4-meters long. For testing of each configuration (e.g., square-shape fast walk) we used 5 long walks and calculate an average error rate over 5 estimated trajectories.

Table 3. Average error rate of estimated position of the physics-based approach vs. ProbIN using models trained after EM iteration 1, 2 and 3. The phone is carried in the hand in front the body.

Type	Speed	Physics	EM1	EM2	EM3
L	slow	348.7%	18.3%	17.2%	16.3%
L	normal	194.6%	23.0%	22.1%	22.3%
L	fast	118.2%	26.7%	24.1%	25.6%
S	slow	2158.3%	4.0%	3.9%	4.4%
S	normal	800.3%	3.6%	3.6%	4.4%
S	fast	463.9%	1.8%	1.9%	2.0%

As the results show the error rate of the physics-based positioning approach is significantly higher than the error rate of ProbIN's approach. The reason is that the mobile phone is held in the hand and not mounted on the foot. Therefore, ZUPT cannot be applied. Thus, errors in the physics-based approach rapidly accumulate over time whereas ProbIN bypasses the step of double integrating the acceleration and is, therefore, more robust against sensor noise.

Similar to the findings reported by [9], the main source of error in ProbIN comes from the incorrect heading information. The low-cost sensors from the mobile phone are less stable and they are more likely to be interfered by local magnetic fields. Therefore, the magnetometer readings are easily biased from their true headings. In our experiments, the basketball court seems to have a stable local magnetic field which gives the magnetometer a constant bias. For example, reporting 12 degree north-east while the phone is heading north and always have +12 degrees to the true headings later on. This explains why the error rates of the square-shaped walks are lower than the error rates of L-shaped walks. In L-shaped walks a bias in the heading causes that the distance between the user's estimated ending point and the user's reference ending point increases. Thus, the error rate for L-shaped walks also increases. In square-shaped walks, the user travels in a close loop round trip which results in canceling out the error caused by the magnetometer bias. This finding applies to all round trip trajectories which are usually used for evaluating positioning systems as reported in the literature. Based on our analysis, we strongly argue against evaluating a self-contained positioning system only with round trip trajectories as this design might be blind of heading errors and can be misleading.

Table 4. The phone is carried loosely in the hand and in the pocket

Type	Position	Physics	EM1	EM2	EM3
L	hand	4435.3%	25.1%	25.4%	34.9%
L	pocket	2900.0%	30.6%	25.2%	21.9%
S	hand	19993.5%	16.5%	34.4%	25.5%
S	pocket	13435.8%	8.1%	9.4%	13.4%

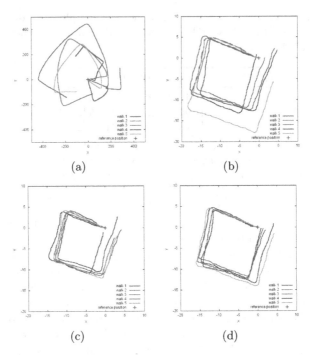

Fig. 8. The trajectories calculated based on the physics-based positioning (a) and on ProbIN statistical model in EM iteration 1 (b), 2 (c) and 3 (d)

Figure 8(a) shows trajectories estimated by the physics-based approach on square-shaped walks in normal speed. It differs notably from the true trajectory shown in Figure 6(c). On the other hand, the trajectories in Figures 8(b) - 8(d) confirmed our expectation that the error rate can be significantly reduced by utilizing ProbIN statistical model.

In the second experiment we explore the remaining two settings of the phone (Table 4). First, the user holds the phone loosely in the hand and is not look-ing at the display. Second, the phone resides in the pocket. In both cases the sensors of the phone sense the oscillating motions during a walk as shown in Figure 7(b). This motion generates additional noise which causes the increase of the estimation error.

7   Conclusion

In this paper we introduce ProbIN, a novel statistical dead-reckoning approach of mapping sensor readings to user's position for indoor positioning applica-tions. Our approach relies solely on the sensors provided by the consumer mo-bile devices. Thus, our positioning system can be deployed in any environment. Furthermore, ProbIN adapts its statistical models to the characteristics of the sensor and the user's walking patterns. Thus, even with the noisy sensor readings the estimated position can be relatively accurate. In addition, ProbIN does not require the phone to be mounted to the body. Users can just hold the phone in the hand or put it in the pocket which is more casual for real life applications.

For future work, we plan to conduct experiments with different type of movements (e.g., running, jumping, crawling, etc.) and with longer distances. This will allow the usage of the system in more challenging scenarios such as running in a forest or crawling in a tunnel. Moreover, the calculated error will also include the altitude in order to optimize the system for trajectories taking place on different floors.

Additionally, our system will be extended by utilizing external infrastructures such as GPS or Wi-Fi when they available. The existing indoor maps can be used for implementing the point-to-point navigation will be implemented. Moreover, the estimated trajectories can be corrected by employing state-of-the-art map-matching techniques.

Acknowledgements. This research was supported by CyLab at Carnegie Mellon under grants DAAD19-02-1-0389 and W911NF-09-1-0273 from the Army Research Office.

References

[1] Beauregard, S.: Infrastructureless pedestrian positioning. PhD thesis, University of Bremen (2009)

[2] Beauregard, S., Haas, H.: Pedestrian dead reckoning: A basis for personal positioning. In: Proceedings of the 3rd Workshop on Positioning, Navigation and Communication (WPNC 2006), vol. 06, pp. 27–35 (2006)

[3] Beauregard, S.: Omnidirectional pedestrian navigation for first responders. In: Workshop on Positioning, Navigation and Communication, pp. 33–36. IEEE (March 2007)

[4] Brown, P.F., Cocke, J., Pietra, S.A.D., Pietra, V.J.D., Jelinek, F., Lafferty, J.D., Mercer, R.L., Roossin, P.S.: A statistical approach to machine translation. Computational Linguistics 16(2), 79–85 (1990)

[5] Brown, P.F., Pietra, V.J.D., Pietra, S.A.D., Mercer, R.L.: The mathematics of statistical machine translation: Parameter estimation. Computational Linguistics 19(2), 263–311 (1993)

[6] Collin, J., Mezentsev, O., Lachapelle, G.: Indoor positioning system using accelerometry and high accuracy heading sensors. In: Proceedings of the 16th International Technical Meeting of the Satellite Division of the Institute of Navigation ION GPS/GNSS 2003, pp. 1–7 (2003)

[7] Dempster, A.P., Laird, N.M., Rubin, D.B., et al.: Maximum likelihood from incomplete data via the EM algorithm. Journal of the Royal Statistical Society. Series B (Methodological) 39(1), 1–38 (1977)

[8] Feliz, R., Zalama, E., García-Bermejo, J.G.: Pedestrian tracking using inertial sensors. Journal of Physical Agents 3(1), 35–42 (2009)

[9] Fischer, C., Muthukrishnan, K., Hazas, M., Gellersen, H.: Ultrasound-aided pedestrian dead reckoning for indoor navigation. In: Proceedings of the First ACM International Workshop on Mobile Entity Localization and Tracking in GPS-less Environments (MELT 2008), vol. 31 (2008)

[10] Germann, U., Jahr, M., Knight, K., Marcu, D., Yamada, K.: Fast decoding and optimal decoding for machine translation. In: Proceedings of the 39th Annual Meeting on Association for Computational Linguistics, vol. 39, pp. 228–235. Association for Computational Linguistics (2001)

[11] Kaufman, L., Rousseeuw, P.J.: Finding groups in data: an introduction to cluster analysis, 9th edn. WileyBlackwell (March 2005)

[12] Lin, H., Zhang, Y., Griss, M., Landa, I.: WASP: an enhanced indoor locationing algorithm for a congested Wi-Fi environment. In: Proceedings of the Workshop on Mobile Entity Localization and Tracking in GPS-less Environnments, pp. 183–196 (2009)

[13] Nguyen, T.-L., Zhang, Y., Griss, M.: Probin: Probabilistic inertial navigation. In: 2010 IEEE 7th International Conference on Mobile Adhoc and Sensor Systems (MASS), pp. 650 –657 (November 2010)

[14] Ojeda, L., Borenstein, J.: Non-GPS navigation for security personnel and first responders. The Journal of Navigation 60(3), 391–407 (2007)

[15] Randell, C., Djiallis, C., Muller, H.: Personal position measurement using dead reckoning. In: Proceedings of Seventh IEEE International Symposium on Wearable Computers, pp. 166–173 (2003)

[16] Shannon, C.E.: A mathematical theory of communication. ACM SIGMOBILE Mobile Computing and Communications Review 5(1), 55 (2001)

[17] Vogel, S., Zhang, Y., Huang, F., Tribble, A., Venugopal, A., Zhao, B., Waibel, A.: The CMU statistical machine translation system. In: Proceedings of MT Summit, vol. 9 (2003)

[18] Welch, G., Bishop, G.: An introduction to the Kalman filter, pp. 1–16. University of North Carolina at Chapel Hill, Chapel (1995)

Secure and Privacy-Preserving Cross-Layer Advertising of Location-Based Social Network Services

Michael Dürr, Florian Gschwandtner,
Corina Kim Schindhelm, and Markus Duchon

Mobile and Distributed Systems Group, Department for Informatics,
Ludwig-Maximilians-University Munich, 80538 Munich, Germany
{michael.duerr,florian.gschwandtner,corina-kim.schindhelm,
markus.duchon}@ifi.lmu.de

Abstract. We present a novel cross-layer protocol design which integrates in our decentralized *Online Social Network Vegas* and allows for secure and privacy-preserving advertising and communication of *Location-based Social Network Services* over WiFi. Our proposal requires minimal modifications to the MAC Layer and could be easily integrated into upcoming standards like IEEE 802.11u.

Keywords: Security, Privacy, Mobile Social Networks, Cross-Layer, WiFi, Beaconing.

1 Introduction

Due to the skyrocketing participation in *Online Social Networks* (OSNs) like *Facebook Places* and *Foursquare*, a remarkable increase of *Location-based Social Network Services* (LB-SNSs) can be observed. Unfortunately, mobile users still suffer from limited 3G connectivity or restrictive pricing plans. In order to continue the ongoing LB-SNS, they attempt to switch to private WiFi access networks or public WiFi hotspots. As mobile users often have to choose between a plethora of WiFi access points (APs) (e.g. provided by coffee shops, shopping malls, or private persons), switching to one of them turns out to be complex and cumbersome. Present WiFi installations are subject to heterogeneous authentication schemes like WPA or WebAuth which results in a trial-and-error procedure when a mobile device does not automatically select the preferred AP. As a result, once associated with an AP, a mobile device cannot receive useful information (e.g. load statistics of neigboring APs) from other APs in radio range. Chandra et al. [1] recently identified this problem and proposed different approaches to code such information into IEEE 802.11 beacon frames. The upcoming standard IEEE 802.11u attempts to provide a general solution as it facilitates unauthorized access to an AP in case a mobile device has another authorizing relationship to an external network. In addition, new features like transparent Layer 2 support for authentication in combination with access to

J.Y. Zhang et al. (Eds.): MobiCASE 2011, LNICST 95, pp. 331–337, 2012.

external profile information from OSNs allow for novel location-based and personalized mobile services. Such services could comprise of consumer-selective
product advertisements as well as personalized voucher and coupon distribution of nearby businesses, individual public transport schedule broadcasts from
nearby bus- or suburban train stations, or community-restricted content sharing through private APs. Although these opportunities appear promising for the
commercial domain, from a consumer perspective, they cause severe privacy and
security concerns.

We present a secure and privacy-preserving cross-layer protocol that facilitates
the advertisement and utilization of LB-SNSs. The protocol is tailored for our
OSN architecture Vegas, a decentralized OSN that has been developed based on
our previous work [2]. A Vegas-based LB-SNSs was recently published in [3].

2   Protocol Design

We identify three different situations that our protocol must be able to deal
with: *a)* the mere recognition and authentication of an advertised service, *b)* the
interpretation and processing of the advertised content, and *c)* the establishment
of an optional reverse channel from a mobile device to the corresponding AP for
advanced services. We decided to split a service advertisement into two parts.
Service advertisement identification information is broadcasted within a Layer
2 MAC frame, whereas the advertisement itself is carried within a Layer 7 UDP
packet. This helps to minimize data sent within a beacon frame necessary to
identify the advertised type of service and still allows for simple authentication
of the broadcasting AP.

2.1   Vegas Design

As we focus on security and privacy, we decided to integrate our solution into
our decentralized, secure and privacy-preserving OSN Vegas. Vegas does not
allow for communication between participants that are not directly connected
by an edge of the underlying social graph. This restriction is motivated by a
problem we termed *social network pollution* [2]. To give a few examples of social
network pollution, present OSNs offer the possibility for search operations on
their social graphs, provide unsolicited friendship recommendations, and offer
support for non-authorized linkage of a friend's friends. This causes a multitude
of unwanted friendship establishments, i.e., links in the social graph which not
necessarily represent a real friendship. It should be stressed that Vegas does not
prohibit friends that do not represent human identity. A Vegas friend can also
map to the profile of a company or any organization from the civilian domain.

Figure 1 illustrates the communication model of Vegas. Each user interacts
with the OSN through one or more mobile or stationary clients. Vegas applies
an asynchronous message exchange scheme based on the concept presented in
[4]. We rely on well known services like email, SMS, or instant messaging which
can be exploited to implement the *exchanger* instance. An exchanger represents

the abstract concept of a message queue which is used to transmit messages or any other kind of content. Any two Vegas friends A and B are aware of one or more such exchanger addresses of each other. A datastore represents the abstract concept of a user-writable storage space with world-readable access (e.g. some web space). Each user provides one or more datastores to place individually encrypted and signed profile for each of his friends.

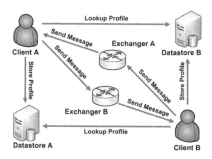

Fig. 1. In Vegas all exchanged information is encrypted and signed. Each user maintains one or more client instances and performs encrypted messaging over one or more exchanger instances. A user publishes individual profiles for each friend at one or more datastores.

2.2 Vegas Operation

Vegas communication and profile distribution works as follows: Two Vegas friends A and B generate a unique public key pair which must not be applied for messaging and profile generation except in the context of A and B. We term such a key pair a *link-specific* key pair. As user A holds a unique key pair $K_{A \to X_i}^{-}/K_{A \to X_i}^{+} (i \in 1, \ldots, n)$ for each of his n friends $X_1, \ldots, X_n$, a key pair simply represents a directed edge in the overall social graph. The notion of a key $K_{A \to X_i}^{-(+)}$ means that this key is a private (public) key generated by A for exclusive communication with X_i. A utilizes X_i's public key $K_{X_i \to A}^{+}$ to encrypt messages as well as profile information intended for X_i. In order to allow X_i to map a received message to its originator A, a fingerprint of A's public key $K_{A \to X_i}^{+}$ is included into each message sent to X_i. In case A wants to send a message to X_i, A applies X_i's public key $K_{X_i \to A}^{+}$ to encrypt the message content. After signing the message with $K_{A \to X_i}^{-}$, A delivers this message via an exchanger to X_i. X_i identifies sender A through his attached public key fingerprint. Since X_i is the only user that knows about this fingerprint, he represents the only user that is able to map it to the identity of A. We apply the same Vegas operations for the placement and update of profile information which we use to send messages.

2.3 Cross-Layer Protocol

As we aim at individual advertising and the deployment of personal and commercial services on top of ubiquitous WiFi APs, we necessitate a novel communication protocol which allows for secure services that smoothly integrate into Vegas. Figure 2 illustrates our protocol including all interactions between the involved parties. For simplification, we use the same identifiers C, AP, and S to either refer to a service (or a device) involved in the protocol or to the organization or person operating the correspondent service. At the beginning, a service provider S has to configure an access point AP that is envisaged to advertise a certain service (1). First, AP generates a public key pair K^-_{AP}/K^+_{AP} and presents S with the public part. In case S does not trust AP, AP can optionally provide K^+_{AP} encapsulated as a certificate signed by a trusted CA. S then generates a certificate $c_{(K^-_S)}(K^+_{AP})$ from K^+_{AP} (e.g. signed by his own certificate $c_{(Self)}(K^+_S)$) and sends $c_{(Self)}(K^+_S)$, $c_{(K^-_S)}(K^+_{AP})$, a service identifier ID_S, and the actual content M that will be advertised back to AP. To support mobile users in choosing relevant offers, ID_S also includes a semantic description of the service. A user C that wants to recognize and validate service advertisements from S has to establish a Vegas friendship with S in advance. To become Vegas friends, C and S rely on a (semi-) trusted out-of-band (OOB) channel to exchange their public keys ($K^+_{S \to C}$, $K^+_{C \to S}$), their exchanger addresses (Ex_S, Ex_C), and their datastore addresses (DS_S, DS_C) (2). In case C and S do not require detailed profile information of each other, exchanger and datastore addresses need not to be exchanged. Exchanging the public keys always suffices

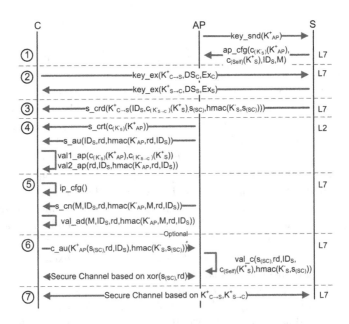

Fig. 2. The cross-layer protocol steps: *1)* Access point setup; *2)* Vegas key exchange; *3)* Provision of service credentials; *4)* Layer 2 service advertisement and authentication; *5)* Layer 7 service broadcast and integrity validation; *6)* Optional (advance services): User authorization; *7)* Optional (advance services): Service tunneling.

to facilitate service provider authentication and service consumer authorization. After C and S became Vegas friends, S sends an s_cred message to C including all information that is necessary to interact with AP (3). This always comprises ID_S and a certificate $c_{(K^-_{S \to C})}(K^+_S)$, which holds K^+_S and which is signed by the link-specific private key $K^-_{S \to C}$. Optionally, s_crd includes a shared secret $s_{(SC)}$ and a cryptographic hash $hmac(K^-_S, s_{(SC)})$ (generated based on K^-_S) which can be used as credentials to services beyond a simple advertisement service (see step 6). After AP has been configured it starts to broadcast service advertisements (4). We decided to overload IEEE 802.11 beacon frames with new IEs which carry all information necessary to authenticate the advertised service (see Section 2.4). Independent of the advertised service, AP repeatedly broadcast certificate message s_crt which includes $c_{(K^-_S)}(K^+_{AP})$. The service identifier and credentials are broadcasted in a separate message s_au which consists of the service identifier ID_S, a random value rd, and an cryptographic hash $hmac(K^-_{AP}, rd, ID_S)$ over both values based on K^-_{AP}. rd will change periodically and can be used to identify advertisements replayed by an attacker long after the advertised service shut down. AP always keeps a list of the most recent values of rd as this value can also be used by C during his authorization (see step 6). We separate the broadcast of AP's certificate $c_{(K^-_S)}(K^+_{AP})$ from S's service advertisements. This prevents redundancies as S may decide to broadcast advertisements for more than one service via AP. As soon as C comes into radio range of AP, C can receive the overloaded beacon frames. In case C recognizes a service description ID_S and already received a complete copy of $c_{(K^-_S)}(K^+_{AP})$, C can easily perform an authenticity and integrity check of the received advertisement: Procedure $val1\_ap$ validates the signature of $c_{(K^-_S)}(K^+_{AP})$ by applying $K^+_{C \to S}$ to $c_{(K^-_{S \to C})}(K^+_S)$ and K^+_S to $c_{(K^-_S)}(K^+_{AP})$ and procedure $val2\_ap$ validates the advertisement by recalculating the cryptographic hash of rd and ID_S and comparing the result to $hmac(K^-_{AP}, rd, ID_S)$. Only in case both validations succeed, a service description can be considered authenticated. In case validation succeeds, C applies procedure ip_cfg which configures an IP address. This is critical, since IP configuration, e.g. via DHCP, might demand for upstream Layer 2 authentication. However, the upcoming IEEE 802.11u standard will strongly simplify this task. By calling procedure val_ad, C can authenticate a service advertisement content M of any broadcast message s_cn that is related to ID_S. AP just has to ad ID_S, rd, and a cryptographic hash $hmac(K^-_{AP}, M, rd, ID_S)$ to val_ad in order to allow C to validate the hash. Due to the possibility to multiplex services with distinct service identifiers, steps (1) – (5) already suffice to facilitate simple services like community-centric and privacy-preserving advertisement, voucher, and coupon broadcasts. In case C also received a shared secret $s_{(SC)}$ and a cryptographic hash $hmac(K^-_S, s_{(SC)})$ (step 3), C optionally can access advanced services (6). To prove his service access authorization, C sends a message c_au which includes all credentials encrypted with K^+_{AP} necessitated by AP. AP then calls a procedure val_c which identifies the requested service by ID_S, recalculates the $hmac(K^-_S, s_{(SC)})$ to validate the originator of $s_{(SC)}$, and verifies that this is no replay by proving the freshness of rd. Now C and AP can both calculate a shared key $xor(s_{(SC)}, rd)$ which can be used to establish a secure channel. As long as AP and S are not operated by one and the same identity, AP cannot infer further information about C. Assuming an Internet connection to S and the case where a service requires detailed profile information about C, it is even possible to establish a secure channel between C and S (7).

2.4   Information Element Structure

To facilitate Layer 2 service advertisement recognition and authentication, we decided to overload standard IEEE 802.11 beacon frames by introducing two new IEs. We utilize the *LB-SNS Certificate Fragment* (LCF) IE to broadcast AP certificates and the *LB-SNS Identity and Authentication* (LIA) IE to broadcast service identifiers and the corresponding authentication information (see Figure 3a). To indicate a custom ID, the field *Element ID* is set to 0xDD and the field *User ID* to 0x123456. The *Length* field indicates the width of the Value field, which has a maximum size of 252 exclusive the User ID field. Value fields of the LCF and LIA IEs are depicted in figures 3b) and 3c). LCF and LIA both include a *Type* field which is used to distinguish LCF IEs from LIA IEs. As a commonly applied public key already has a size of 2048 bit and a Value field is limited to 252 byte, we apply LCF IEs to broadcast only fragments or AP certificates $c_{(K_S^-)}(K_{AP}^+)$. To be able to reassemble a certificate, each LCF IE carries an identifier *Cert ID* to map the LCF IE to the corresponding certificate, a sequence number *Seq ID* to describe the ordering of the fragments, a fragmentation flag *Flag* which indicates the end of a certificate, and the certificate fragment *Cert Frag* itself. Service advertisements are carried in the LIA IE which holds an identifier *Cert ID* indicating the certificate $c_{(K_S^-)}(K_{AP}^+)$ that must be used to prove AP authenticity, a service identifier *Service ID* and a random value *Rand* field, and an *HMAC* field, which holds a cryptographic MD5 hash $hmac(K_{AP}^-, rd, ID_S)$ to prove authenticity of the Service ID and Rand fields.

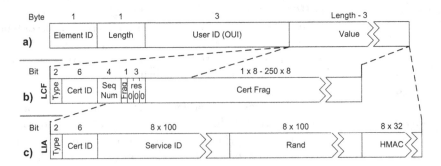

Fig. 3. New IEs: *a)* Common structure of the new information elements (IEs); *b)* Structure of the *LB-SNS Certificate Fragment* (LCF) IE; *c)* Structure of the *LB-SNS Identity and Authentication* (LIA) IE.

Due to space constraints, we omit a detailed explanation of the Service ID field which is necessary to recognize and multiplex advertised services.

References

1. Chandra, R., Padhye, J., Ravindranath, L., Wolman, A.: Beacon-Stuffing: Wi-Fi Without Associations. In: Hotmobile 2007 (2007)
2. Dürr, M., Werner, M., Maier, M.: Re-Socializing Online Social Networks. In: Proc. of GreenCom–CPSCom 2010. IEEE (December 2010)
3. Dürr, M., Marcus, P., Wiesner, K.: Secure, Privacy-Preserving, and Context-Restricted Information Sharing for Location-based Social Networks. In: ICWMC 2011, pp. 243–248. IARIA (June 2011)
4. Werner, M.: A Privacy-Enabled Architecture for Location-Based Services. In: Schmidt, A.U., Russello, G., Lioy, A., Prasad, N.R., Lian, S. (eds.) MobiSec 2010. LNICST, vol. 47, pp. 80–90. Springer, Heidelberg (2010)

A Parallel Approach to Mobile Web Browsing

Kiho Kim, Hoon-Mo Yang, Cheong-Ghil Kim, Shin-Dug Kim

Yonsei university, Department of Computer Science
School of Engineering, C532, Shinchon-dong, 134, Seoul 120-749, Republic of Korea
heavyarms3@gmail.com, {hmyang,sdkim}@yonsei.ac.kr,
cgkim@nsu.ac.kr

Abstract. This paper present a parallel approach about mobile web browsing, especially layout and paint parts. Web browser is one of the most frequently used applications in mobile devices and performance of web browser is an important factor affecting mobile device user experience. From our previous research, we found that layout and paint takes significant portion of web browser execution time and has similar execution characteristics. In this paper, we propose parallel render tree traversal algorithm for layout and paint parts in web browser: creating thread for sub-tree traversal processing. Moreover, to validate proposed Algorithm, we design a simple simulation implementing parallel tree traversal with web page render tree. The experiment results show that execution time is reduced average 28% in dual-core, 32% in quad-core compare to single-thread execution in paint simulation. In layout simulation, average 38% in dual-core, 57% in quad-core execution time is reduced.

Keywords: mobile web browser, parallel algorithm, multi-core, tree traversal.

1   Introduction

Web browser is a software application for retrieving, presenting, and traversing information resources on the World Wide Web. With the wide spread of networking infra structures, internet usage increases extremely and web browser becomes one of most frequently used applications. Many software companies are struggling to achieve more market share in web browser marketplace and web browser performance is one of the most important factors on this browser war. Recently, many smart-phone makers released new smart-phones or tablet-PCs, installed multi-core processor. These smart-phones are designed with dual-core chips now, but as time goes by, quad-core and many-core chips will be used in smart-phones same as in desktop systems[2]. Thus, with the trend towards the multi-core processors in mobile processors, we focus on parallelizing web browser for high performance web browsing. To utilize extra cores, we exploit parallelism using multi-thread library.

In this paper, we propose a parallel render tree traversal algorithm: thread creation for sub-tree traversal for mobile web browsing layout and paint functions. To validate our proposed algorithm, we design a simple simulation environment that has similar processing pattern to layout and paint functions and do experiment. According to our simulation results, the execution time is reduced by average 28% in dual-core, 32% in

J.Y. Zhang et al. (Eds.): MobiCASE 2011, LNICST 95, pp. 338–344, 2012.

quad-core for paint simulation. In layout simulation, execution time is reduced by average 38% in dual-core, 57% in quad-core. If we create more threads or sub-tree traversal, we can get better performance and the more cores are used, the better performance we can achieve. The rest of paper is organized as follows: Section 2 presents the background work that we've done before this research and other related works. Section 3 shows our parallel algorithm for mobile web browsing. Section 4 describes validation of our parallel algorithms. In Section 5, performance analysis of this parallel approach is provided. Finally, we conclude in Section 6.

2   Background

We choose target web browser engine: WebKit[3], and analyzed it. WebKit is an open source web browser engine and used for many desktops and mobile web browsers such as Apple Safari and mobile Safari browser[4], Google Chrome browser[5], and so on. Android web browser is also based on WebKit. The basic work flow of web browser is shown in Figure 1: load HTML, download resources, scan and parse documents, generate its corresponding document object model (DOM) tree and render tree[6, 7], and layout and paint render tree. After the initial page load, scripts respond to events generated by user input and server messages, typically modifying DOM, causing page re-layout and re-paint. We also did WebKit performance profiling over several hardware platforms and custom benchmarks for web pages. We categorized WebKit into several major functions: HTML parsing, CSS parsing, CSS style update, Javascript Processing, layout, and paint. Then we measure the execution time of each major function in real system using WebKit function and Linux system call modifying WebKit source code. Figure 2 shows our profiling results.

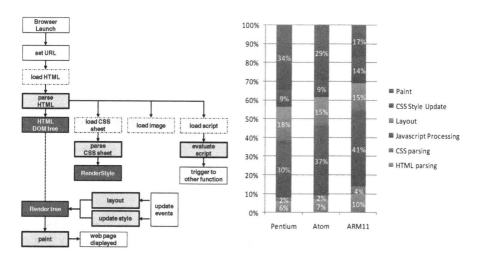

Fig. 1. Basic work flow of web browser   **Fig. 2.** Major function execution time ratio

There are few studies about web browser performance [8], parallel web browser [9], [10], and mobile browsers[11]. In [8], author also evaluates performance of web browser in various platforms. In [9], author introduces brief idea that how to parallelize each part of web browser: front-end, page layout, and scripting. In [10], author introduces new algorithms for CSS selector matching, layout solving, and font rendering. In [11], author introduces mobile web paradigms, mobile web rendering engines, various mobile browsers, and future of mobile web.

Based on our previous research and other related issue about performance of web browser, we propose a new parallel algorithm for layout and paint functions. In the following sections, details of algorithm will be described.

3   Proposed Algorithm

3.1   Task to Parallelize

To parallelize web browser, we need to find suitable sub-tasks to parallelize and we focus on layout and paint functions. First, the overall execution time to process layout and paint functions takes average around 40% of the entire execution time when measuring the performance under Pentium Dual Core 1.6GHz processors. Since these two functions take a significant portion of execution time, we can get more performance improvement when parallelizing these two. Moreover, layout and paint functions have similar execution characteristics, as the render tree traversal shown in Figure 3. Layout and paint functions recursively visit render tree nodes and perform their own tasks at each node. This means layout and paint functions just work for itself alone, not interacting with other data structures or functions. In other words, we don't need to worry about typical synchronization problem in multi-thread programming within these two functions.

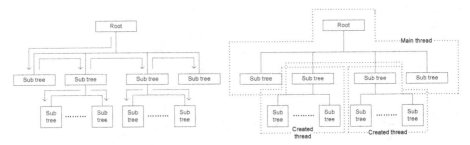

Fig. 3. Render tree traversal   **Fig. 4.** Sub tree traversal with created thread

3.2   Structure of Render Tree

A web page is parsed into a tree of nodes, called the document object model (DOM). Document, elements, and text will can be nodes of this tree. Render tree is very similar to the DOM, where it is a tree of objects and has style information of elements derived from CSS. Web page is composed of a group of boxes and some boxes belong to other boxes. Boxes are represented as tags in html document, elements in DOM, and render tree nodes in a render tree. Since a big box contains several small boxes, overall structure of render tree is formed as unbalanced tree as shown in Figure 5. In this web page, selected two big boxes take most of nodes in render tree and these two boxes also contain several small boxes. The box positioned in below forms bigger sub-tree than the above one since it contains more small boxes than above one.

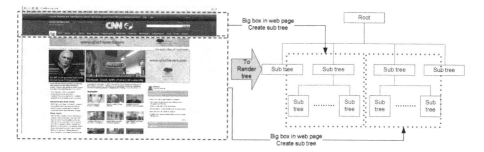

Fig. 5. Overall structure of render tree

3.3 How to Parallelize

We propose a way to create multi-threads for processing sub-tree traversal as shown in Figure 4 using POSIX thread library[12]. For example, when web browser paints web page on screen, browser will draws one box at a time but if we create threads for sub-tree processing, we can draw several boxes at a time. However, there is a problem that render trees are formed as unbalanced trees as we mentioned above and that will cause an unbalanced load balancing problem among threads. To solve this load unbalancing problem, the number of nodes in each sub-tree is used. While a thread visits nodes in the render tree, if the number of nodes in this sub-tree is greater than factor(named as Thread Factor: TF), as another threshold, and has siblings, the thread creates new threads and created-threads will handle this sub-tree.

4   Simulation for Algorithm Validation

To validate the effect of this algorithm we design a simulator implementing our parallel render tree traversal algorithm. When simulator visits each node, it performs assigned tasks. For the input of simulation, we use WebKit DumpRenderTree tool to get the render tree of real web page. WebKit DumpRenderTree prints render tree of web page to the console and we convert it into text file to use it as the input of simulation. To make simulation more similar to real web browser, we differentiate each node's task. For example, image sizes of web pages are very various and displaying big sized image will need more calculation than small sized image. We also found that leaf nodes of render tree are nodes of real images or texts, and inside nodes are wrapper box block. Therefore, we assume that leaf nodes will consume more processing power than inside nodes when browser does painting. So we use each node's type and size to reflect the characteristics of web browsing, since DumpRenderTree gives each node's type and size also. However, layout function doesn't need task differentiation. Layout function performs decision function of each node's position and size. Therefore, job done at each node is not quite different unlike paint function. So, we use same iteration number at each node for layout function simulation. The number of iterations is named as Layout Factor (LF).

For the task that will be performed at each node, we use arbitrary memory allocation, integer and string calculations and execute them repetitively. For the differentiation of each node's task, the number of iterations at each node is used. Calculation method of iteration number is shown as follows:

Table 1. Iteration number

Node type	Inside Node	Leaf Node
The number of Iterations	Inner Node Factor (INF)	x size*y size*Leaf Node Factor (LNF)

5   Experiment Result

We choose 20 web pages to simulate and get Render tree of them. Most of pages have 1000~1500 render tree nodes. Experiments were performed in Intel i7 2600 processors that drop the clock speed to 1.6GHz and 4GB memory, running ubuntu 10.0.4. We use gettimeofday() function to get elapsed time of executing program. We measure execution time of simulator and compare the single thread version with multi thread version. We use dual-core to quad-core, and using Intel Hyper-Threading(HT)[13] technique to see the correlation between number of core and performance improvement.

Table 2. Factor for experiment

Factor	high	mid	Low
INF	10	10	10
LNF	4	3	2
LF	1500	3000	4500

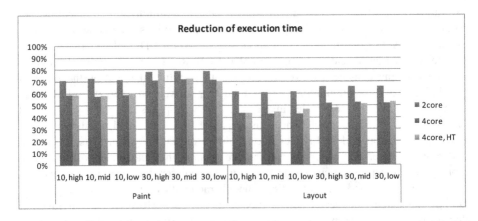

Fig. 6. Reduction of execution time in paint simulation

Figure 6 shows reduction of execution time in paint and layout experiments. On average, reduction of execution time is 28% in dual-core, 32% in quad-core in case of TF is 10 in paint. As shown in figure, if TF is smaller, execution time reduction is bigger. In dual-core, TF 10's performance is average 7% better than TF 30's. Same trend is shown in quad-core also. Moreover, quad-core's performance improvement is better than dual-core's performance improvement. When TF is 10, average 13% better performance improvement we can get in quad-core compare to dual-core. However, HT doesn't give impact because we use just integer calculation, string calculation and memory allocation in this experiment, there is not enough functional units to allocate. In addition, INF and LNF don't give significant impact to performance. Execution time reduction of high, mid, and low is almost similar. On average, reduction of execution time is 38% in dual-core, 57% in quad-core in case of TF is 10 in layout. Compare with paint experiment, we can get better performance in layout experiment. Since layout experiment's per node iteration is same, so load balancing among threads is much better than paint. Except that, overall trend of experiment result is similar to paint simulation. LF also doesn't give significant impact to performance.

6   Conclusion

In this paper, we proposed a parallel approach about mobile web browsing, especially layout and paint parts. We parallelized layout and paint parts by implementing parallel render tree traversal algorithm. Moreover, to validate this algorithm, we design a simple simulation environment that has similar processing pattern to layout and paint functions. The experiment results show that execution time is reduced average 28% in dual-core, 32% in quad-core for paint simulation. In layout simulation, execution time is reduced average 38% in dual-core, 57% in quad-core. By using this parallel algorithm, we can utilize multi-core processor in mobile devices for most frequently used application and offer better user experience.

Acknowledgments. This research is was supported by the MKE(The Ministry of Knowledge Economy), Korea and Microsoft Research, under IT/SW Creative research program supervised by the NIPA(National IT Industry Promotion Agency) (NIPA-2010-C1810-1002-0023

References

1. Gartner Press Releases,
   http://www.garthner.com/it/page.jsp?id=1689814
2. Strategy Analytics Press Releases,
   http://www.strategyanalytics.com/default.aspx?mod=pressrele
   aseviewer&a0=4998
3. The WebKit Open Source Project, http://webkit.org
4. APPLE Safari, http://www.apple.com/safari/
5. Google Chrome,
   http://www.google.com/chrome/intl/en/make/features.html

6. W3C Document Object Model, http://www.w3.org/DOM/
7. WebCore Rendering 1-The Basics,
    http://www.webkit.org/blog/114/webcore-rendering-i-the-basics/
8. Meyerovich, L.: Rethinking Browser Performance. Login 34(4), 14–20 (2009)
9. Jones, C.G., Liu, R., Meyerovich, L., Asanovic, K., Bodik, R.: Parallelizing the Web Browser. In: HotPar 2009 Proceedings of the First USENIX Conference on Hot Topics in Parallelism (2009)
10. Meyerovich, L., Bodik, R.: Fast and Parallel Webpage layout. In: WWW 2010 Proceedings of the 19th International Conference on World Wide Web (2010)
11. Hernadez, E.A.: War of the Mobile Browsers. IEEE Pervasive Computing 8, 82–85 (2009)
12. POSIX Threads Programming,
    http://computing.llnl.gov/tutorials/pthreads
13. Intel® Hyper-Threading Technology,
    http://www.intel.com/technology/platform-technology/hyper-threading/index.htm

SoundBoom: Breaking App Barriers

Rachel Gawley, Jonathan Barr, and Michael Barr

JamPot Technologies Limited, Mobile Computing Research Department,
405 Holywood Road, Belfast, UK
{rachel.gawley,jonathan.barr,michael.barr}@jampot.ie

Abstract. Cross-platform application development is a rapidly increasing area of research. SoundBoom is a mobile application created using innovative cross-platform development techniques. SoundBoom provides a unique ability to create a custom soundboard on a device, utilising the device capabilities such as the camera and microphone. Subsequently, the soundboard assets can be uploaded to the cloud. These assets can populate the SoundBoom app on another device, potentially on a different platform, via the cloud using web services. This population of a native app with dynamic content from the cloud is the first step towards on-device application creation.

Keywords: Mobile applications, app creation, cloud, web services, cross-platform, HTML5.

1   Introduction

Increasing smartphone sales are helping the development of a mobile apps culture [1]. With over 10.9 billion applications (app) downloads occurring in 2010 alone [2], the 'apps culture' is just beginning and is expected to peak in 2014 [2] with 76.9 billion downloads. This anticipated rapid increase in demand for mobile apps has associated issues. One of the biggest problems for both the end-user and mobile application developer is the ability to access the same application on different devices and platforms. This is a well-known issue [3] and usually requires the development of an app for each platform. Ideally, an application should be available on many platforms/devices; however, developing the same application for multiple platforms is not a trivial task. The ultimate goal is to write an application once and deploy to any mobile screen. The closest solutions currently available are collectively known as cross-platform approaches. These approaches rely on web-based technologies [4], [5] or known languages [6], [7], which produce hybrid or native cross-compiled applications. There are limitations of these approaches, especially regarding rich-media content and deploying to multiple platforms. Most approaches are capable of producing mobile applications for a subset of mobile platforms. The SoundBoom project was created to test the limits of cross-platform techniques, which are proprietary to JamPot Technologies Limited, and in the process break some of the app development barriers.

J.Y. Zhang et al. (Eds.): MobiCASE 2011, LNICST 95, pp. 345–348, 2012.
© Institute for Computer Sciences, Social Informatics and Telecommunications Engineering 2012

2   SoundBoom

The SoundBoom application [8], [9], [10], [11], [12] was created to test cross-platform technologies when producing a media-rich application. The aim of the project was to produce an application that:

- Works consistently on as many platforms/devices as possible and has been produced from the same code.
- Enables users to create dynamic content using device capabilities (camera and microphone), which can be viewed on a different device within seconds. The assets can be shared via the cloud and downloaded to a different device on a potentially different platform.

The SoundBoom application meets these requirements by providing:

- A soundboard that plays a sound when each image icon is clicked.
- A means of creating a custom soundboard using the device capabilities (camera, microphone and asset library).
- The ability to save a custom soundboard to the cloud via web services with a unique PIN.
- The option to download a custom soundboard from the cloud using a unique PIN.

The SoundBoom application works on the following platforms:

- iOS
- Android
- BlackBerry Playbook
- MeeGo
- Samsung Smart TV
- WeTab
- Mac OS X
- Windows (XP, Vista, 7)

3   SoundBoom Demonstration

The demonstration will consist of presenting the SoundBoom application on a variety of devices: iPhone; iPad; Android mobile phone; Android tablet; BlackBerry Playbook; MeeGo tablet; WeTab; Mac OS X; Windows. The demo will proceed as follows:

- A custom soundboard will be created on one of the devices using pictures taken and sounds created at the demo.
- The assets will be uploaded to the cloud from the device.
- The assets will be downloaded from the cloud to all the other devices. This whole process will take less than a minute.

- A participant will be invited to choose any of the devices, which will have the newly made custom soundboard and asked to change one of the items (both sound and audio) and upload it to the cloud.
- The changes made on the one device will be populated to other devices within seconds.

The demo highlights the power of a cross-compiled application that can interact with the cloud as a means of uploading and downloading content.

3.1   Wider Audience Participation

To encourage participation, the audience will be provided with information on how to download SoundBoom from the app stores to the their personal devices. SoundBoom will be free for the duration of the conference, where possible. Users will be provided with a PIN to download JamPot's custom soundboard – uploading will be disabled on this PIN. Up to 50 participants will be provided with a unique PIN, which permits write access to the JamPot cloud to store custom soundboards. Each PIN will allow 3 uploads (saves) and unlimited downloads.

3.2   Equipment

JamPot will provide all technical equipment. A stand or table is required to display all the devices. A Wi-Fi connection is required to enable the devices to connect to the cloud via web services.

3.3   HTML5 SoundBoom

As part of an experimental project, a read-only (download only) version of SoundBoom was created in HTML5. The web address to the HTML5 version of SoundBoom will be provided to the users. The PINs that work on the native application will also work on the HTML5 version.

4   Conclusion

The creation of SoundBoom is the result of a novel approach to the development of cross-platform mobile applications. The biggest technological advance in SoundBoom is the proof of concept that application assets created on one device can easily populate a different device on a different platform, via the cloud, in real-time. This addresses the issue identified by Gartner in May 2011[3].

"Every time a user downloads a native app to their smartphone or puts their data into a platform's cloud service, they are committing to a particular ecosystem and reducing the chances of switching to a new platform"

A user no longer has to commit to a specific platform or ecosystem using this approach. SoundBoom is the first step in a much bigger project aimed at making cross-platform app creation possible. The ultimate goal is to create an on-device app-builder aimed at non-technical users.

References

1. The Rise of Apps Culture, `http://pewinternet.org/Reports/2010/The-Rise-of-Apps-Culture/Overview.aspx`
2. IDC study, `http://www.idc.com/research/viewdocsynopsis.jsp?containerId=225668`
3. Gartner press release, `http://www.gartner.com/it/page.jsp?id=1689814`
4. Appcelerator Titanium, `http://www.appcelerator.com/`
5. Phone Gap, `http://www.phonegap.com/`
6. Mono, `http://www.mono-project.com/Main_Page`
7. Adobe Flash Player, `http://www.adobe.com/products/flashplayer/`
8. SoundBoom iTunes, `http://itunes.apple.com/gb/app/soundboom/id429903896?mt=8`
9. SoundBoom BlackBerry App World, `http://appworld.blackberry.com/webstore/content/38624?lang=en`
10. SoundBoom Android Market, `https://play.google.com/store/apps/details?id=air.ie.jampot.SoundBoomPro&feature=search_result#?t=W251bGwsMSwxLDEsImFpci5pZS5qYW1wb3QuU291bmRCb29tUHJvIl0`
11. SoundBoom Amazon, `http://www.amazon.com/JamPot-Technologies-Ltd-SoundBoom/dp/B004X6GU56/ref=sr_1_1?ie=UTF8&s=mobile-apps&qid=1303284579&sr=1-1`
12. SoundBoom Intel AppUp, `http://www.appup.com/applications/applications-SoundBoom`

Interdroid Versioned Databases: Decentralized Collaborative Authoring of Arbitrary Relational Data for Android Powered Mobile Devices

Emilian Miron, Nicholas Palmer, Roelof Kemp, Thilo Kielmann, and Henri Bal

VU University Amsterdam, The Netherlands
emilian.miron@gmail.com, {palmer,rkemp,kielmann,bal}@cs.vu.nl

Abstract. Complex interactions in software development have led to the creation of *version control systems* to manage source code. These systems have become increasingly flexible and support *disconnected* and *decentralized* operations.

However the authoring of other types of data has remained behind and often relies on centralized and online solutions. This is a big problem in the mobile market where applications are encouraged to use relational databases to store their information but little help is offered to allow synchronization and collaboration with peers.

The Interdroid Versioned Databases (IVDb) framework is an integrated solution for collaboratively editing and sharing of arbitrary relational data on the Android mobile platform. It is a reusable framework that addresses the storage, versioning and synchronization needs of applications, freeing developers of considerable design and programming effort.

1 Introduction

People today may own and use several computing devices including personal desktop computers, laptops, netbooks, tablets, and smartphones. Such devices are paving the way for what pervasive and ubiquitous computing advocates have long described[9]. It is certain that the way we communicate and collaborate today has significantly changed to include and take advantage of these devices.

In particular *digital collaborative authoring* of many forms has become popular. The most familiar examples of such collaborations include collaborative web applications such as Wikipedia or Google Docs, but businesses are also increasingly using collaborative workflows to design presentations, prepare documents, create software models and author source code. One can think of even more common things that are managed digitally and shared between members of a family or community including shopping and todo lists, personal financial accounting, and even medical records.

One would like to bring these kinds of collaborative applications to mobile devices. However, due to frequently changing connectivity status on these

J.Y. Zhang et al. (Eds.): MobiCASE 2011, LNICST 95, pp. 349–354, 2012.

devices, it is important for applications to offer *disconnected* and *decentralized* operation. Unfortunately, writing a system which supports these modes of operation requires a large development effort for the application's data storage and synchronization layer. Because of the difficulties of distributed synchronization, applications often settle for centralized and online solutions which do not meet the needs of mobile users and introduce single points of failure.

The system presented in this paper addresses these problems by leveraging the power of version control systems to bring decentralized collaborative editing of relational databases to the mobile platform. This system is based on the popular Git version control system and the Android[1] mobile platform. The end result of this work is the Interdroid Versioned Databases (IVDb) framework which provides a platform for distributed authoring of relational data.

The IVDb framework is an integrated solution for collaboratively editing and sharing of arbitrary relational databases on Android. It is a reusable framework that addresses the general storage, versioning and synchronization needs of applications which require data storage, freeing developers of considerable design and programming effort.

The API of this system was designed for the Android platform and with developer familiarity in mind. Versioning blends naturally with the existing data access mechanisms built into the platform. The framework also includes most tools needed to bootstrap a collaborative editing application in the form of user interface activities that deal with versioning related tasks and can easily interface with pluggable data editing components written by the application developer.

The unique set of features offered by this system unlocks the door for collaborative applications using structured data stores on mobile devices.

2   Background

Git is fundamentally a content oriented filing system with version tracking. Git has the ability to track the state of a filing system based entirely on the hash of the content of the filing system. Git is also able to track multiple branches of a given history, and provides access to the history of commits as well as to individual commits in a given branch. With this structure, and feature set, Git is able to solve a portion of the problems we face when building a distributed collaborative editing system for structured data.

Android[1] is an open source software stack designed for mobile phones. Developers can write custom applications in the Java programming language by using the same platform features that the core applications use. The Android application framework provides several abstractions specifically designed for the platform. Of primary importance for this paper is an integration with the existing content provider interface.

Content providers are an abstraction of the Android application framework used for storage and retrieval of data across applications. Android uses it to expose platform data such as contacts and media information, while applications can use existing content providers or write new ones. The content providers differ from relational databases in how the tables are named. Instead of the flat names and the notion of cross product joins, the tables of content providers are presented within a URI scheme of content://. Each content provider corresponds to an authority, while the path represents either a table or a table + row identifier. In addition to the relational database operation the content provider interface also associates a MIME type for each content URI. These MIME types are used in conjunction with the intent system, in order to allow the Android framework to select viewing and editing activities for specific URIs.

3   Design

The design of the system is driven by the vision of enabling collaborative editing of structured data stores. We thus require the system to enable applications to perform the following activities: provide access to read and modify data, save and access historical versions, branch and merge, and share data with others. Finally, we require the system to integrate well with the Android platform, provide tools for easily transitioning existing applications, work well on resource constrained platforms, and operate in a complete decentralized fashion.

The collaboration and versioning features are an extension to the Android content provider data abstraction interface. Our solution keeps track of versioning information alongside the existing non-versioned data abstraction. For instance, the branch or commit we are accessing can be embedded in either the URI passed to the content provider or via the parameters of the operation. We have chosen for the former because it is more natural to think of a particular row in a particular version as a given resource rather than as an aspect of the operations on the resource. Furthermore, this decision also reduces the effort to migrate existing applications because most often content URIs are generated using a fixed prefix and thus the system allows application programmers to alter that prefix in a single place rather than having to alter every operation. Thus, the framework makes use of a URI scheme which embeds the versioning information inside the URIs.

All URIs begin with a "content" scheme. They then specify the "authority" for the given data, which can be thought of as a namespace, and then follow with a path for the given data item or items. In the case of IVDb all repositories are served using the same authority. The first path component is therefore the

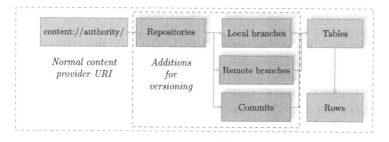

Fig. 1. Versioned Content Provider URIs

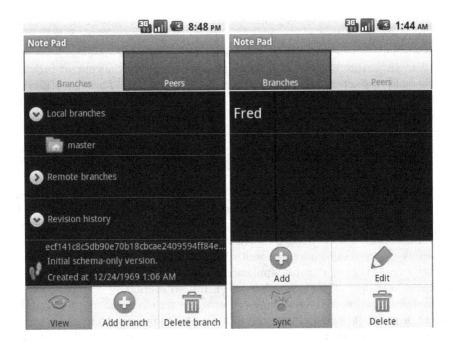

Fig. 2. Screen Shots: On the left is a shot of our Version Browser, and on the right the IVDb Sharing Manager

repository. Following this is the branch type identifier, and then the actual branch identifier. When migrating a legacy application the URI prefix can be easily changed from the content schema and authority to the default local master branch in the framework provider. Finally, the remaining path identifies the table and optional row identifier. This design is pictured in Figure 1.

4 User Interface Components

IVDb includes several reusable user interface components (activities and views) which can be used for bootstrapping a new or existing application with the versioning related user interface. With these components, application developers can focus on writing application specific data visualization user interface components. (See Figure 2.)

The activities in the framework handle the following tasks: (a) Version browser: manage local branches (add, delete), view list of versions (local branches, remote branches and historical versions), commit changes as well as (b) Sharing manager: manage remote peers, synchronize with others. The activities launch related activities based on Intents with URIs from the uniform versioned Content Provider URI scheme.

The custom application components and the activities from the framework can easily interface with each other by using Android's intent mechanism.

5 Evaluation

In order to evaluate the framework the Notepad Content Provider sample from the Android platform development kit was modified to use the framework while keeping the same data model.

The utility of the API can be quantified in lines of code saved when providing the same features using the framework versus when not using the framework. The ease of use is correlated with the utility but is more difficult to quantify as it involves how well the framework integrates with the platform and how familiar the interfaces are to developers. In general we found the modification to be extremely easy to perform. We add 55 lines of code to the user interface code in order to deal with viewing read only data which the original application did not support. However, the content provider implementation was reduced from 204 lines of code to just 70, a significant savings for this application. We anticipate applications with more complicated data types to have a higher percentage of savings in the content provider.

We feel that a small addition in lines of code to the UI in order to add explicit commit, branching, synchronization and viewing of historical versions is a very small price to pay, particularly when offset by the significant reduction in complexity of the content provider implementation. In total the codebase for the versioned application was smaller than the original application while providing more features. This shows that the framework has powerful abstractions that lower development effort while at the same time providing additional versioning features developers would otherwise not write.

6 Related Work

A great deal of work has been done on both synchronization and collaborative editing on mobile devices.

The closest system to ours with regards to data format is Bayou[6]. It is a replicated mobile database that provides eventual consistency over relational data, however, the requirement to have deterministic conflict resolution programs is admittedly very hard or even impossible without user intervention.

Byong et al[3] advocate that many collaborative writing scenarios require asynchronous disconnected operations. They developed a synchronization system for XML documents, which limits the applicability of their solution.

In Syxaw[5] the authors give a general synchronization system for files based on merging of XML data. However, their work mainly deals with optimizing bandwidth usage because of their focus on file system synchronization. Closest to IVDb is their sample collaborative XML editor called Captio which aids users by providing better merging alignment and visualization.

DocX2Go[7] makes use of optimistic replication just as IVDb does, and can work in a fully decentralized way with support. However, the XML focus of the platform, as with other related work can make it inappropriate for many applications.

Several authors emphasize the importance of differencing for the merge problem. Ronnau et al.[8] devise an algorithm that differentiates XML documents generated by the OpenOffice application in a way that notices structural differences as opposed to variability of the format. They also advocate the use of history aware merging such as the one we provide. In [4] Tancred proposes a theoretical model to XML document merging from which he devises a three-way merge algorithm.

In the Disco[2] framework the authors explore how applications can handle operation of collaborative systems in the face of disconnections. This system focuses more on handling disconnection in synchronous systems and not on data representation and versioning.

7   Conclusions

This paper presented IVDb, a framework for the development of collaborative editing applications using structured data for mobile devices. It offers developers of collaborative applications a simple way to structure and build their application, which can be used to significantly reduce development overhead, while also offering versioning features that would otherwise be very demanding to develop.

References

1. Android-Developers-Guide: What is android?,
   http://developer.android.com/guide/basics/what-is-android.html
2. Gutwin, C., Graham, T.N., Wolfe, C., Wong, N., de Alwis, B.: Gone but not forgotten: designing for disconnection in synchronous groupware. In: CSCW 2010: Proceedings of the 2010 ACM Conference on Computer Supported Cooperative Work, pp. 179–188. ACM, New York (2010)
3. Lee, B.G., Chang, K.H., Narayanan, N.H.: An integrated approach to version control management in computer supported collaborative writing. In: ACM-SE 36: Proceedings of the 36th Annual Southeast Regional Conference, pp. 34–43. ACM, New York (1998)
4. Lindholm, T.: A three-way merge for xml documents. In: DocEng 2004: Proceedings of the 2004 ACM Symposium on Document Engineering, pp. 1–10. ACM, New York (2004)
5. Lindholm, T., Kangasharju, J., Tarkoma, S.: Syxaw: Data synchronization middleware for the mobile web. Mob. Netw. Appl. 14(5), 661–676 (2009)
6. Petersen, K., Spreitzer, M., Terry, D., Theimer, M.: Bayou: Replicated database services for world-wide applications. In: Proceedings of the 7th SIGOPS European Workshop, pp. 275–280. ACM (1996)
7. Puttaswamy, K.P., Marshall, C.C., Ramasubramanian, V., Stuedi, P., Terry, D.B., Wobber, T.: Docx2go: collaborative editing of fidelity reduced documents on mobile devices. In: MobiSys 2010: Proceedings of the 8th International Conference on Mobile Systems, Applications, and Services, pp. 345–356. ACM, New York (2010)
8. Rönnau, S., Scheffczyk, J., Borghoff, U.M.: Towards xml version control of office documents. In: DocEng 2005: Proceedings of the 2005 ACM Symposium on Document Engineering, pp. 10–19. ACM, New York (2005)
9. Satyanarayanan, M.: Pervasive computing: Vision and challenges. IEEE [see also IEEE Wireless Communications] Personal Communications 8(4), 10–17 (2001)

Demonstration of Mobilewalla

Anindya Datta and Kaushik Dutta

Mobilewalla.com, Singapore
&
College of Computing, National University of Singapore, Singapore
{datta,dutta}@comp.nus.edu.sg

Abstract. With the popularity of mobile apps on mobile devices based
on iOS, Android, Blackberry and Windows Phone operating systems,
the number of mobile apps in each of the respective native app stores
are increasing in leaps and bounds. Currently there are almost 700,000
mobile apps across these four major native app stores. Due to such enormous number of apps, both the constituents in the app ecosytem, consumers and app developers, face problems in terms of 'app discovery'.
For consumers, it is a daunting task to discover the apps they like and
need among the huge number of available apps. Likewise, for developers,
making it possible for users to discover their apps in the large number of
available apps is a challenge. To address these issues, Mobilewalla(MW),
provides an independent unbiased search engine for mobile apps with
semantic search capabilities. It has also developed an objective scoring
mechanism based on user and developer involvement with an app. The
scoring mechanism enables MW to provide a number of other ways to
discover apps - such as dynamically maintained 'hot' lists and 'fast rising' lists. In this paper, we demonstrate some of the key functionalities
of MW.

Keywords: Mobile App, Search Engine, Semantic Similarity.

1 Introduction

Consumer software applications that run on smartphones (popularly known as
mobile apps, or, simply, apps) represent the fastest growing consumer product
segment in the annals of human merchandising [1,2]. The absolute number of
apps currently in existence, as well as their rates of growth, are remarkable. At
the time of writing, there are 404126, 274555, 30784, 19796 apps available in Apple, Android, Blackberry and Windows platforms respectively. Since December,
2010, the app growth rates for the Apple and Android platforms are nearly 4%
and 7% on monthly basis respectively.

This scenario creates a number of problems for the two key constituencies in
the app ecosystem, the consumers and the developers. For consumers, there are
simply too many apps and far too much fragmentation in these apps (e.g., a large
number of categories). The analogy we often use to describe the confusion faced
by a mobile app consumer is to imagine a customer walking into a grocery store,

J.Y. Zhang et al. (Eds.): MobiCASE 2011, LNICST 95, pp. 355–360, 2012.

needing only a few items, and finding that all aisles and category labels have been eliminated, and every product has been thrown into a pile on the floor. It is a similarly daunting task for a consumer to navigate native app stores [3,4] and discover apps they need and like, as has been widely discussed in media forums in the recent past [5,6].

For application developers, the situation is far worse. There are almost 700,000 mobile apps between Apple and Android alone and most smartphone owners only can only identify a handful - this is a nightmare scenario for developers whose success is contingent upon getting their apps "found" by consumers. "How will my apps be discovered?" is the number one question in the mind of app developers. This issue, known as the "app discovery" problem, has received wide attention in the media as well [7,8].

In response, there is intense interest in creating independent unbiased search systems for mobile apps. One of the earliest entrants in this space is Mobilewalla (MW) (www.mobilewalla.com). In this paper we demonstrate some of the key functionalities of Mobilewalla.

2   Screen Shots and Descriptions

The Mobilewalla architecture is flexibly implemented using a JSON interface. The application server provides a set of JSON APIs that can be invoked by any client over HTTP. Currently, the clients supported include iOS devices (i.e., iPhone/iPod/IPad), Android devices and desktop web applications. All these clients communicate with the Mobilewalla server application using the same JSON API set, but differ in the user interface offered to the end user. We will now proceed to demonstrate some of the important functionalities of the Mobilewalla application by using desktop web application as an example (the user may interact with this application at www.mobilewalla.com).

When the user arrives at the Mobilewalla application, the first step is to choose a platform of interest, i.e., the user must specify which smartphone platform is of interest to the user – iPhone/iPod, iPad, Android, Blackberry or Microsoft (the user may also choose a "don't care" option, marked as "All" in Mobilewalla). Once a platform is chosen the user will be directed to the main "splash page".

From this screen, the user may choose to navigate the app world in a number of ways. The first, and the most common method of interaction is by entering a search query in the keyword input box. Let's assume the user enters the search term "earth photo". Mobilewalla returns a set of apps that fit the user's interest as shown in Fig 1 – in this view Mobilewalla provides not only the app name, but also a number of other core features such as author and price. One notable feature of this view are the *relevance* and *Mobilewalla meter* (*MW Meter*) indicators present in each app box. Relevance indicates the quality of "fit" of that app with respect to the input seach query, whereas *MW Meter* is an encapsulation of the "goodness" of the app as measured by Mobilewalla (this is based on the Mobilewalla Score metric described earlier). Also, while not shown the screenshot, we also segment the apps by Free and Paid and allow a number of options to sort the result set (the user may view these by visiting mobilewalla.com).

Fig. 1. Keyword Search Results Page

The user may choose any app from the app-list view just described and delve into its details. Let us assume the user chooses the Google Earth app. In this case she will be presented with the detail view of this app, shown in Fig 2. In this view, Mobilewalla displays details such as the app description and screenshots and also allows the user to view a number of other interesting artifacts related to this app, such as "Apps by Author" (other apps created by the author of the app detail being viewed), "Mobilewalla Score"(the Mobilewalla score history related to this app over the past 14 days), "Comments", and "Similar Apps" (similar to the "if you like this, you might also like" feature in Amazon). The screenshots corresponding to the "Apps by Author" and "Similar Apps" for the app Google Earth are shown in Figs 3 and 4.

The above two paragraphs decsribes how a user might interact with Mobile-walla by performing a keyword search and then drilling down on the results. However, keyword search is just one of many ways that the user can navigate Mobilewalla. He might also choose to view apps by categories, or choose one of the many "pre-defined" list options such as "Hot Apps", "Fast Movers" and "New Apps". Choosing the "Bowse my category" option reveals a number of category icons from which the use may navigate the app world – Fig 5 shows the results of choosing the "Maps & Navigation" category.

Similarly choosing "Hot Apps" displays the list of the top 1000 apps ordered by their Mobilewalla Scores, while "Fast Rising" apps are those whose Mobile-walls scores have demonstrated the steepest ascent, i.e., apps getting hot the fastest. "New Apps" are those that are less than a month old. In every case a number of sort options are available that allow users to manipulate the result set along various dimensions.

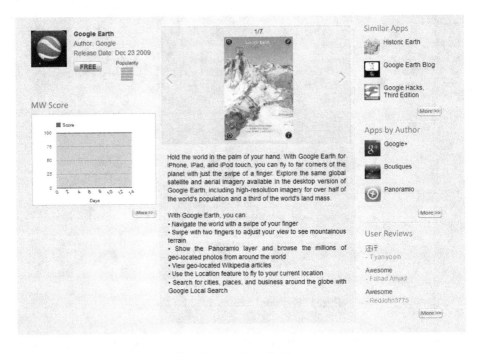

Fig. 2. App Details Page

Fig. 3. Apps By Developer Page

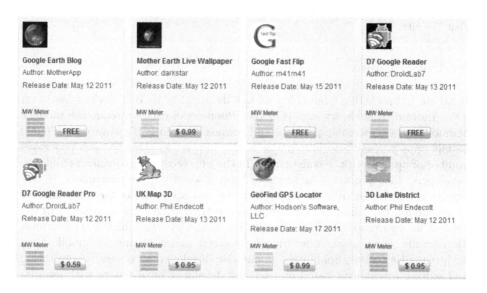

Fig. 4. Similar App Page

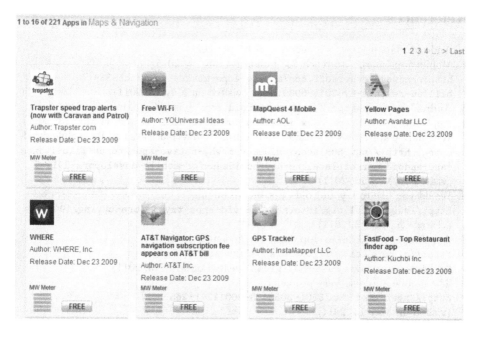

Fig. 5. Category Search Results Page

While Mobilewalla has a number of other interesting features, it is infeasible to describe them in this paper due to length restrictions. We invite the user to visit the site.

3   Conclusion

With the skyrocketing popularity of mobile apps on mobile devices based on iOS, Android, Blackberry and Windows Phone operating systems, the number of mobile apps is increasing in leaps and bounds. Currently there are over 700,000 mobile apps across these four major native app stores. Due to such enormous number of apps, both the constituents in the app ecosytem, consumers and app developers, face problems in terms of 'app discovery'. For consumers, it is a daunting task to discover the apps they like and need among the huge number of available apps. Likewise, for developers, getting their apps discovered in the pool of an enormous number of apps is a challenge. To address these issues, Mobilewalla provides an independent unbiased search engine for mobile apps with semantic search capabilities. It has also developed an objective app rating and scoring mechanism based on user and developer involvement with an app. Such scoring mechanism enables MW to provide a number of other ways to discover apps - such as dynamically maintained 'hot' lists and 'fast rising' lists.

References

1. Android market grows a staggering 861.5 per cent
2. Mobile apps market to reach $38 billion revenue by 2015,
   http://news.brothersoft.com/mobile-apps-market-to-reach-38-billion-revenue-by-2015-6089.html (visited on May 13, 2011)
3. Android market, https://market.android.com/ (visited on May 13, 2011)
4. Apple app store, http://www.istoreus.com/home.html (visited on May 13, 2011)
5. Why native app stores like itunes and android marketplace are bad for mobile developers, http://www.businessinsider.com/why-native-app-stores-like-itunes-and-andoid-marketplace_are-bad-business-for-mobile-developers-2011-5 (visited on May 13, 2011)
6. Would you like to try android apps before buying?,
   http://www.labnol.org/internet/android-apps-try-before-buying/19422/ (visited on May 13, 2011)
7. Appsfire scores $3.6m as app discovery demands grow,
   http://gigaom.com/2011/05/30/appsfire-scores-3-6m-as-app-discovery-demands-grow/ (visited on May 13, 2011)
8. The mobile app discovery problem,
   http://news.cnet.com/8301-30684_3-20011241-265.html (visited on May 13, 2011)

An User-Centric Attribute Based Access Control Model for Ubuquitous Environments

Fei Li[1], Dasun Weerasinghe[1], Dhiren Patel[2], and Muttukrishnan Rajarajan[1]

[1] Centre for Cyber & Security Sciences,
School of Engineering and Mathematical Sciences,
City University London, Northampton Square, London, EC1V 0HB
{Fei.Li,R.Muttukrishnan}@city.ac.uk
[2] Computer Engineering, NIT Surat, India, 395007
dhiren29p@gmail.com

Abstract. The recent developments in mobile platforms are significant, both on the hardware and software fronts. With the huge success of the iPhone and Android phones, more and more companies are entering the mobile application market. However, there are increasing security threats for mobile phone users due to the new generation of attacks targeted purely on mobile environments. Several solutions have been proposed to date, which can generally handle consent in a fixed and coarse-grained way. However, with the increasing usage of mobile devices for high value transactions, the future access control from mobile devices should be based on 'user-centric' challenge response techniques based on the freatures of mobile platforms.The authors present the MLive© framework, a novel approach to establish mutual authentication between the users and the service providers using unique mobile based attirbutes to solve the threats in the mobile environments.

Keywords: Attributes based access control, XACML, privacy, security, mobilepolicy.

1 Introduction

The number of mobile applications based on Android and iOS platforms has an increasing presence in the mobile application stores over the last five years. Online social networks (OSNs) like Facebook, YouTube, and MySpace are encouraging the users of the latest smartphones to download applications onto their handsets to add extra functionalities. These OSNs make the user to be the content producer and are encouraging new users to join the OSNs. Currently there are more than 250 million active users accessing Facebook through their mobile devices [1]. People that use Facebook on their mobile devices are twice as active on Facebook than non-mobile users [1]. Today mobile clients are becoming dominant platform for web browsing and accessing OSNs. The OSN providers collect a large number of users' data. Users usually share their location (including home address, work place etc.) with their friends. These sensitive data should not be collected by the OSN providers. Users

J.Y. Zhang et al. (Eds.): MobiCASE 2011, LNICST 95, pp. 361–367, 2012.

should have the right to decide whether to disclose these data to the others. Hence privacy should be preserved in the OSNs' environments.

Security, privacy and trust as well as the closely related issue of identiy management are considered as important in the mobile user-generated services. The security framework for mobile platform should be flexible, scalabe and interoperable. The Attributes Based Access Control (ABAC) based on XACML (eXtensible Access control Markup Language) can substantially improve the security and management of access control rights on sensitive data. The large adoption of XACML in the access control systems shows the huge success of XACML [2].

In this paper, we present our novel MLive© framework that achieves mutual authentication between both the user and the online service providers. At the same time, users are able to define their personal policies for disclosure of sensitive data, which is a flexible and user-centric approach. Section 2 presents the related work on mobile web-services security. Section 3 describes the MLive© framework in detail. Section 4 discusses the evaluation of the architecture. Section 5 summarizes the work presented in this paper with a short.

2   Related Work

Ubiquitous e-business is one of major topics in intelligent manufacturing system. Ubiquitous e-business environment requires security features including access control. An Ubi-RBAC model [3] which is based on the RBAC model adds new components such as space, space hierarchy, and context constraints. The Ubi-RBAC covers the context awareness and mobility of subjects (human users), which are the key issues of access control in the ubiquitous e-business environment.

There are three major widely used identity management solutions, namely the Liberty Alliance, OpenID and CardSpace from Microsoft. Ahmed et al. [4] analyzed 3GPP standardized OpenID with Generic Bootstrapping Architecure (GBA) protocol which allows cellphone users to use OpenID services based on SIM credentials. The security analysis suggests that the inter-networking of OpenID with GBA is secure in the ProVerif model [5]. However, the protocol breaks under strong adversarial model. The authors in [6] discuss how telecom operators can be part of a mobile security evolution and exploit it commercially by facilitating the adoption of OpenID. They propose a service architecture where the operator is able to exploit the growing acceptance and user base of OpenID by combining it with SIM-authentication.

The CardSpace is a browser and operating system extension that presents a particular user login experience using a wallet-and-identity-card metaphor. However, most of the browsers installed on the cellphones do not have complete functions.

The Liberty Alliance specifications like the Liberty Identity Federation (ID-FF), Identity Web Services Framework (ID-WSF) and Identity Service Interface Specification (ID-SIS) are mainly concerned on federated identity of Internet applications in the current wireless technology especially in mobile networks [7]. Other than OpenID and CardSpace, the Liberty Alliance is based on the notion of federated identity. A federation context is represented by a circle of trust that is constituted by service providers (SPs) and Identity Providers (IdPs) having mutual trust relations. In 2009, it moved to a new organization named Kantara.

3   MLive© Framework

There are five main actors: the consumer, the service providers (SPs), policy evaluation component (PEC), attributes authority (AA) and the identity provider (IdP).

In this scenario, AA is the trusted third party that stores all the attributes, including both the SPs' and the consumers' attributes. Usually, if a SP register at the AA, it will be allocated a unique Service Provider Identity (SPID) as an identity stored at AA. In ABAC systems, a user will be granted access for certain resources based on the related attributes. For the mobile customer, several attributes can be used, such as the *International Mobile Equipment Identity (IMEI), the IP Multimedia Private Identity (IMPI), First Name, Last Name, Email Address, Street, City, State, Country/Region, Postal Code, Home Phone, Date of Birth, Gender, Location and Time.*

In some countries, people have a unique number for their own identity verification. In China, there is an identity card number. In the UK, people have the National Insurance (NI) number. These numbers can be used as a personal identifier for the mobile users. This paper introduces a Unique Identity Number (UIdN) as an important attribute for MLive© security framework. The SPs are registered at the AA and allocated with a SPID. The consumers when registering need to exchange their personal attributes including the UIdN. In our architecture, such sensitive information is stored at AA, and users are able to apply user-defined policies to control the access requests from other entities which are considered un-trusted by the users.

The IdP and the AA has an existing trust relationship. The IdP is a trusted third party. The PEC is the core component of the AA. It will format all the requests as XACML request, evaluate the policies, and perform the access decisions.

The consumer is assumed to access the data and services from the service provider. All transmission of the data and web services are performed over HTTP. The consumer invokes the web service from the SP and needs to register with the IdP first. After registration, the user's details including user name and password will be stored in the IdP and the more sensitive attributes will be stored in AA. In this case, UIdN is the attribute that is stored in the AA.

For a registered consumer, the first step of the schema is to login into the system. Once the IdP receives the request, it will authenticate the user with user name and password method. The consumer will generate a response message and send it to the IdP. If the challenge response is successfully verified, the IdP will generate a local security context for the request. The context contains the information for the consumer, the SP, and the requested sources. After the AA receives the request, it will handle and process the request at three stages.

1. Retrieve the information of the SP, query the AA for the attributes of the SP to check the authenticity of the SP
2. Retrieve the information of the consumer, query the AA for the attributes of the consumer for verification
3. Evaluate the request based on the policies stored in the Policy Repository

Figure 1 shows the main framework. For a registered user, the main message flow will be as illustrated in Figure 2.

For most of the e-business transactions, sometimes the consumers will save their credit/debit card details at the online merchants' web sites as a normal payment in order to save time. However, it is a high risk approach as someone who has the account details of the user could easily carry out an online transaction without any consent.

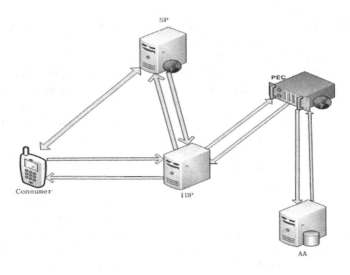

Fig. 1. Proposed Architecture

4   Policy Evaluation

Policy Evaluation Component (PEC) takes charge of XACML policy authentication and authorization. There are 4 main functional components in PEC: the Context Handler (CH), the Policy Enforcement Point (PEP), Validating Point (VP), the Policy Decision Point (PDP), Request Generator (RG), and the Policy Repository.

When a mobile user purchases an item from the SP, he/she needs to request the mobile banking services. Generally, the user is concerned about the authenticity of the SP. At this time, the user needs to check whether it is the real SP that he/she wants to communicate with.

In order to do this, the Validating Point (VP) will compare the attributes of the SP that is received from the IdP and the AA. If the SP is verified, RG will generate a challenge message based on the UIdN received from the AA. PEP will forward the request to the consumer via the IdP. The Consumer's mobile handset will display this request and the user needs to input the correct UIdN. This step is to insure that it is the actual account holder. A response message is generated and will be sent to the PEC. The PEP forwards the response to the VP, if the validation is successful. The CH will format a XACML request and send it to PDP for the policy evaluation. Since the consumer's attributes are collected, these can be used for the further policy evaluation. The PDP will make the decision based on the policies in the policy repository. After this, the PDP sends the results to the PEP.

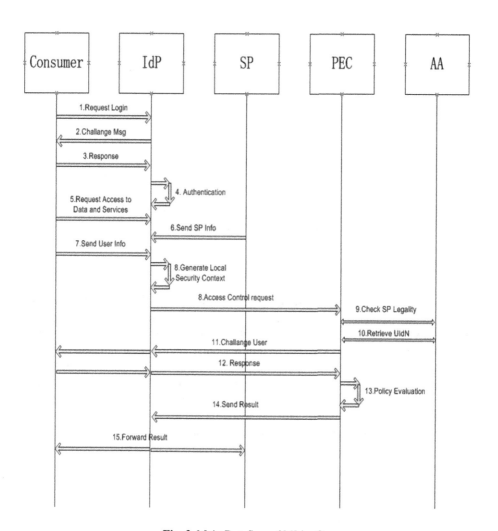

Fig. 2. Main Dataflow of MLive©

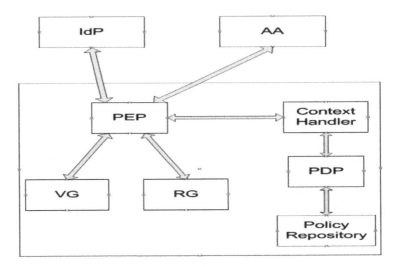

Fig. 3. Policy Evaluation Component (PEC)

5   Conclusion

Attributes based access control, which makes access decisions based on the attributes of requestors, resources, and environment can provide greater flexibility in today's mobile environment. This paper proposed the MLive© framework for access control based on attributes using XACML within a mobile environment domain. XACML defines the security definition and evaluation policies. By using specific attributes that are provided by the mobile users and the service providers in the future, a very secure mobile web services environment can be established and can help to grow the customer confidence and also provide seamless access to their mobile financial services from anywhere, anytime at the touch of a button.

References

1. Facebook Press Room (2010),
   http://www.facebook.com/press/info.php?statistics
2. Ardagna, C.A., De Capitani di Vimercati, S., Paraboschi, S., Pedrini, E., Samarati, P.: Ac XACML-based privacy-centered access control system. In: Proceedings of the First ACM Workshop on Information Security Governance, New York, NY, USA (2009)
3. Oh, S.: New role-based access control in ubiquitous e-business environment. Journal of Intelligent Manufacturing 21(5), 607–612 (2010)
4. Ahmed, A.S., Laud, P.: Formal Security analysis of OpenID with GBA protocol. In: Proceedings of the 3rd International ICST Conference on Security and Privacy in Mobile Information and Communication Systems, Aalborg, Denmark (May 2011)

5. Ahmed, A.S., Laud P.: ProVerif model files for the OpenID with GBA protocol (2011), http://research.cyber.ee (last accessed March 30, 2011)
6. Jrstad, I., Johansen, T.A., Bakken, E., Eliasson, C., Fiedler, M., Do van Thanh, M.: Releasing the potential of OpenID & SIM. In: Intelligence in Next Generation Networks. ICIN (October 2009)
7. Srirama, S.N., Jarke, M., Prinz, W.: A Performance Evaluation of Mobile Web Services Security. In: 3rd Internation. Conference on Web Information Systems and Technologies, March 3-6, pp. 386–392. INSTICC Press (2007)

Are You Burning Fat?

Vishnu Dantu[1] and Srikanth Jonnada[2]

[1] Clark High School, Plano Independent School District, Plano, TX 75075, USA
[2] University of North Texas, Denton TX 76203, USA

Abstract. Obesity is the major contributor of several diseases and results in higher healthcare cost to our society. Diet and exercise can improve fitness level and hence better health. But, people need an easy way
of knowing if they are in their fat-burning zone during exercise. In addition, the measuring device needs to be non-invasive and ubiquitous. In
this project we devised a technique of detecting the right heart zone and
we believe this can be achieved at no-cost by using the "always-available"
mobile phone. We used the camera and flash in NexusOne mobile phone
for capturing the color intensity of finger pulse during heartbeats. In
addition, we are able to extract the respiratory pattern from the heartbeats. From this, we are trying to find the anaerobic threshold of person
using the variation in Inhalation and Exhalation during exercise. With
this we will be able to find the heart rate zone at which a person stops
burning his fat and starts burning his carbohydrates. To our knowledge
there is no research reported on the analysis of burning fat based on the
measurements from a mobile device.

Keywords: Mobile phone, Respiratory patterns, Anaerobic Threshold.

1 Introduction

Over the past 20 years, there has been a startling increase in the amount of obese in
America. Statistically, almost 3 out of every 10 adults are obese as of 2009 (26.7%
of America's population). This is up from 2007 which showed a percentage of 25.6.
Obesity is a medical condition that is easy to recognize, however, there are no
treatments for obesity. Between 16 and 33 percent of children are obese currently.
Soon enough, there will be an overwhelming of Americans (adults and children)
who will be obese in 20-30 years [1]. Among these are our children and the next
generation of Americans. These numbers will continue to increase until something
drastic is changed in their lifestyle. A common and natural treatment of obesity is
exercise. Many obese people looking to lose weight try exercise, however not many
obese people actually lose a significant amount of weight after lengthy periods of
exercise. Aerobic Exercise is a traditional way of burning fat. Aerobic exercise is
not meant to be intense. During aerobic exercise, a person reaches their anaerobic
threshold. A person's anaerobic threshold is the threshold when they stop burning an efficient amount of fat and they start to burn carbohydrates. When people
exercise, they naturally pass this threshold, and from that moment forward, they
are not burning a significant amount of fat [2]. There is a corresponding heart

J.Y. Zhang et al. (Eds.): MobiCASE 2011, LNICST 95, pp. 368–373, 2012.
© Institute for Computer Sciences, Social Informatics and Telecommunications Engineering 2012

rate to a person's anaerobic threshold, if this heart rate is not surpassed then the person will burn the fat that they are looking to burn from their exercise. If a person could know their anaerobic threshold, then they could burn fat rapidly over a few weeks and months instead of years. It is always beneficial to know the heart rate corresponding to the anaerobic threshold during exercise. A person's anaerobic threshold changes constantly based on the fitness level; this is why it needs to be continuously monitored if one wants to continue to burn fat (also not carbohydrates) and achieve their weight-loss goal. The world's society looks at smart phones as if a necessity in our time. This is one of the advantages a smart phone contains; its abundance in our world and the heavy use of it in our society. This is why the smart phone is a special no-cost-device compared to special-purpose devices made by vendors. In particular, there is one tool that the smart phone has to offer that makes it useful to many researchers; this is the camera of a smart phone. The heart is the main organ of the human body which is in charge of pumping blood to all of the limbs of the body. When the finger is placed under a close light fixture, it is possible to analyze a person's blood flow to the finger. Figure 1 shows the locations where pulse can be found on human body.

Fig. 1. Where pulse can be found on human body

The finger glows bright red under heavy light fixture. Analyzing the finger-image under this light fixture, a person can see when the heart is pumping blood into the finger through the arteries. When observed, a person can see the finger blinking periodically. This is because of the heart pumping blood into the finger and then returning the blood back towards the heart to refill it with oxygen from the lungs and then to pump it to another limb in the body. When the finger-image is blinking, this also represents the beats of the heart pumping blood to the limbs of the body.

Fig. 2. Measurement being taken with finger on the camera lens

When the finger is placed on the camera 2 and flash, a video of the finger is being taken. This allows us to analyze the finger more clearly.

2   Methodology

A smart phone is used to analyze the respiratory pattern of a person during exercise. When a smart phone camera along with a flash is placed on the finger of a person, it will be able to capture the blood flow i.e., the variation of color intensity of blood in the finger. This process is similar to the Photoplethysmography(PPG) technique [3] without using the wavelength of light for analysis. Using the intensity variations, we are able to capture the pulse from the finger. This model works on a principle that, every heart beat pertains to a rush of blood in the blood vessels, even in the capillaries at the finger-tips. Whenever the capillaries are rich in blood during a systolic pulse, more light is getting absorbed by the blood, leading to low reflective index and darker frame intensities. Likewise, during a diastolic pulse, most of the light gets reflected leading to bright frames. This change in intensity of light which can pass through the finger creates an alternative pattern of waves similar to a pulse. Figure 3 shows the pulse wave obatined through video by placing the finger on the camera lens.

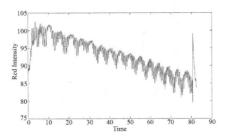

Fig. 3. Pulse waves obtained from finger

Figure 4 shows the analyzed area in a video frame. Initially the video frames were split into four quadrants and only the first quadrant was considered for analysis, since we observed most of the changes and fluctuations are predominant in that region. Every pixel information on each frame was split into individual Red(R), Blue(B) and Green(G) components. For accuracy of plots, we considered only the Rc in video frames. The average intensity of pixels for every frame was calculated as its frame intensity.

Breathing pattern can be obtained from the pulse waveform [4]. The derivation of breathing pattern requires filtering of pulse wave. In the derivation of respiratory pattern, we passed the camera feed from the subject's finger through a 10th order running median averaging filter implemented as a smoothing function. Figure 5 shows the working of respiratory pattern detection from finger pulse. The inhalation and exhalation patterns are split from a breath basing on the peak and time stamp of a breath wave. Figure 6 shows how the Inhalation and Exhalation patterns are divided from a breath wave. Research is in

Fig. 4. Area under analysis

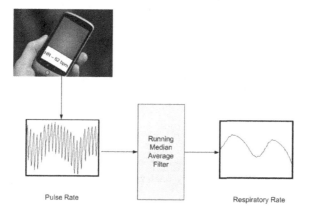

Fig. 5. Model of respiratory pattern with mobile phone

progress to analyze the anaerobic threshold of a person basing on the Inhalation and Exhalation variation. Once we are able to find the Exercise Intensity from the variation in Inhalation and Exhalation pattern [5] we will be able to find the anaerobic threshold of a person [6]. We are calculating the area of Inhalation and

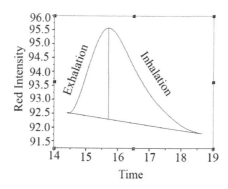

Fig. 6. Inhalation and Exhalation from a breath wave

Exhalation for analyzing the variation between them. Video frames are collected from different people of different age, fitness are being analyzed.

3   Results

Respiratory patterns of a person were calculated at different situations. Figure 7 shows the respiratory pattern during deep breathing. We can observe that all the breaths are similar during deep breathing. Figure 8 shows the respiratory pattern of a person during exercise at a heart rate of 144bpm. In Figure 9 we can clearly observe that the person is gasping for air, as there is a short exhalation and long inhalation immediately.

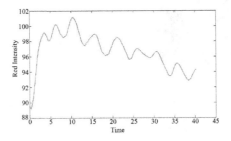

Fig. 7. Respiratory pattern of deep breathing

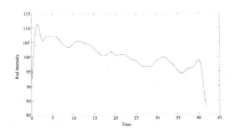

Fig. 8. Respiratory pattern during excercise

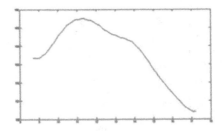

Fig. 9. Inhalation and Exhalation while gasping for air

4   Future Work

We are analyzing the Inhalation and Exhalation pattern of people during exercise which could help in deriving the anaerobic threshold of a person. Different categories of people of age, fitness are being considered for analysis. With the variations in Inhalation and Exhalation patterns we will be able to derive a formula for calculating the anaerobic threshold in terms of heart rate

5   Conclusion

The analysis pattern explained in the paper could lead to an efficient technique which could help us in finding the anaerobic threshold of a person. This could be of high benefit for the obese people who are trying to burn their fat but could not due to lack of awareness of exercise pattern. This application will be available for free to everyone and easily accessible by all categories of people.

References

1. http://www.cdc.gov/obesity/data/trends.html
2. http://www.rice.edu/jenky/sports/anaerobic.threshold.html
3. Allen, J.: Photoplethysmography and its application in clinicalphysiological measurement. Physiol. Meas. 28, R1–R39 (2007)
4. Johansson, A., Stromberg, T.: The respiratory Induced variation of the photo plethysmogram. J. Clin. Monit. 16, 575–581 (2000)
5. Park, S.H., Jang, D.G., Son, D.H., Zhu, W., Hahn, M.S.: A biofeedback-based breathing induction system. In: 3rd International Conference on Bioinformatics and Biomedical Engineering, pp. 1–4 (2009)
6. Rapoport, B.I.: Metabolic factors limiting performance in marathon runners. PLoS Computational Biol. 6(10), e1000960 (2010)

Cognitive Load Based Adaptive Assistive Technology Design for Reconfigured Mobile Android Phone

Gahangir Hossain and Mohammed Yeasin

Electrical and Computer Engineering, The University of Memphis,
Memphis TN, USA
{ghossain,myeasin}@memphis.edu

Abstract. In assistive technology design, it is indispensible to consider the sensory, physical and cognitive level of target users. Cognitive load is an important indicator of cognitive feedback during interaction and became the critical research issue in designing assistive user interfaces, incorporated with smartphone based assistive technology like in the android platform. In this paper, we proposed a cognitive load based user interface integrated with reconfigured mobile android phone (R-MAP) based on user's cognitive load level. We performed some cognitive tasks within a small group of sighted but blindfolded people and blind people or visually impaired using R-MAP. Based on task performance and cognitive load levels we manually annotated some data of 24 participants and finally applied some machine learning algorithms to automate the mobile interface. Based on our novel design and experimental finding, we recommended that "cognitive load enabled feedbacks based assistive user interface" would be a useful assistive tool for the people who use mobile phone for their daily operations.

Keywords: Assistive technology, android phone, cognitive load, virtual sound, user interface.

1   Introduction

Smart phone as an assistive technology tool became popular to the users who are mostly dependent on them. Blind people or visual impaired feel more comfortable using feedback enabled user interfaces for day-to-day operations. In this study we used Reconfigured Mobile Android Phone (R-MAP), a fully integrated standalone system that has an easy-to-use interface to reconfigure an Android mobile phone with assistive virtual sound (VS) feedback [1]. The ultimate goal of this study is to design an automated feedback enabled mobile phone user interface based on cognitive load of the people who use it as an assistive technology tool. Along this direction, the very first objective we considered is to measure cognitive load. The second objective was to map different task based on task-complexity. The third challenge considered was to use machine learning algorithms to automate the user interface. Hence, the objective set was to find relatively better algorithm based on cognitive load classification performance.

J.Y. Zhang et al. (Eds.): MobiCASE 2011, LNICST 95, pp. 374–380, 2012.
© Institute for Computer Sciences, Social Informatics and Telecommunications Engineering 2012

Cognitive load [3][4] refers to the amount of working memory load imposed on the human cognitive capacity when performing a particular task. Measuring cognitive load of people who are blind or visually impaired can be considered different, because of their different memory model, their more active phonological loop and special sketchpad rather than visuospatial sketchpad [5][6].

People having problem with any one organs are categorized in assistive group. The memory model of assistive technology user is therefore different and their cognitive capabilities demand special consideration in designing technology tools using mobile phone.

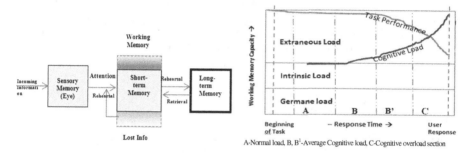

Fig. 1. Human memory system

Fig. 2. Working memory capacity and cognitive load

In particular working memory is considered very sensitive to extraneous load. When working memory capacity exceeds the available resources for a task, we feel cognitively overloaded. The scenario can be explained by a simple graph in Fig. 2. It is the job of user interface designer to make the layout and presentation material as simple as possible for the user to better understand with few working memory resources and to reduce extraneous cognitive load.

In this study two types of cognitive load measurement are considered. The objective method we adopted into R-MAP is the secondary task based performance rating with VS feedback. Another method is the subjective rating of formative questionnaires representing three types of cognitive load index (intrinsic load, extraneous load and germane load) that is administered during post experiment interview [8].

The rest of the paper is organized as following: Section 2 describes a brief literature review on cognitive load, assistive technology tools and relationship of human memory model. In Section 3 the design of R-MAP interface is explained. In Section 4 the experimental protocol is explained. Finally in section 5 experimental results are explained with discussion and possible future improvements.

2   State of the Art

Measuring cognitive load in ordinal cognitive load scale is important in designing an optimal interaction approach between humans and assistive technology systems in order to produce the highest task performance. These loads deal with mental processes of learning, memory and problem solving. Sweller [14] defined the Cognitive Load theory. There are three types of cognitive loads [15][16], namely intrinsic, extraneous and germane. The cognitive load theory suggests increasing the germane load while decreasing intrinsic and extraneous load. In task description, decision task involves different form of Boolean or fuzzy based decisions. Memory retrieval task involves query and information retrieval from main memory or secondary memory. Presentation format is the representation of task materials which is organized (with data structure) or unorganized form.

Recently, Pradipta and Rabinson [13] proposed a novel approach, user interface simulator, to designing and evaluating inclusive systems by modeling users' performance with a wide range of abilities. Another method with i-phone touch screen based cognitive interfaces is researched by Young et al.[12], expecting the future generation of computer based system will need cognitive user interfaces to achieve sufficient, robust and intelligent human interaction.

3   Design of Interface

In our study we applied a similar approach using assistive technology tool R-MAP [1], and our own designed user interface to discover the similarities and differences of cognitive performances shown by blindfolded and blind subjects. A mini-shallow structure user interface like Fig. 3 in R-MAP is experimented.

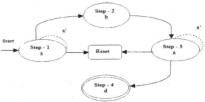

Fig. 3. R-MAP mini-shallow structure interface Layout

Fig. 4. Automata of R-MAP operation (interface interaction)

Considering space of the interface operation, only two /three special locations are selected for operational execution. In depth of interface operation only two layer of information, same locations are used twice for two steps. For example, step 2 and step 4 works in same location. In addition to these two locations for the secondary task purpose a third location 'a' that is basically instructional shifted location of 'a' (dashed marked box in the figure) is included in this design. Therefore, it is a mixed mini-shallow structure layout of interface. An automaton of this interface is shown in Fig. 4.

4   Experiment and Data

4.1   The Experiment

Twenty four subjects (20 sighted but blind-folded and 4 blind people) participated in this study. Among them 12 subjects (including 2 blind people) are selected as expert based on their prior smart phone use experience. All subjects had first a quick tutorial to learn how to use the system. In each session, the R-MAP and a text book is provided to the subject.

In primary task, subjects are asked to use the assistive tool (R-MAP) for their daily purpose; reading labels of text in object and location, reading from text book etc. The secondary task consisted is an interruption task (dual-task) to keep track of the shift of the operational location with continuous visual monitoring task. More specifically, in this experiment the primary task was set to read a text from a book provided to them. They were asked to open the book and to reach any text location. The operation of R-MAP with four steps and sound feedback is shown in Fig. 5.

Step-1, 3

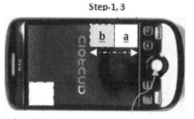 

Step-2, 4   **Reset button**

Fig. 5. RMAP with virtual sound feedback for secondary task
Step-1: Open application, // *Virtual sound alert (VS1 or VS2)*, **Step-2:** Enter into capture mode. **Step-3:** Capture image,   // *Virtual sound alert (Vs1 or VS2)*,   Pause for 5-20 sec. **Step-4:** Speech (Voice o/p).

In secondary task, R-MAP operation was changed a little with guidance of two virtual sounds (VS_1 and VS_2) following speech based cognitive load measurement technique [9][10]. A special shift of first push location (*'a' to 'b' or 'b' to 'a'*) in R-MAP (Fig. 5) was made with VS_1. The second virtual sound VS_2, instructed subject to push the reset button to cancel secondary task mode. The task performance was scored by the examiner in 0-5 range. The more mistakes means subjects were cognitively overloaded. The highest score 5 which indicates the subject were fully loaded with secondary task. The cognitive load scores were then computed separately. Z-score normalization was used before computing the cognitive load index. Dependent variables considered for the secondary task were reaction times (RTs) and accuracy. We computed cognitive load index to find tentative cognitive load of a person performed all three tasks or partially one or two tasks. CLI was calculated by cumulative averaging of task performance and normalizing with respect to total task scores. We also followed an annotation guideline of overload (High load –HL), average load (AL) and Low Load (LL) from some earlier literature [4]. For simplicity and useful operation, we ignored LL and consider only AL and HL as a feature for our classification. The four blind people spontaneously participated in all tasks and showed good performance with significant load. Based on their task performance and cognitive load level we manually labeled all data of 24 participants and finally applied three machine learning algorithm (J48, Random forest and Naïve Bays) from Weka toolbox [7].

4.2   Data

A sample of data we collected is shown in Table 1 below. The task value -1 indicates that participant did not participate in that task. Error value is the cumulative sum of number of errors a participant did in three different tasks.

Table 1. Sample data

UsersID	Age	Ethnicity	Subjects	Gender	Smart Phone User	# of Tasks	Task types	Task-1	Task-2	Task-3	Error	CLI	Load Type
User-1	29	Asian	BF	M	N	1	E	3	-1	-1	3	3	HL
User-4	31	American	BF	F	Y	3	E,M,C	0	1	3	4	1.333333	AL
User-7	30	African	BF	F	Y	2	E,M	0	4	-1	4	2	HL
User-10	30	American	BF	M	N	2	E,M	0	3	-1	3	1.5	AL
User-25	42	American	BP	M	Y	3	E,M,C	0	1	2	3	1	AL

*n- novice user, y- expert user, M- Male, F- Female, BF- Blind-folded, BP- Blind People,
E- Easy, M-Moderate, C-Complex, CLI – cognitive load index, HL – high load (Overload), AL – Average load.

5   Results

We applied Welch's *t-test* with 95% confidence interval and standard error calculation on the preprocessed data before application of machine learning algorithms for classification. The result is shown in Table 2a and Table 2b.

Table 2a. Cognitive load score comparison between Non-expert group and Expert group

	Cognitive Load (Subjective)		Cognitive Load (Secondary Task)	
	M	SD	M	SD
Non-Expert (N=12)	6	2	3.73	0.79
Expert (N=12)	3.33	0.65	2.73	0.90
t-value	4.391		0.361	
p-value	0.0007		0.0123	

Table 2b. Cognitive Load Score comparison between blindfolded and visual impaired

	Cognitive Load (Subjective)		Cognitive Load (Secondary Task)	
	M	SD	M	SD
Blind Folded (N =20)	5.2	0.95	3.65	0.93
VP (N =4)	6.312	0.77	4.25	0.96
t-value	2.5193		1.1489	
p-value	0.0532		0.3146	

Table 2a. shows the *t* values during error calculation and two-tailed p-value for significance judgment. As non-expert subjects do not have prior smart phone use experience, the result shows that in all case of cognitive load measure, difference between non-expert and expert are statistically significant. For same test on blindfolded versus visually impaired people (Table 2b) shows significant differences. In case of subjective cognitive load, the difference is considered not quite statistically significant and same for the secondary task performance. Box and whisker diagram (Fig. 6) are also plotted to see the impression of sample data.

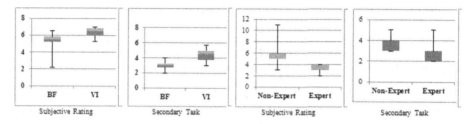

Fig. 6. Cognitive Load assessments between sighted but Blindfolded (BF) and Visual Impaired (VI)

J48, Random Forest and Naïve Bayes classifiers were used with 10 fold cross validation. Random Forest shows relatively better performance. The performance classification is shown in table 3.

Table 3. Performance Classification

Classifier	Accuracy (%)	Kappa
J48	72	3.91
Random Forest	78	4.32
Naïve Bayes	67	3.56

6   Conclusion

This study signifies the difference of blindfolded subjects to act as a blind people during cognitive experiment through android phone based assistive interface. It also supports the evidence of different cognitive map, sometimes superior performance shown by people who are blind or visually impaired based on smart phone use experience. As a novel step to automate an assistive interface, the random forest algorithm found better to classify cognitive load indices based on the sample data. In future we are working with more blind subjects and different methods for load measurement and adaptation to improve the existing ststem.

Acknowledgment. This project is partially funded by National Science Foundation (NSF-IIS-0746790), USA.

References

1. Shaik, A., Hossain, G., Yeasin, M.: Design, development and performance evaluation of reconfigured mobile Android phone for people who are blind or visually impaired. In: ACM SIGDOC 2010, pp. 159–166. ACM, New York (2010)
2. Klatzky, R.L., Marston, J.R., Giudice, N.A., Golledge, R.G., Loomis, J.M.: Cognitive load of navigating without vision when guided by virtual sound versus spatial language. Journal of Experimental Psychology: Applied 12, 223–232 (2006)
3. Paas, F., Tuovinen, J.E., Tabbers, H.K., Van Gerven, P.W.M.: Cognitive load measurement as a means to advance cognitive load theory. Educational Psychologist 38(1), 63–71 (2003)
4. Paas, F., Merriënboer, J.J.G.: Instructioqnal control of cognitive load in the training of complex cognitive tasks. Educational Psychology Review 6, 51–71 (1994)
5. Pylyshyn, Z.: Return of the mental image: are there really pictures in the brain? Opinion. TRENDS in Cognitive Sciences 7(3) (March 2003)
6. Chen, M., Huang, C., Wang, C.: Difference on Spatial Working Memory between the Blind and Sighted People. In: APIEMS 2008 Proceedings of The 9th Asia Pasific Industrial Engineering & Management Systems Conference (2008)
7. Weka Machine Learning tool, http://www.cs.waikato.ac.nz/ml/weka/
8. Yin, B., Chen, F., Ruiz, N., Ambikairajah, E.: Speech-based cognitive load monitoring system. In: Proc. IEEE ICASSP, pp. 2041–2044 (2008)
9. Cierniak, G., Scheiter, K., Gerjets, P.: Explaining the split-attention effect: Is the reduction of extraneous cognitive load accompanied by an increase in germane cognitive load? Computers in Human Behavior 25, 315–324 (2009)
10. Brunken, R., Steinbacher, S., Plass, J.L., Leutner, D.: Assessment of cognitive load in multimedia learning using dual-task methodology. Experimental Psychology 49(2), 109–119 (2002)
11. Welch, B.L.: The significance of the difference between two means when the population variances are unequal. Biometrika 29, 350–362 (1938)
12. Young, S.: Cognitive User Interfaces. Signal Processing Magazine 27(3), 128–140 (2010)
13. Biswas, P., Robinson, P.: Automatic evaluation of assistive interfaces. In: International Conference on Intelligent User Interfaces, Hong Kong (February 2010)
14. Sweller, J., Chandler, P.: Why some material is difficult to learn. Cognition and Instruction 12(3), 185–233 (1994)
15. Su, J., Rosenzweig, A., Goel, A., de Lara, E., Truong, K.N.: Enabling the Visually-Impaired to Use Maps on Touch-Enabled Devices. In: Proceedings of MOBILECHI (2010)
16. Miller, G.A.: The Magical Number Seven, Plus or Minus Two: Some Limits on Our Capacity for Processing Information. The Psychological Review 63, 81–97 (1956)
17. Thomas, C.: Real-Time Sound/Image Manipulation and Mapping in a Performance Setting.pdf. Music/Special Studies, Brown University, http://www.ciufo.org/media/sound_image.pdf
18. Keogan, A.: Flowing Rhythms – The Creation of a Rhythm-based Imager and Lumia, masters thesis, Interaction Design Centre, Dept. of CSIS, University of Limerick, Limerick, Ireland

Towards Location and Trajectory Privacy Protection in Participatory Sensing

Sheng Gao[1], Jianfeng Ma[1], Weisong Shi[2], and Guoxing Zhan[2]

[1] Xidian University, Xi'an, Shaanxi 710071, China
[2] Wayne State University, Detroit, MI 48202, USA
{sgao,jfma}@mail.xidian.edu.cn, {weisong,gxzhan}@wayne.edu

Abstract. The ubiquity of mobile devices has facilitated the prevalence of participatory sensing, whereby ordinary citizens using their private mobile devices to collect regional information and share with participators. However, such applications may endanger users' privacy by revealing their locations and trajectories information. Most of existing solutions, which hide a user's location information with a coarse region, are under *k-anonymity* model. Yet, they may not be applicable in some participatory sensing applications which require precise location information for high quality of service. In this paper, we present a method to protect the user's location and trajectory privacy with high quality of service in some participatory sensing applications. Then, we utilize a new metric, called *Slope Ratio (SR)*, to evaluate the method we proposed. The analysis and simulation results show that the method can protect the user's location and trajectory privacy effectively.

Keywords: participatory sensing, location privacy, trajectory privacy, similarity.

1   Introduction

Participatory Sensing [1] is the process whereby individuals and communities use evermore-capable mobile phones and cloud services to collect and analysis systematic data for use in discovery. However, when a user asks for a certain application, she uploads the request data to servers which are invariably tagged with the location (obtained from the embedded GPS in the phone or using Wi-Fi based localization) and time when the readings are recorded. The mobile sensor data may reveal the user's location at particular time which is related to the user's identity information. It may invade the user's privacy information seriously. We also consider that the user's motion pattern may reveal her trajectory privacy. *Background knowledge attack* [2] exploits the prior knowledge about the user to conclude her privacy information.

In this paper, we aim to protect a user's location and trajectory privacy in participatory sensing applications which require precise location information. We exploit the user's partners to construct an anonymous set, called an equivalence class. The user and her partners send the same service request and their precise locations information to Application Server for high quality of service. The user's location can be concealed by the equivalence class. To protect the user's trajectory privacy, we construct the mapping relationship between the two equivalence classes. The partners'

J.Y. Zhang et al. (Eds.): MobiCASE 2011, LNICST 95, pp. 381–386, 2012.
© Institute for Computer Sciences, Social Informatics and Telecommunications Engineering 2012

trajectories should be similar to the user's trajectory so that it cannot be distinguished by adversary. Also, we utilize a new metric *Slope Ratio (SR)* to evaluate the method we propose and implement the simulation system with practical data.

2   Related Work

K-anonymity is originally proposed by Sweeney [3] in the database community to protect sensitive information from being disclosed. This can be achieved by sending a sufficiently large *"k-anonymous region"* that encloses *k* users in space, instead of reporting a single GPS coordinate. Much work has been done to protect location privacy based on *k-anonymity* model [4, 5]; whereas, little work has been done to achieve privacy protection while providing precise location information.

2.1   Coarse-grained Locations Privacy Protection

Tang et al [6] presented ASGKA protocol to build safe group and design a cycle-like structure to make group member have safe status. However, they didn't consider the user's mobility. Beresford and Stajano [7, 8] proposed Mix Zone concept in which a trusted proxy removes all samples before it passes location samples to Application Server. The degree of privacy offered by the Mix Zone was evaluated for pedestrian traffic under the assumption that an adversary used empirical linking. The concept of tessellation was first introduced in AnonySense [9] to protect user's privacy when reporting context information. Tessellation partitions a geographical area into a number of tiles large enough to preserve the user's privacy and each user's location is generalized to a plane in space which covers at least *k* potential users.

2.2   Fine-grained Locations Privacy Protection

Kido et al. [10] proposed a way to anonymize a user's location information. The personal user of a location-based service generates several false position data (dummies) sent to the service provider with the true position data of the user. Because the service provider cannot distinguish the genuine position data, the user's location privacy is protected. Huang et al. [2] proposed a simple modification to tessellation based on micro-aggregation. They presented an application——PetrolWatch which allows users to automatically collect, contribute and share petrol price information using camera phones. Dong et al. [11] proposed a method to preserve location privacy by anonymizing coarse-grained location and retaining fine fine-grained locations using Attribute Based Encryption.

2.3   Trajectory Privacy Protection

You et al [12] proposed two schemes, namely, *random pattern scheme* and *rotation pattern scheme,* to generate dummies that exhibit long-term user movement patterns. The random scheme randomly generates dummies with consistent movement pattern, while the rotation pattern explores the idea of creating intersection among moving trajectories.

3   Methodology

3.1   Basic System Structure

The very basic architecture of a participatory sensing system consists of collection of mobile nodes (MNs), some Access Points (APs), Report Server (RS), and Application Server (AS). In Participatory Sensing, MNs collect relevant regional information and send these reports to RS to aggregate, and then send the reports to AS which is showed by Figure.1.

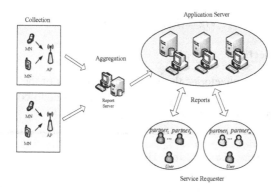

Fig. 1. The basic structure of participatory sensing

3.2   Location Privacy with High Quality of Service

In this section, we present a method to solve the contradictory between the location privacy and high quality of service. Given that no trust server is available, meanwhile, wireless networks are only responsible for communication and won't reveal a user's locations privacy. A user forms an equivalence class by selecting a certain number of partners. The process of partners' selection will be discussed in Section 3.3. There are six partners in the equivalence class which is shown by Figure.2. We argue that the partners won't reveal the user's location information to the AS. The user sends relevant information including her identity signature and requirement to her partners. They verify the user's legality and obtain each coordinate through GPS which are listed as follows: $(L_1, L_2...L_6)$.

(Step1.Service Request) In order to obtain high quality of service and protect privacy information at the same time, the user and her partners send the same service request to the servers which describe as $(L, Request), (L_1, Request), (L_2, Request)... (L_6, Request)$.

(Step2.Service Query) In participatory sensing applications, the AS exploits the information shared by the mobile sensing devices to provide services. Through the precise locations information, it gets the result reports which describe as follows: $(L, Result), (L_1, Result_1), (L_2, Result_2)... (L_6, Result_6)$. Then the AS returns the service result reports to the equivalence class.

(Step3. Service Distribution) All members in the equivalence class receive the result reports. Only the user can pick out the result she desires with her precise location information. The possibility the user can be distinguished will be analyzed in Section 4.

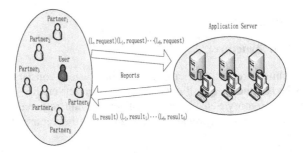

Fig. 2. The Process of Service

3.3   Partners Selection

In order to produce the trajectories those are similar to that of the user. In this paper, we adopt distance-based method to select partners. The pseudo code of the partners' selection is given in Algorithm as follows:

```
T: The public time interval
Input: (Map information, User information)
Output: Partners of the user
```

```
1.  Procedure
2.    Do {
3.      For i=1: k
4.        Convert map information into Coordinate axis;
5.        User's location (x, y) && Destination location (m_i, n_i)
6.        D (i) = sqrt ((x-m_i)^2+(y-n_i)^2);
7.      End;
8.        Sort (D);
9.        Send (signature (UsrID));
10.  If signature (UsrID) & participators haven't been selected;
11.      Location [1: k] =response (PartnerLocation, PartnerID);
12.  End;
13.  Select k different participators as the user's partners;
14.  Record their coordinates to form an equivalence class;
15.    } while (User's next location! =User's current location);
```

3.4   Trajectory Privacy Protection

In this section, we focus on the user's trajectory privacy protection. We exploit the user's partners to construct two equivalence classes. Through mapping the two equivalence classes, we can produce the partners' trajectories that are similar to that of the user in an interval time *T*. Since the crooked trajectory can be divided into several linear trajectories, we assume the user's trajectory is linear in an interval time *T*. When she moves from a to b showed by Figure.3, she selects several partners in the two equivalence classes separately by the algorithm we propose in section 3.3. We can hide the user's trajectory by constructing the partners' trajectories between the two equivalence classes. Based on the distance between the user and her partners, the partners' trajectories we construct are similar to that of the user. We will utilize a new metric *Slope Ratio (SR)* to evaluate the similarity between the user's trajectory and that of her partners. It will be discussed in section 4.

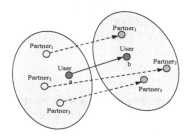

Fig. 3. The trajectories of the user and her partners

4   Experiment and Results

4.1   Theoretical Calculation

The user takes k partners to construct an equivalence class. When she moves to another location, she follows the same operation to form another equivalence class including m partners. At present, we get two equivalence classes in the interval time T. Through the mapping relationship, we can get $min \{(k+1), (m+1)\}$ trajectories. Only one of them is the user's real trajectory.

We assume the user and her partners can be distinguished at the same probability. Adversary may get all locations and trajectories information.

1) Location probability. There are k and m participators in the two equivalence classes separately, the probabilities the real user's location information can be distinguished are $P_1=1/(k+1)$ and $P_2=1/(m+1)$.

2) Trajectory probability. Since the partners' trajectories are similar to the user's real trajectory, $min \{(k+1), (m+1)\}$ trajectories have been constructed so that the probability of getting the real trajectory is $P_3=1/min \{(k+1), (m+1)\}$.

4.2   System Simulation

We utilize a new metric *Slope Ratio (SR)* to evaluate the similarity of trajectory between the user and her partners.

Definition 1. *(Slope Ratio)* In an interval time T, we assume the user's trajectory is linear. We get the user's source location coordinate $A(x_1, y_1)$ and the destination coordinate $B(x_2, y_2)$. The user's trajectory slope can be calculated by $k= (y_2-y_1)/(x_2-x_1)$. Similarly, we can get the partners' trajectories slope $k_2, k_3 \ldots k_m$. *Slope Ratio* is defined as $\alpha(\alpha = k_i/k_1, i=2,3,\cdots m)$, where when α is within the threshold we define, the two trajectories are considered to be similar.

Definition 2. (*Indistinguishability*) When the ratio α of partners' trajectories slope $k_i (i=2,3,\cdots)$ to the user trajectories slope k_1 is within $[0,+\sigma]$, we consider the user's trajectory and her partners' trajectories cannot be distinguished. σ is a threshold, defined by the user.

We have implemented the simulation system with practical data. Detailed evaluation results are available at the technical report version of the paper [13]. The metric shows that the method can protect the user's location and trajectory privacy effectively.

5   Conclusions

In this paper, we propose a method to protect user's location privacy while providing precise location information. Through selecting a certain number of user's partners to construct an equivalence class, we can hide the user's location. Besides, we propose an algorithm to construct several trajectories that are closer to that of the user, which can effectively prevent adversary from identifying the user's trajectory. Finally, we utilize a new metric *Slope Ratio* to analyze the results in theory and experiment.

References

1. Burke, J., Estrin, D., Hansen, M.: Participatory Sensing. In: Workshop on World Sensor Web: Mobile Device Centric Sensor Networks and Applications, USA, pp. 117–134 (2006)
2. Huang, K.L., Kanhere, S.S., Hu, W.: Preserving privacy in participatory sensing systems. Computer Communications 33, 1266–1280 (2010)
3. Sweeney, L.: K-anonymity: A model for protecting privacy. International Journal Of Uncertainty Fuzziness And Knowledge Based Systems, 557–570 (2002)
4. Gruteser, M., Grunwald, D.: Anonymous usage of location-based service through spatial and temporal cloaking. In: Proceeding of the First International Conference on Mobile Systems, Applications, and Service, pp. 31–42 (2003)
5. Gedik, B., Liu, L.: Protecting Location Privacy with Personalized k-anonymity: Architecture and Algorithms. IEEE Transactions on Mobile Computing, 1–18 (2008)
6. Tang, M., Wu, Q.H., Zhang, G.P., He, L.L., Zhang, H.G.: A New Scheme of LBS Privacy Protection. In: Proceedings of the 5th International Conference on Wireless Communications, Networking and Mobile Computing, pp. 1–6 (2009)
7. Beresford, A.R., Stajano, F.: Location Privacy in Pervasive Computing. IEEE Pervasive Computing 2(1), 46–55 (2003)
8. Beresford, A.R., Stajano, F.: Mix zones: User privacy in location-aware services. In: IEEE Workshop on Pervasive Computing and Communication Security, pp. 127–131 (2004)
9. Kapadia, A., Triandopoulos, N., Cornelius, C., Peebles, D., Kotz, D.: AnonySense: Opportunistic and privacy-preserving context collection. Computer Science (2008)
10. Kido, H., Yanagisawa, Y., Satoh, T.: An anonymous communication technique using dummies for location-based service. In: Proceedings of International Conference on Pervasive Service, pp. 88–97 (2005)
11. Dong, K., Gu, T., Tao, X.P., Lu, J.: Privacy protection in participatory sensing applications requiring fine-grained locations. In: 16th International Conference on Parallel and Distributed Systems, pp. 9–16 (2010)
12. You, T.H., Peng, W.C., Lee, W.C.: Protecting moving trajectories with dummies. In: 2007 International Conference on Mobile Data Management, pp. 278–282 (2007)
13. Gao, S., Ma, J., Shi, W., Zhan, G.: Technical Report MIST-TR-2011-101 (March 2011)

A New Key Delivering Platform Based on NFC Enabled Android Phone and Dual Interfaces EAP-TLS Contactless Smartcards

Pascal Urien and Christophe Kiennert

Telecom ParisTech, 23 avenue d'Italie Paris 75013, France
EtherTrust, 62b rue Gay Lussac Paris, 75005, France
Pascal.Urien@Telecom-ParisTech.fr,
Christophe.Kiennert@EtherTrust.com

Abstract. This paper introduces a new mobile service, delivering keys for hotel rooms equipped with RFID locks. It works with Android smartphones offering NFC facilities. Keys are made with dual interface contactless smartcards equipped with SSL/TLS stacks and compatible with legacy locks. Keys cards securely download keys value from dedicated WEB server, thanks to Internet and NFC connectivity offered by the Android system. We plan to deploy an experimental platform with industrial partners within the next months.

Keywords: Mobile service, security, NFC, smartcards, SSL/TLS.

1 Introduction

Mobile service is a very attractive topic for the deployment of the emerging always on society. It is expected [1] that in 2015, about one billion of smartphones, with full Internet connectivity, will be sold every year. Android is a popular open operating system for mobiles based on UNIX, whose version 1.0 was commercialized by the end of 1998. Twelve years later, fall 2010, the 2.3 version (also refereed as Gingerbread) was released with the support of Near Field Communication (NFC) standard [2]. This technology appears in the first decade of the 21st century.

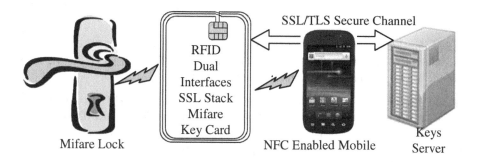

Fig. 1. RFID Lock, new mobile service

J.Y. Zhang et al. (Eds.): MobiCASE 2011, LNICST 95, pp. 387–394, 2012.

It is a radio link, working at the 13,56 MHz frequency and integrated in low power tamper resistant microelectronic chips, usually named contactless smartcards. These devices, battery free and fed by the electromagnetic field, are widely used in Europe and Asia for ticketing, access control and banking purposes. According to the NFC terminology, Gingerbread supports the peer to peer mode (data exchange between two NFC enabled devices), and the reader mode (feeding and communication with an NFC device working in the card mode). Despite the fact that the hardware could also provide the card mode, this feature is not currently supported by Android.

This paper presents an experimental mobile service targeting key delivering for electronic locks. In the legacy service (see for example [3]) electronic locks are equipped with RFID readers, and work with RFID cards (frequently including Mifare [4] components) in spite of magnetic strip cards. A device named the Card Encoder, belonging to a dedicated information system, writes keys values in RFID cards. Our new experimental platform (see figure 1) works with dual interfaces RFIDs (whose structure is detailed by section IV), establishing secure SSL/TLS sessions with a key server. Internet connectivity and human interface is provided and managed by an Android phone. The user is identified by the X509 certificate stored in his key card, and thanks to its smart-phone securely collects a key from the dedicated WEB server. This paper is constructed according to the following outline. Section 2 introduces the NFC and Android technologies. Section 3 describes dual interfaces RFIDs. Section 4 presents basic concepts of the EAP-TLS application for contactless smartcard and gives performances for the prototype platform. Section 5 details the new and secure key delivering services.

2   About The NFC Technology and Android

The Near Field Communication (NFC) technology is a radio interface working at 13,56 MHz. It supports several data encoding schemes, delivering binary throughput ranging from 106 to 848 Kbits/s. The two main classes of such modems are referred as typeA and typeB and are detailed by the ISO 14443 and NFC standards. This technology is embedded in small electronic chips with low power consumption (less than 10mW), which are fed by electromagnetic induction. A device equipped with an antenna and usually named the reader, generates a magnetic field of about 5 A/m, which according to the Lens laws induces a tension of about 2,2V on a rectangular loop with an area of 5x8 cm^2. The working distance of this system is within 10 cm. The RFID components are split in two categories,

- small chips (less than 1mm^2) designed with cabled logic;
- secure microcontrollers chips (about 25 mm^2) equipped with CPU, RAM, Non Volatile Memory, and cryptographic accelerators units.

A good illustration of the first RFID category is the Mifare 1K [4] (1K meaning one KBytes of memory) widely deployed for ticketing applications or RFIDs keys [3]. Electronic passports (normalized by the ICAO standards [5]) include RFIDs belonging to the second category either typeA or typeB.

In this paper we present a highly secure key delivering service dealing with smartphones and dual interfaces RFIDs. These electronic chips equipped with an antenna, support both the Mifare 1K and ISO 14443 (typeA) protocols and embed a secure microcontroller. Today some hotels are already equipped with NFC locks, including a battery and a reader, which read customers' RFID cards. The basic idea of our new service is to get a key from a WEB server thanks to an SSL/TLS stack running in the RFID secure microcontroller and monitored by Android software. This data is afterwards transferred in the Mifare emulated card.

Android [6] [7] [8] is an operating system originally created by the company Android Inc. and supported by the Open Handset Alliance, driven by the Google company. It uses a Linux kernel and provides a runtime environment based on the java programming language. Applications are compiled from JAVA modules, then transformed by the "dx" tool and executed by a particular Virtual Machine called the Dalvik Virtual Machine (DVM). This virtual machine processes code bytes stored in Dalvik (.dex) files, whose format is optimized for minimal memory footprint. An Activity is an application component that manages a screen with which users can interact in order to do something. It may register to the Android system in order to be launched by asynchronous messages named Intent. The list of Intent processed by an application is fixed by an Intent Filter facility. The Android version 2.3, also named Gingerbread, supports NFC software APIs, building an abstract framework over a NFC adapter chip.

3   Dual Interfaces RFID

A dual interface RFID is a secure microcontroller whose security is enforced by physical and logical countermeasures managed by the embedded operating system. Our experimental platform works with a JCOP41 device.

Secure microcontrollers are electronic chips including CPU, RAM, and non-volatile memory such as E2PROM or FLASH [9]. Security is enforced by various physical and logical countermeasures, driven by a dedicated embedded operating system. According to [10] about 5,5 billions of such devices were manufactured in 2010, mainly as SIM cards (75%) and banking cards (15 %). The format of information exchanges with these components is detailed by the ISO7816 standard. It comprises requests and responses whose maximum size is about 256 bytes. Multiple communication interfaces are supported, including ISO7816 serial port, USB, and NFC radio link. Most of operating systems implement a Java Virtual Machine, executing a standardized subset of the JAVA language (see next section). Among them, JCOP (standing for Java Card OpenPlatform) was designed by an IBM Zurich research team [11], and since 2007 is supported by the NXP Company.

According to [12] it uses a Philips hardware chip composed of a processing unit, security components, I/O ports, volatile and non-volatile memories (4608 Bytes RAM, 160 KBytes ROM, 72 KBytes E2PROM), a random number generator, and crypto co-processors computing Triple-DES, AES and RSA procedures. This component also embeds an ISO 14443 contactless radio interface. The JCOP41 operating system (see figure 2) includes a Java Virtual Machine (JVM) implemented over the physical platform via facilities of a Hardware Abstraction Layer (HAL). A JVM works with a subset of the java language; it supports a JavaCard Runtime Execution (JCRE) for Applet processing and is associated with a set of packages standardized by the Java Card Forum (JCF). These software libraries provide cryptographic resources (SHA1, MD5, RSA...), and management of information transfer over the radio interface.

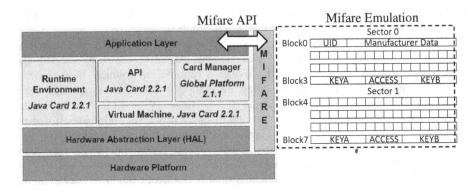

Fig. 2. The JCOP41 Operating system

An application is a set of Java classes belonging to the same package, executed by the JCRE. It is downloaded and installed thanks to the Card Manager component, whose structure is defined by the Global Platform (GP) standard. Our application is written for such javacards, with a memory footprint of about 20 Kbytes; it manages TLS sessions with remote WEB server and transfers keys values in the Mifare sectors.

A Classic Mifare 1K device [4] is a chip working with a TypeA radio interface, which includes a secure 1KBytes E2PROM. This memory (see figure 2, right part) is organized in 16 sectors with 4 blocks of 16 bytes each. Blocks are identified by an index ranging from 0 to 63. The fourth block of every sectors (the sector trailer) stores two 48 bits keys (KeyA and KeyB) ; the remaining four bytes define the access conditions for the blocks. Read and Write operations may be free or controlled by authentication procedures dealing with KeyA or KeyB. The block number 0, named Manufacturer Block, contains a four bytes Unique Identifier (UID) and eleven bytes of manufacturer data. The authentication process uses a three pass protocol based on the so-called Crypto-1 stream cipher, and two random numbers produced by the reader and the Mifare card. A reverse engineering was performed and attacks published in [13]. In a brute-force attack an attacker records two challenge response exchanged between the legitimate reader and a card. This attack takes under 50 minutes for trying 2^{48} keys values using a dedicated FPGA chip. Nevertheless, this device is still widely used for ticketing or keying services. Authentication weakness impact is reduced when these RFIDs store cryptographic tokens that can be freely read, such as those written in magnetic stripes for opening locks.

A dual interface RFID supports both Mifare and ISO 14443 radio protocol. It is often useful for the operating system (i.e javacard applications) to write or read data in Mifare blocks. A dedicated API performs this task; for security reasons the knowledge of KeyA or KeyB is not required. Instead of this value, a parameter called the Mifare Password (MP, [14]) is computed according to the following relation:

$$MP = h(IV) = DES_{DKEY1} \; o \; DES^{-1}_{DKEY2} \; o \; DES_{DKEY1} (IV)$$

Where the parameter IV is an 8 bytes null value, and D_{KEY1} and D_{KEY2} are two DES keys (56 bits each) built from KeyA or KeyB (48 bits) with 8 bits of padding set to zero. The JCOP operating system includes a Mifare API, which internally performs Read/Write operations with the knowledge of the MP.

4   EAP-TLS Smartcard

The SSL (or Secure Socket Layer) and its IETF standardized version TLS (Transport Layer Security) is the de facto standard for the Internet security.

The EAP-TLS protocol [15] was initially designed for authentication purposes over PPP links. It is today widely used in IEEE 802.1x compliant infrastructures (such as Wi-Fi networks) and is supported by the IKEv2 protocol for opening IPSEC secure channels. One of its main benefits is the transport of SSL/TLS messages in EAP (Extensible Authentication Protocol) packets, according to a datagrams paradigm. Therefore it enables the deployment of SSL/TLS services without TCP/IP flavors, and consequently is well suited for secure microcontroller computing platform. The functionalities of the EAP-TLS embedded application are detailed by an IETF draft [16]. More details may be found in [17] and [18]. The EAP protocol provides fragmentation and reassembly services. TLS packets maximum size is about 16384 (2^{14}) bytes. The TLS stack is equipped with an X509 certificate and a RSA private key used for client's authentication in the TLS full mode, illustrated by figure 3 (left part).

A session is initially opened according to a four way handshake (the full mode, see figure 3, left part) in which client and server are mutually authenticated by their certificates. At the end of this phase (the Phase I according to figure 3) a master key has been computed, cryptographic algorithms have been negotiated for data privacy and integrity, and a set of associated ephemeral keys (referred as the keys-block) has been released. These keys are exported from the smartcard to the Android phone that afterwards manages the TLS session, and which typically performs HTTP encryption and decryption operations (referred as Phase II by figure 3).

The TLS resume mode works with a previously computed master secret, according to a three ways handshake (see figure 3, right part). It is based on symmetric cryptography, and reduces the computing load on the server side; by default a WEB server uses a full session only every 10 minutes. A resume session is opened by the EAP-TLS application, which afterwards transfers the keys-block to the mobile phone that performs Phase II procedure. It is important to notice that the TLS master secret is never exported from the smartcard and remains securely stored in the device.

Because RFIDs are low power consumption devices, with small computing resources, and furthermore are driven by operating systems that manage countermeasures, computing performance is a critical topic.

The four ways handshake (Phase I) of a full TLS session (with RSA 1024 bits) costs 11,7s. It requires one encryption with the private key (120 ms) two computations with public keys (2x 26 ms). About 230 MD5 (230 x 2 ms) and SHA1 (230 x 4ms) calculations (dealing with 64 bytes blocks) are performed. It exchanges 2,500 bytes, whose transfer costs 0,125 x 2500 = 310 ms. The remaining time (9,8s = 11,7-1,9) is burnt by the java code execution.

The three ways handshake (Phase I) of a resume session consumes 2,6s. It needs the exchange of 250 bytes (250x 0,125 = 31 ms), and the processing of 75 MD5 and SHA1 that consumes 450ms. The remaining time (2,1s= 2,6-0,5) is spent in the java code execution.

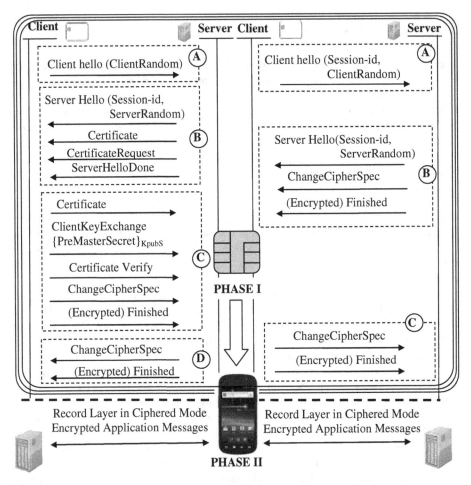

Fig. 3. Phase I and Phase II operations during a TLS session, using an EAP-TLS smartcard

These experimental results show that most of is spent in the embedded JVM. However this is a not a general behavior and other javacards present different figures, in which most of computing times are consumed by cryptographic resources.

5   The Key Delivering Use Case

The key mobile service architecture is illustrated by figure 4. A subscriber owns an Android NFC Smartphone and contactless dual interfaces RFID embedding a

Javacard application (RA) that performs key downloading. The mobile is equipped with a dedicated application (MA). All Dalvik applications must be signed, but the Android operating system allows software downloading from entrusted source, i.e. which are not available from the Android Market store.

Upon detection of the RFID by the Smartphone, the user is prompted to select and start the appropriate (MA) application. The TLS stack embedded in the RFID is activated, the mobile application (MA) opens a TCP socket with the remote server, and thereafter supervises the TLS handshake Phase I between the RFID and the key server. Upon success the keys-block computed by the RFID is transferred to the mobile which fully manages the TLS session Phase II.

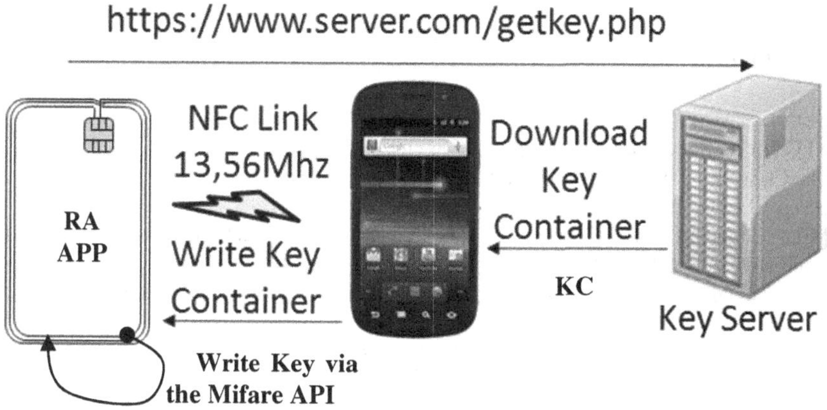

Fig. 4. The Key Delivering Service

The mobile application builds an HTTP request transmitted over the TLS session, i.e. the key repository is identified by an URL such as https://www.server.com/getkey.php. The requested file is located in a server area for which mutual TLS authentication is mandatory. Therefore the RFID is identified by its embedded certificate dynamically recorded (on the key server side) by the PHP variable $_SERVER['SSL_CLIENT_CERT'].

The *getkey.php* script uses the well-known OPENSSL facilities in order to extract the client's RSA public key. It then builds a data structure that we call the Key Container (KC), which securely stores a set of data (the lock key, LK) to be written in one or several Mifare blocks. A container is made of two parts, a header and a trailer.

1. The header is the encrypted value of the key (LK) with the RFID public RSA key, according to the PKCS #1 standard.
2. The trailer contains a PKCS #1 signature of the header with a private key whose certificate is trusted by the RFID EAP-TLS application (RA).

The hexadecimal ASCII dump of the container is returned in the body of the HTTP response, which is collected by the mobile phone. Finally the Key Container is pushed by the mobile application to the RFID. The latter checks the signature with signatory's public Key, and decrypts the LK value with its private keys. It then uses the Mifare API and the associated Mifare Password to write LK in the appropriate blocks.

6   Conclusion

In this paper we presented a new key delivering platform working with dual interfaces smartcards and Android mobile. It is a new class of mobile applications in which the user is equipped with a RFID and a smart-phone. The RFID accesses the Internet via an application running on the mobile, but manages the security of the service. It is afterwards autonomously used, which avoids the lack of battery issue.

References

1. http://www.gartner.com/it/page.jsp?id=1622614
2. NFC Forum Specifications, http://www.nfc-forum.org/specs/
3. The Classic RFID VingCard technology, http://www.vingcard.com/page?id=4380
4. Mifare Standard Card IC MIF1 IC S50, Functional Specification, Revision 5.1, Philips semiconductors (May 2001)
5. International Civil Aviation Organization. Machine Readable Travel Documents, ICAO Document 9303, Part 1,2,3
6. What is android, http://developer.android.com/guide/basics/what-is-android.html
7. Hassan, Z.S.: Ubiquitous computing and android. In: Third International Conference on Digital Information Management, ICDIM 2008 (2008)
8. Enck, W., Ongtang, M., McDaniel, P.: Understanding Android Security. IEEE Security & Privacy 7(1) (2009)
9. Jurgensen, T.M., et al.: Smart Cards: The Developer's Toolkit. Prentice Hall PTR (2002) ISBN 0130937304
10. http://www.eurosmart.com/
11. Baentsch, M., Buhler, P., Eirich, T., Horing, F., Oestreicher, M.: JavaCard-from hype to reality. IEEE Concurrency 7(4)
12. Certification Report, BSI-DSZ-CC-0426-2007 for NXP P541G072V0P (JCOP 41 v2.3.1) from IBM Deutschland Entwicklung GmbH, http://www.commoncriteriaportal.org
13. Nohl, K., Evans, D., Plotz, S., Plotz, H.: Reverse-Engineering a Cryptographic RFID Tag. In: Proceeding of USENIX Security Symposium, San Jose (2008)
14. AN02105, Secure Access to Mifare Memory, on Dual Interface Smart Card ICs, Application Note, Philips semiconductors (January 2002)
15. RFC 2716, PPP EAP TLS Authentication Protocol (October 1999)
16. IETF draft, EAP-Support in Smartcard (August 2011)
17. Urien, P.: Tandem Smart Cards: Enforcing Trust for TLS-Based Network Services. In: Proceeding of ASWN 2008 (2008)
18. Urien, P.: Collaboration of SSL smart cards within the WEB2 landscape. In: Proceeding of CTS 2009 (2009)

Author Index